The publisher gratefully acknowledges the generous support
of the Ahmanson Foundation Humanities Endowment Fund
of the University of California Press Foundation, which was
established by a major gift from the Ahmanson Foundation.

The publisher also gratefully acknowledges the generous support
of Charles and Mary Anne Cooper as members of the Literati
Circle of the University of California Press Foundation.

History and the Testimony of Language

THE CALIFORNIA WORLD HISTORY LIBRARY

Edited by Edmund Burke III, Kenneth Pomeranz, and Patricia Seed

1. *The Unending Frontier: Environmental History of the Early Modern World,* by John F. Richards

2. *Maps of Time: An Introduction to Big History,* by David Christian

3. *The Graves of Tarim: Genealogy and Mobility across the Indian Ocean,* by Engseng Ho

4. *Imperial Connections: India in the Indian Ocean Arena, 1860–1920,* by Thomas R. Metcalf

5. *Many Middle Passages: Forced Migration and the Making of the Modern World,* edited by Emma Christopher, Cassandra Pybus, and Marcus Rediker

6. *Domesticating the World: African Consumerism and the Genealogies of Globalization,* by Jeremy Prestholdt

7. *Servants of the Dynasty: Palace Women in World History,* edited by Anne Walthall

8. *Island World: A History of Hawai'i and the United States,* by Gary Y. Okihiro

9. *The Environment and World History,* edited by Edmund Burke III and Kenneth Pomeranz

10. *Pineapple Culture: A History of the Tropical and Temperate Zones,* by Gary Y. Okihiro

11. *The Pilgrim Art: Cultures of Porcelain in World History,* by Robert Finlay

12. *The Quest for the Lost Nation: Writing History in Germany and Japan in the American Century,* by Sebastian Conrad; translated by Alan Nothnagle

13. *The Eastern Mediterranean and the Making of Global Radicalism, 1860–1914,* by Ilham Khuri-Makdisi

14. *The Other West: Latin America from Invasion to Globalization,* by Marcello Carmagnani

15. *Mediterraneans: North Africa and Europe in an Age of Migration, c. 1800–1900,* by Julia A. Clancy-Smith

16. *History and the Testimony of Language,* by Christopher Ehret

History and
the Testimony
of Language

Christopher Ehret

UNIVERSITY OF CALIFORNIA PRESS

Berkeley Los Angeles London

University of California Press, one of the most distinguished university presses in the United States, enriches lives around the world by advancing scholarship in the humanities, social sciences, and natural sciences. Its activities are supported by the UC Press Foundation and by philanthropic contributions from individuals and institutions. For more information, visit www.ucpress.edu.

University of California Press
Berkeley and Los Angeles, California

University of California Press, Ltd.
London, England

Library of Congress Cataloging-in-Publication Data

Ehret, Christopher.
  History and the testimony of language / Christopher Ehret.
    p. cm.
  Includes bibliographical references and index.
  ISBN 978-0-520-26204-1 (cloth : alk. paper) —
  ISBN 978-0-520-26205-8 (pbk. : alk. paper)
    1. History—Methodology.   2. Language and history.   3. Social
history.   4. Africa—History.   I. Title.
  D16.135.E57   2011
  907.2—dc22   2010001040

Manufactured in the United States of America

20 19 18 17 16 15 14 13 12 11
10 9 8 7 6 5 4 3 2 1

This book is printed on Cascades Enviro 100, a 100% post consumer waste, recycled, de-inked fiber. FSC recycled certified and processed chlorine free. It is acid free, Ecologo certified, and manufactured by BioGas energy.

In memoriam Patricia Durousseau, Laura Fliegelman,
Madoda Hlatshwayo, John Ochieng, and Gloria Waite, young
scholars of history, taken from us before their time

CONTENTS

List of Illustrations   *viii*

Acknowledgments   *xi*

PART ONE. EVIDENCE AND METHOD

1. Methods and Myths   3

2. Writing History from Linguistic Evidence   22

3. Historical Inference from Transformations in the Vocabularies
   of Culture   51

4. Historical Inference from Word Borrowing   82

5. Linguistic Dating   105

PART TWO. APPLICATIONS

6. History in the Sahara: Society and Economy in the Early Holocene   135

7. Social Transformation in the Horn of Africa, 500 BCE to 500 CE   170

8. Recovering the History of Extinct Societies: A Case Study
   from East Africa   185

9. Cultural Diffusion in the Atlantic Age: American Crops
   in Eastern Africa   221

Appendix 1. Outline Classification of Afrasian (Afroasiatic):
   Diagnostic Branch Innovations   249
Appendix 2. Proto-Afrasian and Proto-Erythraic Subsistence   251
Appendix 3. Development of Nilo-Saharan Lexicons of Herding
   and Cultivation   253
Appendix 4. Interpreting the Ethiosemitic Cognation Matrix   256
Appendix 5. Cushitic Loanwords in Ethiosemitic Core Vocabulary   261
Index   265

ILLUSTRATIONS

MAPS

1. Early Northern Sudanian Agripastoralists 46
2. Afrasians and Nilo-Saharans, ca. 8500–4000 BCE 157
3. Ethiosemitic Settlement Areas in the Horn, 500 BCE to 100 CE 178
4. Taita Southern Cushites, ca. 1000 CE 216
5. The Diffusion of American Crops in East Africa, 1500–1900 242

FIGURES

1. Nilo-Saharan Family Tree: The Early Divergences 25
2. Nilo-Saharan Family Tree: New Developments in Lexicon from Proto-Sudanic to Proto-Sahelian 44
3. Primary Branches of Savanna Bantu 56
4. Early Divergences in the Kaskazi Branch of Mashariki 57
5. Categories of Word Borrowing 99
6. Family Tree of the Cushitic Subbranch of Afrasian 138
7. Family Tree of Afrasian Branch Relationships 142
8. Outline Classification of the Deep-Level Divisions of Afrasian 147
9. Family Tree of Nilo-Saharan Branch Relationships 152
10. Outline Subclassification of Ethiosemitic 171
11. Outline Classification of Southern Cushitic 188
12. Family Tree of Southern Cushitic 189
13. Expanded Family Tree of Southern Cushitic 207

TABLES

1. English Stock-Breeding Taxonomies   *54*
2. Successive Stages in the Development of Mashariki Bantu Livestock Terminology   *58*
3. Day Sequences in Southern Cushitic Languages   *69*
4. Proto–Southern Cushitic Day-Naming Sequence   *70*
5. Comparative Arm Taxonomies   *73*
6. Comparative Leg Taxonomies   *74*
7. Activity Sequence: Beer Brewing   *76*
8. Activity Sequence: Early Mashariki Grain Preparation   *77*
9. Projected Median Dating Correlations   *127*
10. African Dating Correlations   *128*
11. Representative Sample: Afrasian Cognate Retentions   *143*
12. Adjusted Afrasian Intergroup Median Cognation   *145*
13. Words for Domestic Stock Spread by Word Borrowing   *150*
14. Afrasian Loanwords in Proto-Sahelian   *161*
15. Sample Sahelian (Kir-Abbaian) Loanwords in Beja   *162*
16. Sahelian Loanwords in Ancient Egyptian   *163*
17. Taita Cushitic A Sound Changes: Loanwords in Saghala   *195*
18. Taita Cushitic A Sound Changes: Loanwords in Dawida   *198*
19. Taita Cushitic A Sound Changes: Loanwords in Both Saghala and Dawida   *199*
20. Taita Cushitic B Sound Changes: Loanwords in Saghala   *200*
21. Taita Cushitic B Sound Changes: Loanwords in Dawida   *202*
22. Taita Cushitic B Sound Changes: Loanwords in Both Saghala and Dawida   *202*
23. Shared Sound-Change Innovations of Taita Cushitic: Loanwords in Saghala and Dawida   *204*
24. Diagnostic Rift Branch Sound-Change Innovations: Taita Cushitic Loanwords in Either Saghala or Dawida   *208*
25. Rift-Branch Sound Changes Lacking in Taita Cushitic: Loanwords in Saghala and Dawida   *209*
26. Culture and Economy: Taita Cushitic A   *212*
27. Culture and Economy: Taita Cushitic B   *213*
28. Culture and Economy: Taita Cushitic A *or* Taita Cushitic B   *214*
29. Taita Cushitic A Loanwords in Saghala Basic Lexicon   *217*
30. Taita Cushitic A Loanwords in Dawida Basic Lexicon   *217*
31. Taita Cushitic B Loanwords in Saghala Basic Lexicon   *218*
32. Taita Cushitic A *or* B Loanword in Saghala Basic Lexicon   *218*

33. Taita Cushitic B Loanwords in Dawida Basic Lexicon   219
34. Ethiosemitic Cognation Matrix   257

LISTS

1. Taita Cushitic A Sound-Change Rules   193
2. Taita Cushitic B Sound-Change Rules   197
3. Taita Cushitic Shared Sound-Change Innovations   203
4. Sound Changes in Taita Cushitic Diagnostic of Rift Southern Cushitic Affiliations   205

ACKNOWLEDGMENTS

This work builds on four decades of teaching, research, and writing. It represents the flowing together of innumerable personal and scholarly influences, each widening and deepening my understanding of my disciplines—linguistics and history—and each introducing me to people and places on the linguistic and historical maps and to new ideas and new ways of looking at things. It is people above all to whom I owe thanks.

To my teachers: the late Jack Berry, peerless professor of linguistics and great champion of my combining of history and linguistics in my doctoral studies; Oswald Werner, whose teaching and work widened my vision on the possibilities of linguistics in anthropology; Bruce Trigger, who introduced me to professional archaeology; Jan Vansina, out of whose graduate seminar at the University of Wisconsin came my first published article and whose support helped get me my first university position; and Bethwell Alan Ogot, the dean of historians of East Africa, mentor and liaison in my first linguistic and historical fieldwork. To all of you, I cannot thank you enough.

To those students of mine who in varying ways applied the evidence of historical linguistics, oral tradition, or comparative ethnography in their historical writing (in chronological order): Donald Kilhefner, Allen Thurm, Douglas Werner, Gildas Nicolas, Gary Y. Okihiro, Robert Papstein, Douglas Johnson, Louis Wilson, Douglas Saxon, Gloria Waite, Alice Gold, Mohamed Nuuh Ali, Carolan Ownby, John Distefano, Mary McMaster, David Schoenbrun, Linda Arvanites, Patricia Durousseau, Christine Saidi, Kairn Klieman, Catherine Cymone Fourshey, Rhonda Gonzales, Anita Pfouts, Carolyn Vieira-Martinez, Shiferaw Assefa, and Constanze Weise. Each of you enriched my life as well as my knowledge. Teaching and learning from you and learning from your experiences and discoveries helped me grow in my own mastery of the methods of extracting history from the evidence of language and in my understandings of the ways in which that evidence bears on other kinds of historical testimony.

To those other students of mine who worked primarily from written sources: Robert Edgar, Maryinez Lyons, Stephen Harmon, Steven Rubert, Kendall Radcliffe, Brian Thompson, Gibril Cole, and Amanda McVety. Working with you and guiding you in your dissertations helped keep me in touch with all the regions and more recent eras of African history, from eastern and northeastern Africa to South Africa to Central and West Africa.

To the many colleagues around the world, in varied fields from history to anthropology to archaeology to linguistics, whose work, ideas, and criticisms have shaped what appears here and have widened my horizons on the powers of linguistic testimony in Oceania, East Asia, South Asia, and the Americas, as well as Africa: there are more of you than I can safely name without leaving out someone important. To one and all I offer my deepest gratitude.

The chapters of this book also incorporate numerous original materials from my own field research, carried out in various African nations over the past forty years. I express my thanks to the Social Science Research Council, Ford Foundation, National Science Foundation, Rockefeller Foundation, Fulbright-Hays, Santa Fe Institute, and Council for Research of the Faculty Senate of the University of California at Los Angeles, each of which provided funding for this work at different times over this span. Above all, to the people of Ethiopia, Kenya, Somalia, Tanzania, South Africa, Uganda, and Zambia in particular, and to my many colleagues in those countries, I offer my deepest gratitude for your hospitality and for all the assistance and encouragement you have given me. I only hope that I can eventually give back as much to you.

PART ONE

Evidence and Method

Methods and Myths

GLOBAL HISTORY AND LANGUAGE EVIDENCE

This book is about history and the practical power of language to reveal history. Though it speaks to the disciplines of anthropology and historical linguistics, which pioneered many of the approaches depicted here, it is a book above all for readers and students of history.

It aims to demystify the application of language evidence to history. It is not a treatise on theory, and debating issues of theory is not its brief. Theory receives due attention when it explains or validates method, but method and technique hold the foreground. And it is not a historical linguistics manual. It is a practical book on writing human history from the documentation of language.

The writing of history from language evidence begins with a fact, simple in statement but complex in its implications: every language is an archive. Its documents are the thousands of words that make up its lexicon. Each development of a new word, each shift in meaning or change in usage of an existing word, takes place for a human historical reason. Sometimes the reason may have been an ephemeral factor of taste or fashion no longer recoverable. But more often that not, word histories have practical and discernable causes. New words come into use, and old words change meaning or add new meanings, because change takes place in the particular elements of human knowledge, belief, custom, or livelihood to which they refer.

Word histories directly register the cultural events of human history. From each word's history we can infer different individual elements of the human history that lies behind the changes the word has undergone. From the histories of many words together we can build up a complex understanding of the history of the society as a whole. And from applying this kind of research to regional collections of societies and their languages, we can construct intricate regional histories of the *longue durée*.

Recovering history from the evidence of language is no new enterprise. Scholars of Indo-European studies have drawn on this kind of evidence from the beginnings of their field two centuries ago, and students of American Indian cultural history have pursued studies of this type over an almost equally long span. Edward Sapir's *Time Perspective in Aboriginal American Culture,* the classic presentation of the methods of historical inference from ethnographic as well as linguistic evidence, was published over nine decades ago, in 1916.[1] For most parts of the world, culture historians, ethnologists, and linguists have long produced works applying linguistic evidence in one fashion or another to the uncovering of new knowledge about past human lives and cultures. Historians have not been entirely oblivious to these instruments, but they have wielded them rarely and have tended to put them to only limited use.

From the late 1960s onward, a small group of historians of Africa have taken the lead as practitioners and innovators in the application of linguistic methods and documentation. For this reason, in the chapters that follow, African history provides the primary models for undertaking this kind of work. The scholars who carried the work forward for Africa have repeatedly broken new ground methodologically while deepening and broadening our understanding of early history and bringing to light complex and nuanced regional stories of the *longue durée* in Africa.

Their techniques and methods have global utility. Oceania, interior Asia, southern and southeastern Asia, and pre-Columbian America are prime regions for the application of these approaches in the coming decades, as world history studies expand their reach. For any period or region of history where the written documentation is scanty or simply highly uneven in its coverage, these approaches can fill out the overall historical picture and, often, allow us to finally make sense of ambiguous written testimonies. Medieval European as well as Classical Mediterranean history—and not just premodern non-Western history—would be well served by such endeavors. Even when the written documentation seems extensive, language evidence can open windows into otherwise obscure or inaccessible aspects of the histories of those written about.

The most important feature of the pioneering African studies is that they present history as historians write it. They differ fundamentally from most previous works by anthropologists and ethnographers and by Indo-Europeanists, who have used linguistic evidence and comparative ethnography principally to trace population movements or to reconstruct the origins, development, and spread of particular ideas, rituals, institutions, customs, or elements of material culture. The new African histories have sought, in contrast, to build integrated regional stories of the past. The issues they raise and the questions they seek to answer speak to historians' concerns and historians' sensibilities.

BUILDING THE LIBRARY:
LINGUISTICS IN AFRICAN HISTORY

Introducing the Methods to Historians

The rise, long overdue, of African history to academic standing in the 1960s brought new attention to linguistic, and secondarily to ethnographic, resources for reconstructing the past. This new interest took hold even as the traditional disciplinary homes of this kind of study—in North America, departments of anthropology, and in Europe, departments of ethnology—had begun to lose interest in them. In 1964 and 1968 Jan Vansina introduced historians of Africa to historical inference from comparative ethnography in two articles, "The Uses of Process Models in African History" and "The Uses of Ethnographic Data as Sources for History." In these articles he recapitulated in compact and accessible fashion the principles and procedures of this kind of study. In 1968 I performed a parallel service for linguistic method in history with an article entitled "Linguistics as a Tool for Historians," following this up with a second article in the 1970s, "Linguistic Evidence and Its Correlation with Archaeology."[2] The latter article once again presented the methods of historical inference from language evidence, but it did so in the context of showing how these findings might be linked to the findings of archaeology.

My work in the 1960s and 1970s contributed a new feature as well to the existing methodologies: I began to build interpretive models and analytical procedures for better integrating the evidence of borrowed words into writing history from language evidence.[3] These investigations revealed that the accumulation of word borrowings from one language into another over sustained periods of time tends to fall into definable patterns. These patterns differ with respect to the quantity and rapidity of borrowing and in the semantic distributions of the words borrowed. Each pattern reflects a different historical pattern of contact among the speakers of the borrowing and donor languages of the loans. (See especially chapter 4 for the categories of borrowing and the human histories associated with each.)

Writing History from Language Evidence

Two books and a dissertation in the 1970s put these new directions in African history on a solid footing. The earliest of these, my book *Southern Nilotic History: Linguistic Approaches to the Study of the Past,* from 1971, is an exercise in writing the history of a major region of East Africa and of all the variety of peoples who had lived in that region over a 2,000-plus-year period.[4] It relies on historical linguistic reconstruction, informed by the comparative ethnographic record, to lay out the patterns of cultural and economic change in those societies over time. It draws on a complex array of word-borrowing histories to reveal the multiple histories of cross-cultural encounter that shaped and drove those changes in different periods and places. I consciously structured the book as a model for historians seeking to write a regional *longue durée* history from nonwritten documentation.

At the time scholars were only beginning to clarify the wider patterns of East African archaeology, so *Southern Nilotic History* did not incorporate the archaeological evidence. But by the end of the 1970s, Stanley Ambrose was able to show that the societies and cultural and economic developments unveiled in *Southern Nilotic History*—and in a second, shorter book of mine, *Ethiopians and East Africans*—correlated in detailed ways with the archaeological record.[5]

The second pioneering volume of the 1970s was Jan Vansina's *The Children of Woot* The geographical focus of the book, which appeared in 1978, is the areas around the confluence of the Kasai and Sankuru rivers, where the Kuba kingdom was founded shortly after 1600. Vansina combines histories of cultural lexicons with comparative ethnographic argumentation to reveal the long-term cultural and political developments of these areas from the early and middle first millennium CE (AD) on through the sixteenth century. This approach allows Vansina to give an encompassing context to, as well as to revise and expand on, his own earlier history of the Kuba kingdom, which had been based primarily on Kuba oral tradition.[6] Teasing out the historical implications of the lexical testimony, he adds new depth and enriching detail to the long-term history of whole region. The Kuba state emerges as a new foundation, yet integrally rooted in its institutions and ideas to developments under way for the previous 1,000 years across those areas.

The third groundbreaking work, also appearing in 1978, was the undeservedly still-unpublished doctoral dissertation of J. Jeffrey Hoover, "The Seduction of Ruwej."[7] In this complex work Hoover displays the power of linguistic analysis to tease out historical memory embedded in myth and oral tradition and to trace back, through lexical histories, the particular historical sources and the evolution of the complex web of political, social, and ritual ideas and institutions of the Lunda (Rund) Empire of the seventeenth century. To an extent not realized before, Hoover reveals the Lunda state as a confluence point of major currents of political change, already in motion more widely across the southern savanna belt of Africa for several centuries before 1600.

Two books in the 1980s further expanded the applications of linguistic methods in African history. *The Archaeological and Linguistic Reconstruction of African History* which I edited together with the archaeologist Merrick Posnansky and which was published in 1982, sought to match, by pairing articles on parallel topics by archaeologists and linguist-historians, archaeological findings with language-based history in four different major regions of Africa. In bringing together knowledge in the two fields as it stood at the beginning of the 1980s, this book offered the first pan-African perspective on the correlation between the two kinds of evidence. A second notable book of the 1980s, although very different in being regionally focused, was Derek Nurse's and Thomas Spear's *The Swahili: Reconstructing the History and Language of an African Society, 800–1500*. In its interlinking of language evidence with oral tradition, written records, and archaeology, it contributes to both knowledge and method.[8] Five doctoral dissertations of the early and mid-1980s at the University of California at Los Angeles, none of them yet revised into a book, also broke new ground in applying linguistic evidence to reconstructing the long-term early social and economic histories of such disparate regions of Africa as Somalia, Kwazulu-Natal, the northeastern Congo Basin, and Chad.[9]

New Themes in Writing History
from Language Evidence: 1990–2010

The 1990s ushered in a new generation in the writing of African history from language evidence. Two kinds of advances characterize this period: the application of linguistic approaches to the writing of integrative macro-regional histories, and the expanding of the topical reach of this kind of work. Five books define this new "generation" of studies.

Two works by Jan Vansina provide complementary *longue durée* political histories of western Central Africa. The first of these, in 1990, *Paths in the Rainforests: Toward a History of Political Tradition in Equatorial Africa*, deals with the vast equatorial rainforest zone. Vansina's second volume in this genre, *How Societies Are Born: Governance in West Central Africa before 1600*, published in 2004, expands his perspectives to the regions immediately south of the equatorial rainforests—in particular, to the western parts of the southern savanna belt of Africa.[10] He begins his story in each book with the early consolidation of farming societies across the regions concerned. He then moves on to the long-term histories of how the peoples of these different regions, in time, created a great variety of political institutions with a quite diverse array of political ideologies and widely differing ways of expressing and gaining access to authority and power.

Two other books, both published in 1998, offer historical perspectives on regional and macro-regional history that engage a wider and more inclusive range of historical themes than Vansina's. David Schoenbrun's *A Green Place, A Good Place: Agrarian Change, Gender, and Social Identity in the Great Lakes Region to the 15th Century*, draws on linguistic and other nonwritten types of evidence to integrate technology, agricultural change, and the history of beliefs and ideas into his recounting of 2,000 years of both social and political change among the peoples of the African Great Lakes. My book of the same year, *An African Classical Age: Eastern and Southern Africa in World History, 1000 BC to AD 400*, presents a macro-regional history of the transformation of economy, society, culture, beliefs, and technology all across the eastern side of Africa in the last millennium BCE and the early first millennium CE. It identifies external factors influencing change as well as internally generated developments in life and livelihood, and it situates this "Classical Age" of eastern Africa within the wider context of world history. Both Schoenbrun and I seek out and apply relevant evidence from different scholarly disciplines, drawing on ethnology, anthropology, and archaeology. Schoenbrun, in addition, makes highly effective use of palynology and oral tradition.[11]

Kairn Klieman, in "*The Pygmies Were Our Compass*": *Bantu and Batwa in the History of West Central Africa, Early Times to c. 1900 C.E.,* published in 2003, takes these approaches a step further.[12] Her history of the western equatorial rainforest regions from 3000 BCE to the nineteenth century adds considerable detail to our understanding of the first 3,000 years of Bantu settlement in these regions, a topic more sketchily considered in Vansina's *Paths in the Rainforests,* while painting a different picture of the social history of those regions over the last 2,000 years. She constructs her social history by interweaving the testimonies of linguistic reconstruction, comparative ethnography, archaeology, myth, ritual content and performance, oral tradition, and, for the more recent centuries, written documentation. Klieman's work is especially important for revealing the Batwa, the so-called Pygmies, to have been long-term, crucial participants in the history of these regions and to have played a variety of differing roles in different times and places. The Batwa, as she shows, have *not* been timeless relics of early humankind, as modern-day scholarly writings sometimes seem to imply, but agents of historical change in their own right.

A new generation of books building on these foundations is just now beginning to appear. These studies, mostly by a new cohort of scholars, take historical reconstruction from language evidence in several challengingly new directions. Among other things, they seek to uncover the long-term regional histories of social relations, processes, and institutions, and the topics they engage range from religion and ritual in social and economic history to the changing genderings of work and authority in society and culture.[13] Already they are uncovering new kinds of historical information and bringing new depth, detail, and nuance to the knowledge of the past that historians can extract from the testimonies of language.

Journal Articles

These books from the African field offer a range of possible models for historians to follow in incorporating such resources into the toolkit of the historian's craft. They are, however, far from being the sole contributions of the past 40 years to the drawing of African historical information out of linguistic evidence.

Over the past four decades, a number of articles in journals and in collected works also applied language evidence to the recovering of history in Africa. Articles by historians skilled in linguistic methods have appeared, albeit sporadically and rarely over the years, in leading journals of African history. Jan Vansina published contributions of this kind in the 1960s and again in the 1980s and 1990s, as did David Schoenbrun in the 1990s.[14] Other articles by these scholars and by me have also appeared in the *International Journal of African Historical Studies* as well as in *History in Africa*. Vansina's "The Bells of Kings," published in 1969 in the *Journal of African History*, is especially notable for combining linguistics with ethnographic and archaeological findings to show how the spread of a new item of political regalia—flange-welded double bells—mapped the spread of both new forging technology and new political ideas in Central Africa during the later first millennium CE.[15]

Two articles in the 1970s by Douglas Werner charted a different innovative direction for research, using language evidence to unveil aspects of early African religious history. In one article Werner shows how the spread of new religious ideas partially overlapped with the spread of new political ideologies into Zambia in the seventeenth century. In the other he traces the historical roots and ancient ideological underpinnings of territorial spirit shrines in Zambia and Malawi.[16] Both articles have stood the test of time well and have important things to say to scholars currently interested in exploring the early history of religion in Africa through language and comparative ethnography.

For over a decade and a half, from 1979 to the mid-1990s, a specialist journal, *Sprache und Geschichte in Afrika,* was a major venue for scholarship applying language evidence to African history. Historians trained in linguistic methods contributed a modest proportion of the articles in this journal, although the majority of the articles came from linguists and ethnologists. Unfortunately, since the mid-1990s the journal has appeared only irregularly, with volume 16/17 appearing in 2001 and volume 18 not until 2007.

Contributions of Ethnographers and Linguists

Ethnographers and linguists, following the older models of how to carry out this kind of work, have also continued to bring to light new information that historians can use and benefit from. In each decade from the 1960s to the present, a variety of significant contributions to our knowledge of African history have come from such scholars.[17] In the 1970s a major work of this kind was Derek Nurse's *Classification of the Chaga Dialects: Language and History on Kilimanjaro, the Taita Hills, and the Pare Mountains.* It presents us with 1,000-plus years of history in a crucial region of East Africa and draws on the evidence of reconstructed lexicon as well as loanwords to sketch out its linguistic historical picture. Over the decades since the 1970s, Nurse in particular has continued to be a major contributor to the reconstruction of eastern African history from language evidence.[18]

On a different note, Marianne Bechhaus-Gerst's *Sprachwandel durch Sprachkontakt am Beispiel des Nubischen im Niltal,* published in 1996, offers an important theoretical contribution to language method in history.[19] She explores issues in the interpretation of linguistic evidence of a particular kind—namely, the extensive lexical and grammatical borrowing generated by a many-centuries-long period of intensive contact between a ruling society and a suppressed majority people. As a by-product of investigating this theoretical issue, her book presents important new insights into the social history of Nubia during the Nubian Christian era that have not yet been taken fully into account by most historians and archaeologists of the region.

A major recurrent theme in the writing of African history from language evidence has been the so-called Bantu expansion. Today languages of the Bantu subgroup of the Niger-Congo language family are spoken across perhaps a third of Africa. The question that this distribution raised early in the minds of historians was how it came about. That interest has generated extended debates and an extensive historical and linguistic literature over the past four decades.[20] Although the tendency of early investigators was to attribute the spread of Bantu languages to a single era of rapid, large-scale population movements, historians now understand the latter-day distributions of Bantu languages to have been the result of a complex array of different developments covering several millennia. For one historian's overview of the several thousand years of social, agricultural, and cultural developments among Bantu-speaking peoples, so long oversimplified as "the Bantu expansion," the reader may wish to turn to the article "Equatorial and Southern Africa, 4000 BCE–1100 CE," in volume 2 of the *Berkshire Encyclopedia of World History*.[21]

In addition, over the past 10 years studies of the histories of single elements of culture or of particular suites of culture have given new life to the older ethnographic tradition of using language evidence to uncover individual elements of the past. The history of a highly important food crop in equatorial Africa is the topic of Gerda Rossel's *Taxonomic-Linguistic Study of Plantain in Africa*. More recently, Koen Bostoen has brought to light important new information on the history of ceramic technology in Central and eastern Africa in his book *Des mots et des pots en Bantou: Une approche linguistique de l'histoire de la céramique*.[22]

The study of the origins and spread of particular cultural items has a long pedigree in the Indo-European and ancient Middle Eastern history fields, going back well before the twentieth century. Sapir already in 1916, in *Time Perspective in Aboriginal American Culture*, could take into account long-known examples from Native American history.[23] Africanist scholars, for their part, have mapped word distributions in tracing the origins and spread of such diverse features of culture as musical instruments, domestic animals, and crop cultivation.[24] One scholar, Roger Blench, has been particularly active since the mid-1980s in publishing lexical evidence relating to the histories of a wide array of domestic animals and crops in Africa. His 2006 book, *Archaeology, Language, and the African Past* is a valuable contribution because it brings most of this work together in one place.[25]

But Blench's book is also a salutary reminder that the outward appearances of the linguistic testimony can often mislead. To confidently infer history from lexical evidence it is necessary to situate that evidence in systematic phonological reconstructions of the languages and language groups in which the words appear. Systematic phonological reconstruction provides the critical apparatus—namely, the histories of regular sound change in languages—essential to determining whether superficially similar words in different languages are old retained cognates, borrowings from one language into another, or mere chance resemblances. Chapter 2 describes in simplified fashion how the criteria of regular sound correspondence operate. The works by Rossel and Bostoen, for example, rest on this kind of solid foundation. Blench's findings sometimes do, but more often they do not.[26]

The essential foundations for applying language evidence to history in Africa or anywhere else are systematic historical linguistic reconstructions. If such reconstructions do not exist for a region of historical interest, then the scholar seeking to draw historical information from the language evidence must build those foundations. For Africa the systematic application of the comparative method of historical linguistics has already been widely applied. This kind of study in Africa began with Carl Meinhof's work on the Bantu languages at the end of the nineteenth century and the beginning of the twentieth.[27] The works of many other scholars over the past 100 years have turned that beginning into an established and extensive archive for those who seek to apply language evidence to history across the whole of the southern and middle third of Africa, in which the Bantu languages are spoken.[28]

For the wider Niger-Congo family, to which Bantu belongs, a detailed phonological reconstruction does not yet exist. But initial reconstructions of a number of the West African subgroups of the family do exist, and these provide preliminary bases for historians to build histories of the particular peoples whose languages belong to those subgroups.

For the Nilo-Saharan and Afrasian (Afroasiatic) language families,[29] spoken across other large portions of the continent of Africa, there also now exist major historical comparative reconstructions for important branches of these families as well as for the families as a whole. A large number of scholars have contributed to the work of reconstructing Nilo-Saharan: Franz Rottland for Southern Nilotic; Rainer Vossen for Eastern Nilotic; Bernd Heine and I for Rub (Kuliak); Robin Thelwall for Daju; Marianne Bechhaus-Gerst for Nubian; Pascal Boyeldieu and I for the Central Sudanic branch; and I for the Nilo-Saharan family as a whole. In the case of Afrasian, there now exist two competing reconstructions of the family In addition, provisional reconstructions of the Chadic, Berber, Omotic, and Cushitic branches of this family are available, along with a solidly established and rather full reconstruction of the Eastern Cushitic subbranch and also a reconstruction (in need of revision) of the Southern Cushitic subbranch.[30] An established reconstruction of the Semitic branch of the family, of course, has long existed. Together these studies provide foundations for applying linguistic evidence to historical reconstruction across large parts of the African continent.

MYTH AND METHOD

In view of all that has already been accomplished in applying language evidence to history—and the summary coverage here does not do justice to the volume and variety of work for just Africa alone—there remains a surprising lack of familiarity among historians, not just of the methods but of the extensive historiography that applies the methods. Because of that general unfamiliarity, myths and misconceptions about what linguistic reconstruction involves also abound.

One myth in need of dispelling right off is the idea that to be a linguist is to be qualified to evaluate the applications of the linguistic historical method to history. Although the application of language evidence in revealing the human past forms its own long-standing field of scholarship, its methods tend to be peripheral these days to the training of most linguists or anthropologists. Relatively few linguists outside of those in Indo-European studies or in some non-Western language fields get significant training these days in deriving history from language. Even most historical linguists, although well trained and practiced in the theory and technical aspects of reconstructing language history in and of itself, tend to have a "book" acquaintance with how to apply these findings to human history.

A second myth is that language evidence is somehow more imagination than substance. It surprises many that something seemingly as immaterial as the words people speak can be hard evidence of the past. But this impression reveals a misunderstanding of the nature of the evidence.

Words, indeed, cannot be held in the hand like the stones and bones of archaeology. Nevertheless, we can turn them into chronologically anchored historical documents. We can do this because it is possible systematically to situate words and their histories in linguistic stratigraphies. Chapter 2 introduces this topic in greater detail. Creating such a stratigraphy depends on a particular, fundamental characteristic of all living languages: when changes in phonology arise, they evolve according to regular rules. The regularity of sound changes allows us to formulate the changes as rules, seriate the order in which particular rules came into effect in the history of a language, and apply them in constructing a linguistic historical stratigraphy of each language. We can then trace the existence of particular words in that language back to earlier periods in the stratigraphy. We can situate their existence at particular places in the stratigraphy according to whether or not particular sound changes affected the sounds found in those words. If a word shows a particular regular sound change, then it was a word known and used by the speakers of the language at the time the sound change took place. If it fails to show an expected sound change, then it must have been adopted into the language *after* the change ceased to be productive.[31]

The traceability of a word back to any particular stratum in a language's history yields a well-founded historical conclusion. It tells us that the thing itself—the idea, cultural practice, or object connoted by the word, or the knowledge of that thing— necessarily existed among the people who spoke the language at that period in history. Similarly, any change in the meanings or usage of a word between two different strata registers a change in the significance or use of the thing that took place between those two periods.

A third myth worth challenging is the idea that writing history from language evidence is mysterious and surpassingly difficult. There are two levels to the study of the historical testimony of language. The more demanding level, because it requires additional training, is the primary processing of the linguistic data itself. Processing the data to make it history-friendly includes working out the sound-change histories and the relationships of languages. To do this work does require special training, but then so does learning the statistical methods of quantitative history. In this writer's experience as a teacher, acquiring the methods of linguistic historical reconstruction is no harder, and probably easier, for most people than mastering statistical approaches. For those who are interested in learning more, a book on historical linguistic method that is especially helpful for nonspecialists, because of the accessibility and clarity of its presentation, is Terry Crowley's *An Introduction to Historical Linguistics*.[32]

METHODS AND APPLICATIONS

Once a historical linguistic reconstruction of a group of related languages has been produced, however, and once numerous word histories have been reconstructed for the languages, the lexical data processed in this fashion now constitute an "edited" body of historical documentation. Part 1 of this book—comprising chapters 2 through 5—aims in particular at introducing historians to this kind of documentation and to the ways in which one can apply the canons of the historian's craft in reconstructing human history from it. Part 2—comprising chapters 6 through 9—applies these methods in a wide geographical and chronological range of African regional histories.

Intended to make the basic ideas and techniques accessible to the general historical reader, chapter 2 proceeds step-by-step through the principles and procedures that guide historical inference from language evidence. The opening portion of the chapter introduces the basic definitions and frameworks for inferring history from linguistic testimony. It describes what "genetic" relationship among languages means, how the divergence of mother languages into daughters takes place historically, and how the descent of languages connects to the historical evolution of the societies that spoke those languages. Applying these concepts, it then shows how the hierarchy of relationships among the languages of a family can be converted into a stratigraphy of the language history. The linguistic stratigraphy in turn provides the essential chronological framework of the history of the societies that spoke those languages.

The middle portions of chapter 2 introduce the reader to the next set of key themes—that words and their histories are historical artifacts. This section describes in broad strokes the varieties of word histories and their differing implications. In simplified fashion it takes the reader through the nitty-gritty of how one fits word histories into a linguistic stratigraphy and then infers change in culture, society, and economy from the distributions that emerge. It performs this task by presenting a case study involving a sequence of periods in the early history of the Nilo-Saharan-speaking peoples of Africa. The successive developments, stratum by stratum, of new sets of words in the lexicon of subsistence reveal that a succession of fundamental economic transformations took place during those periods, shifting these peoples stage by stage from a hunting-gathering to a fully pastoralist way of life.

The latter portions of chapter 2 round out the introduction to method with three further arenas of historical argumentation: inferring the probable earlier locations of languages, and thus of the earlier societies that spoke them; estimating how far back in time such communities existed; and correlating archaeology with the overall linguistic historical findings. The case study of the sequence of subsistence transformations implied in the Nilo-Saharan lexical stratigraphy, presented in the chapter, brings together all these areas of inference—earlier locations, time depth, and correlation with archaeology. The particular subsistence developments implied in the Nilo-Saharan evidence almost precisely parallel those attested in the early Holocene archaeological sequence of the southern eastern Sahara, the very region in which the arguments from linguistic geography would place those early Nilo-Saharan communities.

Deciphering the changes affecting individual words and situating these changes in the linguistic chronology, as described in chapter 2, is equivalent, after a fashion, to the deciphering and historical editing of an obscure text. Just as with the written document, once the linguistic "editing" has been completed—once the histories of the individual artifacts, the words of the language, have been worked out—the second level of study, historical interpretation, comes into play. The historian is now in a position to ask the question, What do the identified changes in the meanings and the uses of particular words, and in the timing of those changes, reveal about historical developments in the culture, economy, and ideas of the people who used those words?

Chapters 3 and 4 introduce that next stage in the analysis. Chapter 3 focuses on the systematic investigation of the semantic histories of lexicons. It examines, in particular, how transformations in the semantic structuring of the sets of words relating to particular fields of knowledge or belief, or to particular suites of cultural and economic practices, reveal the changing and complex ways in which people in the past understood their world and exploited its possibilities. Chapter 4 displays the power of another major type of linguistic historical evidence: loanword histories. This evidence not only reveals the cultural and ideological consequences of interactions between different societies, but allows one to estimate the relative population sizes of the communities involved in the interactions and to assess their social and political prestige or power relative to each other.

The historical interpretation of lexical testimony, as chapters 3 and 4 show, calls on the same skills and ways of thinking that historians apply in historically understanding any other artifact of the past, written or material. Linguistic historical study may indeed require a specially trained historian to "edit" and chronologically situate the documentation—that is, establish and validate the individual word histories. But if that work has been done, other historians should then be able to understand, and even raise their own reasoned disagreements with, the arguments about what the historical artifacts of this kind of research—the words and their histories—reveal.

A striking demonstration of the feasibility of this kind of crossover already exists in the historical literature—Jay Spaulding's 1990 article "The Old Shaiqi Language in Historical Perspective." Spaulding applied the loanword categorizations developed by me (see chapter 4) to the history of the region between the fourth and fifth cataracts of the Nile.[33] From the overall evidence of word borrowing, he established the Nubian ethnic origins of the currently Arabic-speaking Shaiqi of Upper Nubia. What is more important is that the evidence, interpreted in the light of loanword categories (for which see chapter 4), allowed him to then construct a historical overview of the ways in which the shift in language and ethnic self-identification proceeded.

Chapter 5 closes out the methodological and theoretical considerations of part 1. It surveys the issues of dating history from language evidence and presents an extended body of argument and evidence, based on more than twenty African case studies, on the validity and utility in Africa of a particular procedure, known as *glottochronology,* for generating median estimates of time depth in language history. Glottochronology has faced wide criticism over the years, but almost always for the wrong reasons. In general, the critiques have homed in on misrepresentations, misunderstandings, and overblown expectations, propagated as much by glottochronology's advocates as by its opponents, rather than on what the technique actually entails and actually does.

Putting to practical use the method and theory of historical reconstruction from language evidence is the theme of the remaining four chapters, which make up part 2. Employing a wide variety of the tools with which historians process language testimony, chapters 6 through 9 explore the history of four different African regions and time periods in which language evidence has been the crucial resource. The time ranges of these studies include, variously, the early Holocene of 12,000 to 7,000 years ago (chapter 6), the centuries between 500 BCE and 500 CE (chapter 7), the period of the later first and early second millennia CE (chapter 8), and the era from the sixteenth to the nineteenth century (chapter 9). The geographical scope of the four contributions extends from the Sahara (chapter 6) and the Horn of Africa (chapters 6 and 7) to eastern Africa (chapters 8 and 9).

Applying the methods is essential to consolidating one's command of any methodology. The studies in chapters 6 through 9 have that goal. They build on the lessons of part 1 from a variety of angles. In presenting numerous examples additional to those offered in the chapters on methodology, they provide repeated practice in applying and understanding the interpretive principles. They often require, as well, more nuanced interpretations than the methodological chapters offer. They also raise new or unexpected interpretive issues that are historically specific to the regions or to the time periods involved. In still other instances, they pose new variations on old issues. Together these contributions complement and supplement each other in exemplifying the wide variety of ways in which we can reconstruct history from the testimony of language.

Chapter 6 in particular, however, is directly and profoundly important for the world history field, because it upends a long-held Western presumption about the relations of African to ancient Middle Eastern history and to world history as a whole. Simply put, the Afrasian language family, to which both ancient Egyptian and the Semitic languages belong, originated in Africa. The historical linguistic evidence is overwhelming on this point. Within the continent the most probable origin areas of the family lay well to the south, in the Horn of Africa or in the Red Sea Hills areas immediately north of the Horn. The communities that brought the earliest ancestral forms of ancient Egyptian into Egypt, before the age of agriculture, most probably came specifically from the Red Sea Hills region; and the earliest speakers of Semitic had a northeastern African background as well. These are *not* new historical conclusions. They have been generally accepted among the linguists of the African language families for more than fifty years. It is long past time for historians or, for that matter, other scholars, such as geneticists, whose work bears on historical scholarship, to begin taking full account of this information. Chapter 6 seeks to set this process in motion.

PURPOSE AND CONTENT OF THIS BOOK

How are linguistic methods of history to gain the attention they merit from historians? One way forward would be to offer the readers and writers of history an accessible introduction to the methods and principles of this kind of study and to illustrate the applications with a selection of historical studies that have benefited from these approaches. That is the intent and the modus operandi of this book.

The chapters both on method and on application rely almost entirely on evidence from African history. But the principles and approaches have applicability to history anywhere and, in particular, in all regions and eras of global history for which written documentation is lacking, scanty, or highly uneven in its coverage. Even for recent centuries and where written sources may seem extensive, language evidence can reveal unsuspected detail, and it can unveil hidden information on the often-majority segments of society whom we otherwise learn about only by reading our documents "against the grain." Jay Spaulding's article on Nubian history in the seventeenth to the nineteenth century, "The Old Shaiqi Language in Historical Perspective," is a case in point.[34]

My intention and hope in this book is to inspire a widening application of linguistic evidence in world history as well as in the African field and, in the longer run, to encourage the ongoing critical expansion and refining of methods, theory, and application. Anthropologists and linguists will continue to have much to contribute. But the tools for extracting history from language evidence are, in the end, historical tools. They deserve a place in the accepted repertories of the historical discipline. They need to be wielded by historians if they are to yield in full the kinds of information and understanding of the past that historians seek.

NOTES

1. E. Sapir, *Time Perspective in Aboriginal American Culture,* Canadian Geological Survey, Memoir 90, Anthropological series, no. 13 (Ottawa: Government Printing Bureau, 1916).

2. J. Vansina, "The Uses of Process Models in African History," in J. Vansina, R. Mauny, and L. V. Thomas (eds.), *The Historian in Tropical Africa* (London: Published for the International African Institute by the Oxford University Press, 1964), pp. 375–389; idem, "The Uses of Ethnographic Data as Sources for History," in T. O. Ranger (ed.), *Emerging Themes of African History* (Nairobi: East African Publishing House, 1968), pp. 97–124. C. Ehret, "Linguistics as a Tool for Historians," in B. A. Ogot (ed.), *Hadith* (Nairobi: East African Publishing House for Historical Society of Kenya, 1968), 1:119–133; idem, "Linguistic Evidence and Its Correlation with Archaeology," *World Archaeology* 8, no. 1 (1976): 5–18. Bernd Heine updated the title and theme of my 1968 article in his Raymond Dart address, "Language as a Tool for Reconstructing the African Past," delivered at the University of the Witwatersrand in Johannesburg in 1993.

3. C. Ehret, *Southern Nilotic History: Linguistic Approaches to the Study of the Past* (Evanston, IL: Northwestern University Press, 1971); idem, *Ethiopians and East Africans: The Problem of Contacts* (Nairobi: East African Publishing House, 1974); and in a number of articles published in the 1970s and 1980s and in more recent years. (See in particular chap. 4 in this volume.)

4. See n. 3.

5. S. H. Ambrose, "Archaeology and Linguistic Reconstructions of History in East Africa," in C. Ehret and M. Posnansky (eds.), *The Archaeological and Linguistic Reconstruction of African History* (Berkeley and Los Angeles: University of California Press, 1982), pp. 104–157; C. Ehret, *Ethiopians and East Africans: The Problem of Contacts* (Nairobi: East African Publishing House, 1974).

6. J. Vansina, *The Children of Woot* (Madison: University of Wisconsin Press, 1978); idem, *Geschiedenis van de Kuba: Van ongeveer 1500 tot 1904* (Tervuren, Belgium: Musée Royal de l'Afrique Centrale, 1963).

7. J. J. Hoover, "The Seduction of Ruwej: Reconstructing Ruund History" (Ph.D. diss., Yale University, 1978).

8. C. Ehret and M. Posnansky (eds.), *The Archaeological and Linguistic Reconstruction of African History* (Berkeley and Los Angeles: University of California Press, 1982); D. Nurse and T. Spear, *The Swahili: Reconstructing the History and Language of an African Society, 800–1500* (Philadelphia: University of Pennsylvania Press, 1985).

9. D. E. Saxon, "The History of the Shari River Basin, ca. 500 B.C.–1000 A.D." (Ph.D. diss., UCLA, 1980); M. N. Ali, "History in the Horn of Africa, 1000 B.C.–1500 A.D." (Ph.D. diss., UCLA, 1985); C. P. Ownby, "Early Nguni History: The Linguistic Evidence and Its Correlation with Archaeology and Oral Tradition" (Ph.D. diss., UCLA, 1985); J. A. Distefano, "The Precolonial History of the Kalenjin of Kenya: A Methodological Comparison of Linguistic and Oral Traditional Evidence" (Ph.D. diss., UCLA, 1985); M. A. McMaster, "Patterns of Interaction: A Comparative Ethnolinguistic Perspective on the Uele Region of Zaire, ca. 500 B.C. to 1900 A.D." (Ph.D. diss., UCLA, 1988). Each work offers an integrated regional history extending from as early as the first millennium BCE up to 1500 CE. Ownby's and Distefano's works follow a tack similar to that of Jan Vansina's *Children of Woot*, in that they show how their linguistic findings link up with the oral traditions in mutually substantiating fashions. Ownby's "Early Nguni History" especially effectively integrates the evidence of historical comparative reconstruction with the evidence of word borrowing. Ali is currently at work bringing his work up-to-date and converting it into a book. McMaster's "Patterns of Interaction" and Distefano's "Precolonial History of the Kalenjin" were provisionally accepted for publication in the early 1990s, but for various reasons neither author submitted a final manuscript.

10. J. Vansina, *Paths in the Rainforests: Toward a History of Political Tradition in Equatorial Africa* (Madison: University of Wisconsin Press, 1990); idem, *How Societies Are Born: Governance in West Central Africa before 1600* (Charlottesville: University of Virginia Press, 2004).

11. D. Schoenbrun, *A Green Place, a Good Place: Agrarian Change, Gender, and Social Identity in the Great Lakes Region to the 15th Century* (Portsmouth, NH: Heinemann, 1998); C. Ehret, *An African Classical Age: Eastern and Southern Africa in World History, 1000 BC to AD 400* (Charlottesville: University of Virginia Press, 1998).

12. K. Klieman, *"The Pygmies Were Our Compass": Bantu and Batwa in the History of West Central Africa, Early Times to c. 1900 C.E.* (Portsmouth, NH: Heinemann, 2003).

13. Among these works are R. M. Gonzales, *Societies, Religion, and History: Central East Tanzanians and the World They Created, c. 200 BCE to 1800 CE* (New York: Columbia University Press, 2009); and C. Saidi, *Women's Authority and Society in Early East-Central Africa* (Rochester, NY: University of Rochester Press, 2010). Saidi's work, in particular, has critical implications for anthropological theory and comparative history. Specifically, its findings raise questions about long-held orthodoxies on the subordination of women and on the nature of matriliny and its place in human history.

14. J. Vansina, "Western Bantu Expansion," *Journal of African History* 25, no. 5 (1984): 129–145; idem, "New Linguistic Evidence and 'the Bantu Expansion,'" *Journal of African History* 36, no. 2 (1995): 173–195; D. Schoenbrun, "We Are What We Eat: Ancient Agriculture between the Great Lakes," *Journal of African History* 34, no. 1 (1993): 1–31.

15. E.g., among others, C. Ehret and M. Kinsman, "Shona Dialect Classification and Its Implications for Iron Age History in Southern Africa," *International Journal of African Historical Studies* 14, no. 3 (1981): 401–443; C, Ehret, "Bantu Expansions: Re-envisioning a Central Problem of Early African History," *International Journal of African Historical Studies* 34, no. 1 (2001): 5–41; D. Schoenbrun, "Gendered Histories between the Great Lakes," *International Journal of African Historical Studies* 29, no. 3 (1996): 461–492; J. Vansina, "Government in Kasai before the Lunda," *International Journal of African Historical Studies*

31, no. 1 (1998): 1–22; idem, "Bantu in the Crystal Ball," *History in Africa* 6 (1979): 287–333; 7 (1980): 293–325; idem, "The Bells of Kings," *Journal of African History* 10, no. 2 (1969): 187–197.

16. D. Werner, "Some Developments in Bemba Religious History," *Journal of Religion in Africa* 4, no. 1 (1971): 1–24; idem, "Miao Spirit Shrines in the Religious History of the Southern Lake Tanganyika Region: The Case of Kapembwa," in J. M. Schoffeleers (ed.), *Guardians of the Land* (Gwelo, Zimbabwe: Mambo Press, 1979).

17. Two early articles of note were J. H. Greenberg, "Linguistic Evidence for the Influence of the Kanuri on the Hausa," *Journal of African History* 1, no. 2 (1960): 205–212; and Christopher Wrigley, "Linguistic Clues to African History," *Journal of African History* 3, no. 2 (1962): 269–272.

18. D. Nurse, *Classification of the Chaga Dialects: Language and History on Kilimanjaro, the Taita Hills, and the Pare Mountains* (Hamburg: Buske Verlag, 1979). In the 1980s Gérard Philippson further advanced our knowledge of the same region with his book *"Gens des bananeraies": Contribution linguistique à l'histoire culturelle des Chaga du Kilimanjaro* (Paris: Éditions Recherches sur les Civilisations, 1984) by adding comparative ethnographic evidence to the linguistic findings. Notable examples of Nurse's contributions include "Segeju and Daisu: A Case Study of Evidence from Oral Tradition and Comparative Linguistics," *History in Africa* 9 (1982): 175–208; "History from Linguistics: The Case of the Tana River," *History in Africa* 10 (1983): 207–238; "Reconstruction of Dahalo History through Evidence of Loanwords," *Sprache und Geschichte in Afrika* 7, no. 2 (1986): 267–305; "Extinct Southern Cushitic Communities in East Africa," in M. Bechhaus-Gerst and J. Serzisko (eds.), *Cushitic-Omotic: Papers from the International Symposium on Cushitic and Omotic Languages* (Hamburg: Buske Verlag, 1988), pp. 93–104; "The Contributions of Linguistics to the Study of History in Africa," *Journal of African History* 38, no. 3 (1997): 359–391.; and, with Franz Rottland, "Sonjo: Description, Classification, History," *Sprache und Geschichte in Afrika* 12/13 (1991/92): 171–289.

19. M. Bechhaus-Gerst, *Sprachwandel durch Sprachkontakt am Beispiel des Nubischen im Niltal: Möglichkeiten und Grenzen einer diachronen Soziolinguistik* (Cologne: Köppe, 1996).

20. Publications in African history journals on this theme go back to Malcolm Guthrie's article "Some Developments in the Prehistory of the Bantu Languages," *Journal of African History* 4 (1963): 9–21. A large literature debating various issues relating to the theme developed thereafter in historical and linguistic journals of the field, including, among others, several contributions by Jan Vansina; by Bernd Heine and his colleagues; by Derek Nurse; and by me. See, for example, Vansina, "Bantu in the Crystal Ball"; idem, "Western Bantu Expansion"; idem, "New Linguistic Evidence"; B. Heine, "Zur genetische Gliederung der Bantu-Sprachen," *Afrika und Übersee* 56 (1973): 164–185; B. Heine, H. Hoff, and R. Vossen, "Neuere Ergibnisse zur Territorialgeschichte der Bantu," in W. Möhlig, F. Rottland, and B. Heine (eds.), *Zur Sprachgeschichte und Ethnohistorie in Afrika* (Berlin: Reimer, 1977), pp. 57–72; D. Nurse, "Bantu Expansion into East Africa," in Ehret and Posnansky, *Reconstruction of African History*, pp. 199–122; idem, " 'Historical' Classifications of the Bantu Languages," *Azania* 29/30 (1994): 65–81; C. Ehret, "Bantu Origins: Critique and Interpretation," *Transafrican Journal of History* 2, no. 1 (1972): 1–9; and idem, "Bantu Expansions." The topic has stimulated the convoking of international scholarly conferences (e.g., Wenner Gren Research Conference on Bantu Origins in Sub-Saharan Africa, held at the University of Chicago, March 24–29, 1968; and the colloquium L'Expansion bantoue, held at Viviers, France, April 4–17, 1977) as well as an interest in mathematical modeling of how the "expansion" of the Bantu languages might have taken place—notably, Y. Bastin, A. Coupez, and B. de Halleux, "Classification lexicostatistique des langues bantoues (214 relèves)," *Bulletin des Séances, Académie Royale des Sciences d'Outre-Mer* 27, no. 2 (1983): 173–199; and Y. Bastin, A. Coupez, and M. Mann, *Continuity and Divergence in the Bantu Languages: Perspective from a Lexicostatic Study* (Tervuren, Belgium: Koninklijk Museum voor Midden-Afrika, 1999).

21. W. H. McNeil and others (eds.), *Berkshire Encyclopedia of World History*, vol. 2 (Great Barrington, MA: Berkshire Publishing Group, 2005), pp. 664–670.

22. G. Rossel, *Taxonomic-Linguistic Study of Plantain in Africa* (Leiden: Research School CNWS, School of Asian, African and Amerindian Studies, 1998); K. Bostoen, *Des mots et des pots en Bantou: Une approche linguistique de l'histoire de la céramique* (Frankfurt am Main: Lang, 2005). A work along the lines of Bostoen's is Gabriele Sommer's *Sprachhistorische Rekonstruktionen zu den Ursprüngen von Getreidenutzung und Gartenbau in Nordostafrica* (Cologne : Rüdiger Köppe Verlag, 2001), which investigates aspects of the ancient history of crops in the Horn of Africa.

23. See n. 1.

24. Notable examples from the 1950s through 1980s include T. J. Nicolas, "Origine et valeur du vocabulaire désignant les xylophones africains," *Zaire* 11 (1957): 69–89; G. Kubik, "Generic Names for the Mbira," *African Music* 3 (1964), 3; J. H. Greenberg, "Historical Inferences from Linguistic Research in Sub-Saharan Africa," in J. Butler (ed.), *Boston University Papers in African History* vol. 1 (Boston: Boston University Press, 1964), pp. 1–15; and C. Ehret, "Historical/Linguistic Evidence for Early African Food Production," in J. D. Clark and S. Brandt (eds.), *From Hunters to Farmers* (Berkeley and Los Angeles: University of California Press, 1984), pp. 26–35.

25. R. Blench, *Archaeology, Language, and the African Past* (Lanham, MD: AltaMira Press, 2006).

26. Blench is certainly not alone in mixing valid with mistaken identifications because his evidence was not situated in a systematic reconstruction. Several of my own early articles suffer from this weakness and have been wholly superseded by better-founded work, and at least one article—C. Ehret, "Patterns of Bantu and Central Sudanic Settlement in Central and Southern Africa," *Transafrican Journal of History* 3, nos. 1/2 (1973): 1–71—should never have been published.

27. C. Meinhof, *Grundriss einer Lautlehre der Bantusprachen, nebst Anleitung zur Aufnahme von Bantusprachen* (Leipzig: F. A. Brockhaus, 1899); also idem, *Grundzüge einer vergleichenden Grammatik der Bantusprachen* (Berlin: Reimer, 1906).

28. For this archive, see *Bantu Lexical Reconstructions 3*, www.metafro.be/blr.

29. I follow the lead here of I. M. Diakonoff, the preeminent Russian scholar of this language family, in applying to it the name *Afrasian*. Diakonoff, Letter to the Congress regarding recent work in the USSR on the comparative historical vocabulary of Afrasian, in T. Bynon (ed.), *Current Progress in Afro-Asiatic Linguistics: Papers of the Third International Hamito-Semitic Congress* (Amsterdam and Philadelphia: John Benjamins, 1984), pp. 1–10, forcefully and cogently argued that the name *Afroasiatic*, common in much of the literature, gave undue prominence to the single Asian offshoot of the family, Semitic, in a language family that was overwhelmingly African and originated in Africa.

30. F. Rottland, *Die südnilotischen Sprachen: Beschreibung, Vergleichung und Rekonstruktion* (Berlin: Reimer, 1982); R. Vossen, *The Eastern Nilotes: Linguistic and Historical Reconstructions* (Berlin: Reimer, 1982); B. Heine, *The Kuliak Languages of Eastern Uganda* (Nairobi: East African Publishing House, 1976); C. Ehret, "Revising Proto-Kuliak," *Afrika und Übersee* 64 (1981): 81–100; R. Thelwall, "The Daju Language Group" (Ph.D. diss., New University of Ulster, 1981); M. Bechhaus-Gerst, "Sprachliche und historische Rekonstruktionen im Bereich des Nubischen unter besonderer Berücksichtigung des Nilnubischen," *Sprache und Geschichte in Afrika* 6 (1984/85): 7–134; P. Boyeldieu, *Identité, tonale et filiation des langues Sara-Bongo-Baguirmiennes (Afrique Centrale)* (Cologne: Rüdiger Köppe Verlag, 2000); C. Ehret, *A Provisional Reconstruction of the Consonants and Vocabulary of Proto-Central Sudanic* (in preparation); idem, *A Comparative Historical Reconstruction of Proto-Nilo-Saharan* (Cologne: Rüdiger Köppe Verlag, 2001). For Afrasian, see idem, *Reconstructing Proto-Afroasiatic (Proto-Afrasian): Vowels, Tone, Consonants, and Vocabulary* (Berkeley and Los Angeles: University of California Press, 1995); and V. Orel and O. Stolbova, *Hamito-Semitic Etymological Dictionary: Materials for a Reconstruction* (Leiden, New York: E. J. Brill, 1995). For Chadic, see P. Newman, "Chadic Classification and Reconstructions," *Afroasiatic Linguistics* 5, no. 1 (1977): 1–42; and H. Jungraithmayr and D. Ibriszimov, *Chadic Lexical Roots*, 2 vols. (Berlin: Reimer, 1994). For Berber, see M. Kossmann, *Essai sur la phonologie du proto-Berbere* (Cologne: Rüdiger Köppe Verlag, 1999). For Omotic, see Ehret, *Reconstructing Proto-Afroasiatic*, chap. 2;

and M. Lionel Bender, *Comparative Morphology of the Omotic Languages* (Munich: LINCOM Europa, 2000). For Cushitic. see C. Ehret, "Proto-Cushitic Reconstruction," *Sprache und Geschichte in Afrika* 8 (1987): 7–180. For Eastern Cushitic, see idem, "Revising the Consonant Inventory of Proto-Eastern Cushitic," *Studies in African Linguistics* 22, no. 3 (1991): 211–275. For Southern Cushitic. see idem, *The Historical Reconstruction of Southern Cushitic Phonology and Vocabulary* (Berlin: Reimer, 1980).

31. Because of recent advances in historical linguistic reconstruction in Africa, we can now build exceedingly intricate linguistic (and therefore societal and historical) stratigraphies of African languages and language groups. For an especially complex set of examples, see C. Ehret, "Language Contacts in Nilo-Saharan Prehistory," in Henning Andersen (ed.), *Language Contacts in Prehistory: Studies in Stratigraphy* (Amsterdam and Philadelphia: John Benjamins, 2003), pp. 135–157.

32. T. Crowley, *An Introduction to Historical Linguistics,* 3rd ed. (Oxford University Press, 1997).

33. J. Spaulding, "The Old Shaiqi Language in Historical Perspective." *History in Africa* 17 (1990): 283–292. See chap. 4 of this book for the criteria he uses; see also C. Ehret, "The Demographic Implications of Linguistic Change and Language Shift," in C. Fyfe and D. McMaster (eds.), *African Historical Demography,* vol. 2 (Edinburgh: Centre for African Studies, 1981), pp. 153–182.

34. See n. 33.

Writing History from Linguistic Evidence

LANGUAGE HISTORY AND HUMAN HISTORY

Every language contains a wealth of historical documentation on the people who have spoken it in the past. What do we mean by this claim? Just what are the data that a language provides for the writing of human history?

Every language is an archive of many thousands of individual artifacts of the past. These artifacts are the words of the language. Each language contains the full range of vocabulary necessary to express the whole gamut of knowledge, experience, and cultural practice pursued by the various members of the society that speaks the language. As ideas, behaviors, and practices changed in the earlier history of that society, the vocabulary that described these elements of life necessarily underwent changes—in the meanings applied to existing words, through the adoption or deriving of new words, and via the loss or obsolescence of older words. The history of past change and development across that gamut of culture and economy leaves its imprint on the histories of the thousands of individual words with which the members of the society express all the various elements of their lives.

The evidence of language history is a democratic resource. It does not normally allow one to identify individual characters in history, but it provides a powerful set of tools for probing the widest range of past developments within communities and societies as a whole, and it lends itself well to studies of history over the long term.

The materials in this chapter have previously been published in C. Ehret, "Language and History," in B. Heine and D. Nurse (eds.), *African Languages: An Introduction* (Cambridge University Press, 2000), pp. 272–297.

For although the linguistic reconstruction of history does not allow precise dating, its data relate directly to the whole array of cultural elements that constitute the longer-term trends and sustained courses of human development.

ESTABLISHING A LINGUISTIC STRATIGRAPHY

How does one uncover and make sense of the testimony of the myriad individual word histories in a language or in a group of languages? The essential first step is to establish what is often called a *linguistic stratigraphy.*

The most basic form of such a stratigraphy can be represented by a family tree of the relationships among the languages being studied. The technical linguistic aspects of establishing a family tree, and the complications that often arise in carrying out the task, are not something that can or should be dealt with at length here.[1] But the historical meaning of such "genetic" relationships among languages is something that does need explaining here if we are to understand how human history can be recovered from linguistic documentation.

At its most fundamental level, the genetic metaphor implies a linguistic relationship like that found in many single-cell organisms. Two or more languages are related because they descend from a common mother language, called a *protolanguage.* This protolanguage evolved at an earlier time in history into two or more daughter languages: it diverged into its daughters, much as the mother cell splits into daughter cells. The daughter languages each can subsequently become protolanguages themselves, diverging at later periods into daughter languages of their own; and this process can of course repeat again and again over the long run of language history.

It is very important when describing language history to use terms like *diverged* and *evolved,* which imply extended processes of development. The straight lines of a family-tree diagram sometimes mislead people into thinking that sharp language splits are involved. But in fact the breakup of a mother language into daughters is always gradual. Language change is an ongoing process in any living, spoken language. It consists of the slow, progressive accumulation of many small changes— in vocabulary, in grammatical usages, and in pronunciation—as time goes on. In the special case of linguistic divergence, a language begins initially to undergo different changes in different parts of its speech territory. These diverging courses of change lead at first to the emergence of different dialects of the language in different areas, and then, over a period of centuries, to the evolving of these dialects into distinct languages, no longer intelligible to each other's speakers.[2]

The mitotic metaphor for linguistic relationship and divergence, drawn from biology, is an apt one in most respects. The most important insight we discover is that the mother language diverges into its daughters, just as the microscopic mother single cell in biology splits into its own daughters. As differentiation proceeds, the dialects gradually become no longer mutually intelligible, and so finally become separate daughter languages. As also with mitotic division, the mother persists only in its daughters, so that no existing spoken language can be described as older than any other still-spoken language. Daughter languages can become mother languages themselves, and their daughters in turn mother languages, and so on through history. Whether a particular language will diverge in such a manner or continue as a single, though continually changing, language through a particular period of time depends, of course, on the particular historical circumstances of the language and the society that speaks it. There is one notable difference between the metaphor and its concrete biological referent: the mother language can sometimes give rise to several daughters during the same period of time, whereas mitotic division normally produces just two daughter cells out of one mother cell.[3]

CONSTRUCTING A LINGUISTIC CHRONOLOGY: AN AFRICAN EXAMPLE

The Nilo-Saharan language family of Africa offers an illustrative case study in the application of these principles. Beginning with an outline classification of the deepest levels of relationship in the Nilo-Saharan family, we can use these considerations to build a linguistic stratigraphy of the history of the early speakers of Nilo-Saharan languages:

I. Koman
  A. Western Koman
  B. Gumuz (single language)
II. Sudanic
  A. Central Sudanic
  B. Northern Sudanic
    1. Kunama (single language)
    2. Saharo-Sahelian
      a. Saharan
      b. Sahelian

The division of a family into successively narrower subgroups, as depicted in this outline classification, reflects the history of successive language divergences undergone by the family. We can best visualize this unfolding linguistic history if we convert the classification into a family tree diagram (figure 1).[4]

In this diagram we identify a series of historical periods. First, the original "mother" language, which we call Proto-Nilo-Saharan, diverged into two daughter languages, Proto-Koman and Proto-Sudanic. Subsequently, Proto-Koman evolved into Proto–Western Koman and a sister language distantly ancestral to modern Gumuz. Proto-Sudanic, the other original daughter language of Proto-Nilo-Saharan,

Figure 1. Nilo-Saharan Family Tree: The Early Divergences

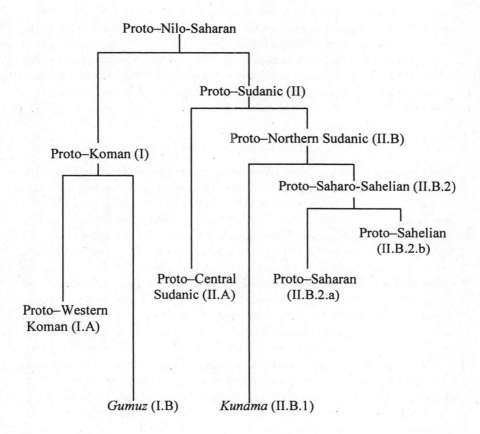

evolved into two daughters of its own, Proto–Central Sudanic and Proto–Northern Sudanic. Proto–Northern Sudanic then gave rise to Proto-Saharo-Sahelian and the earliest form of the Kunama language. Still later, Proto-Saharo-Sahelian diverged into Proto-Saharan and Proto-Sahelian. A complex and varied array of still-later divergences took place in the history of this family of languages,[5] but for the sake of clarity only the earliest developments are presented here.

This sequence of periods constitutes the basic linguistic stratigraphy of the early ages of Nilo-Saharan history. The first stratum, affecting all of the family, is the period of history represented by Proto-Nilo-Saharan. Thereafter each branching line of descent follows its own separate stratigraphic sequence. For the Koman language group, the second stratum is the period of evolution of Proto-Koman out of Proto-

Nilo-Saharan, and the third stratum covers the era during which Gumuz and Proto–Western Koman became distinct. But if, in contrast, we follow the chain of eras that leads down to the Saharan subgroup, the second stratum is formed by the period in which Proto-Sudanic came to be spoken; the third covers the evolution of the separate languages Proto–Central Sudanic and Proto–Northern Sudanic out of Proto-Sudanic; and the fourth is marked by Proto–Northern Sudanic's divergence into its Proto-Saharo-Sahelian and Kunama branches. The fifth stratum in this historical sequence comprises the period of the emergence of Proto-Saharan, along with Proto-Sahelian, out of Proto-Saharo-Sahelian.

LANGUAGES AND SOCIETIES

There is one more step we must take before we can begin to situate our linguistic historical evidence in our linguistic stratigraphy: we must understand the social historical dimensions of language relationship. To do this we must first visualize how language and society connect to each other. Through most of human history, a language could exist only because there was a society to which that language belonged and whose members used it as their vehicle of social and cultural communication. When, for whatever historical reason, people lose the sense that they belong to a commonality distinct from those of other peoples, the language they speak soon ceases to be passed down to younger generations and so begins to die out. Conversely, the continuing existence of a language over a long span of time reveals a corresponding long-term societal continuity of one kind or another among the speakers of the language, extending right across the different periods of its history.

The longer the period of time since the divergence of a daughter language out of the protolanguage, the more varied and diverse the ways in which the accompanying history of social continuities is likely to be played out. Most often a language is transmitted through direct historical lines of societal descent, even though as the centuries pass the society itself may change out of all recognition, and even though at times the disruptions of war or internal societal strife, or the challenges of nature, may greatly attenuate the connection.

Much less commonly, a lateral transmission of a language can take place. Dahalo, a language of the Southern Cushitic subgroup of the Afrasian (Afroasiatic) language family spoken in Kenya, provides an good example. Originally, sometime before 2,000 years ago, the Dahalo people were gatherer-hunters who spoke a language belonging to the Khoesan family. After a probably long period of close relations with a neighboring, dominant Southern Cushitic–speaking herding society, the Dahalo gave up using their original Khoesan language. They began instead to speak the Southern Cushitic language of their neighbors, although they continued to follow their older food-collecting ways of life. They also carried along many words of their old language into their new one, and this is how we know today that they used to speak a Khoesan tongue. Then during the first millennium CE, the Southern Cushitic farmers were all assimilated into another Cushitic herding society, the Garree. Only the Dahalo continued to speak the Southern Cushitic language. Because they still maintained their economically distinct way of life, they were able to retain the adopted language, despite having a new society move in all around them.[6]

So the history of related languages is at one and the same time a history of societies. When we reconstruct the relationships among a group of languages, we simultaneously establish the historical existence of the societies that spoke the languages. We also establish that some sort of societal continuity connects the histories of the speakers of each language right back in time to the people who spoke the ancestral language (the protolanguage) of the family as a whole. Our tree of relationships among the Nilo-Saharan daughter languages is a history of a succession of Nilo-Saharan-speaking societies. It forms a social historical as well as linguistic stratigraphy.

WORDS AS HISTORICAL ARTIFACTS

Once we have used the evidence of language relationship to lay out the historical links among the related societies and to formulate the linguistic stratigraphy of this history, we are ready to tackle the most challenging and most rewarding part of the enterprise of recovering history from language evidence. We are ready to position the individual artifacts of history, the words that make up the vocabularies of the languages of our topic of study, in our stratigraphy. Two criteria guide our placement of the artifacts.

Situating Words in a Linguistic Stratigraphy

One criterion is the actual distribution of the words in particular modern-day languages. To derive an extant word from a root word used in an earlier protolanguage, the modern-day forms of the root (its *reflexes*) must appear in at least one language in each of two primary branches of the family. To be considered, for instance, a Proto-Nilo-Saharan root word, the word must have reflexes in at least one language of each of the two primary branches of Nilo-Saharan: Koman and Sudanic.

The process of determining whether a modern-day word can be traced back to an intermediate daughter language, such as Proto–Northern Sudanic, has an additional wrinkle. The most obvious basis for reconstruction would be for the root word, as before, to have reflexes in at least one language in each of the two primary divisions of Northern Sudanic—namely, in Kunama and Saharo-Sahelian. But the criterion could be satisfied just as well in another fashion. If the same root word occurred in a language of the Central Sudanic group, it would need only to be found either in Kunama or in any one of the Saharo-Sahelian tongues to be considered a Proto–Northern Sudanic item. The reason is obvious if we refer back to the tree diagram of the Nilo-Saharan family. To trace a modern-day word back to an earlier protolanguage is to say that the word was transmitted from that protolanguage via the direct line of social and linguistic descent of the language in which it is found in later times. If we follow the outlines of the Nilo-Saharan family tree, we see that the lines of descent that link Kunama and Proto-Saharo-Sahelian to Central Sudanic connect back through two successive intermediate daughter languages, Proto–Northern Sudanic and Proto-Sudanic. The only way a word could be part of the common inheritance of both a Central Sudanic language and Kunama, or of both a Central Sudanic language and a Saharo-Sahelian one, would be if it also had been present in the Proto–Northern Sudanic language.

Regular Sound Change in Language History

A second criterion must be met, however, if we are to consider such root forms to be fully valid reconstructions, and this is the criterion of regular sound correspondence. Regular sound correspondence allows us to determine whether two closely similar words are cognates or borrowings (or just chance resemblances).

What do we mean by regular sound correspondence? As part of the normal course of history in any language, there arise from time to time changes in how particular sounds are pronounced. When such a sound shift, as it is called, takes hold, it tends to affect all cases of the sound in question. For instance, if a *b* becomes a *p* at the end of one word in a language, it normally does so because of the operation of a sound-shift rule that changes all cases of former word-final *b* into *p*. In other words, sound change in any language proceeds, on the whole, according to regularly formulated rules.

Because of this characteristic, history always creates a regular correspondence of sounds between related languages. Let us chose an example from the Bantu branch of the Niger-Congo language family. A Proto-Bantu consonant represented by linguists as *b regularly became a *w* in the daughter language Swahili and dropped out of pronunciation entirely in another daughter language, Gikuyu, spoken in highland Kenya. An asterisk preceding a sound or a word or morpheme identifies that item as the reconstructed earlier pronunciation of the item based on systematic sound-correspondence rules. By two other sound shifts, the Proto-Bantu consonant sequence *nt changed into simple *t* in Swahili while becoming *nd* in Gikuyu. And by two further sound change histories, original Bantu *a remained *a* in both languages, and original *u stayed *u* in Swahili while producing a sound spelled *ū* (but pronounced like *o*) in Gikuyu. Thus we say that Swahili *w* regularly corresponds to Gikuyu Ø (zero); that the instances of Swahili *t* that derive from Proto-Bantu *nt correspond regularly to Gikuyu *nd*; and that Swahili *a* and Gikuyu *a* and also Swahili *u* and Gikuyu *ū* show regular sound correspondences. Reflecting these regularities, the Proto-Bantu root word *bantu 'persons, people' evolved into the modern-day words *watu* in Swahili and *andū* in Gikuyu.

Regular sound change allows us to identify the words in the related languages that have been preserved in a direct line of descent from the vocabulary of the common mother language, or protolanguage. It enables us, consequently, to distinguish from such inherited items the words that a particular language has adopted—or, as linguists say, *borrowed*—from other languages over the course of its history. If the sound correspondences are regular *throughout* in the words being compared—as they are in the instance of Swahili *watu* and Gikuyu *andũ* just cited—then the probabilities are usually exceedingly high that the words are cognates, directly inherited in each language from their distant, ancestral protolanguage. In linguistic terminology, they are each a regular reflex of the same root word. If sound correspondences fail even in any one of the sounds in the two words being compared, then some other kind of history, usually involving the borrowing of the word into one or both languages, may have to be invoked instead.

VARIETIES OF WORD HISTORIES

So the essential intermediate step in tracing the history of any word is to test its sound correspondences. From that exercise we discover whether the word is likely to be part of the long-term inheritance of a language or an item originally adopted ("borrowed") into the language from another language. But that only begins the process of unveiling its history. If the word is old in the language, we must then determine whether the word has undergone meaning changes or changes in its grammatical form. If the word was borrowed, we must consider it in relation to other loanwords in the language. Is it one of a wider set of loanwords borrowed during a particular era from a particular language, and if so what kinds of words make up that set? Have they a wide variety of meanings, or do they tend mostly to refer to a particular category of human activity, such as farming or religious ideas or the like? Each kind of word history reveals something different about the history of the people who used the word.

Inherited Words

Some words occurring today in the daughter languages will prove to have been in use, with the same meanings, ever since the time the mother language was spoken. They will thus attest to long-term cultural continuities—to areas and elements of retention in culture and life. The widespread use in Bantu languages of the Niger-Congo family, for instance, of an old, inherited word for "goat," *-bólì—which reconstructs back to the Proto-Bantu period and, in fact, to even earlier in Niger-Congo history—shows that the Proto-Bantu people without a doubt knew of goats and that their descendants maintained the knowledge of this animal from that period down to the present.

In contrast, the semantic derivations of words often reveal older, now lost, ways of thinking or former ways of doing things. For example, in the Proto-Mashariki language, a daughter language of Proto-Bantu spoken near the great Western Rift valleys of Africa at around 1000 BCE, a new word for "to plant (crops)" came into use. Because this verb previously in Bantu history meant "to split," its new meaning tells us that the Proto-Mashariki people continued to emphasize a particular, earlier, rainforest-based agricultural technique. This technique, protective of fragile soils, involved cutting a narrow slit in the ground and planting a new cutting from a yam or other similar food plant in the slit. Over the next several centuries after 1000 BCE, the settlement of Mashariki people in lands with richer soils, along with changes in their crops, led to the complete loss of this practice among their descendants. Without this piece of linguistic testimony, an insight about earlier agricultural technology would have been lost.

Other words of ancient use in a language family will have undergone meaning shifts in one or another daughter tongue. In the Horn of Africa, several words in Proto-Soomaali, a language of the Afrasian language family, originally referred to the different life stages of cattle. In the daughter language of Proto-Soomaali that we call Maxay (or Northern Soomaali), these words came instead to refer to the equivalent life stages of camels. The meaning shifts reveal the replacement of cattle by camels among the early Maxay, who about 1,200 years ago spread their settlement into very dry parts of the Horn, where camels, but not cattle, could thrive.[7]

Other kinds of meaning change can reveal the appearance of new ideas or the development of new economic or social practices. We will consider examples of this kind of historical inference. Among these are an ancient Nilo-Saharan verb *kʰáy 'to break off, tear off', which, after the inception of cultivation, took on a more specific application to the clearing off of vegetation, and another early Nilo-Saharan verb, *ndʸɔ̀, which shifted its application after the adoption of cattle raising from "to squeeze, press out" in general to the technical meaning "to milk."

In still other cases a derivational affix may be added to an old root word to create a new term. For example, among the early Mashariki Bantu of about 3,000 to 2,500 years ago in the African Great Lakes region, a new word for "salt," *-ínɔ́, came into use. Its derivation from an ancient Bantu verb, *-ín- 'to dip', indicates that the early Mashariki had begun by then to extract salt from certain briny lake deposits— somewhat earlier than the archaeology can yet confirm.[8]

Borrowed Words

Still other words will turn out to have been "borrowed"—that is, adopted—into a particular language from another language rather than inherited from the protolanguage. Borrowed words—or *loanwords,* as they are also called—reveal cross-cultural influences. Many different kinds of word borrowing have taken place in history.

The patterns of word borrowing between languages fall into a variety of categories and subcategories, and each of these reflects something different about the historical interactions among the peoples involved in this adoption of new words. The borrowing, for instance, of a single word often indicates the adoption of the item named by the word. The generic term -*kal* for "camel" in Turkana of northern Kenya, for example, is a loanword from Rendille *gaal*, showing that the Turkana first learned of these animals from speakers of that language.

At the other extreme, a very large number of words may have been borrowed, all in a relatively short period of time, from one language into another. Very often this kind of word borrowing tells us that large numbers of the people who formerly spoke the donor language of the loanwords were assimilated into the society of the people who adopted the words.

Between these extremes lie a variety of other patterns of word borrowing over time among languages. The differences in the kinds, quantity, and rapidity of borrowing fit into a range of categories, each of which reveals a different kind of longer- or shorter-term human history of social, economic, intellectual, and demographic change. Identifying and giving historical voice to the differing categories of word borrowing present in a language are essential to making the fullest use of the historical testimony of language evidence. The contributions of this kind of historical inference are the province of chapter 4, which explores this theme in depth.

Systemic Semantic Shift in Word Histories

A very different but also highly productive approach to the grouping together of word histories takes account of the findings of ethnoscience. The scholars of this branch of anthropology have shown that societies, each in their own various culture-specific ways, systematize their knowledge and their understanding of the cultural and natural worlds in which they operate. The folk epistemologies of a society reveal themselves in the semantic patternings of the words that deal with the different subsets of human knowledge. Because of that fact it becomes possible to elicit the modern folk systems of peoples who speak related languages and then to seek to reconstruct from these data the earlier systems of their common ancestors. From the individual word histories within a semantic subset, we can make further inferences about how ideas and beliefs have changed between earlier and more recent periods. Both inherited and borrowed vocabulary may figure in this type of investigation. The borrowed words in particular reveal whether the cultural shift owes wholly or in part to influences from neighboring societies.[9]

The religious history of the Southern Nilotic peoples in the first millennium BCE offers a fairly straightforward example of this kind of historical inference. The Proto–Southern Nilotes of about 800–500 BCE took over a new set of ideas about the realm of spirit from their Southern Cushitic neighbors in central Kenya. Before 1000 BCE the beliefs of the Southern Nilotes were those of the Sudanic religion. Most other related Nilotic peoples, such as the Maasai and the Dinka, still follow this belief system today. In the Sudanic religion there is a belief in a Spirit or spiritual Power in the universe, called by names that scholars usually translate into English with the word *Divinity*. Divinity is the source of good and evil; the bad happenings of life are the result of Divine retribution, visited upon people for the wrongs they or their parents before them have committed. In religious metaphor, Divinity is identified with the sky and with rain and lightning.

The Proto–Southern Nilotes, however, changed their belief system sometime between 800 and 500 BCE. They adopted a new identification of Divinity with the sun, and they also began to recognize the existence of lesser, dangerous spirits, able to bring about bad happenings to people. The Southern Cushitic societies of East Africa followed virtually the same division of the realm of spirit into two categories, in which Divinity or God was identified with the power of the sun, and lesser spirits were believed able to cause harm. It seems clear that one of the two peoples must have obtained their ideas from the other.

But how do we know that it was in fact the Southern Nilotes who adopted the new views from the Southern Cushites? We know this from the testimony of word histories. The Proto–Southern Nilotes acquired at least one key word in their new religious terminology from the Southern Cushites, their word for "Divinity" or "God," *asiis. This word was a borrowing of the old Southern Cushitic term for "sun" and in fact meant both "sun" and "Divinity/God" in the Proto–Southern Nilotic language.[10]

This sort of analysis has the potential to reach into every corner of the history of human cultures, in the widest sense of that term. Chapter 3 takes up this theme at length, casting a wide net on what the historical testimony of systemic semantic shifts in languages can bring to light.

APPLYING THE PRINCIPLES OF LINGUISTIC RECONSTRUCTION TO HISTORY

With this broad survey of linguistic methods for history now in hand, we can consider the practical applications of these approaches to historical discovery. As an integrative case study, we will explore certain aspects of very early Nilo-Saharan history, showing how we can use a linguistic stratigraphy of key changes in vocabulary to plot the course of social and economic change.

Periodizing the Testimony of Language

The Nilo-Saharan family has undergone a complex history of repeated divergence into subgroupings and languages, a history that took at least 12,000 years to unfold. Over those thousands of years, great shifts in human economies and in customary life and political and social institutions have taken place in Africa, as well as all across the world, and Nilo-Saharan-speaking peoples have been at the center of many of the most important reshapings of life and livelihood on the African continent. Their languages, as would be expected, have time and again mirrored those changes. A particularly striking and telling range of examples of how linguistic historical methods and techniques work out in practice can be adduced if we restrict ourselves to the period from 11,000 to 7,000 years ago, when most Nilo-Saharan peoples shifted from gatherer-hunter to herding and cultivating economies.

Nilo-Saharan societies took on key roles in the earliest creation and spread of agricultural ways of life on the African continent, and the evidence of this history provides a striking illustration of the power of linguistic evidence in unveiling the ancient past. But we can go further in the case of early Nilo-Saharan agricultural history: we can correlate the history inferred from the linguistic evidence with the findings of archaeology. In this instance we discover that virtually the same sequence of changes appears in the archaeological record of the eastern Sahara as in the linguistic record of the Nilo-Saharan family. The correlation of the linguistic and archaeological stratigraphies then allows us to pinpoint in time and place the common set of developments apparent in both records.

The linguistic evidence and arguments for Nilo-Saharan history are extensive and complex, and the history itself was long and immensely varied, and so only a simplified sampling of the relevant data can be presented here. In the word histories cited in the next sections, the regularity of sound correspondences can be assumed to have been established,[11] except where irregularities are specifically noted. The Nilo-Saharan family tree (see figure 1) provides us with the basic linguistic stratigraphy for tracing the lines of descent of the particular reflexes of each root word. To assist the reader in identifying these descent lines, each citation of a reflex and its language has its branch of Nilo-Saharan also listed. (A fuller presentation of the evidence relating to early Nilo-Saharan peoples and their place in the long-term history of Africa appears in chapter 6.)

Stratifying Nilo-Saharan Word Evidence for Food Production

In the first two stages Nilo-Saharan language history, represented by the Proto-Nilo-Saharan and Proto-Sudanic strata (see figure 1), the societies that spoke the Nilo-Saharan languages were apparently still all gatherer-hunters in economy. No vocabulary diagnostic of any type of food production can be traced back to those two eras. In the Proto–Northern Sudanic language, however, the first words diagnostic of the deliberate tending of animals came into use. Then in the subsequent Proto-Saharo-Sahelian era, a whole set of words indicative of cultivation were innovated. In addition, the Proto-Saharo-Sahelians developed a new residential lexicon, revealing them to have become builders of large sedentary homesteads with round houses, thornbush cattle pens, and granaries. Finally, in the Proto-Saharan and Proto-Sahelian eras, the evidence of word histories shows the addition of sheep and goats to the domestic economy in those times.[12]

The histories of the individual root words that compose this body of evidence are of several types. Sometimes we simply cannot as yet track the words back before the beginnings of food production. The earliest term for a cultivated field, traceable to the Proto-Saharo-Sahelian language, is such a case:

1. *oɗʸomp 'cultivated field' (318)[13]

II.B.2.a. Saharan: KANURI də́mbà 'bed for sweet potatoes, small irrigation dike'
II.B.2.b. Sahelian: TEMEIN ɔjɔm, pl. kɔjɔm '(cultivated) field'
  Nilotic: JYANG dom, pl. dum '(cultivated) field'

In many other instances, however, the words turn out to be older roots shifted in meaning to denote activities or things connected to livestock raising or to crop cultivation. Examples of this kind of word history include several Proto-Nilo-Saharan (PNS) verb roots that originally referred to activities not specifically involving cultivation. One of these (*kʰay) formerly denoted breaking or tearing off of any kind, but at the Saharo-Sahelian stage it took on the technical meaning of cutting and clearing away plant material, particularly in relation to cultivation. The second (*tɔɔk) appears originally to have meant "to stick into the ground," without implying cultivation. But in all its forms in the Saharan and Sahelian languages it became a word for farming activities. The third verb (*dʸiip or *dʸiip') would seem to have meant simply "to dig" in early Nilo-Saharan, but its known occurrences in the Saharo-Sahelian group similarly apply only to the work of cultivation.

2. *kʰày 'to break off, tear off (tr.)' (1015)

I.A. Koman: Western Koman: OPO kai- 'to break'
II.A. Central Sudanic: Proto–Central Sudanic *ke *or* *k'e 'to tear off'
II.B.2.a. Saharan: KANURI cè, kè 'to plow, remove earth'
II.B.2.b. Sahelian: FOR kauy- 'to weed; to skin'
  SONGAY kèyè 'to weed field a second time'
  NYIMANG kai 'to chop (vegetation in clearing land)'
  Nilotic: Proto–Western Nilotic *kay 'to harvest'
  Rub: IK kaw- 'to cut (e.g., with ax), to clear land'

3. *tɔ́ɔ́k 'to stick in the ground' (785)

II.B.1. KUNAMA tokai- 'to dig the ground with a spear' (*tok-ay-, stem plus extended action suffix in *y)
II.B.2.a. Saharan: KANURI dòwóp 'to sow, plant' (*dogop, stem plus *p extended action)
II.B.2.b. Sahelian: SONGAY dóogó 'to weed'
  Rub: Proto-Rub *tokob 'to cultivate' (stem with same suffix as in Kanuri)

4. *ɗʸìip or *ɗʸììp' 'to dig' (304)

    II.A. Central Sudanic: Proto–Central Sudanic *ɗʸi *or* *ɗi 'to dig' (second consonant is missing because Proto–Central Sudanic deleted all word-final consonants)

II.B.2.a. Saharan: KANURI jìwá 'to weed, harrow'

II.B.2.b. Sahelian: GAAM dʸìw- 'to sow seeds'

The fact that each of these verbs derives from a root word that earlier in Nilo-Saharan language history had a nonagricultural meaning suggests that the cultivation of crops may well have begun as a set of independent inventions among the Proto-Saharo-Sahelians.

    If we turn our attention to word histories relating to livestock raising, an equally varied picture emerges. Again some root words cannot yet be traced back to earlier pre-food-producing periods—as, for example, a verb for "to drive herd" used as early as the Saharo-Sahelian period:

5. *yókw "to drive herd" (1501)

II.B.2.a. Saharan: KANURI yók 'to drive, herd'

II.B.2.b. Sahelian: SONGAY yógó 'to bustle, stir, move about in order to gather the herd and send it to pasture'

        Nilotic: Proto–Eastern Nilotic *-yok 'to herd'

           Proto–Southern Nilotic *yɑkw 'to herd'

    But again also, other old root words specifically do reveal in their histories the transition to animal domestication. For instance, the earliest verb indicative of driving livestock to pasture, which can be tracked back to the Proto–Northern Sudanic stratum in our linguistic stratigraphy, was formed by attaching the Nilo-Saharan causative suffix *k to the older Proto-Nilo-Saharan (PNS) verb *sʸuu 'to lead off, to start off':

6. *sʸúúk 'to drive (animals), e.g., to pasture' (1205)

    (from PNS *sʸúú 'to lead off, start off' plus *k causative [1201])

    II.B.1. KUNAMA sugune- 'to cultivate, to raise animals' (back-formation from an earlier noun, consisting of stem plus noun suffix in *n)

II.B.2.a. Saharan: KANURI sùk 'to drive (many things), to speed horse'

II.B.2.b. Sahelian: Nubian: DONGOLAWI shuug 'to drive along, off'

The particular animals driven by the people of the Proto–Northern Sudanic stage appear to have been cattle. The newly coined word testifying to this point is yet another example of the derivation—taking place from the proto–Northern Sudanic period onward—of new food-production terms from old Nilo-Saharan root words that originally had meanings not associated with cultivation or herding:

7. *yááyr 'cow, head of cattle' (1485)
   (*from PNS *yàày 'meat' plus *-[V]r noun suffix [1484]*)

   II.B.1.   KUNAMA aira, aila 'cow'
             (ara 'wild cow, antelope, small buffalo': loanword from Nara language
             [see II.B.2.b])
   II.B.2.a. Saharan: BERTI eir 'cow'
   II.B.2.b. Sahelian: SONGAY yàarù 'bull'
             NARA ar, PL. are 'cow'
             Nilotic: Proto–Southern Nilotic *(y)eeʀ 'male cattle'

Most interestingly, this latter root word can be derived, by addition of a Nilo-Saharan noun suffix *-(V)r, from a still earlier Proto-Nilo-Saharan term, *yaay 'meat'. This semantic history suggests that the Northern Sudanic people used cattle as their main source of meat. The indigenous derivation of the word would fit with a history in which the Northern Sudanic people themselves domesticated cattle, rather than adopting them from elsewhere, although it does not require such a history.

The Kunama term *ara* 'wild cow' belongs to a large set of Nara loanwords in Kunama, of the kind characterized as "heavy general" (see chapter 4, figure 5, category 3B). Such borrowing implies a long history of close interactions and cultural assimilation between the speakers of the earlier forms of the Kunama and Nara languages.

Still other root words dealing with livestock raising have histories that include their having been borrowed from one language to another. Histories of this kind, of course, indicate the diffusion of the things or ideas from one early society or group of societies to another. A most instructive instance is provided by the earliest verb for "to milk." The history of this word involves both its derivation by meaning shift from an earlier Nilo-Saharan pre-food-production root word that did not mean "to milk" and its later spread by borrowing, with its new meaning, from one Nilo-Saharan branch to another. Originally meaning "to squeeze," the root word added a verb suffix in *w at the Northern Sudanic stage in our linguistic stratigraphy (producing an underlying shape *ndʸɔw-) and, along with that suffixation, took on a new technical meaning, "to milk."

8. *ndʸɔ 'to squeeze' (356)
   II.A.   Central Sudanic: Proto–Central Sudanic *nzʸɔ 'to squeeze out, press out'
             (Proto-Central Sudanic *zo 'to milk': loan from Sahelian language)
   II.B.1.   KUNAMA shu- 'to milk' (< *show-, stem plus *w focused-action
             extension)
   II.B.2.b. Sahelian: TAMA juuw- 'to milk' (stem plus *w focused-action extension)
             GAAM dʸə-n- 'to milk' (stem plus *w focused-action extension plus *n
                durative extension)
             Rub: Proto-Rub *'jut 'to milk' (stem plus *w focused-action extension
                plus *tʰ continuative extension)

In languages of the Central Sudanic branch of Nilo-Saharan this verb appears in two forms—with regular sound correspondence and the meaning "to press out" and in a borrowed form with the meaning "to milk." The borrowed shape, of course, fits the category of a single-word borrowing (see chapter 4, figure 5, category 1): it reflects the diffusion of a new cultural item to the Central Sudanic peoples. It is one of a number of similar word histories in Central Sudanic languages implying that the early Central Sudanic people, who diverged along a separate line of historical development before the Northern Sudanic period, did not participate in the original establishment of livestock raising among Nilo-Saharan peoples. The ideas and practices of herding diffused to them from other Nilo-Saharan societies only much later in time.

Even more arresting is the evidence dealing with the raising of sheep and goats. Here the histories of a number of key early root words show that the keeping of these two animals did not originate among the Nilo-Saharans at all, but spread to them *after* the Proto-Saharo-Sahelian period in our stratigraphy. The sources in each case were languages of the Afrasian family. For instance, the generic term *tam for "sheep" in the Kanuri language of the Saharan group was an ancient loanword from the Chadic branch of Afrasian. Similarly, the Proto-Sahelian root word for "goat," *ay, came originally from the northern, Beja subgroup of the Cushitic branch of the Afrasian family, spoken along the African side of the Red Sea.[14] These borrowings again belong to the category of single-word borrowings, indicative of the diffusion to the early Sahelian and Saharan peoples of the new subsistence items, the goat and the sheep, named by those words.

9. *áy 'goat' (1508)

II.B.2.b.   Sahelian: FOR déí, pl. keita 'he-goat'

TEMEIN kai 'goats (suppletive plural)' (*k plural prefix plus stem -ai)

Daju: Proto-Daju *aise 'goat' (stem ai- plus *s noun suffix)

Surmic: Didinga-Murle *eeθ 'goat' (stem ee- from earlier *ai- plus *s noun suffix [*s becomes *θ in this group; θ is the sound written *th* in English])

The linguistic inferences conform to the zoological and archaeological evidence that goats and sheep were domesticated in far southwestern Asia. An Asian origin for the two animals requires that they would have to have spread to the Nilo-Saharan-speaking societies via the Afrasian-speaking territories to their north and east, accounting for the adoption of Afrasian words for the animals in Nilo-Saharan languages. The placement of the new goat and sheep terminology in the Nilo-Saharan stratigraphy tells us also that these animals reached the various Northern Sudanic communities two long historical stages after the Northern Sudanic domestication of cattle.

One important caveat must be kept in mind in assessing this kind of testimony. Lack of evidence is not, in and of itself, evidence of lack. Might some of the words indicative of herding or cultivation have once existed with the same meanings in the two earlier-diverging branches of the Nilo-Saharan family tree, Koman and Central Sudanic (see figure 1), but happened to have been entirely lost in just those branches? One key characteristic of the evidence rules against this possibility. Namely, the newly evident terms at each node form semantically coherent cultural suites:

1. at the Proto–Northern Sudanic node, a set of verbs and nouns specifically for herding of, apparently, cattle;
2. at the Proto-Saharo-Sahelian node, a set of verbs and one noun specifically for cultivation activities, along with a suite of terms depicting sedentary settlements; and
3. at the Proto-Sahelian node, separate suites of nouns specifically for goats and for sheep.

The probability that chance preservation accounts for the observed culturally coherent semantic patterns is vanishingly small. Moreover, whenever any of these particular terms is traceable back to earlier stages in Nilo-Saharan history, in each case it previously had a nonherding or noncultivating meaning.

To recapitulate, the nine word histories sampled here are part of a much larger body of word histories demonstrating that, in the earliest periods of the linguistically recoverable history of Nilo-Saharan peoples, their societies were gatherer-hunters in economy. Food production took hold among them later on, during three successive historical eras. First, the Proto–Northern Sudanic communities began to tend cattle. The only vocabulary of residence we yet have for this period suggests a transhumant style of life for the Proto–Northern Sudanians. To this era also dates the earliest verb for making pottery (appendix 2). Next the cultivation of crops was taken up by the Proto-Saharo-Sahelians. In addition, the Proto-Saharo-Sahelians developed a vocabulary indicative of the existence of large sedentary settlements, including words for thornbush cattle pens, large homestead yards, round houses, and granaries. Finally, in the periods represented by the Proto-Sahelian and Proto-Saharan stages in the Nilo-Saharan linguistic stratigraphy, terminology relating to goats and sheep came into use.

The historian can visually depict this kind of lexical history in the stratigraphy itself. Figure 2 (presented later in this chapter) illustrates how this can be done for Nilo-Saharan history. Focusing in particular on the strata leading from Proto-Sudanic down to Proto-Sahelian, figure 2 identifies the new kinds of words present at each stratum and draws a link attaching each set of new lexicon to the stratum in which it first occurred. These data draw on a fuller list than just the nine word histories sampled above. This fuller list appears in appendix 3. Episodes of word borrowing as well as episodes in the development of new words and new meanings for old words can be depicted in this fashion. Lexical changes in the stratum leading to the Proto-Sahelian node on the Nilo-Saharan tree, for example, included the adoption of loanwords from an Afroasiatic language.

LOCATING PAST SOCIETIES:
AN EXAMPLE FROM NILO-SAHARAN HISTORY

To turn the linguistic findings into satisfactory history we must correlate them with other datable evidence of the past, such as archaeology or written documents. To accomplish this correlation, two other lines of linguistic historical argumentation must be applied. One is to use the more recent locations of the languages of a family to argue for the most probable areas in which their earlier protolanguages would have been found. The other is to apply glottochronology to estimate the broad time frame within which particular protolanguages would have been spoken.

Locating Societies in Place

In arguing for earlier language locations, the most probable historical scheme is the one that requires the least population displacement and the fewest population movements to account for the modern locations of the languages of the family. The sequence of argumentation begins with the most recent branchings among the languages and moves backward in time. We sometimes call this approach by its own name—*the principle of fewest moves*—but it is simply a version of the usual scientific principle of Occam's razor, adapted to historical argumentation from linguistic evidence.

In many cases a very close determination of high probability can be made on the basis of this criterion. The Kalenjin language, for instance, consists of four primary clusters of dialects.[15] Three of these are spoken in a compact region of western Kenya, while the fourth, South Kalenjin, occurs several hundred kilometers away in central Tanzania. It is immensely improbable that four peoples should spread out of some third area, or for that matter out of central Tanzania, and all by mere chance end up tightly clustered in another place altogether. It is so improbable that no solution can reasonably be entertained other than that Proto-Kalenjin was spoken somewhere in the area of western Kenya defined by the three clustered dialect groupings, and that the South Kalenjin spread via population movements from there.

More complex applications of the same basic principle have been made in plotting the spread of the Bantu peoples,[16] Ubangian-speaking peoples,[17] and the Austronesians.[18] Other important applications have been made in Native American history.[19]

What does this principle reveal about the geographical history of the Nilo-Saharan development of food production? The latest of the three stages we have identified for this history took place among the Proto-Sahelians. (See the Nilo-Saharan family tree in figure 1.) With the exception of a single subgroup, Eastern Sahelian—which extends from the Nubian languages of the Nile in the northern Sudan to the Maasai language of north-central Tanzania—all the Sahelian groups today are located in the Sahel geographical belt, along the southern edges of the Sahara Desert, extending from Songay, spoken in Mali near the interior delta of the Niger River, to the For language of the Marra Mountains in Sudan. The most parsimonious history of population movements is therefore one that places the lands of Proto-Sahelian broadly somewhere along the southern edge of the Sahara region.

At the next previous stage in this history, Proto-Sahelian diverged as a sister language of Proto-Saharan out of their common ancestor, Proto-Saharo-Sahelian. The modern-day distribution of the daughter languages of Proto-Saharan reaches from the Sahara Desert fringes north of the Marra Mountains—where Zaghawa and Berti are spoken—to the Tibesti region of the east-central Sahara Desert—occupied by the Tibu people—and to the Chad Basin at the south edge of the central Sahara, in which the Kanuri and Kanem languages are spoken. The Proto-Saharan speech territory therefore most probably lay in the southern or southeastern parts of what is today the central Sahara Desert. If we combine the arguments for locating the Proto-Saharan and Proto-Sahelian territories, the simplest history we can construct would attribute the wide spread of the Sahelian languages to a single early east-west expansion, with that expansion beginning from a region adjacent to the proposed Proto-Saharan lands in the east-central or southeast-central Sahara.

Finally, we consider the first of the three stages. In that period the Proto–Northern Sudanic language diverged into two branchings: Proto-Saharo-Sahelian, whose lands in our reckoning would best be placed in the east-central or southeast-central Sahara; and Kunama, today a single language spoken just beyond the far southeastern edge of the Sahara Desert, in the far northwestern part of the Ethiopian Highlands. The simplest account of this historical stage would involve either:

a. the expansion of the speakers of the Proto-Saharo-Sahelian daughter language of Proto-Northern Sudanic westward from the southeastern Sahara;
b. the expansion of the speakers of the earliest form of the Kunama language eastward from the southeast-central Sahara; or
c. the spreads of both groups outward from a common center somewhere in the eastern half of the southern Sahara regions.

Locating Societies in Time: A Linguistic Approach

Having made the case for the most probable locations of the earliest Northern Sudanic speech communities, we turn to the issue of dating. One way to give a dating framework to this history is to apply the technique with the unprepossessing name *glottochronology.* Deriving dates for linguistic history will be the topic of chapter 5, and the issues, problems, and criticisms of glottochronology will be taken up there. But a preliminary mention of the approach is necessary here. Glottochronology uses detailed empirical findings from a variety of language families from far-flung parts of the world, which reveal a recurrent pattern of lexical change in what has been called "basic" or "core" vocabulary. Scholars have used standard lists, commonly called "Swadesh" lists, of one hundred or two hundred meanings that are basic and nearly universal in the world's languages, to uncover this pattern. Everywhere investigations have been carried out, the proportions of words for those meanings that a language replaces over particular time spans tend to cluster around the same *median* percentages.

Note the emphasis on the word *median.* What takes place in core vocabulary is the accumulation of many changes that are individually *random and unpredictable.* The accumulation of lexical replacements in different languages then becomes describable by statistics and distribution curves. Glottochronology does not at all postulate regular, predictable change, although both its supporters and detractors have often made that claim; rather, it describes the cumulative outcome of many unpredictable events. This sort of phenomenon is, of course, quite familiar to sociologists and political scientists studying human behavior, but it is perhaps a bit exotic to linguists, some of whom have talked as if they thought a mystical regularity was being imputed to language change. The recent blanket dismissal of glottochronology by the influential historian Jan Vansina[20] shows that linguistically trained historians, too, can be susceptible to such misunderstandings.

To return to the key findings, repeatedly verified from language families around the world: the proportions of lexical replacement in core vocabulary over particular spans of time appear to distribute around the same median figures in the Americas, Europe, Asia, and Africa. The findings apply equally well to the Bantu languages of eastern and southern Africa as to the Nilotic languages;[21] to the languages of the very distantly related Semitic and Cushitic branches of the Afrasian family;[22] to the Turkic language group; to Carib and Numic in the Americas; to Japanese; and to a variety of Indo-European cases.[23] Nor does the size or social complexity of the speech community appear to modify the long-term outcome of this kind of vocabulary change.[24]

In the case of the Northern Sudanic branch of Nilo-Saharan, the languages of its two coordinate subbranches, Kunama and Saharo-Sahelian, have very low cognation percentages with each other in the one-hundred-meaning list, centering around 3–5 percent.[25] With 5 percent as the median figure for a 10,000-year period, these counts project a very, very rough date for the divergence of Proto–Northern Sudanic at somewhat earlier than 10,000 years ago—in other words, at around the eleventh millennium BP, consistent with the indications of the archaeological correlations.

Locating Societies in Time by Correlating Stratigraphies

But glottochronology by itself offers only a broad projection of the most probable time frame of the linguistically attested history. We make a far stronger case for our dating if we are able to establish detailed correlations of the kinds and sequence of developments revealed in our linguistic stratigraphies with those found in particular archaeological stratigraphies. One of the most complex and sophisticated exercises in this kind of correlation is that of Stanley Ambrose for the archaeological and linguistic history of early food-producing societies in East Africa. A recent example is Christine Saidi's book on gender in early African history, which shows how archaeology and language history dovetail point for point in southeastern Central Africa over the past 2,000-plus years.[26]

To establish correlations of this kind, we need three kinds of linguistic discovery:

1. inferences from the linguistic geography of language families as to the most probable earlier locations of the speech communities whose archaeology we are looking for;
2. proposed broad dating frameworks for those communities, arrived at through glottochronological projections; and
3. linguistic reconstruction of numerous word histories predicting the elements of material culture we can expect to find in the archaeology of those communities.

Our cases for correlation become even richer when we have available to us significant bodies of loanword evidence, as both Ambrose and Saidi have in their studies. This kind of resource often reveals the particular material cultural transmissions that took place between peoples and that therefore can be expected to leave traces in the archaeology. For the early Northern Sudanic communities, the borrowing at the Proto-Sahelian and Proto-Saharan eras in the stratigraphy of words for goats and sheep are such an instance.

In the case of the Northern Sudanic speakers and their descendants, the three kinds of linguistic discovery prove to be powerful tools. The arguments from Nilo-Saharan linguistic geography indicate that we should look for correlative archaeology where the Northern Sudanic peoples most likely lived: in the southern half of the eastern Sahara. The projected glottochronological dates direct our attention specifically to the next 2,000 or 3,000 years after approximately 9000 BCE. The reconstructed lexicon of material culture identifies the specific changes in the features of subsistence and residence to look for in the archaeology and shows that these changes took hold over three successive eras of time.

And in fact, for just the periods from 8500 BCE onward in the history of the eastern Sahara—then a land mostly of steppe, grassland, and dry savanna environments—the very same sequence of developments can be identified in the archaeology as in the linguistic evidence of early Nilo-Saharan food production.[27] In areas that included far southwestern Egypt, a three-stage development of food production took place between about 8500 and 6000 BCE:[28]

1. Food production began with the tending of cattle by people making pottery and living in relatively ephemeral settlements between 8500 and 7500 BCE. The lexical evidence of economy and residence allows us to identify the inventors of this new subsistence tradition specifically with the speakers of the Proto–Northern Sudanic language.
2. That development was followed in the later 7000s BCE by the appearance of prima facie evidence—including complex settlements with cattle pens, large homesteads, round houses, and granaries—for a second development in food production: cultivation. Here our correlative linguistic stratigraphy attributes this era of change in subsistence and, most strikingly, in residential patterns to the Proto-Saharo-Sahelian society.
3. At a still later point in time, between 6500 and 6000 BCE, the first evidence of sheep and goats appears in the material record. This development, from our linguistic stratigraphy, can be placed in the period after Proto-Saharo-Sahelian society had begun to break up into its daughter Proto-Sahelian and Proto-Saharan societies (figure 2 and map 1).

A different sort of correlative dating of language evidence involves being able to show: (1) that a word contains a particular sound change; and (2) that the sound change in question occurred before or after historical events that are datable on other grounds. If the word has the sound change, then it would have come into use in the language—and it would reflect an idea or thing known to the speakers of the language—before the time at which the sound change operated. If it does not show the expected sound change, then the inference is that the word came into the language after the sound change.

An especially illustrative African example relates to the history of the spread of new kinds of political complexity in the past 700 years in southern Central Africa. The relevant sound change was a tonal switch in the Luba language of Katanga, with high tones changing to low and low tones changing to high. The Luba word for "tribute paid from a lesser chief to a higher chief or king," musónkó, was adopted into the Nyanja-Cewa language of Malawi in a form without that sound change. Its adoption by Nyanja-Cewa speakers therefore reflects the spread of royal institutions from the Luba at a time prior to the sound shift. The oral traditions relate that ruling families of Luba descent settled and began building kingdoms in Nyanja-Cewa areas in Malawi around the fourteenth century. In contrast, the same noun was borrowed, but *with* the tone-reversing sound change present, into the Sabi languages of eastern and central Zambia, thus revealing a wave of Luba influence there dating *after* the sound change. The Zambian oral traditions also record the spread of Luba

Figure 2. Nilo-Saharan Family Tree:
New Developments in Lexicon from Proto-Sudanic to Proto-Sahelian with Parallel Archaeological Sequence

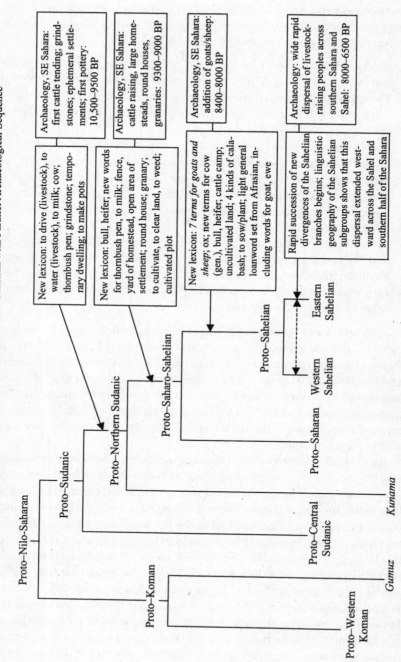

political influence but, in line with the linguistic indications, date that impact to around the seventeenth century. Together the two borrowings of the word for "tribute" require that the Luba Katanga tonal shift happened between roughly 1400 and 1600.[29]

The sound change in this instance is uniquely informative, because it affected not just some but all the words of the language. If, as is probable, words other than just musónkó passed at these periods from Luba to Nyanja-Cewa and to the Sabi group, those words and the specific cultural adoptions they represent will also be datable to before or after the period of the tonal sound change. Historical inference from this kind of language evidence is likely to be similarly productive elsewhere in the world where tonal languages are spoken; East and Southeast Asia come readily to mind.[30]

CONSTRUCTING A HISTORICAL NARRATIVE FROM LANGUAGE EVIDENCE

The examples from early African history illustrate the basic techniques of the historical reconstruction of history from linguistics and show how archaeology and linguistic findings can be combined in satisfying ways. The cases cited from Nilo-Saharan history, in particular, familiarize us with some of the long-established methods and formats to follow in this kind of historical study. They give us a first awareness of just how far-reaching and valuable this work can be.

But the really important advances and the most sophisticated and original applications of linguistic methods in African history writing have dealt with the past 3,000 to 4,000 years. Notable recent exemplars, already described in chapter 1, are Jan Vansina's Paths in the Rainforests, David Schoenbrun's A Green Place, a Good Place, Kairn Klieman's "The Pygmies Were Our Compass," and my book An African Classical Age.[31] Each of these works intertwines the evidence of many hundreds or, in some cases, even thousands of word histories. Each marshals a great body of comparative ethnographic evidence to evoke and articulate the complex social and cultural changes those word histories reveal. Each engages the long-term social and political developments as well as the multiple trajectories of agricultural and technological history and the consequences of trade and the diffusion of things and ideas over longer and shorter distances. Each integrates the available archaeology into its story, and Schoenbrun's book brings in, as well, the contributions of paleo-environmental studies.

The importance of these books reaches beyond just the uncovering of the African past. They offer models for the writing of full and satisfying social and economic histories of large regions—or political histories, in the case Vansina's book—applicable to any region of the world where written documentation is lacking and to many parts of the world for which written documentation exists but is sparse and uneven.

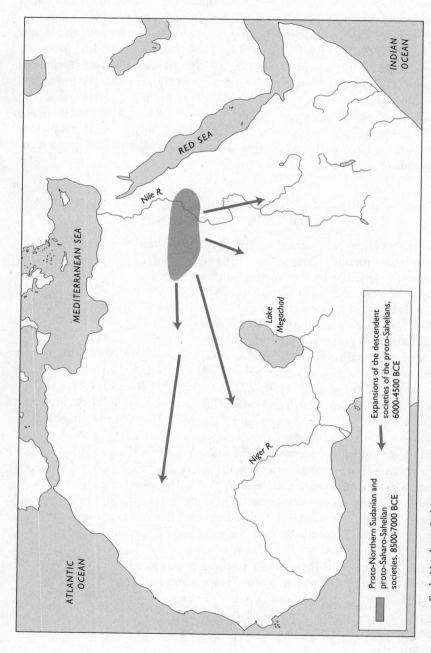

MAP 1. Early Northern Sudanian Agripastoralists

Each work demonstrates the great power of language evidence in displaying the history of the inner as well as the outer lives of those societies. Vansina constructs the *longue durée* evolution of political institutions among the Bantu peoples of the equatorial rainforest regions of Africa, a story of ancient genesis and great complexity and longevity. Klieman's book revisits that history, bringing new detail to the early periods and turning a bright light on the previously neglected social and ritual history of those regions and on the Batwa as salient historical actors. Schoenbrun's study dissects the complex histories of change in thought, ritual, and institutions over 1,500 years that laid the foundations for the rise of states in the African Great Lakes region in the second millennium CE. *An African Classical Age* depicts the complex unfolding of cross-cultural interactions in eastern Africa in the last millennium BCE, involving peoples of all four of the major African language families, and the emergence out of those interactions of a new cultural, social, and economic synthesis and its spread in the early first millennium CE all across the eastern and southern sides of the continent. It sets that history, as well, within the wider African and world historical contexts of its times.

Other scholars are now pursuing similarly new directions in their work,[32] and we can confidently expect further exciting advances in the coming years. What has been discussed here only scratches the surface of what linguistic techniques can bring to the study of history in Africa—and to the building of rich and deep understandings of all the neglected histories of preliterate or otherwise underdocumented societies around the world.

NOTES

1. As noted in chap. 1, an especially useful introduction for historians to the relevant range of historical linguistic issues is T. Crowley, *An Introduction to Historical Linguistics,* 3rd ed. (Oxford: Oxford University Press, 1997).

2. In many cases, as a mother language begins to differentiate into daughters, an intermediate period may ensue during which the language consists of mutually interacting dialects. If speakers of the different dialects do not move off to settle in distant areas, and if no irruptive movements of other peoples break up the continuity of the language area, then the dialects may continue for centuries to be spoken by contiguous communities each able to understand each other's speech; that is, the communities will form a dialect network or chain.

In such a network of related but diverging communities, a tendency will exist for changes, such as lexical innovations, that arise in one dialect to spread to one or more of its neighboring dialects. Because of this contact phenomenon, even centuries later the daughter languages that developed out of neighboring dialects will share more linguistic features with each other, including higher percentages of old cognates—words retained in common—than with daughter languages that derived from dialects more distant from each other in the original dialect continuum. The original geographical distribution of the dialects into which the mother language initially diverged can thus often be inferred from the variations in the percentages of cognation between the various daughter languages. The Romance languages in Europe are a prime example of this phenomenon.

3. My own work on African languages supports the position, generally followed by historical lin-

guists since Antoine Meillet's work in the early twentieth century, that there is no such creature as a true *Mischsprache*—a language formed from the equal merging of two or more languages. Every language has a fundamental inherited core, plus differing degrees of admixture, sometimes extensive and far-reaching, of elements adopted from other languages with which that language has interacted during its history. Sarah Grey Thomason and Terrence Kaufman's book *Language Contact, Creolization, and Genetic Linguistics* (Berkeley and Los Angeles: University of California Press, 1988), by raising theoretical issues about how to classify languages with very high degrees of admixture from other languages, gave an initial impetus to a revival in the 1990s of the idea of *Mischsprachen* among a number of scholars.

A very few cases of extreme admixture do exist in the world. The African instance most commonly cited over the years has been the Southern Cushitic language Ma'a. Maarten Mous (most recently in *The Making of a Mixed Language: The Case of Ma'a/Mbugu* [Amsterdam and Philadelphia: John Benjamins, 2003]) has particularly championed the conclusion that this language is a true mixed language. But it would seem that he worked with a jargon based on Ma'a, not on the same Ma'a language that I worked with in my field research in the 1960s and again in the 1970s. Besides observing Ma'a in home use, I have studied long oral historical texts in the language, gathered by Professor Steven Feierman in the late 1960s. These texts reveal a functioning, living Ma'a language with differing syntactic features from the Bantu languages that have so deeply influenced it. For example, in contrast to Bantu languages, it is a prepositional language. It is also possible, from the phonological history of this language, to seriate the progressive intrusion of more and more Bantu grammatical features into the language and to see that the admixing took place by stages over an extended period of time. The comparative method of historical linguistics thus applies quite well to deciphering the history and descent of this language (as evidenced in detail in C. Ehret, *The Historical Reconstruction of Southern Cushitic Phonology and Vocabulary* [Berlin: Reimer, 1980]) and allows the Ma'a evidence to be deployed in the usual fashions in reconstructing the history of its speakers. (See also chap. 8 of this book.)

4. This subclassification is constructed from detailed lexical, semantic, and grammatical innovation histories in C. Ehret, *A Historical-Comparative Reconstruction of Nilo-Saharan* (Cologne: Rüdiger Köppe Verlag, 2001). An alternative Nilo-Saharan subclassification, different in several key aspects, is followed in M. L. Bender, *The Nilo-Saharan Languages: A Comparative Essay* (Munich: LINCOM Europa. 1997), and elsewhere. The differences derive primarily from the fact that Bender uses a less wide range of classificatory evidence and a superficial, impressionistic, and only partial phonological reconstruction of Proto-Nilo-Saharan.

5. Each of these many later strata preserves its own complex body of evidence on the history of Nilo-Saharan societies over the past seven millennia. These immense historical resources still remain largely unused by historians.

6. C. Ehret, *Ethiopians and East Africans: The Problem of Contacts* (Nairobi: East African Publishing House, 1974).

7. M. N. Ali, "History in the Horn of Africa, 1000 BC to 1500 AD" (Ph.D. diss., UCLA, 1985).

8. C. Ehret, "Linguistics, Historical," in J. Middleton (ed.), *Encyclopedia of Africa South of the Sahara* (New York: Charles Scribner's Sons, 1997), vol. 2, pp. 579–580.

9. C. Ehret, "Historical Inference from Transformations in Cultural Vocabularies," *Sprache und Geschichte in Africa* 2 (1978): 189–218.

10. C. Ehret, *An African Classical Age: Eastern and Southern Africa in World History, 1000 BC to AD 400* (Charlottesville: University Press of Virginia, 1998).

11. Ehret, *Historical-Comparative Reconstruction of Nilo-Saharan*.

12. C. Ehret, "Nilo-Saharans and the Saharo-Sudanese Neolithic," in T. Shaw and others (eds.), *Archaeology of Africa: Foods, Metals and Towns* (London and New York: Routledge, 1993), pp. 104–125; idem, "Who Were the Rock Painters? Linguistic Evidence for the Holocene Populations of the Sahara,"

in Alfred Muzzolini and Jean-Loïc Le Quellec (eds.), *Symposium: Rock Art and the Sahara*, in *Proceedings of the International Rock Art and Cognitive Archaeology Congress News 95* (Turin: Centro Studi e Museo d'Arte Preistorica, 1999); idem, *Historical-Comparative Reconstruction of Nilo-Saharan*.

13. After this root word, as well as after each other root sampled here, a number is given in parentheses. This is the root's number, allowing it to be easily looked up in the Nilo-Saharan etymological dictionary in Ehret, *Historical-Comparative Reconstruction of Nilo-Saharan*. The reader will discover that several of the roots are written slightly differently in this article from how they appear in the etymological dictionary of Nilo-Saharan in order to make them more readable for the nonlinguist. This root, for instance, appears as *tɔ:k in the dictionary. The colon indicates that the utterance of the vowel was stretched out longer than for a single *o* by itself, such as we see in the root *yókw (#5). But that fact would not be obvious to most readers. For that reason the root was rendered here as *tóók, with an additional *o* to express the lengthening of the vowel. The acute accent over the vowels indicates high tone; an accent grave, as in the root word *kʰày (#2), denotes a low tone. The lack of a tone mark means that the tones of the word cannot yet be reconstructed.

14. Ehret, "Nilo-Saharans"; idem, "Who Were the Rock Painters?"

15. John Albert Distefano, "The Precolonial History of the Kalenjin of Kenya: A Methodological Comparison of Linguistic and Oral Traditional Evidence" (Ph.D. diss., UCLA, 1985).

16. Chapter 1, note 20, surveys the important sources on this topic.

17. Douglas E. Saxon, "The History of the Shari River Basin, ca. 500 B.C.–1000 A.D." (Ph.D. diss., UCLA, 1980).

18. Robert A. Blust has taken up this topic in several of his works, and his lead has been followed by other scholars of the Austronesian family. One branch of the Austronesian family, Oceanic, has been treated to an especially thoroughgoing application of the techniques of lexical reconstruction of the history of all aspects of culture: Malcolm Ross, Andrew Pawley, and Meredith Osmond (eds.), *The Lexicon of Proto-Oceanic: The Culture and Environment of Ancestral Oceanic Society*, 5 vols. (Canberra: Pacific Linguistics: Research School of Pacific and Asian Studies, The Australian National University, 1998–2007).

19. S. Lamb, "Linguistic Prehistory in the Great Basin," *International Journal of American Linguistics* 24 (1958): 95–100. This article, in which Lamb applies these principles in tracking the spread of a particular set of societies—the Numic subgroup of Uto-Aztecan speakers—is a particularly well known example of this kind of work in Native American history. Edward Sapir, *Time Perspective in Aboriginal American Culture* (Ottawa: Canadian Geological Series, 1916), provides the classic overall introduction to both linguistic and comparative ethnographic methods, including inference of history from distributional patterns.

20. J. Vansina, *How Societies Are Born: Governance in West Central Africa before 1600* (Charlottesville: University of Virginia Press, 2004).

21. See chap. 5 below.

22. S. Ambrose, "Archaeology and Linguistic Reconstruction of History in East Africa" in C. Ehret and M. Posnansky (eds.), *The Archaeological and Linguistic Reconstruction of African History* (Berkeley and Los Angeles: University of California Press, 1982), pp. 104–157; Ehret, *African Classical Age;* C. Saidi, *Women's Authority and Society in Early East-Central Africa* (Rochester, NY: University of Rochester Press, 2010); Ehret, *Historical-Comparative Reconstruction of Nilo-Saharan*.

23. For more of the relevant sources, see C. Ehret, "Language Change and the Material Correlates of Language and Ethnic Shift," *Antiquity* 62 (1988): 569.

24. Very few studies have sought to apply actual evidence to disprove glottochronology. One kind of substantive work dealt with individual languages in which the apparent rate of change in basic vocabulary was significantly less that expected by the method. (K. Bergslund and H. Vogt, "On the Validity of Glottochronology," *Current Anthropology* 3 [1962]: 115–153, is a notable case.) But these languages

each had a long history of being associated with the special social preservation and recital of the older literary forms, a situation that provided a strong and recurrent potential for feedback from those ancient literary sources to the spoken language, thus reinforcing the use of older vocabulary and slowing the replacement of old words by new. The results of these studies do not after all contradict the expectations of the method and do nothing that brings into question the utility of glottochronology in the study of unwritten languages.

Other scholars have been bothered by the fact that lesser apparent rates of change apply to neighboring languages in a chain of contiguous, closely related dialects. But those instances derive from histories in which the society that spoke the mother language underwent an incomplete divergence into daughter communities, and in which the intersocietal boundaries did not become well defined. Such histories regularly produce a recognizable patterning of percentages allowing them to be easily identified and understood. Normally the dialects located farthest apart, at opposite end of the chain, have cognate percentages with each other that fit well with the glottochronological expectations. The dialects located in between them have percentages that are skewed higher in direct proposition to how close they are to each other, with adjacent dialects sharing the highest percentages of all.

25. M. L. Bender, "The Languages of Ethiopia: A New Lexicostatistical Classification and Some Problems of Diffusion," *Anthropological Linguistics* 13, no. 5 (1971): 165–288; C. Ehret, unpublished pdf documents, available from the author on request. This latter document revises the word lists in Bender according to the criteria of regular cognation in Ehret, *Historical-Comparative Reconstruction of Proto-Nilo-Saharan,* and includes data from additional languages.

26. Ambrose, "Archaeology and Linguistic Reconstruction"; Saidi, *Women's Authority.*

27. R. Kuper and S. Kröpelin. "Climate-Controlled Holocene Occupation in the Sahara: Motor of Africa's Evolution," *Science* 313 (11 August 2006): 803–807.

28. F. Wendorf, R. Schild, and A. Close (eds.), *Cattle Keepers of the Eastern Sahara: The Neolithic of Bir Kiseiba* (Dallas: Southern Methodist University Press, 1984); F. Wendorf and R. Schild, "Nabta Playa and Its Role in Northeastern African History," *Anthropological Archaeology* 20 (1998): 97–123; F. Wendorf, R. Schild, and associates, *The Archaeology of Nabta Playa,* Holocene Settlement of the Egyptian Sahara, vol. 1 (New York: Kluwer Academic/Plenum Publishers, 2001).

29. C. Ehret, "Linguistic Evidence and Its Correlation with Archaeology," *World Archaeology* 8, no. 1 (1976): 5–18.

30. The diagnostic power of tonal sound changes is most relevant to historicizing the diffusion of culture and ideas when both the loaning and the borrowing languages are tonal. It does not have the same significance in cases in which borrowing goes from a tonal to a nontonal language, such as from Chinese to Japanese. On the other hand, the loss of consonants so evident in the evolution of Chinese provides an alternative kind of strong diagnostic sound-change evidence for dating the successive layers of Chinese loanwords in Korean and Japanese.

31. J. Vansina, *Paths in the Rainforests: Toward a History of Political Tradition in Equatorial Africa* (Madison: University of Wisconsin Press, 1990); D. Schoenbrun, *A Green Place, a Good Place: Agrarian Change, Gender, and Social Identity in the Great Lakes Region to the 15th Century* (Portsmouth, NH: Heinemann, 1998); K. Klieman, *"The Pygmies Were Our Compass": Bantu and Batwa in the History of West Central Africa, Early Times to c. 1900 C.E.* (Portsmouth, NH: Heinemann, 2003); Ehret, *African Classical Age.*

32. E.g., Saidi, *Women's Authority;* R. M. Gonzales, *Societies, Religion, and History: Central East Tanzanians and the World They Created, c. 200 BCE to 1800 CE* (New York: Columbia University Press, 2009).

3

Historical Inference from Transformations in the Vocabularies of Culture

Building historical chronologies from language evidence and periodizing the lexical documents of cultural practice and knowledge were the brief of chapter 2. By setting this linguistic historical framework in place, the historian opens up a wide variety of further pathways toward inferring history from language. This chapter explores in particular what the study of semantic transformation in cultural lexicons can reveal about the history of the ideas and the organization of knowledge and activities of life in earlier times and places.

AXIOMS IN UNDERSTANDING
SHIFTS IN SEMANTIC SYSTEMS

The vocabulary of any language contains words to express the whole range of culture and information entertained by the society that speaks the language. When culture or information changes, vocabulary change, however subtle or slight, must occur, too. Transformative change in a particular area of economy, customs, cultural knowledge, or the material circumstances of life inevitably leads to fundamental changes in the vocabulary of those areas of life and livelihood.

The lexicon of culture can change through the addition of new vocabulary:

An earlier version of this chapter appeared as C. Ehret, "Historical Inferences from Transformations in Culture Vocabularies," *Sprache unde Geschichte in Afrika* 2 (1980): 189–218. It has been revised here to bring it up to date in its linguistic information, its naming of groups, and its language classifications; used by permission of Rüdiger Köppe Verlag.

1. by borrowing words from other languages; and
2. by deriving new terms from old root words already present in the language.

Cultural lexicon also evolves:

3. through the creation of new meanings and usages for existing words; and
4. through the dropping from common use, and eventually from the language altogether, of words that are no longer culturally salient.

If a full-fledged transformation of some aspect or portion of culture has taken place, then a systemic transformation of semantic patterning in the lexicon relating to the transformed segment of culture can be expected as well.

On the other hand, change in vocabulary does not necessarily imply cultural change or the addition of new information. Words and meanings can change or shift in application for a variety of causes and pressures that we can link together under the rubric of *fashion*. For example, if a particular social or ethnic group is considered prestigious, its prestige will generally lead to the adoption of many of its words and semantic patterns by neighboring groups, whether or not relations with the prestige group leads to significant culture change. Similarly, periods of extensive bilingualism between two culturally similar societies, where relatively equal prestige of the two participant groups obtains, can yield the exchange of different vocabulary elements. But the social determinants of which particular words get borrowed in which particular directions may be difficult to discern in such a case. Even the individual displacements over the centuries of one word or meaning by another, as part of long-term random change within the vocabulary of a particular language, are probably each favored or preconditioned, however indirectly, by the conscious or unconscious social predilections of the era. An especially visible and hence commonly noted form of such social causation is the propensity of taboo subjects to bring about rapid lexical turnover in the subsets of vocabulary dealing with them.

Every vocabulary change can therefore be suggested to be a response in some manner or another to historical developments or to conditions or attitudes at the time of the change, and every such shift is thus a potential indicator of a past situation affecting the speakers of the language. There is no possibility of ever tracing the entire lexical and semantic history of a language, but in nearly every case the history of a large and broadly representative proportion of vocabulary can be traced back over a considerable period of time through historical linguistic methods. As with all historical endeavors, the historian simply makes use of the data still recoverable and reconstructs the portion of history that those data allow.

The discoveries of ethnoscience add a further potential level of information to what a historian can extract from lexical evidence. The insight that all peoples organize and categorize their knowledge, whether or not they have professional philosophers and scholars, offers a diagnostic context for judging the import of particular vocabulary changes. Individual additions to general knowledge and new fashions that do not upset wider cultural adjustments in a society will be reflected in the integration of new words into existing categorizations and semantic patterns. In contrast, a cultural transformation, being by definition a transformation of perceptions and usages across a whole area of activity in a society, commonly leads to a semantic resystematization of the vocabulary dealing with that area of culture. From the resulting changes in semantic patterning, and from the histories of the individual words that contribute to the shifted pattern, we can often infer a great deal about the dimensions and nature of that transformation.

TRANSFORMATIONS IN TANGIBLE CULTURE

The Example of Livestock Terminologies

The least difficult cultural transformations to identify from this sort of perspective are those with tangible vocabulary referents, for the reason that the lexemes of a categorization—and thus also the taxonomy they form—describe concrete, visually definable objects and so are relatively simply elicited. The principal criteria of synchronic inference in livestock subsistence areas of culture can be illustrated by (now partially obsolete) English breeding taxonomies (table 1).[1]

The four major subsistence animals—the cow, sheep, pig, and chicken—all have (or had) categorizations consisting of at least five simplex terms, including those for "gelded male." This kind of categorization is diagnostic of the subsistence importance of the animal. Two animals—the cow and chicken, whose females provide another food product in addition to meat (milk or eggs)—even had seven-term breeding taxonomies, distinguishing not-yet-mature females and males.

In contrast, animals of secondary significance for subsistence tend to have more limited breeding taxonomies. Among English speakers, geese and ducks were given four-term breeding taxonomies, in which the generic term doubled as the word for mature female. Another animal of low importance, as well as low esteem— the goat—once had a three-term taxonomy, with *goat* as generic, *buck* for the male, and *kid* for young. Only *goat* and *kid* lasted into early English as terms specifically applicable to the animal, although compounds of recent coinage turn up in jocular or storytelling contexts—that is, *nanny goat* and *billy goat*.

Animals without significance for subsistence, even an animal as widely bred and favored by the English as the dog, had very simple breeding taxonomies. In the case of the dog, two subgeneric simplex terms existed, *bitch* and *puppy*. For the disrespected donkey, there was just the compound term *jackass*. It is possible also to apply subgeneric terminology of horses to donkeys in a few cases, although only in compound or implied compound form—for example, "(donkey)-mare." But these are only descriptive extensions of the effective folk taxonomy of a far more important animal: the horse.

Table 1. English Stock Breeding Taxonomies

generic	cow	sheep	pig	chicken	horse	goose	duck
male	bull	ram/ tup	boar	cock	stallion/ stud	gander	drake
gelded male	ox/ steer	wether	*hog	capon	gelding		
young male	bullock		shoat	cockerel	colt		
bearing female	cow	ewe	sow	hen	mare	goose	duck
young female	heifer		shoat	pullet	filly		
young (gen.)	calf	lamb	farrow	chick	foal	gosling	duckling

The horse was the one nonsubsistence animal (nonsubsistence in England, at least) that had fully as complex a breeding terminology in English as any of the subsistence livestock. This situation is accounted for by the extraordinarily prestigious role of horse ownership in earlier British social systems and its surpassing importance in work, war, and social display.

In addition to possessing a primary breeding taxonomy, domestic animals in some societies may be defined according to a crosscutting taxonomy based on factors of appearance. Most commonly the defining elements are skin-coloration patterns, but sometimes horn formation contributes additional terms in the case of horned stock. Such a classification is always supplementary to and never occurs without the primary breeding taxonomy. It indicates that the animals so named—in addition to being, or in distinction to being, subsistence resources—act as signs or tokens of social and economic position and power in the society and that they bear an intrinsic value above and beyond their practical usefulness in subsistence or work. In English livestock terminology, simplex coloration taxonomy is preeminently equine—for example, *roan, bay, sorrel,* and so on. In many parts of Africa, cattle long ago acquired this kind of prominence and social significance and so are accorded categorization by color and other factors of appearance.

Finally, animals can also be distinguished by breed names. Breeds and, in the case of plants, varieties tend to be regional developments. As well, interbreeding normally rearranges breed and variety relationships, so that the particular terms used tend to be relatively short-lived. The contemporary distributions of such names can often provide evidence for contacts and adoptions dating to the last few centuries, but they tell little about earlier transformations of subsistence life. David Lloyd's history of the Avongara-Azande agriculture in the eighteenth and nineteenth centuries, based on field studies undertaken in the 1970s, provides an especially illustrative case study of how effective the evidence of crop-variety names, when combined with the testimony of oral tradition, can be in recovering very recent eras of agricultural change and innovation.[2]

Transformations in Livestock Terminology: Stratifying the Data

We turn now to a particular set of historical examples in African history. The successive transformations of livestock nomenclature over the time between approximately 1000 BCE and 500 CE among the East African peoples who spoke daughter languages of Proto-Mashariki provide an especially broad range of the diachronic applications of such criteria as these to the reconstruction of culture history. The Mashariki group is a subbranch of the Savanna branch of the Bantu languages. Nearly all the Bantu languages spoken today from Uganda and Kenya south to Zimbabwe and South Africa belong to this subbranch.

To extract the historical meaning of the lexical evidence, the first step must be to lay out the linguistic historical stratigraphy into which the relevant word histories fit. We can visualize the stratigraphy of Mashariki Bantu history through the construction of two tree diagrams. The first tree, with proposed approximate dates (figure 3), depicts the background stages of history leading up to the Proto-Mashariki society, which existed at around 1000 BCE.[3]

The second tree (figure 4) gives the stratigraphy of the Kaskazi, or northern, group of the Mashariki subbranch of Savanna Bantu. During the early history of Kaskazi-speaking societies, major semantic resystematizations in the lexicon of livestock taxonomy took place, the implications of which we will now explore.

The speakers of Proto-Kaskazi resided in or near the Western Rift region of Africa, perhaps especially in areas around the northern parts of Lake Tanganyika, in the early first millennium BCE.[4] As their descendants began to spread out over a widening expanse of lands between 1000 and 500 BCE, their speech gradually diverged into the eight dialects shown on the tree: Proto-Rukwa, Proto-Rufiji-Ruvuma, Proto-Njombe, Proto-Takama, Proto-Northeast-Coastal, pre-Langi, Proto-Upland, and Proto–Great Lakes.[5] By the later middle of the first millennium BCE, the Proto–Great Lakes dialect community itself began to diverge, giving rise to four daughter societies, Proto–East Nyanza, Proto–Luhyia, Proto–North-Nyanza (*PNN* on the Kaskazi tree), and Proto–Western Lakes (*PWL* on the tree).

For some centuries all these various dialects would have continued to be spo-

Figure 3. Primary Branches of Savanna Bantu

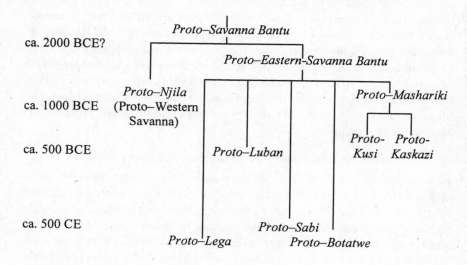

ken in areas near Lake Tanganyika and Lake Nyanza (Lake Victoria). But over time, as the various dialect communities moved out into new areas, new geographical clusters of these communities took shape. Speakers of the early Kaskazi dialects often continued to reside in neighboring areas and to have close interactions with each other. Though speaking distinct dialects, they nevertheless influenced each other linguistically, and new words that developed in one dialect often spread to other dialects in same geographical cluster. Table 2 gives examples of shared developments in livestock vocabulary, reflective of the existence of these interacting clusters of early Kaskazi communities.

Because the Kaskazi communities were growing in numbers and moving into new areas of settlement all through this time, the regional clusters of communities underwent several changes in composition over the period. On the Kaskazi tree (see figure 4), four horizontal dash lines ending in arrows identify the succession of dialect clusters that arose because of these historical processes.

Earliest in time, probably in the first half of the last millennium BCE, four Kaskazi dialect communities, the Proto-Rufiji-Ruvuma, Proto-Njombe, Proto-Takama, and Proto-Northeast-Coastal, formed such an interacting cluster of communities. This regional dialect grouping has been called the Southern Kaskazi cluster (see again figure 4).

Sometime later, probably in the centuries around the middle of the millennium, the Proto-Rufiji-Ruvuma moved away and settled eventually in the southern parts

Figure 4: Early Divergences in the Kaskazi Branch of Mashariki

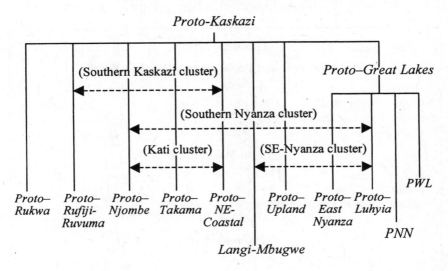

of modern-day Tanzania. The three communities that stayed behind then came into close relations with four other expanding Kaskazi dialect communities, probably in the areas southwest of Lake Nyanza. Together they developed into a new geographical cluster, the Southern Nyanza areal cluster (marked by the second horizontal dash line in figure 4). The communities participating in the second era of close interactions were the Proto-Njombe, Proto-Takama, and Proto-Northeast-Coastal, along with the Proto-Upland people, the Proto-Langi-Mbugwe, and people speaking two subdialects of Proto–Great Lakes, the Proto-Luhyia and the Proto–East Nyanza.

Somewhat later, possibly late in the second half of the millennium, the Southern Nyanza cluster broke up into two smaller areal groupings. One of the two, the Southeast-Nyanza cluster, comprised the ancestral Proto–East Nyanza, Proto-Luhyia, and Proto-Upland dialect communities and possibly the Proto-Langi-Mbugwe. The other, called the Kati cluster, consisted of the Proto-Northeast-Coastal, Proto-Njombe, and Proto-Takama speakers. The two lowest horizontal arrow lines in figure 4 link together the ancestral communities involved in these close cultural interactions. Finally, late in the first millennium BCE, these two clusters broke up, too, as some of the member communities of each cluster left the Great Lakes region altogether, moving to other, distant parts of East Africa.[6]

With the overall historical sequence of dialect clusters now laid out, we have a chronological framework for considering the specific developments in livestock

Table 2. Successive Stages in the Development of Mashariki Bantu Livestock Terminology

(goats)		(sheep)		(cattle)	
Proto-Savanna and Proto-Eastern-Savanna Bantu					
*-buli	goat				
*-boko	billy goat				
*-sampa	young female goat				
Proto-Mashariki					
*-buli	goat			*-gombe	cow
*-pongo	billy goat				
*-sampa	young female goat				
Proto-Kaskazi					
*-buli	goat			*-gombe	cow
*-pene	goat				
*-pongo	billy goat			*-kambako	bull
*-buguma	nanny goat			*-buguma	cow
*-sampa	young female goat				
Southern Kaskazi areal cluster					
*-buli	goat			*-gombe	cow
*-pene	goat				
*-pongo	billy goat			*-kambako	bull
*-kondolo	goat wether				
*-buguma	nanny goat			*-buguma	cow
*-sampa	young female goat				
Southern Nyanza areal cluster					
*-buli	goat	*-gondi,	sheep	*-gombe	cow
*-pene	goat	*-gondu			
*-pongo	billy goat	*-tulume	ram	*-kambako	bull
				*-jagamba	bull
*-buguma	nanny goat			*-buguma	cow
*-sampa	young female goat	*-keese	ewe-lamb?		

(continued)

Table 2 *(continued)*

Kati cluster					
*-buli	goat	*-gondi	sheep	*-gombe	cow
*-pene	goat	*-kolo	sheep		
*-gulata	billy goat	*-tulume	ram	*-jagamba	bull
*-pongo	billy goat			*-kambako	bull
*-diila	young billy goat?	*-keese	young ram?	*-jeku, *-jiku	young bull
*-palala	sterile billy goat?	*-palala	sterile ram?	*-kongolo	sterile bull
*-buguma	nanny goat	*-buguma	ewe	*-buguma	cow
*-taasa	sterile goat ewe	*-taasa	sterile ewe	*-taasa	sterile cow
*-togoota	young female goat	*-sampa	ewe-lamb	*-dama	heifer

Southeast-Nyanza areal cluster					
*-buli	goat	*-gondi, *-gondu	sheep	*-gombe	cow
*-pongo	billy goat	*-tulume	ram	*-jagamba	bull
*-laafu	goat wether	*-laafu	wether	*-laafu ?	steer
*-subeeni	young female goat	*-subeeni	ewe-lamb	*-mooli	heifer
*-meeme	kid	*-keese	lamb		
*-saata	barren nanny goat	*-saata	barren ewe	*-saata	barren cow
				*-koolo	black and white cow
				*-samo	speckled cow

vocabulary that took place during those eras and to the historical interpretation of those changes. Table 2 presents the specific stages in the development of those vocabularies of goat, sheep, and cattle raising, starting from the Proto–Savanna Bantu era and carrying down to the period of the dispersal of the early Kaskazi communities across East Africa.[7]

Interpreting History from Developments in the Cultural Lexicon

The successive developments in livestock terminology, as presented in table 2, reveal not just a growing complexity and variety of livestock raising among the Bantu-speaking societies of Central and eastern Africa after 1000 BCE. They also reveal changing attitudes and valuations of livestock raising among these communities, and they provide definitive evidence as well for the impact of non-Bantu peoples in stimulating many of the changes.

For the Proto-Savanna and Proto-Eastern-Savanna Bantu periods, only three livestock-classification terms can yet be reconstructed. These three terms—the generic word for "goat," the word for a male goat, and the word for a female who has not yet borne offspring—originally formed a breeding taxonomy of goats. The element within this set that is diagnostic of the raising of goats is the term for a young female that has not yet borne offspring. A term with this meaning is sufficient evidence on its own for the firm assertion that goats were not simply known to, but were raised in, Proto-Savanna and Proto-Eastern-Savanna communities as a food source. The lack in this particular taxonomy of a second kind of term, for the castrated male, which is similarly by itself diagnostic of the raising of an animal, suggests, however, that goats were not kept in such great numbers that competition among males had to be constrained. The lack of any terminology at all for sheep or cattle is entirely consistent with other evidence, which shows that sheep were later introductions and that cattle, although apparently known to the very earliest Bantu north of the forest, had long ceased to be part of the knowledge of their southerly descendants.[8]

This taxonomic pattern persisted into the Proto-Mashariki period, although with a notable addition—a generic term for a new animal: the cow. The existence of this word shows that the Proto-Mashariki knew of cattle. But the lack of any other vocabulary additions implies that they cannot have had much more than a passing acquaintance with the cow and did not actually raise the animal themselves.

In the immediately following period, the Proto-Kaskazi descendants of the Proto-Mashariki added two further cattle terms, for "bull" and "cow" (bearing female). Neither term can be considered specifically diagnostic of a Proto-Kaskazi raising of cattle. Still, the adoption of the two words does suggest that cattle were becoming a considerably more familiar animal to them and that perhaps a few Mashariki individuals kept cows in very small numbers.

The insignificant position of cattle in the economy appears to have remained unchanged on into the subsequent era of the divergence of the Proto-Kaskasi and the development of the Southern Kaskazi areal cluster of communities. On the other hand, a growing importance of goat raising is suggested by the adoption of a new practice by the Southern Kaskazi communities: the gelding of excess males. This is reflected in the coining of a new word, *-kondolo, for a goat wether. The derivation of *-kondolo from an earlier Bantu verb, *-kond- 'to strike repeatedly', tells us that the gelding was most probably accomplished by the striking and crushing of the goat's testicles between two stones—a method still practiced in a number of East African areas in more recent centuries.

During the third era, dating possibly to around mid–first millennium BCE, the new Southern Nyanza areal grouping of Bantu communities added a major new component to their livestock raising: sheep. That these communities in fact possessed sheep is evident in their development of a breeding taxonomy for the new animal, including a term most likely referring to a young sheep that had not yet borne young. This is one of the two meaning categories, the other being gelded male, described earlier as being normally diagnostic of the raising of the animal named. Two of the new terms, *-gondi/*-gondu 'sheep (generic)' and *-tulume 'ram,' are Southern Cushitic in origin; the third term, *-keese 'young sheep', comes from a Southern Nilotic language.[9] These word borrowings reveal dual sources for the adoption of sheep raising by the Southern Nyanza areal cluster of communities.

The breakup of the Southern Nyanza areal cluster into two clusters of communities, Southeast-Nyanza and Kati, appears to have marked a major historical threshold, after which livestock raising took on a much greater importance than previously, with major changes in the livestock terminology accompanying this shift.

One distinctive difference between the Southeast-Nyanza and Kati peoples appeared in the area of cattle coloration nomenclature. The beginning stages of the development of color classifications are attested for the early Southeast-Nyanza cluster of communities—for example, in the adoption of the terms for "black and white cow" and "speckled cow."[10] From this we can argue that, among the early Southeast-Nyanza peoples, cattle were already taking on the sort of high valuation that we see so commonly in more recent East African societies. Both these terms are Southern Nilotic loanwords, revealing Southern Nilotes to have been the source of this new perception. But for the Kati network of communities no similar reconstructions can be picked out. Several Kati societies did eventually develop such terminological systems, but they must be attributed to later historical developments.

In addition, the taxonomic reconstructions show that the ancestral Kati transformed the semantic patterning they inherited from their earlier Proto-Kaskazi and Mashariki ancestors. The Proto-Kaskazi and the Southern Nyanza communities of the immediately preceding period had fitted new terms into their inherited taxonomic system—some for the new animals—the cow and the sheep—and others replicating or supplementing existing subgeneric terminology. The resulting accumulation of synonyms and semantically overlapping names, such as we see in the pair of terms for "bull" in the Southern Nyanza lexicon and for "bull" and "billy goat" in the Kati lexicon in table 2, is typical of a transition period in cultural transformation. It represents the addition of knowledge not yet systematized and integrated with the old and/or competition between old and new conceptualizations of existing knowledge. As the new systematization of the knowledge set begins gradually to attain general acceptance, the presence of coexisting synonyms progressively declines through the assignment of different technical applications to some members of the synonym sets and through the obsolescence and eventual dropping from use of other remaining redundancies.

The result for the early Kati cluster of communities was that they shifted from the older Mashari taxonomy—generic, male, mature female, and young female approaching maturity—toward a distinctly different conceptualization: *generic*, plus a male/female parallelism in three subtaxonomic categories: *bearing adult, non-bearing adult,* and *young that has not yet borne.* This is the pattern evident in the Kati terms for goats, sheep, and cattle.

Some of the particular semantic reconstructions in that set of terms remain provisional because of gaps in the evidence. But the overall pattern seems clear for cattle taxonomy where the collected data is fullest; and the general import of the available evidence is that the same pattern, in most of its particulars, probably extended to the lesser livestock. The Kati communities removed one potential redundancy, created by the addition of a new term for 'young she-goat', *-togoota, by apparently narrowing the application of the older *-samba root to just the young female sheep. Redundancies in the terms for "goat," "sheep," and "he-goat" were eliminated over a longer period: as the descendants of the early Kati cluster spread out and differentiated into a variety of communities in distant parts of Tanzania, the various groups eventually settled on certain of the synonyms as their primary terms, with the alternative forms becoming obsolete and finally dropping from use.

Was the new taxonomy merely a reworking of the logic of livestock nomenclature in response to growing familiarity with domestic grazing animals? The kinds and amount of word borrowing that accompanied the reshaping strongly suggests that it was instead an adoption of a new organization of knowledge from the people with whom the early Kati cluster of communities interacted—specifically, from a Southern Cushitic society. The Southern Cushitic word borrowings in the new nomenclature predominantly serve to enunciate the new distinction of "not-yet-bearing female animal" versus "not-yet-bearing male animal"—that is, *-diila 'young billy goat' versus *-togoota 'young she-goat' and *-jeku/*-jiku 'young bull' versus *-dama 'heifer'.[11] In contrast, the "mature male" and "bearing female" categories, which were left over from earlier Mashariki era, often retained their earlier Mashariki names: note in particular *-kambako 'bull' and *-buguma 'mature female cow'.

Among the communities of the Southeast-Nyanza cluster, in contrast, a partial reinforcement of the taxonomic system of earlier Bantu took place, but with the addition of terms of reference specifically to gelded males. Again the taxonomic pattern that developed came to be applied to the full range of domestic animals.

The reason for the different patterns is that a different source of new livestock information—a Southern Nilotic population—predominated in the external relations of the Southeast-Nyanza areal cluster of communities. The reconstructed Southern Nilotic pattern of about 2,500 to 2,000 years ago had these primary semantic divisions: generic, male, castrated male, female that has not yet borne, young generic, old female, and barren female—the last two possibly specifically referring to cattle. That pattern appears in the general structure of the new Southeast-Nyanza nomenclature, and what is more, a specific Southern Nilotic lexical impact is evident in the borrowed roots for "heifer" (*-moori) and "young female goat/sheep" (*-subeeni), both of which are Southern Nilotic loanwords.[12] Most of the older Bantu terminology dropped out in Southeast-Nyanza languages. The root for "billy goat," *-pongo, lasted to the present only in Chaga, where it was reapplied to the male donkey.

Probing the Historical Context

Two further questions may be asked of the data. One is to query the wider social historical context of each set of evidence. The other is to ask if the data imply any specific changes in knowledge or practice. The Kati period of borrowing of livestock terminology from Southern Cushitic belongs to a broader loanword set reflecting a general heavy Southern Cushitic impact on Kati culture, evident in many other cultural and even basic vocabulary loanwords in the Kati languages of later eras.[13] The transformation of livestock knowledge was part of a broader ethnic transformation through the assimilation of many erstwhile Southern Cushites into Kati-speaking communities.

But the Southeast-Nyanza word borrowings from Southern Nilotic tend to be a much more limited set, in which livestock terms predominate. The relations of the ancestral Southeast-Nyanza network of communities with Southern Nilotes were those, then, of neighbors, which led to the adoption of useful subsistence expertise. Surely intermarriage and trade encouraged this process, but the evidence does not require the sort of ethnic merger that the Kati data suggest.

One set of changes in the practices associated with livestock raising seems also probably attributable to this era. The Proto-Mashariki Bantu of ca. 1000 BCE seem surely not to have gelded their animals. The gelding of goats cannot be traced earlier than the period of the Southern Kaskazi areal cluster of communities of the first half of the last millennium BCE. By the late first millennium BCE, the Southeast-Nyanza cluster of communities were well acquainted with the practice, as their specific term for "wether" and "goat wether" (possibly applying also to "steer") shows. The Kati communities, if they did practice gelding, do not demonstrate that fact in their breeding taxonomy, which was more interested in the sterility of an animal in general than in whether sterility was specifically due to human agency or not. A possible explanation is that the number of animals of all kinds kept by the early Kati communities was small enough that it was not commonly necessary or wise to geld excess males. It is true today that, among a number of eastern African peoples, sheep are sufficiently rare that the gelding of rams is not practiced and that therefore no specific terms for "wether" exist in their languages.

Information from related vocabulary—in this case, the verb "to geld"—supports the inference of relative lateness of gelding among the Eastern Bantu. Often no term specifically and only meaning "to geld" occurs in a language; rather, a term meaning "to pound" or "to remove" is applied to the process, depending on the particular technique preferred in the particular society. Where a specific verb can be found, it is not reconstructable to the era of the Kati cluster or to earlier times but is limited to narrower subgroups of Mashariki Bantu. Thus it can be argued that the Proto-Mashariki did not normally castrate or geld the animals they did have; but only later did descendant communities take up the practice in different forms at different times and places. The relatively early development of vocabulary naming gelded animals among the Southeast-Nyanza cluster of communities suggests that at least some members of those groups were beginning to accumulate fairly large herds. The contrary lack of similarly strong evidence as yet for gelding among the early Kati groups of the late last millennium BCE points to an opposite conclusion: that they did not yet keep livestock on the same scale.

Summing Up the Steps in the Analysis

The particular histories of vocabulary change we have just considered provide examples of how the histories of lexical and semantic change reveal:

a. the growth of knowledge;
b. the acquisition of new things;
c. the development of new ways to do things; and
d. the integration of old and new knowledge into new patterns of thinking and categorizing.

From these examples we can identify the series of steps we need to take in identifying the historical developments that these kinds of data reflect and in integrating those developments into the wider picture of change and transformation in the history of ideas and practices of culture. The six steps of analysis as presented here are the following:

1. To reconstruct, through the application of historical linguistic techniques, the actual vocabularies and their meanings at different points in time.
2. To analyze the implications of each taxonomy for the history of cultural knowledge and associated activities.
3. To compare chronologically successive taxonomies in order to uncover the particular transformations in culture and in the structuring of knowledge that can be inferred from the vocabulary transformations.
4. To look for the specific sources of words within taxonomies. Did they come into the language through word borrowing from another language, or through modifying the meanings of existing words in the language? Or are they words newly derived from older words already in the language? Southern Kaskazi *-kondolo 'goat wether', for example, derives from an early Bantu verb, *-kond- 'to strike repeatedly'. It therefore attests to the existence already at that period of the practice of gelding by crushing the testicles between two stones.
5. To investigate semantically related vocabulary outside the central taxonomy for the light it might shed on issues related to the cultural item in question.

The development of a verb for "to geld," for example, indirectly reveals that the herds have grown sufficiently in number that fighting between males over access to females needs to be controlled.

6. To evaluate the significance of vocabulary change in the particular area of culture being studied, by placing it in the context of patterns of change elsewhere in vocabulary during the same era.

The inference that different kinds of ethnic interaction surrounded the growth of livestock raising among the ancestral Southeast-Nyanza and Kati areal clusters of communities—apparently involving mostly interethnic contacts in the first case but the merger of peoples in the latter—illustrates the contribution that this last criterion can making toward revealing the wider historical context of cultural change.

These steps in the historical analysis of vocabulary evidence have, of course, equal applicability to the study of transformation in other areas of material culture. Cuts of meat, forms of milk, and kinds of pasture are additional possible sets of vocabulary that reveal aspects of change in livestock raising. Crop classifications, field nomenclature, and structural taxonomies of particular plants, such as bananas and grain, can similarly provide basic evidence for agricultural transformations. Taxonomies of tools, containers, weaponry, wildlife, house structure, and residential layout, among others, all constitute suitable areas of investigation.

TRANSFORMATIONS IN NONTANGIBLE CULTURE: POLITICS, RELIGION, AND SOCIETY

These approaches are equally applicable to the study of transformations in nonmaterial culture. The greater difficulty in working out the individual semantic domains and linkages within nonmaterial taxonomies means that more time must be spent to obtain the same quantity of results, but the greater frequency of revealing metaphors and similes in the derivations of particular words adds a potentially unmatched richness of insight into earlier concepts and ways of thinking. These latter comments apply especially to the areas of religious belief and practice[14] and to social and political structure. Histories of subsistence transformation tend be revealed through word borrowing, semantic change in existing words, or the coinage of new words, but in investigating transformation in such areas as religion, social structure, and politics, it is often the derivation of new figurative usages via metaphor and simile that provides the most telling insight into past modes of thought.[15]

David Schoenbrun's A Green Place, A Good Place offers especially wide and varied demonstrations of the use of this kind of evidence in reconstructing the long-term history of political ideologies and ritual institutions in the African Great Lakes region. Rhonda M. Gonzales's Societies, Religion, and History similarly enlists semantic histories in revealing the roles of religious ideas and observances in social history in eastern Tanzania. For the western equatorial rainforest regions of Africa, Kairn Klieman's article "Of Ancestors and Earth Spirits" is a particularly engaging demonstration of how one can apply word histories in uncovering and making sense of the historical layering of ideological change in ritual and religious institutions across a whole region.[16] In each of these works, the authors confront themes and issues of universal significance in historical studies, and they illustrate and put into use methods and techniques that have great potential for enriching our historical understandings in many other parts of the globe.

Linguistic reconstruction of the history of kinship in all its variety gives historians another extraordinarily informative entrée into long-term social and economic history. At the level of family and the extended relations of a family, customary kin relations govern marriage patterns, inheritance, and access to authority and power. At the level of the society, in a majority of the communities in earlier human history and even among many peoples today, the institutions through which people identify themselves and govern their relations with others are kin groups of claimed distant common ancestry to which they belong—that is to say, clans or lineages based on unilineal descent.

Different terminological systems go with different kinds of social histories and social relations among peoples. To reconstruct change and development in kin terminologies across the centuries is to uncover the history of the kin relationship across time and, from that history, to discover the changing patterns of access to authority and wealth across those spans. For example, so-called Crow kin systems, in which the same term is used for both the father's sister and the father's sister's daughter, consistently accompany matrilineal descent. To reconstruct the former existence of a Crow terminology in a society is to reconstruct, by implication, the former existence of matrilineal descent and inheritance. In contrast, the former presence of Omaha cousin naming, defined by the use of the same term for mother's brother and mother's brother's son, is an equally certain indicator of not just patriliny, but especially strong patrilineal descent and inheritance customs.

The empowering feature of inference from kin-term reconstructions is that semantic shifts tend to be unidirectional. The fit of kin terms within overall terminological systems limits the directions and varieties of meaning change possible. The basic guideline is this: in general, kin relations with concrete individual referents—father, mother, sibling, and child—can be extended to collateral relations of the same or alternate generations; but the opposite direction of shift, extending a term for a secondary relation to apply to a primary one, does not normally take place. Words for "father" in a great many cultures around the world, for example, have been extended in meaning to include father's brothers. Once that extension has taken place, the term can extend further, from father's brother to mother's brother, reflecting a cultural shift from a collateral to what is called a generational identification of parent's brothers. But an opposite expansion of the kin category, in which a word originally referring solely to father's brother developed into the primary term for "father," is highly improbable.

Similar constraints govern the directions of semantic extension in the history of cousin terms. An old root word for "sibling" can take on the additional meaning "parallel cousin." A parallel cousin is the child of one's father's *brother* or one's mother's *sister* (the child of the same-sex sibling of one's parent). From there the word can undergo a yet further meaning extension to include cross cousins as well. Cross cousins are the children of one's father's *sister* and one's mother's *brother* (the children of the opposite-sex sibling of one's parent). But the opposite direction of change does not happen. When one and the same term is used for both brother and all male cousins, and one term also for sister and all female cousins, we must normally presume the sibling meanings to have been original.

A second normative semantic directionality is from blood to marriage relationships, but not the other way around. If we find, for instance, that the term for spouse's sibling in language A is cognate with the term for cross cousin in a related language B, we can make two culture historical inferences: (1) the underlying root word originally connoted the cross cousin, a blood relative; and (2) language A at some earlier point in history added the meaning "spouse's sibling" in a society in which marriage to cross cousins was customary. Because the cross cousin in that case is also one's potential spouse, the spouse's brother or sister is therefore a potential sibling-in-law as well as an actual cross cousin. Cross cousin, as the blood relationship, is therefore the original meaning, and the application to sibling-in-law is secondary.[17]

Similarly, if we discover that a word for "mother's brother" in one language is cognate with the term for "spouse's father" in a related language, we know that prescriptive cross-cousin marriage existed in the ancestral society that used the word for the spouse's father. In a society in which cross-cousin marriage is common, one's spouse is likely to be the child of one's mother's brother or father's sister. The mother's brother is thus conventionally the father-in-law, and the father's sister is the mother-in-law. Hence the meaning shift, "mother's brother" to "spouse's father," noted just above becomes possible. Cross-cousin marriage has been a long-term and powerful shaper of social history in a number of parts of the world—notably, all through the Dravidian-speaking societies of India.[18] Being able to reconstruct in this fashion the more ancient presence of such a custom is thus of great importance in extending the range and power of the historian's ability to interpret the often fragmentary evidence relating to early social history.

A different combination of kin and marriage developments can be discerned 6,000 or more years ago in the history of Semitic-speaking peoples.[19] The Proto-Semitic term for "father-in-law," *ham-, derives from the much more ancient Proto-Afrasian root word for "father's brother."[20] This meaning shift, of course, reflects a preference highly unusual in the world as a whole, but ancient and widespread among Semitic speakers, for marriage with the father's brother's daughter. The reconstruction of this meaning shift to at least as early as the Proto-Semitic language shows that the custom was very ancient indeed, going back to the end of the Neolithic in the Middle East in the ancestral line of social and linguistic descent leading to Proto-Semitic. It has a second implication as well: this kind of custom is associated with highly patriarchal societies, with significant restrictions on the autonomy of women. The semantic history of *ham- implies that strong patriarchy is of unusual antiquity among Semitic speakers.

Fairly wide application of these kinds of inference has already been made to the African language families, with the Nilo-Saharan family as the most extensively studied. Although patriliny characterizes the majority of Nilo-Saharan societies today, matrilineal descent turns out to be the ancient and original pattern. It was possibly in existence among the speakers of the Proto-Nilo-Saharan language, but certainly in being by the time of early cattle raising among the Proto–Northern Sudanic descendants of the Proto-Nilo-Saharans. (See chapters 2 and 6 for this history.) Matriliny then persisted for thousands of years in most of the Nilo-Saharan lines of societal and language descent, giving way to patriliny often only in the past 2,000 years and in some cases persisting down to the present. The kin lexicon histories demonstrate also that cross-cousin marriage was anciently present and persisted for thousands of years among most of the Nilo-Saharans.[21]

The history of kinship among the Nilo-Saharans is highly important for studies in world history, because its testimony brings into question certain common assumptions. First and foremost, the ancientness, back to before 8000 BCE and possibly long before that, of matriliny and its long persistence among Nilo-Saharan speakers takes issue with ideas that matriliny is no more likely than patriliny to be the earliest development of unilineal descent, or that matriliny "naturally" gives way to patriliny. Second, this history disputes an idea in recent scholarship that livestock raising enhances men's authority and leads necessarily to the adoption of patrilineal descent and inheritance.[22] Many different Nilo-Saharan peoples were strongly pastoral for millennia and nevertheless maintained matrilineal descent and inheritance.

RECONSTRUCTING CONCEPTUALIZATIONS OF TIME

It is also possible to approach the history of time concepts from the perspective of systematic semantics. Consider the present-day Southern Cushitic classifications of days with respect to the center point "today" (table 3), which take a variety of forms.[23] Simply from the semantic patterning in the extant languages, it is possible to argue for an original Proto–Southern Cushitic unbalanced naming of either four or five days into the future and only one day into the past. The Southern Cushitic languages

Table 3. Day Sequences in Southern Cushitic Languages

	Iraqw	Burunge	Kw'adza	Dahalo	Ma'a
5th day before today		balgeera			
4th day before today	balangaros	hoto?inayle	samalituko		
3rd day before today	balaŋ	hatiri?ile	ha?a?uko		
day before yesterday	lat?aŋ	bolotiri	balitiko	ɗammo-suma	wasuhu
yesterday	isaʕ	saʕale	sa?anko	ɗammo	osa
today	lari	leetuti	wa?uko	?aḍokkʷa	wa'a
tomorrow	matlo	hetlalu	ayitlo	hiimane	ɬenu
day after tomorrow	baloqa	bolotiray	balitiko	hiimane ?isu?u	huɣo
3rd day after today	baldane	hatiray	lemeyiko	tuhiini	
4th day after today	toqoni	hoto?inay	samaliko	?iṭṭaanṭooni	
5th day after today		tidane		ṭo?a	

divide into three deep branches—one consisting of Dahalo alone, one of Ma'a alone, and the third, Rift Southern Cushitic, to which the other three languages in table 3 (Iraqw, Burunge, and Kw'adza), along with two other languages not cited, belong (see chapter 8 for a more comprehensive linguistic stratigraphy of Southern Cushitic). For two of the three branches, Dahalo and Rift Southern Cushitic, names that are currently, if not historically, simplex occur up to the fifth day after today. The Rift languages also extend this pattern to days before today, but in general all such names

Table 4. Proto–Southern Cushitic Day-Naming Sequence

*ʔaasaʕ-	'yesterday'
*waʔ-	'today'
(?)	'tomorrow'
*-suhu	'day after tomorrow'
*tuɦi	'third (or fourth?) day after today'
*toʔ-	'fourth (or fifth?) day after today'

for days before yesterday are secondary derivations from names for equivalent days on the future side of today or, as in Iraqw, transparently recent constructions.

What apparently happened was that various Rift languages, to at least some extent independently, brought logical balance into their inherited system of time reckoning by extending the names of specific days as far back into the past as they previously extended into the future. Maʼa, in contrast, adopted the semantic system of neighboring Bantu groups, creating an alternative logical balance by dropping names for days after the day after tomorrow and constructing a new term for the day before yesterday. Dahalo apparently preserved the ancient Southern Cushitic categorization, with the single addition of a recent and still transparently compound term for the day before yesterday (*dammosuma*, consisting of *dammo* 'yesterday' plus *suma* 'before'). Reconstruction of the specific Proto–Southern Cushitic day names confirms the implications of the semantic patterning (table 4).[24]

In itself the proposed history of day nomenclature among Southern Cushites is simply another element in the history of perception and organization of information in their societies. But the implications of their views on time for other aspects of history look like an intriguing proposition to explore. Did Southern Cushites tend to plan their activities more precisely than is usual among preindustrial communities? Had they certain social observances based on five-day or perhaps four-day spans? Did, then, the Rift development of equally long chains of day reckoning back from today reflect some transformation in social perceptions of the value of time, or only a tendency to bring taxonomies into logical balance?

The evidence available to us at present does not allow solutions or even a better statement of these questions. But the issue points up something of importance to this sort of study of transformation in culture—that the essential correlate of establishing taxonomies of nonmaterial culture, if we are to produce meaningful reconstructions of earlier cultural transformations, is thorough mastery of the ethnographic context of the taxonomies. Establishing the nature and role of time concepts in modern Southern Cushitic cultures may well yet offer insight into why such an asymmetric reckoning of past and future existed in ancient Southern Cushitic time terminology.

TRANSFORMATIONS IN THE CONCEPTUAL ORGANIZATION OF UNIVERSAL SETS

Besides these many spheres of knowledge that are culture specific, there are also things universally encountered by human beings but for which categorization can vary according to the particular viewpoints of different societies. The same six steps in analysis can be applied to such materials, but the range of possible inferences tends to be more limited. Anatomical taxonomies, for instance, describe universal human characteristics. The transformation of some portion of the categorization is unlikely to represent a transformation in knowledge, therefore, but it can result from an internal reworking of the logic of the anatomical concepts of the society. Or, alternatively, it can result from the adoption of an alternative conceptualization from influential neighbors. The culture historical information in this sort of case will tell about people's viewpoints or their wider cultural historical milieu and not at all about the history of the things themselves.

Anatomical conceptualizations indeed seem to be fairly resistant to pressure for change from competing patterns. For example, the Bantu languages in Kenya and Tanzania have generally failed to take up Southern Cushitic limb taxonomies despite being heavily affected by influences on other areas of knowledge or practice (as is evident, for instance, in livestock terminology; see table 2). In tables 5 and 6, Swahili terms of limb nomenclature are listed as an example of Bantu patterns and compared with evidence from several Southern Cushitic languages and from Proto–Southern Cushitic. The English glosses are in boldface italic type; a triple hyphen (---) represents the lack of an equivalent in the language; and question marks indicate a current lack of specific data.[25]

The typical East African Bantu pattern is to have single generic terms for the whole of the respective upper and lower limbs of the body and to lack any distinguishable units equivalent to English *hand* and *foot*. The common contemporary, as well as reconstructed, Southern Cushitic pattern is, instead, the division of the upper limbs into two segments of similar scope to English *arm* and *hand* but, interestingly, the unification of the parts of the lower limbs under a single generic term. The West Rift languages, represented here by Iraqw, shifted, however, to a pattern like that typical of Bantu languages by ceasing to distinguish "hand" from "arm." The complete lack of Bantu loanwords in Iraqw limb terminology shows, though, that Bantu influence cannot be invoked here. Rather, the West Rift shift appears more likely to have been an internally motivated change in conceptualization to bring upper-limb terminology into logical parallelism with that of the lower limb.

A second typical contrast between Bantu and Southern Cushitic limb taxonomies is in the treatment of the digits. Bantu languages recognize, in general, five fingers/toes on each limb—applying a single simplex term, in other words, to cover the whole set. A few Bantu languages have a distinctive word for "toe," but they do not have a separate simplex term distinguishing the thumb or big toe. The Southern Cushites, on the other hand, originally demarked the thumb/big toe by a special simplex name of its own, different from the word for "finger/toe." The exception is Ma'a, where the reconstructed finger/thumb distinction was dropped, probably during the period of intense influence of neighboring Bantu groups during the past few centuries. Ma'a as a whole shows both extensive lexical and intensive grammatical interference from two Bantu languages, Asu and Shambaa. In the data noted here, a number of Bantu loanwords in subgeneric terminology, though not in the generic terms, appear—for example, the words for "elbow," "palm," and "shin."

Word borrowings also turn up in subgeneric limb terminology in Dahalo. The Dahalo word for "palm" is a Soomaali loanword, while the words for "finger" and "forearm" are also loans from Bantu tongues, the former from a northern Swahili dialect and the latter from an unidentified Bantu language. Yet despite the apparently universal bilingualism of the present-day Dahalo in their own language and Swahili, the Dahalo hand/arm and even finger/thumb distinction continues to co-exist in their thinking with the very different limb conceptualization they take up whenever they speak Swahili.

A second element of patterning to note in anatomical taxonomy is the repetition of the same particular lexeme in different genera. Such occurrences tell us something of the analogies of appearance, function, and placement made by the speakers of a language. Recognizing such patterns makes it possible sometimes to demonstrate a cultural influence in which a simile is borrowed from one language into the other, but not the specific word that encapsulates the simile.

Several obvious potential applications of the same word to different organs come to mind: finger = toe, wrist = ankle, palm = sole, knee = elbow. In fact, palm and sole, and elbow and knee, are probably always expressed by different words in East African languages. Finger and toe are usually but by no means always called by the same word, and in Southern Cushitic languages the same word usually covers both big toe and thumb. Wrist and ankle are usually different words in Southern Cushitic languages but are not uncommonly expressed by the same word in Bantu languages.

Some other linkages not so obvious to English speakers turn up, some widely

Table 5. Comparative Arm Taxonomies

	arm	upper arm	elbow	forearm
Swahili	mkono	shavu	kikoo	kigasha
Iraqw	dawa	ʕutla	gongoxi	?
Burunge	daba	?	tluħiya	?
Asa	moŋgok	?	ndaguleet	?
Kw'adza	mudzaʔikuto	poʔoti	dumayituko	?
Dahalo	miggi	?	t'eeðe	ngalo
Ma'a	harega	c-aŋila	ki-gokora	---
proto-S.Cush.	*miggɨ	*haraka	?	?

	wrist	hand	palm	fist
Swahili	kiwiko	---	kiganja	konde
Iraqw	gonoħamo	---	tsaʕay	kunday
Burunge	kwaħi	---	?	?
Asa	?	dab	naaldab	?
Kw'adza	kolotiko	tsaʔamuko	bongolaʔe	?
Dahalo	ʕoło	ɖaβa	babaʔa	ʈuɳʈumu
Ma'a	n-konyoko	i-zogera	ki-fumba	kundi
proto-S.Cush.	*konkoolo?	*daba	?	*kund-

	finger	thumb	knuckle	fingernail
Swahili	kidole	kidole gumba	---	kucha
Iraqw	tsitsa	dugno	diqay	fuqno
Burunge	dinca	dugunino	?	carafu
Asa	seŋgetok	?	?	seŋgete
Kw'adza	nigunituko	?	kongolaʔe	tseʔuko
Dahalo	caanɖa	ndodi	?	tsoolo
Ma'a	ki-satu	---	kunge	xemu
proto-S.Cush.	*t'aʕ-	?	*kung-	*c'araf-

Table 6. Comparative Leg Taxonomies

	leg	thigh	knee	back of knee
Swahili	mguu	upaja	goti	---
Iraqw	yaʔe	oriya	gurungura	kanu
Burunge	yaʔe	tlana	gurugunda	kanu
Asa	yeʔe	?	ŋuluet	?
Kw'adza	yaʔo	gemayi	kunguluʔiya	dilinga
Dahalo	ḍakaʕa	luka	gilli	?
Ma'a	ku-saʔame	?	imure	igoroto
proto-S.Cush.	*saʔama	?	*gili̵	?

	calf	shin	ankle	foot	sole
Swahili	shavu	goko	kiwiko	---	wayo
Iraqw	nawee	tsiʕi	gonoħamo	---	digir
Burunge	micoko	?	kwaħi	---	dagara
Asa	?	?	mugwara	---	?
Kw'adza	dzulutiko	?	guhuluko	---	paʔamuko
Dahalo	ṭahara	konkoolo	googontlima	---	?
Ma'a	?	lu-gula	kungu	---	lu-bame
proto-S.Cush.	?	?	*mukʷ-	---	*p'aʔam- *dagir-

	heel	toe	big toe	toenail
Swahili	kisigino	kidole	kidole gumba	kucha
Iraqw	kolo	tsitsa	dugno	fuqno
Burunge	gobina	dinca	dugunino	carafu
Asa	tutunyo	seŋetok	?	seŋete
Kw'adza	fuguluko	nigunituko	?	tseʔuko
Dahalo	gimp'o	caanḍa	ndodi	tsoolo
Ma'a	ki-haga	ki-satu	---	xemu
proto-S.Cush.	gaymp'-	*t'aʕ-	?	*c'araf-

spread and others not—for example, shoulder blade and wrist. Seen in West Rift Burunge kwaħi 'wrist' and Iraqw kwaħa 'shoulder blade', this relation seems to reflect the recognition of the participation of both joints in the action of wielding or throwing, as their separate derivations from a Proto–Rift Southern Cushitic verb, *kwaħ-'to throw', implies.[26]

The comparative historical study of anatomical taxonomies, because of the great complexity that a full taxonomy can attain, would seem to have considerable potential as a gauge of the scale of cultural transformation inferable from change elsewhere in vocabulary. But anatomy is not the only set of natural characteristics that humans find the need to categorize. Taxonomies of geographical features, of cloud forms, and of tree and plant parts are similarly more likely to change because of the influence of contrasting or competing systems of organizing such knowledge than because of changes in information. Soil and mineral taxonomies and classifications of plants and animals, on the other hand, may be transformed as well by the migration of people into new areas with different natural distributions—in other words, because of changes in information.

TRANSFORMATIONS IN THE CONCEPTUALIZATIONS OF SEQUENCE

For the most part, we have been talking about classifications based on perceived spatial divisions. The discussion of time reckoning touched, however, on an alternative mode of classification: by sequential division, in which the linked items can be called an activity sequence. An activity sequence can consist of nouns or of verbs or of both nouns and verbal nouns together.

The best possibilities for historical analysis of culture transformation are sequences that mimic a taxonomic shape, frequently with a verb as the encompassing characterization of the set. An example is beer-brewing terminology, where the "genus" is a verb—"to brew" (or a verbal noun, "brewing")—and the "species" are the series of successive, named conditions of the material being brewed. Consider the Iraqw (Southern Cushitic) and Langi (Bantu) stages of beer making represented in table 7.[27]

There are broad similarities in the processes of making beer from grain across eastern Africa, but nevertheless significant differences in detail turn up, as do differences in the degree of particularization of nomenclature for the steps in the process. The Iraqw and Langi, neighboring peoples in north-central Tanzania, have activity sequences of brewing that are, for all practical purposes, identical. The steps are the same in number and nature; of those stages named in Iraqw, only the specification of beer that is fully fermented but not yet filtered may be lacking in Langi. In no case does the same root appear in both languages, so no direct adoption of ideas by one from the other can be argued. Yet clearly the virtual identity of every

Table 7. Activity Sequence: Beer Brewing

	Iraqw	*Langi*
malt	bimbila	memɛra
mash	daɬo	kolɔvɛka
boiled mash	muqus	ikaya
coarse-ground grain, added to boiled mash	alwaqesi	itanti
coarse-ground grain and mash boiled again	humri	ikaya
mixture with more malt added, left to ferment	luʔmi	camɔtwa
unfiltered fermented beer	xwanti	(no term?)
beer	bura	irusu

stage of the process and the manner in which the stages are conceptualized requires the postulation of at least a wide regionally shared approach to beer making, of ancient enough provenance that each language has developed its own vocabulary for something common to both. In other instances of brewing terminology in East Africa, though, loanwords do occur. A wider comparative study of brewing activity sequences, following the steps of analysis laid out for taxonomies of material culture, should therefore be a productive historical enterprise, providing evidence of growth and change, contact influences, and the spread of new ideas about food processing.

On the other hand, activity sequences of logical or practical coherence need not be conceptually linked by common subordination to a classificatory term to be worthy of identification and study. An example here would be the preparation of grains for use as food. Typically in eastern Africa the sequence of actions would be:

1. "to thresh," in order to loosen the seeds from their husks and stalks;
2. then "to winnow," by tossing the threshed grain with a basketry winnowing tray and allowing the breeze to carry away the chaff;
3. next "to sift grain," in order to remove small and harder rubbish;
4. fourth, "to pound grain" in a mortar;
5. finally, "to grind grain" into flour—often a two-stage process.

Table 8. Activity Sequence: Early Mashariki Grain Preparation

'to thresh'	*-puul-	(proto-Bantu (PB) *-puul- 'to husk')
'to winnow'	$\left\{\begin{array}{l}\text{*-pep-}\\ \text{*-pepet-}\\ \text{*-pet-}\end{array}\right\}$	(PB 'to blow')
	*-el-	(PB *-(g)el- 'to measure' ?)
	*-pung-	(early Bantu 'to fan')
'to sift grain'	*-sel-	(early Bantu 'to clean')
	*-sekes-	(PB *-seke 'grains (of anything)' plus *-s- verb extension turning it into a verb)
'to pound grain'	*-tu-	(PB 'to pound (food of any kind)')
'to grind grain'	*-si-	(PB 'to grind (a tool)')

For an example of how evidence for cultural transformation can be extracted from such a set of data, we may turn again to early Mashariki Bantu vocabularies. What is particularly significant about the reconstructed Mashariki Bantu grain-preparation activity sequences of the last half of the last millennium BCE is that multiple synonyms were used to express some of these activities. The development of multiple terms for a set of activities is often indicative of a transformation of knowledge or practice. The activities surrounding grain cultivation would have been new to the Proto-Mashariki, because their ancestors, who before 1000 BCE had lived to the west of East Africa, in the equatorial rainforest and woodland savanna zones, had not been growers of grain crops.[28] In particular, unlike the processes of pounding and grinding, winnowing and sifting would not have been required by earlier Bantu kinds of food preparation, so new terms would have had to be innovated. The Mashariki communities of the first millennium BCE variously used the terms listed in table 8 for the several successive stages in the preparation of grain for cooking.

The development of several synonymous verbs—in this particular case, for winnowing and sifting—supports the inference from other kinds of evidence that grain cultivation was a newly adopted farming activity among the early Mashariki. Note, however, that this collection of verbs includes no loanwords from non-Bantu source languages that might reveal where this new cultural knowledge specifically came from.

That fact itself is not surprising. A lack of loanwords in the *verb* lexicon of a transformation, even when the impetus for change clearly comes from outside the society, is not at all untypical. Nouns tend to be considerably more easily borrowed than verbs, so that the confirmation of the suspected diffusion of a new set of practices must frequently be sought by examination of the nouns associated with the relevant activity sequence. In the case of the early Eastern Bantu, the associated noun vocabulary shows that a major transformation of agricultural knowledge was indeed taking place, from the Proto–Mashariki Bantu period down to the beginning of the first millennium CE, with Bantu communities progressively naturalizing the cultivation of grains under the successive influences of several different Nilo-Saharan-speaking groups of peoples.[29]

Still, borrowings of verbs do take place, and where they appear, they amount to stronger evidence for the external causation of cultural transformation than a like number of borrowed nouns would. For instance, the Kati cluster of communities of the late first millennium BCE adopted their primary livestock-raising verb, *-diim- 'to herd', from Southern Cushites, an exceedingly strong confirmation of the conclusions reached on the basis of breeding taxonomies (for which see table 2). This verb, *-diim-, probably stood at the head of its own activity sequence—including verbs with such meanings as "to drive to pasture" and "to drive home from grazing"—and this sequence had its own associated nouns, at least one of which, Proto-Kati *-kwama 'herd', was also a Southern Cushitic loanword.[30]

Once again the techniques of historical analysis of the semantic patterns have wider applicability to a variety of cultural phenomena. We could as well apply them to the successive steps in cultivation, iron working, pottery manufacture, and many other productive activities. A particular usefulness should be in tracing histories of transformation in ritual and ceremonial sequences. A step-by-step comparison, for instance, of the details and precise order of ceremonies of initiation by circumcision in Kenya shows that the Maasai practices trace back to more ancient origins along the southern edges of the highlands of Ethiopia or in northern Kenya. In contrast to the high degree of Maasai cultural indebtedness overall to Southern Nilotes over the past 1,300 years,[31] the influences evident in this set of cultural features may have come at an earlier period directly from Eastern Cushitic peoples.[32]

MEDICAL CULTURE

The topic of transformations in medical culture has been left till last because its investigation touches on such a variety of possible ways in which vocabulary transformation can reflect cultural transformation. How people in different societies identify and distinguish or group together different diseases is an example of human conceptualization of non-human-made things. Yet at the same time disease terminology records human experience, and so the comparative study of disease categories essentially probes the transmission of experience and of people's perceptions of such experience, rather than information per se. The other side of the coin—healing—conceptualizes by both spatial relation and sequence. Medicinal categories classify information about tangible materials and their use. The procedures of the healer for various ailments can, on the other hand, be treated as activity sequences.

Moreover, medical culture ramifies into so many other areas. Past patterns of disease transmission inevitably reflect earlier lines of communication between communities—that is, trade routes or political links, each with their own sets and categorizations of vocabulary, or else routes of population movement. Or they tell us something about the history of human coexistence with nonhuman disease vectors, names for which belong to zoological taxonomies. Vocabularies of medical practice cross-link with plant classification, since medicines commonly consist of plant materials. In addition, the procedures of healing frequently overlap into the domain of ritual activity sequences.

Gloria Waite's *A History of Traditional Medicine and Health Care in Pre-colonial East-Central Africa* pioneered the investigation of this kind of history.[33] Her untimely death cut short her contributions to this field, but her work makes clear the importance of botanical as well as cultural fieldwork for uncovering the medical history of earlier times and places. Her study combines language evidence with oral tradition, written records, and comparative ethnography, backed up by a thorough grounding in the medical botany of healing in Central Africa. Her case studies cast light on such topics, among others, as the spread of medicines and medical ideas with long-distance migration and the roles and predicaments of medicine and medical practitioners in precolonial political struggles. It is clear from her presentations that there is far more that historians could learn from a systematic and detailed historical linguistic investigation of the vocabularies of medicine and healing, especially in conjunction with other kinds of historical testimony. This field of study should be an area of much more urgent interest to historians not just of Africa, but of premodern medical culture in most parts of the world.

In the end, of course, no area of culture stands off entirely distinct from all the rest. Medical culture is simply an area where the multiple connections are particularly obvious. The historical analysis of cultural transformations must begin with the relevant taxonomies, activity sequences, and so forth. Understanding the human history that lies behind the semantic changes within a particular area of culture rests on tasks of both narrower and wider scope. The histories and derivations of individual words in taxonomies and the like reveal changes in particular features of culture and the sources and directions of the acquisition of new things and ideas. Discovering whether the transformations are limited in scope or part of a sweeping historical shift depends on the critical perspective that the patterns of vocabulary change elsewhere in the language offer.

NOTES

1. In table 1, an asterisk denotes an earlier meaning that is no longer current.

2. D. Lloyd, "The Precolonial Economic History of the Avongara-Azande, c. 1750–1916" (Ph.D. diss., UCLA, 1978).

3. *Njila* is a new name for the Western Savanna group, proposed in J. Vansina, *How Societies Are Born: Governance in West Central Africa before 1600* (Charlottesville: University of Virginia Press, 2004).

4. C. Ehret, *An African Classical Age: Eastern and Southern Africa in World History, 1000 BC to AD 400* (Charlottesville: University Press of Virginia, 1998).

5. Modern-day Rukwa languages include Nyakyusa, Safwa, Fipa, and many others spoken in the Malawi-Zambia-Tanzania borderlands of southwestern East Africa. The Rufiji-Ruvuma group includes such languages as Yao, Makonde, Ngindo, Mbunga, Mwera, Matengo, and many others, covering most of today's southeast quarter of Tanzania. The Njombe group consists of Hehe, Bena, Kinga, and Sangu, of the southern highlands of Tanzania, while the Takama group comprises Nyamwezi, Sukuma, Iramba, Rimi, and Kinga of the western third of Tanzania. Northeast-Coastal Bantu is another widespread group of eastern Tanzania and eastern Kenya, including Swahili, Pokomo, Mijikenda, Shambaa, Zigula, Asu, Saghalla Taita, Kami, and Gogo. The Upland group consists of Chaga and the Gikuyu, Kamba, and Meru tongues of eastern Kenya. The East Nyanza languages, which include Gusii, are spoken to the southeast of Lake Nyanza (Victoria).

This division of Kaskazi into eight subgroups revises classification given in Ehret, *African Classical Age*, p. 36, in accordance with the more recent arguments in C, Fourshey, "Agriculture, Ecology, Kinship and Gender: A Social and Economic History of Tanzania's Corridor 500 B.C. to 1900 A.D." (Ph.D. diss., UCLA, 2002).

6. See Ehret, *African Classical Age*, especially chaps. 2 and 6, for this overall history.

7. Many of the data cited in this and subsequent tables appear in the text figures and the appendices to Ehret, *African Classical Age*. Other data in these tables are available in the author's unpublished research document "Compendium of Southern and Eastern African Culture Vocabularies" (n.d., a typescript of around 3,000 pp.).

8. C. Ehret, "Agricultural History in Central and Southern Africa, ca. 1000 B.C. to ca. A.D. 500," *Transafrican Journal of History* 4, nos. 1/2 (1974): 1–25.

9. Ehret, *African Classical Age*, pp. 308, 325.

10. C. Ehret, *Southern Nilotic History: Linguistic Approaches to the Study of the Past* (Evanston, IL: Northwestern University Press, 1971); Ehret, *African Classical Age*, p. 308.

11. C. Ehret, *Ethiopians and East Africans: The Problem of Contacts* (Nairobi: East African Publishing House, 1974), pp. 19–23; Ehret, *African Classical Age*, p. 327.

12. Ehret, *Southern Nilotic History*, appendices; Ehret, *African Classical Age*, pp. 308, 317.

13. Ehret, *African Classical Age*, pp. 68, 327–328.

14. Ibid.

15. C. Ehret, "Language Evidence and Religious History," in T. O. Ranger and I. N. Kimambo (eds.), *The Historical Study of African Religion* (London: Heinemann, 1972), pp. 45–49.

16. D. Schoenbrun, *A Green Place, a Good Place: Agrarian Change, Gender, and Social Identity in the Great Lakes Region to the 15th Century* (Portsmouth, NH: Heinemann, 1998); R. M. Gonzales, *Societies, Religion, and History: Central East Tanzanians and the World They Created, c. 200 BCE to 1800 CE* (New York: Columbia University Press, 2009); K. Klieman, "Of Ancestors and Earth Spirits," in Alisa

LeGamma (ed.), *Eternal Ancestors: The Art of the Central African Reliquary* (New York: Metropolitan Museum of Art; New Haven: Yale University Press, 2007), pp. 33–61.

17. C. Ehret, "Reconstructing Ancient Kinship in Africa," in N. J. Allen and others (eds.), *Early Human Kinship: From Sex to Social Reproduction* (Oxford: Wiley Blackwell), pp. 200–231, 259–269.

18. T. R. Trautman, *Dravidian Kinship* (Cambridge: Cambridge University Press, 1981).

19. See A. Kitchen and others, "Bayesian Phylogenetic Analysis of Semitic Languages Identifies an Early Bronze Age Origin of Semitic in the Near East," *Proceedings of the Royal Society B: Biological Sciences* 276, no. 1668 (2009): 2703–2710, for this dating.

20. Ehret, "Reconstructing Ancient Kinship in Africa."

21. C. Ehret, "Reconstructing Ancient Kinship: Practice and Theory in an African Case Study," in D. Jones and B. Milicic (eds.), *Kinship and Language: Per Hage and the Renaissance of Kinship Studies* (Salt Lake City: University of Utah Press, in press).

22. C. Holden and R. Mace, "Spread of Cattle Led to the Loss of Matrilineal Descent in Africa: A Coevolutionary Analysis," *Proceedings of the Royal Society B, Biological Sciences* 270, no. 1532 (2003): 2425–2433.

23. Most of the Southern Cushitic data in this table are published in C. Ehret, *The Historical Reconstruction of Southern Cushitic Phonology and Vocabulary* (Berlin: Reimer, 1980); other data are taken from the unpublished lexicons of the languages in question, based on field data collected by the author, and are available on request.

24. The roots in table 4 appear in the etymological dictionary in Ehret, *Historical Reconstruction of Southern Cushitic.*

25. For the sources of the Southern Cushitic data in tables 5 and 6, see n. 23.

26. Ehret, *Historical Reconstruction of Southern Cushitic.*

27. Data cited here are from the field collections of the writer.

28. Ehret, *African Classical Age,* chaps. 2, 3.

29. Ehret, "Agricultural History in Central and Southern Africa," has a limited and sometimes incorrect understanding of these processes. The story has now been greatly revised and much more fully presented in Ehret, *African Classical Age.*

30. Ehret, *African Classical Age,* p. 308 and elsewhere.

31. Extensive evidence for these interactions appears in Ehret, *Southern Nilotic History* and idem, *Ethiopians and East Africans.*

32. D. Kilhefner, "Circumcision and Scarification in Initiation: Comparative Linguistic and Ethnographic Study" (seminar paper, UCLA, 1969).

33. G. Waite, *A History of Traditional Medicine and Health Care in Pre-colonial East-Central Africa* (Lewiston, NY: E. Mellon Press, 1992).

4

Historical Inference
from Word Borrowing

A second essential angle of approach to deriving history from lexical evidence is through inference from the histories of word borrowing. Word borrowing is perhaps the single most important category of lexical evidence because from it we uncover the histories of societies in the time spans that lie between the nodal periods of the linguistic chronology. Such evidence not only tracks the spread of ideas and things across the historical landscape, but, more important, enables us to identify the particular kinds of extended historical encounter that took place between societies, and to infer the demography and the demographic outcomes of such encounters.

INTRODUCING THE TOPIC

Many kinds of linguistic change and all language shifts derive in the last analysis from demographic relations.[1] Sociolinguistics has usually been content with recognizing patterns of social relations between different populations and identifying the kinds of language changes that accompany those relations. More basically it is the proportional concentrations of such populations within the social mix that determine the kind of influence each can have on the changes in language that take place. Language history does indeed reflect social history because language is the

This chapter—with a number of refinements, revisions, and additions—builds on C. Ehret, "The Demographic Implications of Linguistic Change and Language Shift," in C. Fyfe and D. McMaster (eds.), *African Historical Demography*, vol. 2 (Edinburgh: Centre for African Studies, 1981), pp. 153–182.

vehicle of social existence. But social history is the outward expression of human accommodations to and manipulation of more fundamental pressures and forces, and so language changes are driven, even if sometimes only indirectly, by those same engines.

Then, too, historical investigations and sociolinguistic investigations start from opposite ends. The sociolinguist asks which language changes accompany which particular sociological situations. The historian comes at the problem from the other direction: if we have evidence of such and such an array of past changes in language, what can we infer about the human situation that engendered those changes?

The motivations of historically significant language change can be grouped under two broad headings: *practical utility* and *social utility* (or prestige). *Practical utility* refers to the learning of a new or additional language to carry on the business of life; to the adoption (borrowing) or coinage of new words by a language to name concepts, things, or processes new to or newly developed by the population speaking the language; and to the simplification of grammar, for facilitating language learning, in the formation of pidgins and creoles.[2] The practical utility of a change does not in every case reflect demographic relations.

Social utility, or prestige motives, can be seen both in the adoption of words, expressions, and manners of pronunciation from prestigious groups and in most shifts of a population from the using of one language to the using of another. The prestige of one language or dialect is usually justified on esthetic grounds by its speakers. The reality is that prestige always reflects power, whether regional and political or over access to desirable things. The speakers of a dialect or language that has a general prestige are numerically preponderant in positions of political and economic power. The speakers of a tongue with prestige limited to one area of culture are the numerically preponderant controllers of access to, or practitioners of, that aspect of culture. Changes for social utility thus always ultimately reflect demographic relations.

Past demographic relations leave linguistic artifacts behind, in the shape of either

1. modifications in a language attributable to contacts with other languages (or other dialects of the same language); or
2. the replacement of one language by another (or of one dialect of a language by another) as the common new idiom.

The first situation can arise without the second development's taking place. The second probably almost never occurs without some effects, however slight, of the first process, in the form of elements taken over from the previous language into the tongue that displaces it.

Words adopted from one language into another language (loanwords) form the core of the historical evidence. Sociolinguists, because they are, after all, linguists and not lexicographers, are wont to emphasize the phonological and grammatical effects of contact. But it is in vocabulary that the effects of contact are first and, in the end, most strongly produced. Analysis of grammatical and phonological adoptions can do little more than corroborate conclusions inferable from vocabulary evidence alone about the intensity, duration, and demography of the contacts involved. Words can be "borrowed" without the borrowing of any grammar or phonology, whereas grammatical and phonological elements probably cannot pass from language to language without an accompaniment of word borrowings. Words, moreover, have specific meanings within culture and therefore are the sole linguistic bearers of specific culture historical information.

Some attempts have already been made at proposing broad categories of language-contact phenomena and relating these categories to different sorts of histories of what are essentially demographic relations over time.[3] Sociolinguistic studies of populations in contact are, of course, essential background to developing such categorizations, but they normally deal with contemporary populations over, at best, very short periods, often close to being a single point in time. What historians need to do is build on this base by developing more cases of what has happened over periods of generations, in culturally and technologically different eras, to languages the history of whose speakers is relatively well documented. From this endeavor we can build up an increasingly reliable base of examples, and test, refine, and apply the resulting categorizations in the historical interpretation of earlier language changes among peoples lacking written or adequate oral documentation.

The usefulness of the provisional categories applied in previous linguistic historical reconstruction has lain in part in the very looseness of their definitions and the carefully vague statements of the histories of population contacts they have been taken to imply.[4] It is time to risk proposing a more detailed specification of categories and a narrower definition and multiplication of the particular patterns of history that can be inferred. As a step in that direction, the following categories and subcategories are proposed. For easy overall reference, figure 5 (at the end of this chapter) sums up the categories of borrowing, their characteristics, and their historical implications.

CATEGORY 1: SINGLE-WORD BORROWING

The borrowing of a single word normally reflects the adoption of the single new item named by the word. Frequently the item has spread by long-range diffusion relatively rapidly, often through trade. A complex set of examples of this kind of word history is dealt with in chapter 9. This sort of borrowing carries no implications about demographic change.

CATEGORY 2: RESTRICTED WORD BORROWING

Subcategory 2A: Semantically Restricted Word Borrowing

A semantically restricted loanword set is one that is limited to words dealing with particular areas of knowledge or activity. The most notable examples in American English are Spanish and Algonkian loanword sets.[5]

The Spanish loans are restricted principally to three semantic areas:

1. natural features—for example, *canyon, arroyo, mesa, sierra, rincon, barranca, potrero, cienaga, and chaparral*;[6]
2. plants and animals—for example, *islay, mesquite, pinyon, toyon, tecolote, coyote, javelina, jaguar*, and the like; and
3. techniques and practices related to a particular kind of food production— for example, *ranch, corral, lariat, chaps, rodeo, pinto, bronco, burro, buckaroo, mustang*, and so forth.

A few words, such as *canyon* and *ranch*, have spread into wide use in English through the media of film and novel, but most of them continue to be restricted in effective use to the American Southwest. At least two, *barranca* and *potrero*, are used only in the rural Southern California variety of English of which I am a speaker. The dialectal distributions of the loans would of course pinpoint the areas of interaction between Anglos and Hispanics even if we did not already know from other evidence where the contacts took place.

What matters here, however, is the demography of the contacts. Semantic restriction of borrowings indicates, first, that the donor population had information essential to the borrowing population but not known or not important to them before. In this case we know that the English speakers adopted from the Spanish speakers a way of carrying on subsistence that was possible in the southwestern environment and differed from their previous approaches. In addition, the English speakers moved into an environment with different terrain and quite a different climate from what they previously knew, and with plants and animals new to them. In the second place, semantic restriction indicates failure of the donor population to gain, or their rapid loss of, power in the contact situation. In general, this happens because they are, or rapidly become, a minority in the population mix. In this instance the speakers of English took up the positions of wealth and prestige and in many areas came soon to outnumber the Spanish speakers as well.

The earliest Algonkian contact with Anglo-Americans shows striking parallels. The loanwords dating to this contact are mostly limited to three semantic areas:

1. flora and fauna—for example, *opossum, raccoon, skunk, chipmunk, chickaree, woodchuck, moose, muskellunge, chinquapin, squeteague, pecan, and hickory*;

2. particular elements of food production—namely, *hominy, succotash, pone,* and *squash;* and
3. new items of material culture—for example, *moccasin* and *toboggan.*

The English speakers were moving into an area where the other inhabitants had essential or useful prior information. The climate and terrain were not so different from the previous homeland of the Anglos, except for a greater annual temperature range, but many of the plants and animals were new; and there were valuable new crops, especially maize (called *Indian corn,* later shortened to *corn* in American English), to be adopted. Note, as is sometimes the case in this sort of utilitarian food adoption, that the borrowing language created a name for the crop by analogy to previously known foods, but adopted outright some of the names for ways of preparing maize (*hominy, succotash, pone*).

As in the Anglo-Hispanic contact, the semantically restricted borrowings reflect a history in which the speakers of the acceptor language rapidly eclipsed the donors in power and/or in numbers. A variation that should be noted is that the Anglo-Algonkian contact involved several languages on the donor side, whereas the Anglo-Spanish contact was one-to-one.

Further parallel instances of this kind of history include the Spanish contact with Nahuatl speakers in Mexico and Dutch speakers with Khoekhoe in the Cape. The Spanish-Nahuatl case produced a wide array of

1. new flora and fauna names (e.g., *coyote* and *tecolote,* both of which were secondarily borrowed into American Southwest English); and
2. new food production terms (*tomate, milpa, matate,* etc.).

The Dutch-Khoekhoe case produced mainly flora and fauna adoptions in Afrikaans (*kudu* and *gnu* are the notable large-animal names). The incoming groups rapidly attained political and economic domination in both cases.

In Mexico the previous languages often continued to be spoken and the newly dominant immigrants formed a significant minority rather than an absolute majority. What would seem further to have weakened the ability of those dominated over to have more deeply influenced Spanish was that they spoke a great variety of languages. Spanish speakers soon came to outnumber first speakers of any other single language in the country, even the previously dominant Nahuatl of central Mexico. In the Cape the disintegration of Khoekhoe social units proceeded so rapidly that the local form of Dutch rapidly became the majority language. Its speakers were numerically preponderant even if European physical ancestry was in the minority.

There is a common demographic feature in all these cases that is surely also essential to their characterization. Each acceptor community of semantically restricted loans continued, until that speech community attained majority status, to be part of a politically connected speech community most of whose members lived out of reach of the contact area itself. That tie served continually to reinforce standard usages in most portions of vocabulary and so further limit the impact of the donors on receptor speech.

The lower limit of the subcategory is approached by the case of French loanwords in American English, which number very few indeed:

1. for natural features (*butte, prairie*); and
2. for a particular way of life (*cache, travois*).

Again the set of loanwords reflects the movement of Anglos into a new sort of terrain, to the west of the Appalachians, and the adopting by some Anglos of a livelihood, fur trapping, especially associated previously with French speakers. The smallness of the French loanword set in western American English accords with the smallness of the French minority absorbed by the Anglo advance.[7]

Semantically restricted borrowing sets can also derive from contacts where it was the minority that was intrusive. An especially interesting case of borrowing from an intrusive minority—intrusive by a large number of individual marriages rather than by communal settlement—is that of the Gogo in southern Masailand in Tanzania. The cultivating vocabulary of the Kisonko Maasai of the area is almost completely from Gogo, one of the nearby Bantu languages.[8] The Kisonko do not normally themselves cultivate, but they need the vocabulary to be able to talk about the activities of their neighbors. It turns out that about 50 percent of the Maasai wives in the region were born and raised Gogo.[9] Women among the Gogo are the farmers, and so they have brought into southern Kisonko the vocabulary of the special skills inculcated by their upbringing. On the other hand they are, as women married to Maasai husbands, subordinate members of a society in which men hold the main positions of wealth and power. They are also, even if a majority or near majority of women, a minority in the overall society.

Subcategory 2B: Grammatically Restricted Word Borrowing

Grammatically restricted word borrowing is defined by the occurrence of loanwords from a particular source language that are restricted to particular parts of speech—normally to interjections, adverbials of motion or sound, slang, and extrasystemic utterances. In American English the prime example is a set of words and utterances of apparently African origin; the best known of these is the word *okay*.[10]

African donors to American English formed well over half of the population in their main areas of residence in the American South at the time when these expressions were probably gaining currency. But they came from a great variety of earlier linguistic backgrounds, and many would have been distanced from those backgrounds by an intermediate period of habitation or ancestry in the West Indies. As with the Indian languages vis-à-vis Spanish in Mexico, their languages were individually in the minority against English, even if a greater proportion still knew such languages than is normally supposed. Thus what often could be most readily retained in the new milieu were expressions of pan-regional currency in Africa, like *okay*, which had a regional spread along and inland from the Guinea coast of West Africa.[11]

Grammatically restricted borrowing, it can be suggested, tends to come, via slang, from a collection of suppressed minorities who in toto form a considerable, sometimes majority, portion of the overall population. Enslavement seems to be one environment of this sort of borrowing. The Malay loanword *baie* 'much, many, very' in Afrikaans is an example from South Africa of a word originally coming into a language in this fashion.

Subcategory 2C: Status-Restricted Word Borrowing

The term *status-restricted* connotes loanwords that are jocular, deprecatory, or obscene. They enter a language via slang and are not the standard accepted terms (at least in the beginning) for the thing or action they name. Status-restricted loans seem regularly to come from the language of a looked-down-upon minority into the language of the established majority speech community. Such borrowings do not usually take place at first contact between peoples, nor at a time when the speech community is still in the process of becoming a majority. The minority speech community may be either intrusive or previously established before the majority formed around them.

One notable set in American English consists of Indian loanwords referring to Indians and items of Indian culture. These can be of as late as eighteenth-century entrance into English and often are from Algonkian—for example, *squaw, papoose, wigwam, sachem,* and *sannup.* The first three, used only of Indians, are inherently derogatory, for they treat Indians as something other than fully human, as having squaws instead of women, papooses instead of babies, and wigwams instead of houses. The next-to-last term (*sannup* is generally unknown any longer) came to be used rather jocularly for white political leaders, though originally it was taken over from an Algonkian word for "chief."[12]

Another example in American English is the Yiddish loanword set that includes such words as *nudnik, schmuck, klutz,* and the like. Many of these are still limited to New York City varieties of English, but a few have made it even across the Atlantic. The Yiddish loans entered English via slang, mostly in jocular usage. They seem also interestingly to have, at the same time, the characteristics of a semantically restricted set: a majority of them are insults or deprecations. What probably accounts for the particular kind of wider currency they have gained in recent decades is that many of the major American comics of the twentieth century came from

Yiddish-speaking family backgrounds. Even as the Algonkians had new agricultural information to offer in the seventeenth century, and the Spanish new cattle-raising techniques to be made use of in the nineteenth, so the comedians had something useful to offer—fashionable entertainment, or perhaps just better words with which to vent our spleen on the aggravations of modern life.

One example from earlier English-language history that seems to fit this pattern should be mentioned. Some of the several Welsh loanwords in Middle English or Early Modern English have the appearance of originally peripheral usages brought in to make for more colorful speech, as slang serves us today—for example, *flimsy* and *flummery*. The Welsh were a minority, generally looked down upon, and so the social and demographic conditions match those linked in other cases to status-restricted word borrowing.

The general characteristic of all situations of category-2 borrowing is thus the passing of loanwords from a subordinated or lower-status community to an economically and politically dominant community. The adopting community also forms the considerable majority of the overall population, or is in the process of rapidly becoming the large majority, or forms a large plurality over a combination of minorities (in other words, well outnumbers any single subordinated minority). Different subcategories seem to go with different kinds of contact and with differing population distributions among interacting speech communities.

On the whole, only word borrowing occurs with contacts of the sorts indicated by category 1 and category 2, and often very little of that. The one possible exception seems to be some cases of subcategory-2B borrowing in which the collection of subordinated minorities constitute together a significant majority of the whole population and formerly spoke languages that, though different, belonged to a single linguistic area. That is, the languages had been contiguous and had similar phonological inventories and some grammatical features in common because of long contact or genetic relationship or both. In such cases the strongly suppressed population may still influence the pronunciation and perhaps have some effect on word order or idioms in the language that they adopt from the dominant speech community. These features may be especially strongly present in the dialect of the subordinated community if the social division between it and the dominant community is rigidly maintained. This effect verges on pidginization, for which see category 4.

The key point for subcategory-2B contacts is whether any of these effects are able to pass into the speech of the dominant community, and it seems that they can at times. Examples sometimes proposed include the dropping of final *r* and simplification of word-final consonant clusters (*se'f* for *self*) in Coastal Southern U.S. dialects. On the other hand, similar changes have occurred elsewhere in English, so that the best that can be argued is that African speech patterns reinforced tendencies already emerging in English.

CATEGORY 3: GENERAL WORD BORROWING

General word borrowing is characterized by a wide semantic distribution of the words that one language has adopted from another. Since the pattern manifests itself as a continuum of intensities, from small scatters of loans across a variety of semantic areas up to numerous arrays of borrowed words in almost every part of vocabulary, it is difficult to distinguish clear subcategories. Yet it is quite evident that differing intensities of borrowing reflect differing histories of contact. By dividing up vocabulary according to relative resistance to borrowing, it is possible to define four workable, if not wholly distinct, subcategories: intensive, heavy general, extensive, and light general.

The first distinction that can be made with respect to resistance to word borrowing is between "core" and "culture" vocabulary.

Basic vocabulary can be said to have two degrees—what might be called, respectively, "core" and "peripheral basic" vocabulary. There is no sharp break between the two. Core vocabulary consists of words for universally recognized items, actions, and categories—for example, *nose, tooth, heart, liver, sun, moon, to go, to come, to eat, to drink, I, you,* and so on. The standard *Swadesh* one-hundred- and two-hundred-meaning lists provide convenient lists of basic items.[13] These are often called the one-hundred-*word* and two-hundred-*word* lists, and these terms can be used interchangeably, although strictly speaking, these are lists of meanings.

On the whole the one-hundred-meaning version was well chosen. Experience shows that it contains, as it was intended, most of the words that are most resistant to replacement by new words for those meanings. The words for most of the one hundred meanings are rarely, and some never to my knowledge, borrowed. The two-hundred-word list begins to contain more of "peripheral basic" vocabulary—items fundamental to even simple conversation but much less universal in their semantic boundaries and more subject to modification in meaning and to replacement in usage by other words than truly "core" items. Examples of peripheral basic items not in the two-hundred-meaning list are words like *to gnaw, to nibble, to taste, to swell, to rise, to grow, spleen, waist, shoulder, sky, fog,* and so forth.[14]

Culture vocabulary, on the other hand, consists of the words for the materials of a culture and the ideas and beliefs entertained by a particular society. Culture vocabulary, too, can be seen to have a division into two, at least for the purposes of historical inquiry. Wild-animal nomenclature provides the means of division. What has been discovered is that the names of indigenous large animals tend to be long retained and to be relatively resistant to replacement by borrowing. In African contexts "large" means mammals no smaller than the bushpig; and the larger the mammal, the greater the resistance to borrowing. The word for the elephant is, in fact, for all intents and purposes a core vocabulary item in many parts of Africa. Among reptiles only crocodiles and pythons fit in the loan-resistant set of animal names, while among birds just ostriches (where they occur) belong. Two insect names are particularly retentive. Louse, the universal human pest, has always been in the standard one-hundred-meaning list of core vocabulary: the fly may belong there also, but for now it can be put among the animals whose names resist loaning.

The boundaries between culture vocabulary and peripheral basic vocabulary, and between peripheral basic vocabulary and core vocabulary, are the opposite of hard and fast. Words of peripheral basic vocabulary with corresponding meanings often correspond very inexactly, as readers who have had to translate from one language into another can attest, and that makes them in part culturally variable. Even core vocabulary items can carry cultural overtones and participate in ethnically restricted metaphors. But with these limitations understood, the distinctions are nevertheless historically significant, with differing degrees of penetration of loanwords going along with different demographic and cross-cultural histories.

Subcategory 3A: Intensive Word Borrowing

Intensive word borrowing identifies a history of cross-cultural interaction between societies that not only brings numerous loanwords into the peripheral basic vocabulary of a language and even more into in culture vocabulary, including the nomenclature of large wild animals, but also penetrates significantly into core vocabulary. The borrowing of names of large wild animals is meaningful, provided that the borrowed names refer to animals previously known to both communities. Significant penetration of core vocabulary means usually that three or more loanwords traceable to one particular donor language enter the one-hundred-word list of the receptor language. Intensive borrowing is the most extreme form that word borrowing can take.

Such penetration of loans into parts of core vocabulary, as a wide array of historical examples show, does not take place without relatively heavy word borrowing all across the lexicon. The corollary of this observation is that one need identify in a language only a "significant" body of core word borrowings from a particular donor to be able to infer an earlier era of intensive general borrowing from that donor language. This observation is of especial importance for the historical study of very ancient developments. What happens over a long period in a language is that a considerable turnover in vocabulary takes place, with many words changing meaning, many words dropping entirely out of use, and often many new words entering via subsequent eras of word borrowing. The body of words borrowed in any particular era will thus progressively decline in number as time goes on, but it will decline most slowly in core vocabulary. After several thousand years, most of the culture-vocabulary loans adopted by a language during an intensive borrowing period will be gone, whereas several of the core loans will still remain in use. Their presence is enough to guarantee the onetime existence in the language of an accompanying much larger body of loans from the particular source language and thus to imply a long-ago period of intensive word borrowing.

Intensive word borrowing is often (but by no means always) accompanied by considerable grammatical borrowing, including even the adoption of specific grammatical morphemes (suffixes and prefixes) from the donor language, and by phonological borrowings. But since this sort of borrowing is a sometime accompaniment of, rather than an alternative to, word borrowing, the identification of the loanwords is sufficient and adequate by itself to make the case. Linguists tend to look first at grammatical and phonological interference because that reflects the interests that lead most of them into the discipline in the first place, but for the historian it is just frosting on the cake.

Intensive word borrowing has both chronological and demographic implications for history. Perhaps the most common demographic pattern in which this kind of borrowing takes place is one in which the speakers of the adopting language are universally or virtually universally bilingual in their own language and in the language from which the words come, and may have been so for a period of centuries. Word borrowing with this kind of speech-contact history is normally cumulative. Even the highest rates of borrowing appear to require two or three centuries of contacts to build up a sufficient body of loanwords to fit this subcategory.

The extreme examples in recent East African history are those of minority gatherer-hunter communities who economically coexisted, through their use of different subsistence resources, with dominant pastoral majorities or sometimes cultivating majorities. In all instances where the beginnings of their contacts with their dominant neighbors can be traced to the seventeenth century or earlier—that is, the cases of the Tinderet and certain other Kenya gatherer-hunters among the Maasai and of the Dahalo among the Swahili and Oromo—the loanword sets from the majority languages attain the status of intensive. In one case of an Okiek language in central Kenya the core vocabulary loans from Maasai number nine.[15] Where contact with Maasai began in the eighteenth century, as in the case of Asa (a Southern Cushitic language) and Akie (a Kalenjin dialect) in Tanzania, the penetration of loanwords into core vocabulary was only just beginning to take place in the mid–twentieth century, although word borrowing into peripheral basic culture vocabulary was much further advanced.[16]

Another notable East African case is that of the Ma'a mixed farmers of northeastern Tanzania. Though forming a minority in numbers, they were probably not dominated by the neighboring majorities to the same extent as the Okiek, Asa, and Akie. They appear in earlier centuries to have been more economically distinct from their neighbors than at present, specializing in the raising of cattle for internal trade in the Pare Mountains. So again there was some economic basis for the perseverance of the Ma'a as a separate speech community. Their contacts with the Asu majority of South Pare and so presumably their bilingualism, today universal, in Asu (a Bantu language not to be confused with Asa above) and the Maʾa language can be dated to at least the sixteenth century,[17] and this length of contact, as of the 1960s,[18] was reflected in three word borrowings from Asu in the one-hundred-word list, with another one or two incipient borrowings competing in use with still-current older Maʾa words for the particular meanings. Extensive Maʾa word borrowing from Asu appears in peripheral basic and culture vocabulary and is accompanied by an extraordinary amount of grammatical borrowing from Asu—probably the extreme case of such borrowing in Africa if not in the world.[19]

Since the late eighteenth century, Maʾa speakers have often been trilingual, speaking Shambaa, the present-day majority language, as well as Asu and Maʾa. Shambaa loans, in keeping with contact of less than three centuries, are numerous in culture vocabulary, occur to some extent in peripheral basic lexicon, and provide three or four alternative core vocabulary words, not yet established but competing in use with established Maʾa words; only one, a word for "feather," has pretty much already effectively displaced the older Maʾa word. (Again, this comment refers to the 1960s.) A few verb extensions from Shambaa may be beginning to become productive grammatical elements in Maʾa, but that is all so far. The Asu–Maʾa contact, going back at least 300 years, thus has produced intensive borrowing; the Shambaa contact, which has been strong probably less than 200 years, has not yet done so.

Still another notable African case of intensive word borrowing is that of the Agäw languages spoken in Ethiopia. The number of core-vocabulary borrowings from the now demographically dominant Ethiopian Semitic tongues range from about thirteen or fourteen in Kemant to probably less than five in Awngi.[20] Heavy interaction with speakers of Semitic tongues appears in each case to go back several hundred years and in some cases, like that of Kemant, back 700 or 800 years. Contacts with considerable bilingualism may stretch several hundred years before that, even to the early Axumite period, in some northern areas of Ethiopia, although most of the Agäw languages in actual direct contact with Ethiopian Semitic so early are probably by now long extinct. The least impact shows in Awngi, which has probably had the shortest period of direct Ethiosemitic pressure.

The Agäw examples reinforce the argument that duration is an essential component of the creation of an intensive-borrowing pattern, at least in cases of word borrowing from a dominant majority-community language into a persistent minority-community language. Judging from the evidence of both the Agäw and the Okiek languages, core-vocabulary loans appear to be able to establish themselves in a minority language in this kind of contact situation at rates of about one to three per century.[21]

Different factors may account for an example of mutual intensive general borrowing from early northern East Africa. Two languages spoken about 3,000 years ago, proto-Rub and proto–Southern Nilotic, each acquired an intensive set from the other. Both speech communities persisted through the period, and each embarked on major expansions after the contacts ended.[22] A long-term history of relatively equal relations between peoples living in adjacent and overlapping lands may be the explanation in this instance. In addition, the contacts took place during the early era of agriculture in the region, when very low population densities probably obtained. The lack of comparable examples from eras of fully established and complex agricultural life may be an artifact of an inadequate sample. On the other hand, in early farming eras it may be that long-term stable relations between coexisting communities could endure for periods not possible with the more numerous populations of later times.

Although nearly all cases of intensive borrowing seem to involve significant time spans of interaction, at least two cases from nineteenth-century southern Tanzania, those of the Ngoni and Mbunga, depart radically from this pattern. In both instances, the period of intensive borrowing, with up to five or six loanwords entering the core vocabulary of the borrowing languages, lasted no longer than about two generations.[23] A particular kind of violent, rapid, and unusually intense and radical sociopolitical transformation characterized both these instances and probably explains the exceptional lexical impact. In both cases an incoming, aggressively militarized, small minority community, centralized socially and politically around military institutions, violently conquered a larger preexisting local set of communities. They destroyed the earlier small political units and social relations and incorporated the inhabitants into the new institutional relationships. The languages of the majority incorporated people continued in use; the conquerors' languages died out within three to four generations. But the persisting languages each adopted a great many loanwords, even in core vocabulary, from the conquering society.[24]

The ninth-century Danish invasions of northern and central England provide a third example, from a different part of the world, of just this kind of history with just this kind of impact on vocabulary. Danish armed bands organized for war established their authority all across those regions, with their leaders becoming the local lords. The use of Danish soon died out, although because of continuing contacts across the North Sea, it may have been spoken alongside English two or three generations longer than Ngoni lasted in southern Tanzania. The linguistic impact was the same. Numerous Danish loanwords passed into English, including at least six in the core one-hundred-meaning list—*egg, skin, big, bark, root,* and *die*—and other words often included in core lists, such as *sky* and *leg*.

All three cases, Tanzanian and English, have a common factor, and this factor may be the essential precondition, in combination with conquest, for this unusually rapid type of intensive borrowing. To wit, in each of these histories, the donor language was relatively closely related to the borrowing language, and the two languages involved in each case still shared considerable common vocabulary (although with small pronunciation differences) from their common ancestry. To see the significance of this factor, let us contrast the Danish period with the subsequent era of Norman French conquest of England. In the latter case the conquerors' language continued to be spoken by the elite for almost three centuries, not just four or five generations. Norman rule introduced hundreds of new words into the English language, yet only a single word, *mountain,* into the English core one-hundred-meaning list. What stands out as different in this case was that French, although related to English, was only very distantly related to it and far different in vocabulary.

Subcategory 3B: Heavy General Word Borrowing

Heavy general borrowing is marked off from intensive borrowing by a lack of notable penetration of loans into core vocabulary—that is, by no more than one or two borrowings in the one-hundred-word list. It is differentiated from extensive general borrowing, the subcategory to follow, by the occurrence of loans in the loan-resistant portion of wild-animal nomenclature. Word borrowing is relatively common in peripheral basic as well as culture vocabulary and is often accompanied by phonological influence of the donor language on the receptor and occasionally by a few grammatical adoptions.

Over a very long period of time, a heavy general borrowing set will of course suffer from normal lexical attrition. As happens with an intensive set, the words more resistant to replacement by semantic change and new borrowing will tend to remain when much of the rest have disappeared from use. In this case what will notably remain after a few thousand years will be borrowed names for a very few large wild animals. Since names of such animals, provided they are known to both donor and receptor communities of the loanwords, are normally borrowed only when considerable other vocabulary, both cultural and peripheral basic, are also adopted, their presence will be enough to demonstrate the former existence of heavy general borrowing.

In its historical and demographic implications, heavy general appears to be a transitional subcategory. A heavy general set can result, on the one hand, from the same sorts of demographic and social relations that create an intensive borrowing pattern, but of shorter duration. An example is the Shambaa set of influences on Ma'a, discussed earlier, which includes already a large number of animal names but is only beginning to touch core vocabulary and to have grammatical impact. Similarly the Maasai loans in Asa fit the heavy general pattern. What seems crucial is that the contacts involved in each instance have not yet lasted as long as three centuries.

On the other hand, a heavy general borrowing set can probably be built up by an extended period of the kind of contacts that produce the next subcategory to be discussed, extensive borrowing—in particular in the contact situation in which the language of an established majority community was progressively replaced in everyday use, over a period of several centuries, by the language of what was at first a minority community, intrusive into the area.

Subcategory 3C: Extensive General Word Borrowing

An extensive general set is characterized by numerous loanwords from a particular source language, as much sometimes as a few hundred in all but usually less, in a wide scatter through culture vocabulary, but not including terms for large wild animals, and to a lesser extent touching peripheral basic vocabulary.

What would be left over from an extensive general borrowing set after a very long period had passed, of perhaps 2,000 years or more, probably would be rather similar in appearance to a small light general set (which see below). Only a few of the loanwords would still persist in use and would be semantically scattered. What might nevertheless distinguish it is that some of the loans would be in peripheral basic as well as culture vocabulary.

Extensive general borrowing seems to go with two sorts of histories, one involving language shift and the other long-term prestige dominance of a minority language over the speech of the majority.

The Luhyia loanwords in Kenya Luo form an extensive borrowing pattern attributable to language shift. The Luo began to enter Luhyia-speaking territories in western Kenya early in the second half of the sixteenth century.[25] By the second half of the eighteenth century, they had increased, through the arrival of more Luo immigrant groups, from an intrusive minority into an almost solid block of population, though with still some Luhyia-speaking minorities, on the north side of the Winam Gulf. They spread in considerable part by absorbing the former Luhyia populations of the region. The resulting Luhyia loanword set comes close to the upper limit of what fits the extensive borrowing category because it includes at least one term for a large wild animal (the giraffe).[26] A slower Luo growth into a majority over more than two-plus centuries would have expanded the Luhyia linguistic contribution, conceivably increasing the number of loanwords for large wild animals and so pushing the loanword set over the threshold of the heavy general pattern. A more rapid incorporation of the previous population, of less than two centuries, would presumably yield a lighter extensive set. The demographic correlate here would be one of a majority speech community shifting language to that of an initially minority community. The social requirement would be the full social integration of the two populations. Partial incorporation as a suppressed caste, with the older language being lost, would create quite different, category-2 effects on the replacing language.

The lower extreme of this sort of borrowing—what might be called *light extensive borrowing*—is provided by a case like the Latinization of Gaul. The Celtic language spoken there continued to be used for a few centuries, progressively giving way before the spread of the Roman conquerors' language. The loanwords left in the present-day descendant of northern Gaulish Latin, French, occur in peripheral basic and culture vocabulary; yet even allowing for the passage of time they must always have been fewer than the Luhyia loans in Luo, despite the probably longer period of contact. The salient difference here would seem to be that the intrusive minority remained an integral part of a much larger political unit. The conquered were thus a majority locally but a minority in relation to the larger unit into which they were incorporated. As long as the empire lasted, the intrusive language (all the while becoming gradually the majority language locally) received reinforcement from the forms used in other parts of its wide speech area, and such reinforcement would have tended to drive out of use many of the incipient Celtic borrowings because these could not get established in the language as spoken elsewhere.

At least two kinds of prestige language dominance seem to be able to create extensive borrowing in the opposite demographic direction, from minority to majority speech community.

One history is that reflected by the Germanic loanwords in very early medieval French, by the Arabic loans in Spanish, and by the French loans in Middle English. Indeed, in many cases of conquest this sort of pattern can be seen. The size of the resulting loanword set can vary greatly. Hundreds of French words had taken hold in English by the end of the Middle English period. The determinative factor seems to be the duration of the perseverance of the minority language as the means of political communication and the extent to which the majority must actually become fluent in it to carry on their livelihood. Norman French remained the language of court and nobility for more than two centuries in England, and the prestige and utility of medieval northern French was reinforced by English rule over large parts of France at different times over an almost 400-year period.

The second sort of prestige dominance associated with extensive word borrowing is one in which the minority speech community holds social and economic prestige but not necessarily the direct reins of political power. Religion is commonly a powerful element in the social prestige of the minority language. Even more than for minority rule, long duration seems essential to this kind of contact's producing an extensive borrowing set. An outstanding African example is that of Swahili, where at least 700 and probably more than 1,000 years of Arabic prestige influences[27] have created an extensive set of cultural and peripheral basic loanwords in a Bantu language. Three core vocabulary items (damu 'blood', baridi 'cold', and samaki 'fish') are among the adopted Arabic words in some Swahili dialects, but over the time of contact involved, the adopted Arabic words constitute a rate of borrowing of far less than the one to two words per century suggested to define an intensive set. Borrowings of large animals' names, indicative of heavy general borrowing, are entirely lacking. Soomaali offers a parallel example, having an extensive loanword set again from Arabic adopted for similar reasons. Outside of Africa, one might consider the example of Arabic loans in Persian, where both an initial period of political domination and a long subsequent period of religious prestige have combined to produce an extensive borrowing set. Of course, the Arabic loanwords in both Swahili and Persian, in addition to extensive general borrowings, also include very strong semantically restricted loanword sets (category 2A) in the field of religion.

Subcategory 3D: Light General Word Borrowing

Light general borrowing consists of a small scatter of culture loanwords across a variety of semantic areas. Loaning does not usually extend into peripheral basic vocabulary, let alone core vocabulary, nor does it include names of any large wild animal unless some borrowed metaphorical usage or a lack of previous familiarity with the animal can be invoked. Phonological and grammatical borrowings do not occur. After a few thousand years of language change it may be difficult to find more than one or two words left over from a onetime light general borrowing set.

The causal situations unique to this sort of borrowing can be ones of sustained trade, some intermarriage, and various other forms of cooperation and encounter, not excluding interspersed periods of warfare, between two neighboring and territorially impinging speech communities, both of which continue to persist as separate societies. If one group is more numerous and/or more widespread geographically, the borrowings will pass from its language into that of the smaller group. Examples of histories reflecting this kind of demographic pattern are those of the Luo and Gusii in the nineteenth century and the Maasai and Gikuyu in the eighteenth century.[28] Between communities of more equal size or more equal territorial extent, such borrowing may well take place in both directions, but this possibility needs more investigation.

CATEGORY 4: PIDGINIZATION

Pidginization, the formation of pidgin languages, is a rare and peculiar sort of language change. What happens is an abrupt grammatical modification of a language with a rapid adoption of new vocabulary, often from several different source languages at the same time and having the same appearance as extensive general, heavy general, or intensive word-borrowing sets.

Pidginization is the *last* hypothesis one should turn to in explaining major linguistic change in earlier eras of human history. It appears to happen only in situations that one way or another involve the development, often rapid, of very long-distance trade, and thus must have been a very rare phenomenon indeed before the last several hundred years of European expansion and was perhaps unknown anywhere in the world before 3,000 years ago. Even great grammatical borrowing, like that of Ma'a from Asu, is not pidginization. Ma'a did not in any way undergo abrupt

Figure 5. Categories of Word Borrowing

Category	How the word borrowing takes place	Parts of vocabulary in which the word borrowing occurs	Minimum duration of word borrowing
1— Single-word borrowing	Through contacts among individuals or groups belonging to 2 or more speech communities	An individual word for a new item of culture is adopted	A few hours or days may sometimes be enough
2A— Semantically restricted word borrowing	Through contacts of the members of one speech community with those of another	A set of words dealing with a particular field of technical or cultural knowledge is borrowed	Uncertain; possibly as little as 1–2 generations in some instances
2B— Grammatically restricted word borrowing	From a suppressed collection of minority populations to a dominant speech community	Interjections and some adverbs are borrowed	Uncertain; but probably as little as a century
2C— Status-restricted word borrowing	From a lower-status minority to a dominant majority speech community	Jocular, deprecatory, or tabooed vocabulary is borrowed	Uncertain; but probably 2–3 generations
3A— Intensive word borrowing	From a dominant majority to a co-existing economically distinctive minority speech community; or from intrusive conquering small minority to majority people, closely related in language	Borrowings take place all through vocabulary (basic words are adopted at a rate of about 1–3 percent per century; other vocabulary is borrowed more rapidly)	Usually about 2–3 centuries; just 2–3 generations in instances of conquest by speakers of closely related language

(continued)

Figure 5 *(continued)*

Category	How the word borrowing takes place	Parts of vocabulary in which the word borrowing occurs	Minimum duration of word borrowing
3B— Heavy general word borrowing	According to *first* pattern described in 3A preceding, but of shorter duration than 2–3 centuries; or according to the pattern in 3C following, but of longer duration than 2–3 centuries	Borrowings take place in all parts of vocabulary, *except* for basic vocabulary	If short period of category 3A borrowing: 1–2 centuries; if category 3C borrowing: more than 2 centuries
3C— Extensive general word borrowing	From one speech community to another, as part of the merging of the one community into the other (and the loss of its former language in the process)	Borrowings take place in all parts of the vocabulary, *except* for basic vocabulary *and* terms for large animals	Uncertain; but probably about 1–2 centuries
3D— Light general word borrowing	From one neighboring speech community to another	A sparse, semantically diverse scatter of culture vocabulary is borrowed	2–3 generations
4— Pidginization	By a collection of distinct speech communities thrown together by historical circumstance in the same region; as part of their adoption of a new common language	Rapid and extensive word borrowing takes place in all parts of the vocabulary, accompanied by severe grammatical simplification of the adopted new common language	Less than one generation

structural simplification but instead, over a period of centuries, replaced a major segment of its older grammatical system with a new, borrowed system. From internal reconstruction, one can identify several stages in the Ma'a adoption over the past 300 years of both lexical and grammatical elements from the neighboring Asu and, later, Shambaa languages, and that is quite a different thing from pidginization.[29]

The demographic context of pidginization is one in which a collection of minorities, usually not previously in contact or very little in contact with each other, are thrown together in situations where they need to use the language of one, often especially small minority among them—namely, the language of the economically focal group in the new relationship. This group may be the major carrying merchants or slave masters or both. Once a pidgin becomes the adequate first language of a self-reproducing society (a *creole*), it begins, however, to develop further in the normal fashions described by categories 1–3.

CLOSING CONSIDERATIONS

The various categories and subcategories of word borrowing are not all necessarily mutually exclusive. Some of the subcategories of category 3, for example, can often form a sequence in the development of a language shift. We can easily imagine a history of contact between communities beginning with a period of trade and intermarriage at ethnic boundaries and hence light general word borrowing, followed by a period of spread of one language at the expense of the other, resulting in its taking up of an extensive or, if the process is sufficiently drawn out, a heavy general set of word borrowings from the other. What would remain in the way of evidence at the end of the process would be a borrowing set of the appearance of the second or third sort, because the initial light general borrowings would be indistinguishable from the general culture word adoptions of the later intensification of contact (figure 5).

Although borrowing patterns in accord with different subcategories of category 3 can occur sequentially, as the form of contact and demographic relations between the two shift over time, different category 2 patterns can co-occur with each other and with different category 3 patterns. Subcategories 2B and 2C both describe limited African loan sets in American English, for example.

The combining in a language of limited and general borrowing sets from a particular source language produces a semantic clumping of loans within a wider scatter. What happens is that the general political or prestige dominance of one population group over another is accentuated by that group's demographic concentration in the area of society that has special access to a key area of knowledge or activity. The overall dominance of the group is reflected in the general borrowing array, and its special enabling skill in the subcategory 2A—semantically limited—

borrowings. The two kinds of borrowing both take place, in other words, through one and the same period of time.

One example is that of Norman French in Medieval English, where particular semantic concentrations of loans occur in the vocabulary of feudal governance, law, and warfare—the areas of culture key to the control of England and the lives of its people. Another example is provided by the Arabic loans in Swahili, which have especially high frequency in the vocabulary of religion and formal education. Similarly, the special concentration of Latin and Greek loanwords in the vocabulary of formal knowledge and educated expression in English reflects the former concentration of persons with command of Latin and Greek in the positions of control over education and the creation of new knowledge in the Medieval and early Modern periods. In these sorts of cases, the subcategory of the general loanword set gives us an idea of the proportional demographic relations between the peoples involved; the restricted loanword sets embedded within the general set suggests something of the relations of the different populations to the forces driving the change indicated more broadly by the general set.

The evidence of language contact thus offers us possibilities of uncovering past demographic relations and making inferences about relative (but not absolute) population strengths, and even a view—as in a glass darkly, perhaps—of historical causation. And of course, as chapter 3 shows, the specific words borrowed allow the historian to fill in the details of how ideas and things spread from one people to another and to discover how different societies influenced each other in changing ways over historical time—in material culture, in social custom, in cultural practices, in beliefs, and in the organization of knowledge.

NOTES

1. The expression *linguistic change* as used here refers to changes in vocabulary, phonology, grammar, and the like. *Language shift* is the changeover of a people from using one language to using another as their first language.

2. The processes of rule simplification take place also in normal languages because of pressures toward regularization inherent in the logical structure of a language and in those cases are not attributable to influences from outside.

3. C. Ehret, *Southern Nilotic History: Linguistic Approaches to the Study of the Past* (Evanston, IL: Northwestern University Press, 1971), chap. 2; and idem, "Linguistic Evidence and Its Correlation with Archaeology," *World Archaeology* 8, no. 1 (1976): 5–18.

4. E.g., Ehret, *Southern Nilotic History*, chaps. 4–9; C. Ehret and D. Nurse, "The Taita Cushites," *Sprache und Geschichte in Africa* 3 (1981): 125–168, among other works.

5. The reader will find most good English dictionaries that provide etymologies useful in identifying the Algonkian and many of the Spanish loanwords in recent American English, the Welsh and Norman French loanwords of Middle English, and the Latin and Old Norse loanwords in Anglo-Saxon that are cited here. I have added a few Spanish loanwords from my own rural California and Southwest upbringing that might not be discovered in the typical dictionary.

6. The word *potrero* originally meant a corral in Spanish, but it came to be used in early California Spanish for a particular kind of bowl-shaped valley in the hills that formed a sort of natural corral. It was borrowed into California English in that meaning.

7. The case of French loanwords in English of far southern Louisiana, where French speakers remained locally significant numerically, is a different matter, not dealt with here.

8. Writer's field collections, Kibaya, Tanzania, July 1967.

9. A. H. Jacobs, personal communication, July 1971.

10. Winifred Vass proposes a large number of such cases. Some of these are surely fanciful or chance resemblances, but others may be actual Africanisms, and this field of study deserves to be given more serious investigation: W. K. Vass, *The Bantu Speaking Heritage of the United States*, Afro-American Culture and Society Monograph no. 2 (UCLA, 1979).

11. D. Dalby, "The Etymology of O.K.," *Times* (London), July 19, 1969.

12. *Tipi* or *teepee* and *wickiup* are more technical word borrowings used to distinguish Native American house types. *Wigwam* was apparently used at times also as a technically descriptive term.

13. For which see D. Humes, "Lexicostatistics So Far," *Current Anthropology* 1 (1960): 3–44.

14. The standard word collection list used by Derek Nurse to gather East African Bantu lexicons in the 1970s contains several hundred meanings that fit the idea of peripheral basic vocabulary.

15. Ehret, *Southern Nilotic History*, p. 94.

16. C. Ehret, fieldwork of the 1960s; some of this evidence appears in idem, *Southern Nilotic History*, and idem, *Ethiopians and East Africans: The Problem of Contacts* (Nairobi: East African Publishing House, 1974).

17. I. N. Kimambo, *A Political History of the Pare of Tanzania* (Nairobi: East African Publishing House, 1969), pp. 61–62.

18. For more on this linguistic history, see chap. 2, n. 4.

19. C. Ehret, *The Historical Reconstruction of Southern Cushitic Phonology and Vocabulary*, Kölner Beiträge zur Afrikanistik 5 (Berlin: Reimer, 1980), pp. 130–131.

20. There are problems in determining the exact number of such loans because it is not always easy to distinguish Agäw borrowings from Ethiopian Semitic from the ancient Agäw loans in the Semitic tongues dating from a period when the Semites were still the minority.

21. See chaps. 5 and 7.

22. C. Ehret, "Population Movement and Culture Contact in the Southern Sudan, c. 3000 BC to AD 1000," in J. Mack and P. Robertshaw (eds.), *Culture History in the Southern Sudan*, Memoire 8 (Nairobi: British Institute in Eastern Africa, 1983), pp. 19–48; Heine, *The Kuliak Languages* (Nairobi: East African Publishing House, 1976).

23. I was wrong in certain comments I made about Ngoni in C. Ehret, "Christopher Ehret Responds," *International Journal of African Historical Studies* 34, no. 1 (2001): 82–87, and I wish to express my apologies to Yvonne Bastain for misunderstanding and misinterpreting her analysis of the Ngoni language and its history.

24. R. Gonzales, G. Waite, and C. Ehret, "Strategies for Uncovering and Recovering the Early African Past: History in Southern Tanzania, 500 BCE to 1800 CE" (unpublished paper).

25. B. A. Ogot, *History of the Southern Luo* (Nairobi: East African Publishing House, 1967).

26. Ehret, *Southern Nilotic History*, pp. 187–188, provides a sample of Luhyia loans in Luo.

27. R. Pouwels, *Horn and Crescent: Cultural Change and Traditional Islam on the East African Coast, 800–1900* (Cambridge: Cambridge University Press, 1987).

28. W. R. Ochieng, *The Pre-Colonial History of the Gusii of Western Kenya* (Nairobi: East African Literature Bureau, 1974), pp. 207–217; W. Lawren, "Masai and Kikuyu: An Historical Analysis of Culture Transmission," *Journal of African History* 9 (1968): 571–583.

29. M. Mous, in *The Making of a Mixed Language: The Case of Ma'a/Mbugu* (Amsterdam and

Philadelphia: J. Benjamins, 2003), appears to be dealing with a jargonized version of Ma'a from the late twentieth century, different from the speech of back-country first-language speakers with whom I worked in the 1960s and from whom Steven Feierman collected extensive historical texts, also in the 1960s. S. G. Thomason and T. Kaufman, in *Language Contact, Creolization, and Genetic Linguistics* (Berkeley and Los Angeles: University of California Press, 1988), use Ma'a as an example of a mixed language. Their treatment, however, rests on a secondhand acquaintance with an incomplete body of data, much of it gathered by non–linguistically trained persons in the earlier twentieth century.

5

Linguistic Dating

To establish the linguistic stratigraphy of a language family or branch of a family, as we saw in chapter 2, is to establish the relative chronology of the history of the language group and the peoples who have spoken those languages. How does one assign absolute dates to the relative timescale? Linguistic inquiry, unlike archaeology, does not directly generate independently datable artifacts; hence the importance of the indirect approaches of correlating language testimony with archaeology and other dated forms of historical documentation. Might there nevertheless be ways to build an absolute dating scale more directly from language evidence?

Scholars have pursued this possibility for some time. The principal tools in this effort have been computational.[1] The original method of this type, glottochronology, came into use in the 1950s. In the past decade linguists and biologists have particularly begun applying other computational procedures, pioneered in biology and genetics for building trees of relationship (cladistics) and estimating genetic time depths, to the constructing of linguistic trees and the plotting of time distance in language relationships. As these investigations proceed, they appear likely to add powerful new tools for deriving dates from linguistic distance measures[2] and to have implications everywhere for historians who wish to enrich historical knowledge with linguistic evidence.[3]

For now, however, as a variety of examples from Africa show, the older technique,

This chapter incorporates the article C. Ehret, "Testing the Expectations of Glottochronology against the Correlations of Language and Archaeology in Africa," in C. Renfrew, A. McMahon, and L. Trask (eds.), *Time Depth in Historical Linguistics,* vol. 2 (Cambridge: McDonald Institute for Archaeological Research, 2000), pp. 373–399; used by permission.

glottochronology, remains a productive tool for estimating linguistic time depth. Testing the utility of this approach in African historical dating is the focus of the remainder of this chapter.

UNDERSTANDING THE PROBLEM

Glottochronology, when it was first proposed half a century ago, generated both enthusiastic support and impassioned disbelief among linguists. A large number of articles in the 1950s and 1960s applied the technique to a variety of languages from a number of families and tested the datings of language divergence obtained in this manner against chronologies derived from other sources of evidence. A much smaller number of studies argued against glottochronology on the basis of a few selected cases, in which unusual historical factors were present. The upshot of the debate was the emergence of a relatively small body of scholars who continued to use and sporadically to add examples to the evidence favoring the utility of glottochronology, while the majority of scholars chose to accept, without further critical review, the idea that the exceptional cases disproved the rule.

There is at base probably one key reason that glottochronology has gotten short shrift. To understand this reason requires, with apologies for redundancy, a brief restatement of matters already broached in chapter 2. From reading the articles of the original debate over glottochronology, one gets the sense that neither side had a clear handle on the basic nature of the phenomenon. Both seemed to accept a characterization of glottochronology as involving a *constant* and *regular* rate of lexical change over set periods of time. But what glottochronology actually describes is something different. It in fact identifies, however imperfectly, a real phenomenon with strong analogues in the natural world—namely, the *patterned accumulation of individually random change among quanta of like properties.* The individual lexical changes in basic vocabulary take place randomly—unless particular and usually overtly identifiable historical influences intervene—but the overall accumulation of such random changes over long time periods tends to form normal distributions.[4]

As is implicitly and often even explicitly clear, the unconscious misconception on all sides that, instead, a *constant* and *regular* rate of vocabulary change was involved offended our sense of what being human was all about. As a consequence, as I observed in another context, "the principal form of objection [to glottochronology] has been, dishearteningly, what can only be characterized as assertions of disbelief."[5] At the same time, the proponents failed to respond to the philosophical concern underlying this disbelief and so did little to show their opponents that the aversion was misplaced. The standard retention figures have too often continued to be treated as if they expressed a constant rate of change rather than merely the median of a statistical distribution.

Glottochronology deals with the long-term cumulative effects on lexical history of the innumerable minute choices of usage and vocabulary made all across the years by people in a society as they carry on the everyday give-and-take of conversation and communication. The defined basic vocabulary with which this effect is measured was deliberately constructed of meanings universal or nearly so among humans, so that even the "innumerable minute" choices would not normally themselves be culturally or socially overt, or even aware ones. When overt historical factors do intrude, they manifest themselves as word borrowings in the basic vocabulary.[6] A special version of this problem arises when divergence takes place in a long-term dialect chain or contiguous cluster of dialects. A variety of examples show us that different such histories skew the cognation distributions in predictable, patterned fashions.[7]

AIMS AND GOALS

This chapter, operating from the conceptualization of glottochronology as a measure of cumulative change that is individually random, tests the large number of accepted correlations of language and archaeological cultures in Africa against the expectations of the method. The African cases themselves are drawn from four extremely different language families. In their phonologies, their morphological patterns, and their syntactical tendencies, those families differ from each other as much as Algonkian differs from Indo-European or as Indo-European differs from Sino-Tibetan. The African cases produce consistent results across the board, whichever African family is involved. They indicate that glottochronology is a useful and in fact essential tool in the correlation of language and archaeology. They show that it gives viable, although probabilistic and very rough, absolute datings to linguistic stratigraphies (note that *absolute* does not at all mean "precise"!) and that its findings cannot be disregarded at will by those seeking to correlate archaeology with linguistic history.

We will consider here twenty-four cases in all. These studies come from widely separated parts of the continent of Africa and relate to a variety of different time depths, from as recently as 500 years ago to before 8000 BP. The evidential bases for correlating particular languages with particular societies are varied as well:

1. in a number of instances, the correlation rests on epigraphic evidence; or on direct or indirect written historical testimony as to the timing of cultural divergence; or on mutually confirmatory sets of roughly datable oral traditional evidence; or on a combination of two or more of these sources. Examples include those of the Ethiosemitic speakers and the Oromo of northeastern Africa; the Nubians of Sudan and far southern Egypt; and the Dangme of Ghana.

The greater number of cases are those in which an archaeological culture can be linked to the speakers of a former language for either of two reasons:

2. the archaeology reveals unbroken continuity extending back in time from related speech communities of recent times to the material remains of an earlier archaeological culture or complex; or

3. in the case of several ancient correlations, the material cultural predictions of the linguistic stratigraphy fit in detailed ways with the attested materials in the archaeological stratigraphy.

Most of the correlations from the past 3,000 years are on secure ground because they rest on documentary evidence or archaeological continuities (reasons 1 and 2). The cases of the Nkangala-Nguni, two stages of Shona expansion, the Botatwe, the Central Sabi, the Sabaki, the Northeast-Coastal Bantu, the Maa, and the Maa-Ongamo are each supported by unbroken archaeological continuities back to earlier attested cultures (reason 2). The Swahili example is established by both documentary evidence and archaeological continuity.

For the periods before 3,000 years ago, the examples more often build their correlations from the fit of the linguistic evidence with particular archaeological cultures (reason 3). A majority of the twenty cases involving correlation of language with archaeological cultures were first proposed by archaeologists, and a number of these are already well established in the literature—for example, the correlation of Mashariki (narrow Eastern) Bantu with the Chifumbaze complex.

The examination begins with examples relating to the past 5, 000 to 5,500 years and then moves on to consider several more-provisional correlations proposed for still-earlier periods.

NGUNI AND SHONA HISTORIES IN SOUTH AFRICA

The Nguni

Our first case study involves the Nguni of South Africa. Well-known modern societies of this subgroup of Bantu-speaking peoples include the Zulu and the Xhosa. The pottery styles, residence patterns, and other features of the material culture of the various Nguni groups, as they existed in the eighteenth and nineteenth centuries, show direct archaeological continuities with previous sites across their regions of residence, extending back to the eleventh century.

The eleventh century, however, was a time of sweeping change in the material record of the regions in which Nguni languages were spoken in 1800. A new pottery style took hold at that time, first in central and northern Kwazulu-Natal and then over the next two centuries in the areas of the Transkei and eventually the Ciskei. The previous residence type among the food-producing people of the region had been villages, which were concentrated particularly in association with certain kinds of soils along the river valleys of the overall region. This form of settlement was replaced in the eleventh and twelfth centuries by smaller hamlets, which now began to be found all across the region in all its environments. Previously, in the first millennium, farming supplemented by some livestock raising, especially of smaller livestock, and considerable hunting and fishing had been the pattern. This economic order was replaced in most areas by an economy combining farming, especially reliance on grain cultivation, with extensive cattle and other livestock raising, less hunting, and in many areas, even along rivers, no fishing at all.

Carolan Ownby has shown from a detailed linguistic reconstruction and a large body of data that, corresponding to the two successive archaeological cultures of the Iron Age in the Kwazulu-Natal and Kei regions, two distinct sets of Bantu societies successively inhabited those areas. The first Bantu population spoke a language called "Sala" by Ownby, the closest relations of which were with the modern-day Shona language of Zimbabwe. This language forms a powerful and pervasive substratum in Nguni, deeply affecting both phonology and vocabulary in the latter-day Nguni dialects. The earliest Sala influence on Nguni dates to the Proto-Nguni period. But the fact that Sala peoples previously lived all through the Kwazulu-Natal and Kei regions is evident in the subsequent adoption of still more Sala loanwords, even into basic vocabulary, by each of the Nguni daughter dialects that emerged across those areas.[8]

The pottery tradition in place in the Natal and Kei regions from the second up to the eleventh century can be tied to the Sala people for two reasons. First, only two food-producing cultural complexes, as described above, have existed across that region. The second of these, which displaced the first from the eleventh century onward, is clearly that of the Nguni, leaving the Sala as the only possible candidates for the makers of the earlier complex.

The second reason requires a more complicated statement. One side of the picture is drawn from a wider regional correlation of the language evidence with the archaeology. The pre-eleventh-century culture in the Kwazulu-Natal and Kei regions formed the southern extension of a particular tradition, the Lydenburg, present also during the first millennium in the adjoining regions to the north, between the Vaal and Limpopo rivers. Late in the millennium, from about 900 CE, another offshoot of the wider Kalundu complex, to which the Lydenburg tradition belongs, spread in areas immediately north of the Limpopo and, between then and about 1200, all through Zimbabwe. The ceramic industries of the Shona societies of later centuries can be traced in an unbroken line back to the pottery brought into Zimbabwe by that cultural spread of Lydenburg-related people.[9]

In other words, the evidence is strong that Lydenburg culture, and the Kalundu complex as a whole, were the work of very early Shona-speaking people. The Sala people, as speakers of a language closely related to Shona, can therefore be expected to have made a facies of the Lydenburg tradition or of the broader Kalundu complex to which Lydenburg and its facies belong. Exactly such a facies was present across the regions, in Kwazulu-Natal and the Transkei, in just those areas where

Ownby has decisively shown the Sala language to have formerly been spoken. The linguistic and archaeological evidence in the Natal and Kei regions converges to the same answer: the dominant pre-Nguni food-producing population, the Sala of Ownby's work, spoke a Shona-related language and belonged archaeologically to the Lydenburg tradition or the wider Kalundu complex.

Moving on to the Nguni side of the evidence, the linguistic historical findings depict a two-stage initial divergence of Proto-Nguni. In Ownby's view, Proto-Nguni differentiated initially into four dialects. Three of these dialects were ancestral to the languages of the three Nguni-speaking societies—the Northern Ndebele, Southern Ndebele, and Phuti—that resided in recent centuries on the High Veld, to the north of the Great Escarpment (the Drakensberg). The fourth dialect, Proto-Nkangala, was the ancestor of all the later Nguni languages and dialects spoken across the Kwazulu-Natal and Kei regions, between the escarpment and the sea. The speakers of this dialect broke away from their close relatives on edges of the High Veld by moving into Natal and then spreading out and diverging into a large number of communities. Because the new archaeological continuities beginning in the eleventh century lead in unbroken continuity down to the modern-day speakers of the Nkangala dialects of Nguni, we can identify the Proto-Nkangala as the introducers of the new archaeological horizon. The percentages of cognation that reflect the settlement and initial expansion and divergence of the Nkangala dialects, starting at just after 1,000 years ago, form a distribution range that centers around 72–79 percent, with its median at about 76 percent.[10]

Shona History in Zimbabwe

The establishment of the Shona dialects across Zimbabwe and the adjacent areas to the east in Mozambique supplies still another correlation of lexical change with archaeology. The initial spread into southern Zimbabwe of the Kutama, or Leopard's Kopje, offshoot of the Kalundu complex began about the tenth century.[11] It then spread more widely east and west across southern Zimbabwe by the early eleventh century. The eastern end of this expansion apparently extended into Mozambique, although that aspect remains to be adequately studied by archaeologists. In the twelfth and thirteenth centuries, Kutama offshoots spread over the central and northern Zimbabwe plateau as well. The arrival of the Kutama tradition in each part of Zimbabwe marks a break with the preceding archaeology of the country; but from those points onward, continuous developments without further break took place down to more recent times. Written documentation confirms that, from before the sixteenth century, dialects of the Shona language were spoken through all these regions.

Dialect classification study depicts a three-stage expansion of Shona. The deepest dialect divisions reflect a first stage of differentiation in which four dialects emerged across southern Zimbabwe and the adjacent areas immediately to the east in Mozambique. At the second stage one of the these dialects diverged into a further set of daughter dialects extending from south-central Zimbabwe eastward and east-northeastward into Mozambique. Finally, a third stage of dialect differentiation gave rise to the dialects of central and northern Zimbabwe.[12] The first stage in the dialect history fits the first stage of Kutama establishment across southern Zimbabwe beginning in the tenth century; the third stage maps with the very same areas as the Kutama expansion into central and northern Zimbabwe in the thirteenth and fourteenth centuries. Because of the paucity of archaeology in Mozambique, we lack material corroboration of the intermediate stage indicated in the language evidence.

Reliable data, collected from Shona dialects early in the twentieth century, provide only a truncated version of the one-hundred-word list. The percentages of cognation obtained in this way chart a set of relationships thoroughly congruent, however, with what the main body of evidence for dialect classification requires.[13] These fall into two useful ranges of cognation:

a. 61–80 percent, with a median of 71, for the dialects whose distributions match up with the initial spread of Kutama in southern Zimbabwe, around and after CE 900; and

b. 75–86 percent, with a median of 80, for the dialects that can be correlated with the last stage of Kutama expansion, 1100–1300, across the central and northern Zimbabwe plateau.

THE NAMAKALA AND LUANGWA TRADITIONS AND THEIR CORRELATIONS

In Zambia and the adjacent parts of several neighboring countries, two strong correlations between language and culture have been established. One is of the Botatwe (Ila-Tonga) languages with the Namakala cluster of archaeological cultures, and the other is of the Sabi (Bemba, Bisa, Tabwa, etc.) languages with the Luangwa culture. Both Botatwe and Sabi are subgroups of the Bantu languages.[14]

The Botatwe Case

Namakala appears newly in the Zambian archaeological record in about the seventh century. It may be an offshoot an earlier culture found to the north in southeastern Congo.[15] Between around 700 and 1000 three variants of the Namakala tradition emerged: the Fibobe and the Gundu facies and a third variety, to which archaeologists continue to apply the name Namakala. This second stage of Namakala continued to develop without break into the recent culture of the Ila, speakers of one of the four member languages of the Botatwe group. Fibobe and Gundu, respectively, evolved into the cultures of the Lenje and Tonga—two of the other members of the group. (Another Botatwe society, the Soli people, make a pottery of the Luangwa tradition, because of their special historical relations with Sabi peoples—

a topic we will return to shortly.) The expansion of these three Namakala facies in southern and west-central Zambia progressively displaced the Salumano culture, which had been the dominant archaeological tradition in the region before 600 CE. The full replacement of the Salumano by the Namakala facies took place over a period of several centuries.[16]

The cognation percentages among the Botatwe dialects spoken by the makers of the different Namakala facies—the Ila, Lenje, and Tonga—form a distribution typical of a dialect chain. In this kind of distribution, the adjacent languages in the chain share figures skewed high by their continuing history of direct cultural interaction and consequent linguistic inference on each other during the early periods of their linguistic differentiation out of their common ancestor. Dialects successively further apart in the chain are successively less affected by this drag on the apparent rate of differentiation and so have successively lower cognation counts with each other. For this reason the lowest percentage range, between the most distant members of the chain, can be taken as most nearly reflecting the true depth of differentiation within the chain. In the Botatwe group that figure is 70 percent.[17] As we have just seen, the beginnings of the archaeological divergence of the early Namakala tradition into three closely related successor cultures belongs to the three centuries just before 1000. In other words, a period of about 1,300 to 1,000 years corresponds to the lowest cognation range among the three Botatwe languages, at 70 percent.

The Luangwa Tradition and the Central Sabi Languages

The second cultural complex, Luangwa, consistently links up to the Sabi-speaking peoples. In the first half of the second millennium CE, varieties of this archaeological tradition spread over most of eastern and central Zambia and also could be found to the north in far southeastern Congo. The core regions of this cultural complex are consistently the lands of peoples who speak a Sabi language—specifically, the dialects of the Central Sabi language, such as Bemba, Bisa, Aushi, Lala, Lamba, and Temba, among others. The beginnings of Luangwa expansion across eastern and central Zambia date to around 1000. Luangwa culture spread at the expense of previously established cultures, including Kalambo in northeastern Zambia. An unbroken cultural continuity extends from the inception of the Luangwa period down to the modern-day Sabi peoples of those regions.

A complication we must deal with in the history of the Luangwa culture is the diffusion at different times of major elements of this complex to non-Sabi peoples inhabiting several immediately adjacent, surrounding areas. One such people were the Soli of central Zambia, who retained their Botatwe language but borrowed many Sabi words into it. Other non-Sabi peoples who adopted significant elements of Luangwa culture include the Kaonde, a Luban-speaking people residing on the western edges of the Sabi-speaking regions; the Mambwe and Lungu of far northeastern Zambia; and the early Nyanja-Cewa, who inhabited lands just east of the Sabi areas, in Malawi and southeastern Zambia. In each of these cases, Sabi influences are strongly evident in both lexical and cultural borrowings. In the Malawian instance, the major impact of Sabi peoples and Luangwa culture appears to have accompanied the adoption of new political forms by the Nyanja-Cewa people in the middle centuries of the first half of the second millennium. In northeastern Zambia major political changes appear similarly to be linked to the late spread there, at around the seventeenth century, of Luangwa-related pottery in place of the long-established Kalambo style. The Soli in central Zambia are still another case in which political changes of Sabi origin probably greatly enhanced the impact of the Luangwa culture on a non-Sabi-speaking society.[18]

The overall geographical distribution of the Luangwa culture makes it clear that this tradition arose among the Central Sabi peoples. They are and were consistently the bearers of this culture. The non-Sabi groups who adopted significant material cultural elements from this tradition all reside in immediately adjoining territories, situated around the peripheries of the large contiguous, central block of Central Sabi–speaking societies.

The percentages of cognation among the most distantly related Central Sabi dialects form a distribution centering around the low and middle 70 percents, with the median at 73 percent.[19] This range can thus be taken to reflect the dialect divergence that corresponds to the Luangwa expansion, a cultural spread beginning at around 1,000 years ago.

SWAHILI, SABAKI, AND NORTHEAST-COASTAL BANTU HISTORY

On the coasts and in the coastal hinterlands of Kenya and northern Tanzania lies another region with well-established correlations of language with archaeology. Three case studies can be extracted from these data—one involving the Swahili; the second, the Sabaki group, of which Swahili is a member; and the third, a still-wider subgroup of Bantu languages, Northeast-Coastal, to which Sabaki belongs.

The Swahili and Their Sabaki and Proto-Northeast-Coastal Bantu Ancestry

The Swahili can be tracked back in time, both from the archaeology and from scattered written references, to a founding era along the Kenya Coast, in and around the Lamu Archipelago, dating between 700 and 900. Already by the close of the eighth and the start of the ninth century, Swahili merchants had planted settlements as far south along the Indian Ocean coast as southern Mozambique and had apparently reached the Comoro Islands.

The lexicostatistical data for the Swahili dialects are extensive,[20] but two factors must be corrected for before their implications can be assessed. For one thing, dialect chaining has recurrently skewed the figures for nearby dialects higher than those across the chain as a whole. Second, a considerable number of word borrowings have intruded into the basic lexicostatistical list of each dialect. If one accounts for the borrowings (by either the method used by Embleton or that employed by Ehret)[21] and restricts the comparison of percentages to nonadjacent dialects, a consistent distribution emerges from the processed data. The cognation retention range in the one-hundred-meaning list among the different primary dialect groups of Swahili runs from the high 60 percents to 74 percent. The archaeological dating of the first stage of Swahili expansion, to the late eighth and the ninth centuries, therefore associates the cognation range of high 60s to 74 percent with a time period of just about 1,200 to 1,300 years.

Together the Swahili, the Mijikenda, and another neighboring mainland people, the Pokomo, for whom as yet we have no archaeology, form the Sabaki subgroup of the Northeast-Coastal Bantu. Three other sister subgroups—the Ruvu of east-central Tanzania and the Asu and the Seuta of northeastern Tanzania—complete the makeup of Northeast-Coastal Bantu.

As with the Swahili dialects, the overall Sabaki cognation figures must be adjusted for both old dialect-chaining influences—in this case, often distorting upward the scores of particular Pokomo or Mijikenda dialects with particular neighboring Swahili dialects—and considerable word borrowing in basic vocabulary. Once these factors are accounted for, the cognation percentages among the three major Sabaki languages—Swahili, Mijikenda, and Pokomo—can be shown to range from 63 to 69 percent, with a median of 66.[22] That range thus reflects the initial divergence of the Sabaki subgroup.

Archaeology and the Sabaki and Northeast-Coastal Bantu

The domestic pottery of the early Swahili era belongs to the Tana (or Wenje) tradition, also called the "Triangular Incised Ware" (TIW) tradition.[23] The earliest Tana wares are found in the hinterland of the central and northern Tanzania Coast, where they date to the fourth century. In general this pottery occurs wherever Northeast-Coastal Bantu populations established themselves. Between the fourth and the seventh century Tana ware and its associated cultural tradition became widespread from the Rufiji Delta of the south-central coast to the valley of the Pangani River in the north. All across these regions, peoples of the Ruvu, Seuta, and Asu subgroups of Northeast-Coastal Bantu have long formed the primary populations.

A previously established ceramic tradition, Kwale ware (and a variant of it, Limbo), which had clear links to the ceramics of the earliest Mashariki Bantu of the Great Lakes region, appeared at the East African coast and its immediate hinterland by the last century BCE, persisting in some locales up through the middle of first millennium CE. Both south and north of the Pangani River, the Tana wares associated with the early Northeast-Coastal Bantu began at first to coexist with and then to displace the Kwale tradition by about the fifth century CE. Then, after 500, the Tana culture spread farther north, appearing at the sites of the soon-to-emerge Swahili society on the islands of the Lamu Archipelago, as well as at mainland locations.[24]

This archaeological history exactly fits the societal and language history the linguistic evidence requires. This testimony shows that two successive Bantu populations settled in northeastern Tanzania and coastal Kenya, with the later-arriving early Northeast-Coastal Bantu dialects gradually displacing the prior Bantu languages. The word-borrowing sets reflecting this history are of the kind that accompany a period of coexistence in the same region of an established population with an incoming population (see chapter 4), with the earlier language eventually dropping from use in favor of the newcomers' language.[25]

With such a layering of different settlement groups, here is what one can expect in the archaeological record: At first, one pottery style is present, that of the initial population of the region. As the new set of people move into the region, a coexistence of two ceramic decorative styles, reflective of the commingling of settlements of people from two speech communities, should then appear in the archaeology. Over time, as the earlier language gives way to the new, we may find for a time the presence of both traditions in different neighboring sites or even in the same site. If the language of the new arrivals gradually displaces the earlier language from use, this will be reflected in a growing predominance of the new decorative elements, with the eventual disappearance of the motifs and stylistic arrangements deriving from the earlier population. Just that kind of transition, from Kwale to Tana, can be argued to be present in the history of ceramic styles in the early and middle first millennium in the East African coast and immediate hinterland.

Felix Chami has argued strongly for continuity between the Kwale and Tana (TIW) wares in northeast Tanzania—primarily, it would seem, because of the contemporaneous occurrence sometimes of both decorative styles in single sites. But from the published site descriptions it is evident, as Rhonda Gonzales has demonstrated, that a three-stage history was present. Early in the first millennium Kwale ware was made. In the middle centuries, roughly 400–600, both Kwale *and* Tana were present, coexisting sometimes in different sites and sometimes in the same sites, thus indicating the coexistence of two populations. By 600 and after, TIW began to replace Kwale everywhere, coincident with the dying out of the earlier Bantu dialects and their replacement by Northeast-Coastal Bantu languages.[26]

The northward spread of Tana ware must date to before the second half of the 700s, because, as we have already seen, the Swahili seaborne expansions began probably by then. The archaeology of the appearance of the Tana tradition in the Sabaki-speaking areas would place these events in fact in about the sixth century. South of the Tana River, Tana pottery of the early Sabaki communities continued to be the characteristic style on into the formative period of one of the two societies most closely related in language to the Swahili—namely, the Mijikenda, whose key ritual sites, the *kayas*, provide a further archaeological continuity from 1000 down to the twentieth century.[27]

Sabaki and Northeast-Coastal Bantu Correlations

A still lower percentage figure reflects the divergence of the original Northeast-Coastal society into its descendant Ruvu, Seuta, Asu, and Sabaki subgroups. Again correcting for the problems of word borrowing in the basic word list and for old dialect chain influence—particularly between adjacent languages of the Ruvu and Seuta groups—a core cognation range from 49 up to the low 60 percents can be discerned, with its median at around 58 percent.[28] The early Northeast-Coastal society's overall geographical correlation with the early spread of Tana pottery sets the start of this divergence at around the fourth century.

To sum up, three correlations of cognation counts with archaeology emerge from the Northeast-Coastal Bantu and Tana culture evidence:

a. The initial spread of Swahili, reflected by a percentage range of 68–74 among its most distant dialects, commences in the archaeology in the late eighth and the early ninth centuries.

b. The immediately preceding historical stage, at which Proto-Sabaki spread north from the Pangani to the Lamu region and began to diverge into the dialects ancestral to Proto-Mijikenda, Proto-Swahili, and Proto-Pokomo, is marked by a cognation ranging slight lower, at 63–69 percent (with a median of 66), and can be correlated with the spread of Tana culture into the same hinterland areas at around the sixth and seventh centuries.

c. The still-earlier stage—at which Proto-Northeast-Coastal Bantu communities spread out across the areas of the lower Ruvu and Pangani rivers and began the divergence of which the Proto-Sabaki was one of the offshoots—produced a cognation range centering around the high 50 percents. This period of divergence can be correlated with the earliest Tana-ware sites, dating to the fourth century south of the Pangani River.

MASHARIKI BANTU AND THE CHIFUMBAZE COMPLEX

Nguni, Shona, and Northeast-Coastal Bantu are three among a large number of subgroups belonging to the Mashariki ("Eastern Bantu") division of the Bantu languages. The history of the first stages in the divergences of the Proto-Mashariki language, out of which the ancestral languages of those subgroups themselves emerged, provides us with an example that reaches still deeper into the past. The now generally accepted view is that the early history of the Mashariki group as a whole broadly corresponds in the archaeological record to the spread of a large number of closely related cultures, belonging to what is called the Chifumbaze complex. The earliest Chifumbaze sites were located in the western side of the African Great Lakes region and date to the early first millennium BCE.[29] Late in the millennium the complex spread out across the eastern side of Africa as far east as the Kenya Coast and, in the early first millennium CE, as far south as Kwazulu-Natal.

To assess the linguistic-dating implications of this generally accepted archaeological correlation, we turn to the percentages of cognation among the different primary subgroups of Mashariki. That effort involves a very great number of figures because of the great number of individual languages involved, and as is typical in such instances, the distribution of percentages can be wide. There are also problems of dealing both with languages that have borrowed heavily from non-Bantu tongues, resulting in a lower skewing of their cognation percentages, and with languages that have borrowed heavily from other Mashariki tongues, conversely high-skewing their figures. Once the problems of heavy borrowing are accounted for, we discover that the central clustering of figures between the most distantly related subgroups of the Mashariki languages lies between about 35 and 48 percent, with the median around 39 or 40 percent. Reflective of the first stage of Mashariki language differentiation, these figures thus can be argued to correlate with the earliest attestations of the corresponding archaeological tradition, the Chifumbaze complex, dating to about 3,000 years ago in the western Great Lakes.[30]

NON-BANTU CASE STUDIES FROM EASTERN AFRICA

Further well-established eastern African cases of linguistic and archaeological correlation involve the Southern and Eastern Nilotic and Southern Cushitic peoples and their languages. The most recent in time and best established involves the Maa-Ongamo subgroup of Eastern Nilotes. Test cases earlier in time come from Southern Nilotic and Southern Cushitic history.

Maa-Ongamo History

Cattle-raising people, who had previously resided in far southeastern Sudan, brought the Proto-Maa-Ongamo language south into central Kenya.[31] Their arrival in central Kenya can be correlated with the appearance in the eighth century of a new pottery, Lanet ware, which continued to he used by their descendants down to the twentieth century.[32]

After the initial devolution of the Proto-Maa-Ongamo community into two societies, the Ongamo and the Maa, the Maa descendant language itself subsequently diverged into its three primary present-day dialects: Sampuru, Camus, and Maasai. We know that the Maa-Ongamo separation took shape by or before 1000 CE, because the Proto-Chaga, a Bantu people of the period 1000–1200, were already by those centuries borrowing Maa-Ongamo words with the distinctive phonological features of Ongamo.[33] The subsequent breakup of the Proto-Maa society and the emergence of a distinct Maasai society can be dated to not long before the sixteenth century. This conclusion is based on our extensive knowledge of both the Maasai oral traditions themselves and the correlative evidence of the traditions of several neighboring peoples, whose histories were profoundly reshaped by their encounter with Maasai military prowess.[34]

The cognation percentages for the stages of Maa-Ongamo differentiation provide the following picture. Figures of around 72 percent reflect the initial divergence of the Proto-Maa-Ongamo into Maa and Ongamo societies.[35] From correlations with archaeology and the history of the Proto-Chaga people, this range appears to correlate with a date no later than about the tenth century. For the Maa development into separate Sampuru, Camus, and Maasai peoples, beginning perhaps a century before 1500, the comparable percentages of cognation range from 80 to 85 percent.[36]

Southern Nilotic History

The arrival of the Southern Nilotes on the East African archaeological scene can now be firmly correlated with appearance of the Elmenteitan culture in the western highlands of Kenya in about the ninth century BCE.[37] By the sixth and fifth centuries BCE, a major offshoot of the Elmenteitan moved into the vast Mara and Loita plains south of the western highlands.[38] The Elmenteitan sites in the western highlands show archaeological continuities down to the Kalenjin societies of the Southern Nilotes. The Elmenteitan manifestations of the Mara and Loita areas can be attributed to the ancestors of the southern branch of the Southern Nilotes, the Datoga, a few of whom still reside in the Mara region and the rest of whom lived there until they were driven southward by the advancing Maasai only in the later seventeenth century, during the Il-Tatua wars.[39]

How is this primary division of the Southern Nilotes into Kalenjin and Datoga branches reflected in the cognation counts? The percentages of cognation of the Kalenjin dialects with the Datoga dialects center around 44–49 percent.[40] This range corresponds thus to the archaeological divergence of the Elmenteitan tradition into northern and southern facies at about 2,600 to 2,500 years ago.

Southern Cushitic History

Southern Cushitic history offers correlations stretching back to a still-earlier period. The archaeologist Stanley Ambrose has made a convincing case that early Southern Cushitic–speaking peoples were the makers of several versions of what has been called the "Savanna Pastoral Neolithic" complex.[41]

Peter Robertshaw and David Collett have argued for two major divisions in this complex: Olmalenge and Oldishi.[42] The earliest appearance of this complex was in northern Kenya, east of Lake Turkana, where it dates to 3500–3000 BCE (in calibrated dates). The northern sites and those of later times in the central Kenyan rift valley areas have been attributed to Olmalenge. Oldishi sites appeared between 1800 and 1500 BCE in southern Kenya and central northern Tanzania and by the last millennium BCE had spread very widely across the open grasslands of those regions. From the distributions of the extant Southern Cushitic languages, and from the evidence for extinct Southern Cushitic tongues—whose former locations are attested by numerous loanwords in the Southern Nilotic, Maa-Ongamo, and Bantu languages of East Africa—it is evident that the sites of Oldishi culture appear consistently in the lands where Rift Southern Cushites lived, and those of the Olmalenge culture in areas of Ma'a Southern Cushitic population.[43] The third branch of Southern Cushitic, Dahaloan, was spoken in eastern parts of Kenya not yet satisfactorily explored by archaeologists, and so we cannot as yet give them archaeological identification.

Three ranges of cognation can be attached to this history:

a. Two overlapping ranges mark the earliest divergences of the ancestral Southern Cushitic society—first into Proto-Dahaloan and Proto-Ma'a-Rift communities at 15–22 percent, with a median of 19 percent, and then of Proto-Ma'a-Rift into ancestral Ma'a and Proto-Rift societies at 19–25 percent. These percentages would correlate with the first period of Savanna Pastoral Neolithic sites, beginning sometime around 3500–3000 BCE in calibrated dates, or 5,500 to 5,000 years ago, in northern Kenya.

b. A third range pertains to the Rift group. Rift Southern Cushitic divides into two subbranches, East Rift and West Rift, with the cognation figures between the languages of the two subbranches running 35–42 percent and having a median of 40 percent. The early known examples of the Oldishi culture, which can be geographically correlated with the early locations inferred linguistically for Rift peoples, date to roughly the middle of the second millennium BCE. If, as seems probable, the East and West Rift divergence is an outcome of the Oldishi expansions, then the range of cognation separating East from West Rift languages, running from the mid-30 to low 40 percents, would relate to a time period of about 3,500 years.[44]

NORTHEASTERN AFRICAN CORRELATIONS

In northeastern Africa, along with the archaeology, a different kind of correlative data for linguistic dating is available; that of epigraphy and other kinds of written documentation. In Ethiopia two notable cases can be explored—those of the Oromo and of the Ethiosemitic language group—while the northern Middle Nile Basin provides an additional instance of Nubian history.

Oromo History

The most recent example of correlative data with written documentation is that of the Oromo. From the Ethiopian written sources we can date the onset of the great expansion of Oromo people within the Ethiopian Highlands quite closely: to the two decades preceding 1550. The southward advance of Oromo populations into northeastern Kenya is known, both from exceptionally well-dated oral traditions and from written notices, to have reached as far as the hinterland of the coast between 1550 and 1600.

Even in the 1520s the Oromo formed more than one political community, and consequently they may have spoken more than one dialect. But any dialect differences existing at that time would have been relatively slight, and the main divisions of Oromo seem still to have formed a closely interconnected grouping of people dispersed around the Bali region of Ethiopia. We can therefore date the start of dialect divergence in Oromo to not later than the 1520s, although it might have begun as much as a century or two before 1500. The cognation rates among the major Oromo dialects, as calculated in about 1969–70[45] and corrected by me for intrusive word borrowings, run from 81 to 85 percent, with a median at 84 percent. The minimum time span for the differentiation reflected by this range is thus 450 years (1520–1970), with a possibly somewhat longer time span actually involved.

Ethiosemitic Language History

An instance earlier in time comes from the Ethiosemitic languages. The ancestral language of all the members of this group is attested in epigraphic records dating to the fifth century BCE at ancient sites in modern-day Eritrea and far northern Ethiopia. This language diverged initially into two dialects—one ancestral to the later church liturgical language of Ethiopia, Ge'ez, and to the modern-day Tigre and Tigrinya languages of Eritrea and northern Ethiopia, respectively, and the other ancestral to the remainder of the Ethiosemitic tongues, all today spoken farther south in Ethiopia. This first divergence of Ethiosemitic into two primary subgroups could not have begun very long after the fifth century, because already by the fourth century CE the northern subgroup itself had clearly been divided for some time into two dialects. One was Ge'ez, the written language of that time, the spoken form of which evolved into Tigrinya; the other was the forebear of the Tigre language.[46]

The primary level of divergence in Ethiosemitic, between its northern and southern branches, is reflected by cognation figures that, after correction for word-borrowing effects, fill a tight range from 43 to 52 percent, with its median at 48 percent.[47] These figures therefore correlate with the first divergence of the epigraphic Ethiosemitic, and that divergence, as we have seen, fell in the second half of the last millennium BCE, approximately 2,500 to 2,000 years ago. I have argued from a different kind of linguistic evidence for placing this break at about 2300 BP.[48]

Nubian History

In the case of Nubian history, the Classical written sources locate identifiably Nubian populations along or just west of the Nile south of Egypt from about the third century BCE onward. Already by that time it is evident that several distinct Nubian societies, politically independent of each other, were in existence, indicating, as the archaeologist William Y. Adams and the linguist Robin Thelwall have shown, that the linguistic differentiation of the Nubians was already well under way before 2,300 years ago.[49] In the one-hundred-word lists of the Nubian languages, the lowest cognation range, marking this initial divergence of the Nubian group, runs at 37–51 percent, with a median of 44 percent.[50]

The one exceptional instance is a much higher than expected cognation between the two Nubian languages along the Nile: Nobiin and Dongolawi. In this case a combination of factors has been argued to account for the figures—first, the settlement 2,000 years ago of the early Dongolawi speakers in an area previously Nobiin related in language, and then, between CE 600 and 1300, a period of seven centuries of military, cultural, and literary rule of the Nobiin over the Dongolawi people,[51] bringing about a heavy infiltration of Nobiin word borrowing (category 3A) into Dongolawi and so greatly skewing its figures upward with Nobiin. But the rest of the figures are consistent, putting the low Nubian range of 37–51 percent as equivalent to a divergence dating to at least the early first millennium BCE.

CORRELATIONS FOR NIGER-CONGO LANGUAGES OF WEST AFRICA

On the other side of the continent, in West Africa, a two-stage correlation of the Benue-Kwa branch of the Niger-Congo languages with archaeological change can be proposed.

The Benue-Kwa Divergence

The first set of developments took place in the archaeology of the West African rainforest zone, extending from southeastern Ivory Coast on the west to southwestern Cameroon on the east, beginning around 5000–4000 BCE. Throughout this east-west band of regions, a new set of archaeological manifestations took hold during this period. The characteristic technological addition was the making of polished stone axes,[52] with ceramics as an early part of the overall assemblages, too. The regions involved in the changeover coincide closely with where linguistic historians place the early speech territories of the languages of one particular subbranching of the Niger-Congo family, Benue-Kwa. Everywhere in recent centuries, with the single exception of Ijo, only languages belonging to that subbranch were spoken across all those lands. No other early, similarly sweeping cross-regional archaeological replacement that might account for the distribution of the Benue-Kwa languages has been identified in this zone.

The Benue-Kwa languages of these regions form a diverse group. As calculated by a variety of scholars using overlapping sets of languages, the cognation percentages in basic vocabulary between languages belonging to different of the most distantly related subgroups of Benue-Kwa consistently fall in the teens, centering right around 10–15 percent.[53] Hence, *providing* this provisional archaeological correlation is born out, the dating of the initial Benue-Kwa expansion and diversification in the West African rainforest to around 5000–4000 BCE would correlate with a cognation percentage range in the lower to middle teens.

The First Bantu Expansions

In the fourth and third millennia BCE, new expansions of the polished-stone-ax cultures of the West African rainforest took place southward and southeastward from Cameroon into the equatorial rainforest regions. The as-yet-available evidence for this history is known from scattered locales, but these sites each reveal the encounter of polished-stone ax making and pottery-fashioning people with the quite different tool-making traditions of the previous inhabitants. The earliest stage in this process appears to have involved communities from southwestern Cameroon, who moved down the Atlantic coast as far as the mouth of the Ogowe River possibly before 3000. The second stage began with the movement southeastward from Cameroon of closely related communities, in the third millennium BCE, deeper into the equatorial forest itself. Over the next 1,500 to 2,000 years, the new culture manifestations spread widely across the equatorial rainforest, reaching as far, by 1000 BCE, as the western side of the Great Lakes region.

There is no doubt any longer that these intrusive new communities, sparsely known as they are so far from the archaeology, were the forebears of the later Bantu peoples.[54] In linguistic history the Bantu languages form an offshoot of the Benue-Kwa branching of Niger-Congo. This is the same group to whose speakers we attribute the antecedent polished-stone-ax cultures of the adjacent parts of the rainforest belt in West Africa. The tool-making side of that tradition continued in use down to the establishment of iron technology in the equatorial rainforest in the first millennium BCE.

Kairn Klieman's work on Bantu subclassification supports previous studies, but adds a new twist. It divides "Narrow Bantu" into one branch consisting of a small group found along the Atlantic coast near the mouth of the Ogowe River, to which she gives the name "Coastlands," and a second branch comprising the rest of Narrow Bantu, called "Nyong-Lomami."[55] Klieman's language evidence fits, in other words, with the archaeological indications of two expansions of polished-stone-ax people into the equatorial rainforest, with one branch moving south along the coast itself by 3000 BCE and the other moving into the rainforest farther east after 3000 BCE.

The cognation percentages in basic vocabulary are dual in their indications as well. For the initial divergence between the Coastlands and Nyong-Lomami branches of Narrow Bantu, the distribution of percentages centers on the high teens, with the core range of figures extending from 15 to 22 percent. This range would correspond to the archaeological evidence for the coastal expansion taking place as early as the fourth millennium BCE. The divergences within Nyong-Lomami would have started with the subsequent expansion of this branch of Narrow Bantu into more central parts of the western equatorial rainforest in the third millennium BCE. The range of cognation between languages belonging to different primary subbranches of Nyong-Lomami—reflective of this particular stage of divergence—consistently run in the 20 percents, from rarely as low as 19 or 20 percent up to more usually around the high 20 percents and, at the other extreme, to as high, occasionally, as the middle 30 percents. The median figure of the distribution would be around 26 percent, coinciding with a time span beginning sometime in the third millennium.[56]

The Dangme Dialects: A Recent Correlation from West Africa

One other West African correlation, relating to the past 1,000 years, is worthy of mention here also. The Proto-Dangme people of southern Ghana can be tied through both oral tradition and material cultural traits to a particular development of town life along the lower Volta River, belonging in the archaeology to the period 1200–1400. Beginning in the fifteenth century, this culture diverged into a set of independent polities, most often consisting of a town and its immediately surrounding rural area. The present-day cognation percentages among the Dangme dialects spoken in the particular polities that trace themselves back to this period of dispersal, correlating to a time span of just about 600 years, center around 83 percent.[57]

DEEPER-TIME CORRELATIONS IN AFRICA

We are now ready to move on to consider two additional cases, where the correlations of language and archaeology, *if valid,* reach still further back into the past. These examples come from two of the major African language families: Khoesan and Nilo-Saharan. The archaeological correlations seem quite strong, but the percentages of cognation at such depths are so low as to make it problematic to discriminate between different cognation ranges.

Khoesan Languages and the Wilton Tradition

In the centuries before 8000 BP, a major break in the archaeological sequence took place across a large part of southern Africa. The previously predominant Albany culture in southern areas, focused on large-game hunting and having an only partially microlithic stone-tool technology, came to an end; and a new tradition, the Wilton, based on a more eclectic gathering and hunting, and distinctly microlithic in its tool making, spread south of the Limpopo in the east, and from Namibia and Botswana to the Cape of Good Hope in the west. The predecessor forms of the Wilton tradition had already existed for 10,000 years farther north in eastern Africa.

The correlation of Wilton with the Southern African Khoesan language family rests on strong foundations. First, a variety of historical evidence shows that languages of the Khoesan family were formerly spoken in all of the southern African areas occupied by varieties of the Wilton tradition. As late as the sixteenth century, Khoesan speech territories still covered nearly all of Namibia and Botswana and all of modern-day South Africa south of Namibia and Botswana and west of the Great Fish River. East of those areas, the former predominance of Khoesan languages is attested in place-names and in numerous loanwords adopted into the Bantu languages that displaced them from use at various times in the past 2,000 years. Second, cultural continuities extend from the establishment of Wilton in southern Africa 8,000 or more years ago down to the inception of the Iron Age, and often after it, in that part of the continent. Moreover, whenever we can identify from more direct evidence the language of a Wilton people, it turns out to have been Khoesan in its relationships.

The Southern African Khoesan languages extant in the earlier twentieth century can be classified into three branches: the Zhu (or Northern) branch, the Khoe (or Central) branch, and the Tuu (or Southern) branch. The geographical scatter of these languages, from the Atlantic coast of Namibia in the west to the border of South Africa and Mozambique on the east, provides a representative reflection of the range of differences that formerly characterized Southern African Khoesan, even though a great many of the languages have since become extinct. Recent cognate counts in the one-hundred-word list between languages belonging to different of these three branches give percentages centering around 5–7 percent.[58] The proposed archaeological correlation of Khoesan languages with the Wilton complex implies that this range, 5–7 percent, should correspond to a time depth on the order of 9, 000 to 8,000 years.

Nilo-Saharan History and Eastern Saharan Archaeology

The final example comes from the archaeology and language history of the southern half of the eastern Sahara. It rests on a strikingly detailed material fit between archaeological and linguistic stratigraphies in that region, previously presented in the illustrations of method in chapter 2. This history receives more detailed coverage in chapter 6.

In summary, in far southwestern Egypt, and probably also in the adjoining parts of modern-day Sudan, a series of cultural horizons have been mapped out for the period between 8500 and 6000 BCE. At the earliest stage, from around 8500 down to about perhaps 7200 BCE, there existed in this region a culture that made one of the three earliest potteries of world history.[59] The people of this tradition had ephemeral residential sites, used grindstones to process still apparently wild grasses or grains, and tended cattle. The evidence of fauna and climatic conditions of the time indicate that year-round water resources would not have been naturally available to cattle in the region exploited by this culture and that therefore the cattle were domesticated or in the process of becoming domesticated. By or before 7200 a new stage in this cultural sequence came into being, characterized by large homesteads with round houses, granaries suggestive of incipient cultivation, the digging of wells, and other evidence of sedentarism. These communities raised cattle, and it can be suspected that some grain cultivation, possibly of sorghum, was also present.[60] Finally, between 6400 and 6000 BCE, goats and sheep were added to the animal-raising component of the economy.[61]

The sequence of change in economy and material culture in the three successive Proto–Northern Sudanic, Proto-Saharo-Sahelian, and Proto-Sahelian eras, as revealed in the lexical testimony, almost precisely replicates the archaeological sequence of changes in far southwestern Egypt between 8500 and 6000 BCE. First, at the Northern Sudanic stage, there came into use lexicon for cows, grindstones, and pottery; next, at the Proto-Saharo-Sahelian stage, a set of nouns depicting more complex settlements with round houses, granaries, and wells, some additional cattle terms, and a set of verbs relating to cultivation; and finally, at the Proto-Sahelian period, a suite of goat and sheep terms, along with some additional, new cattle and cultivation terms.[62]

What does the evidence of basic vocabulary cognation between the languages of the relevant divisions of Nilo-Saharan show? The shared retentions of the same old root words for particular core vocabulary meanings in languages related at this kind of time depth are very few. Between Kunama, the one language of its branch of Northern Sudanic, and the languages of its sister branch, Saharo-Sahelian, the shared demonstrable cognates range around 1–6 percent, falling most often at 2–4 percent. The figures for the languages belonging to the Saharan and Sahelian subgroups of Saharo-Sahelian are little different, with ranges overlapping slightly to the high side of the Kunama scores with the Saharo-Sahelian tongues, at 2–8 percent.[63] The proposed linguistic correlations with the archaeology connect these rough, very low ranges of cognation to time spans between roughly 10,500 and 9,000 years ago.

SUMMING UP

The method of glottochronology in its original formulation made use of empirical findings from a wide variety of languages for which solid datings of different stages in the languages' histories were available. These findings suggested that the proportion of words retained with the same meaning in those languages, out of a defined basic vocabulary of one hundred items, tended to distribute itself in very rough fashion around a median figure of 85.5 percent per 1,000 years. In the case of two related languages mutually diverging out of a common mother, each would retain (assuming, for the sake of simplicity, median retention figures for both) a different 85.5 percent of the original vocabulary after 1,000 years of differentiation. The retained vocabulary in each would consist of

1. about 85.5 percent of the subset of 85.5 percent retained in its sister language; plus
2. about 85.5 percent of the subset of 14.5 percent not retained in the other.

Their shared retention with each other could therefore be expected to range around a median figure equal to the square of 85.5 percent, or around 73 percent. This figure, too, was roughly borne out by the empirical findings.

The early practitioners of glottochronology converted this relation into a rigorous-seeming mathematical formula for calculating the dates of language separation directly from the percentages of common retention among the languages involved. But that procedure conveyed a false sense of precision and treated the retention figure as a constant rate rather than as the statistical distribution that, at base, it really is. It tried to be harder science than it was. It seems to me quite sufficient, and less misleading in its implications, to use a standard correlation chart in assigning the highly approximate dating projections allowed by glottochronology. Treating the figures in that fashion, table 9 produces rough linkages between percentages of shared retention in basic vocabulary ("one-hundred-word list") and time depths of differentiation among related languages. Table 10 presents a summary of how the correlations of actual cases in Africa fit in with this scale.

Overall, these counts provide striking support for the results arrived at from other language families elsewhere in the world using other kinds of correlative evidence. Moreover, in and of themselves the African examples come from as diverse an array of languages as can be imagined—in phonology, in morphology, and in grammar in general. Nevertheless, whichever the family, the correlations in Africa of more recent millennia, as well as those back to 7000 BP, consistently give results closely in line with the glottochronological findings elsewhere. With percentages below 10 percent, reflective of time depths on the very rough order of more than 8,000 years ago, the discriminatory capabilities of this tool clearly begin to wane, but it retains its capacity to warn us of the magnitude of the time distances that might be involved in our attempts at correlation.

Interestingly, no indications appear in these data of a need to add a correction factor to handle the differential retentiveness of the different meanings of the one-hundred-word list.[64] It has been observed by a variety of scholars (including me) that certain meanings, such as "eye" and "I," among others, tend to continue to be

Table 9. Projected Median Dating Correlations

Median Time	Cognate Retention
500 BP	86%
1000 BP	73%
1500 BP	63%
2000 BP	53%
2500 BP	46%
3000 BP	39%
4000 BP	29%
5000 BP	21%
6000 BP	15%
7000 BP	11%
8000 BP	8%
9000 BP	6%
10000 BP	4%

expressed in languages by the same root word over especially long periods, whereas the words for other meanings in the list, such as "cloud" and "small," seem much more frequently to be replaced by new words. This observation suggests that the greater the distance of the relationship between two languages—the longer ago they diverged out of a common protolanguage—the more their few remaining shared retentions in core vocabulary should consist of the items on the list that are most resistant to replacement by new words. The rate of loss of common cognates in the one-hundred-word list, as a number of investigators have proposed, should therefore slow down in proportion to how distantly related to each other the languages were. The findings here do not overtly indicate such an effect, suggesting that there may be factors not yet identified that offset the effect, or that the meanings of truly higher retentiveness form such a small proportion of the list as to have little effect on the overall rates of vocabulary change.

Table 10. African Dating Correlations

Historical case	Time period	Cognate Retention
1. Proto-Nkangala Nguni	1000-900 BP	72-79% (median 76%)
2. Shona (1st stage of spread)	1100 BP	61-80% (median 71%)
3. Shona (3rd stage of spread)	900-700 BP	75-86% (median 80%)
4. Proto-Botatwe	1300-1000 BP	70%
5. Proto-Central Sabi	1000 BP	72-74% (median 73%)
6. Proto-Swahili	1200 BP	69-74%
7. Proto-Sabaki	1500-1400 BP	63-69% (median 66%)
8. Proto-Northeast-Coastal Bantu	1800-1700 BP	49-64% (meidan 58%)
9. Proto-Mashariki	3000 BP	35-48% (median 39%)
10. Proto-Maa-Ongamo	1300-1000 BP	72%
11, Proto-Maa	600 BP	80-85%
12. Proto-Southern Nilotes	2600-2500 BP	44-49%
13. Proto-Southern Cushites	5500 BP	15-22% (median 18%)
14. Proto-Rift Southern Cushites	3500-3000 BP	35-42% (median 39%)
15. unified Oromo society	before 450 BP	81-88%
16. Proto-Ethiopic	2500-2300 BP	43-52% (median 48%)
17. Proto-Nubian	before 2300 BP	37-51% (median 44%)
18. Proto-Benue-Kwa	6000 BP	12-16%
19. Proto-Narrow Bantu	6000-5500 BP	15-22%
20. Proto-Nyong-Lomami	5000-4500 BP	19-35% (median 27%)
21. Proto-Dangme	600 BP	83%
22. Proto-Southern African Khoesan	9000-8000 BP	5-7%
23. Proto-Northern Sudanic	10,500-9200 BP	1-6%
24. Proto-Saharo-Sahelian	9200-9000 BP	2-8%

NOTES

1. The classic summation of work in computational linguistics as of the mid-1980s is S. M. Embleton, *Statistics in Historical Linguistics* (Bochum, Germany: Brockmeyer, 1986).

2. A. McMahon and R. McMahon, *Language Classification by Numbers* (Oxford: Oxford University Press, 2005), which dissects the issues, debates, and presumptions people bring to computation linguistics, with specific evidence and case studies, is a major signpost toward the new directions. The McMahons review the literature applying computational measures to grammatical as well as lexical sharings and preview their own and others' applications of such techniques in phonological comparisons. An earlier collected work, C. Renfrew, A. McMahon, and L. Trask (eds.), *Time Depth in Historical Linguistics*, 2 vols. (Cambridge: McDonald Institute for Archaeological Research, 2000), although of mixed usefulness, offers another access point because of the range of disciplines and approaches represented in it.

3. An example is A. Kitchen and others, "Bayesian Phylogenetic Analysis of Semitic Languages Identifies an Early Bronze Age Origin of Semitic in the Near East," *Proceedings of the Royal Society B: Biological Sciences* 276, no. 1668 (2009): 2703–2710, which in applying these methods to the Semitic branch of the Afrasian (Afroasiatic) family produces a relationship tree with striking correlations to the archaeological and epigraphic record.

4. McMahon and McMahon, in *Language Classification by Numbers,* aver that the assumptions underlying glottochonology are false, but by this they mean the assumptions of regularity that this chapter also critiques. So as not "to alienate our colleagues in more traditional historical linguistics," the McMahons suggest halting "attempts at dating now" until scholars establish what the methods they examine in their book "can and cannot validly do" (p. 204). This may be a politic approach to a particular audience they wish to reach. It holds out the prospect of someday attaining a degree of "validity" that will bring that audience along. Against this prospect are the positivist demands this particular audience in the past has made on the evidence. The data and methods examined by the McMahons will, by their nature, always yield probabilistic conclusions, different perhaps in quality but not ultimately in kind from those of lexicostatistical dating.

5. C. Ehret, "Language Change and the Material Correlates of Language and Ethnic Shift," *Antiquity* 62 (1988): 264–274.

6. Embleton, *Statistics in Historical Linguistics,* takes the tack of incorporating the borrowing factor into her calculations. C. Ehret, *Southern Nilotic History: Linguistic Approaches to the Study of the Past* (Evanston, IL: Northwestern University Press, 1971), p. 84; idem, *The Historical Reconstruction of Southern Cushitic Phonology and Vocabulary* (Berlin: Reimer, 1980), pp. 385–38—and more recently Mark Pagel, "Maximum-Likelihood Models for Glottochronology and for Reconstructing Linguistic Phylogenies," in C. Renfrew, A. McMahon, and L. Trask (eds.), *Time Depth in Historical Linguistics*, vol. 1 (Cambridge: McDonald Institute for Archaeological Research, 2000), pp. 189–208—find that loanwords can simply be removed from both terms of the calculation because they are elements extraneous to the kind of change that is being counted.

7. C. Ehret and M. Kinsman, "Shona Dialect Classification and Its Implications for Iron Age History in Southern Africa," *International Journal of African Historical Studies* 14 (1981): 401–443; C. Ehret and M. N. Ali, "Soomaali Classification," in T. Labahn (ed.), *Proceedings of the Second International Congress of Somali Studies (Hamburg, August, 1983)* (Hamburg: Buske Verlag, 1983), pp. 201–269; and K. Klieman, *"The Pygmies Were Our Compass": Bantu and Batwa in the History of West Central Africa, Early Times to c. 1900 C.E.* (Portsmouth: Heinemann, 2003). K. Klieman, "Peoples of the Western Equatorial Rainforest: Economy and Society, 3000 B.C. to A.D. 1880" (Ph.D. diss., UCLA, 1997), presents a range of particularly complex and informative examples of this kind of distribution and how to interpret them historically.

8. C. Ownby, "Early Nguni History: The Linguistic Evidence and Its Correlation with Archaeology and Oral Tradition" (Ph.D. diss., UCLA, 1985).

9. T. N. Huffman, "The Origins of Leopard's Kopje: An 11th Century Difaqane," *Arnoldia* 8, no. 23 (1978): 1–12, presents the initial case for this correlation.

10. Ownby, "Early Nguni History."

11. The name *Kutama* was proposed in Huffman, "The Origins of Leopard's Kopje."

12. Ehret and Kinsman, "Shona Dialect Classification."

13. Ehret and Kinsman, "Shona Dialect Classification." Ehret and Kinsman's dialect classification rests on an extensive quantification of isogloss mappings, a distinct and separate body of evidence from the lexicostatistical counts.

14. The discussion in this section draws on the evidence and findings in C. Saidi, *Women's Authority and Society in Early East-Central Africa* (Rochester, NY: University of Rochester Press, 2010).

15. Huffman, "Origins of Leopard's Kopje."

16. N. M. Katenekwa, "The Iron Age in Zambia: Some New Evidence and Interpretations" (paper presented at Conference on Agricultural Origins in Eastern Africa, Newnham College, Cambridge University, July 1994); Saidi, *Women's Authority,* chap. 2.

17. Saidi, *Women's Authority,* chap. 2. An additional Botatwe dialect cluster, Subiya, is spoken around the interior floodplain of the Zambezi River. Recent dissertations by Anita Pfouts, "Economy and Society in Northern Namibia, 500 BCE to 1800 CE: A Linguistic Approach" (UCLA, 2003), and Kathryn de Luna, "Collecting Food, Cultivating Persons: Wild Resource Use in Central African Political Culture, c. 1000 B.C.E. to c. 1900 C.E." (Northwestern University, 2009), have shed much new light from linguistic evidence on the history of this group, but adequate archaeological information is as yet lacking for the particular areas in which this cluster is found.

18. Ibid.

19. Saidi, *Women's Authority,* develops this evidence in considerable detail.

20. D. Nurse and T. Hinnebusch, *Swahili and Sabaki: A Linguistic History* (Berkeley and Los Angeles: University of California Press, 1993).

21. Embleton, *Statistics in Historical Linguistics;* Ehret, *Southern Nilotic History;* idem, *Historical Reconstruction of Southern Cushitic.*

22. D. Nurse and G. Philippson, *The Northeastern Bantu Languages of Tanzania and Kenya: A Classification* (Dar es Salaam: University of Dar es Salaam, 1974); Nurse and Hinnebusch, *Swahili and Sabaki.*

23. Felix Chami, *The Tanzanian Coast in the First Millenium AD: An Archaeology of the Iron-Working, Farming Communities* (Uppsala: Societas Archaeologica Upsaliensis, 1994).

24. Moreover, a major change in settlement patterns, at least in far northeastern Tanzania, took place in concert with the pottery changeover (Felix Chami, presentation at Conference on Agricultural Origins in Eastern Africa, Newnham College, Cambridge University, July 1994).

25. Ehret, *African Classical Age,* chap. 6.

26. R. M. Gonzales, *Societies, Religion, and History: Central East Tanzanians and the World They Created, c. 200 BCE to 1800 CE* (New York: Columbia University Press, 2009), lays out the evidence and arguments in detail.

27. H. W. Mutoro, "An Archaeological Study of the Mijikenda Kaya Settlements of Hinterland Kenya Coast" (Ph.D. diss., UCLA, 1987).

28. Nurse and Philippson, *Northeastern Bantu Languages.*

29. M.-C. Van Grunderbeek, E. Roche, and H. Doutrelepont, *Le premier âge du fer au Ruanda et au Burundi,* Publication 23 (Brussels and Butare: Institut National de Recherche Scientifique); M.-C. Van Grunderbeek, "Essai de délimitation chronologique de l'âge du fer ancien au Burundi, au Ruanda et dans la région des Grands Lacs," *Azania* 28 (1993): 53–80; Ehret, *African Classical Age.*

30. Different portions of the relevant figures appear in Y. Bastin, A. Coupez, and B. de Halleux, "Clas-

sification lexicostatistique des langues hantous (214 relèves)," *Bulletin des Séances, Académie Royale des Sciences d'Outre-Mer* 27, no. 2 (1983): 173–199; C. Ehret and others, "Outlining Southern African History: A Reconsideration," *Ufahamu* 3, no. 1 (1972), 9–27; D. Nurse, "The Diachronic Background to the Language Communities of Southwestern Tanzania," *Sprache und Geschichte in Africa* 9 (1988): 15–115; Nurse and Philippson, *Northeastern Bantu Languages;* Nurse and Hinnebusch, *Swahili and Sabaki;* D. Schoenbrun, *A Green Place, a Good Place: Agrarian Change, Gender, and Social Identity in the Great Lakes Region to the 15th Century* (Portsmouth, NH: Heinemann, 1998); G. Waite and C. Ehret, "Linguistic Perspectives on the Early History of Southern Tanzania" (unpublished, 1981; accepted for publication in *Tanzania Notes and Records,* but that journal then ceased publication).

31. C. Ehret, and others, "Some Thoughts on the Early History of the Nile-Congo Watershed," *Ufahamu* 5 (1974): 85–112; C. Ehret, "Population Movement and Culture Contact in the Southern Sudan, 3000 BC to AD 1000," in J. Mack and P. Robertshaw (eds.), *Culture History in the Southern Sudan* (Nairobi: British Institute in Eastern Africa, 1983), pp. 19–48; R. Vossen, *The Eastern Nilotes: Linguistic and Historical Reconstructions* (Berlin: Reimer, 1982); idem, *Towards a Comparative Study of the Maa Dialects of Kenya and Tanzania* (Hamburg: Buske Verlag, 1988).

32. S. Ambrose, "Archaeology and Linguistic Reconstructions of History in East Africa," in C. Ehret and M. Posnansky (eds.), *The Archaeological and Linguistic Reconstruction of African History* (Berkeley and Los Angeles: University of California Press), pp. 103–157.

33. C. Ehret, "The Invention of Highland Planting Agriculture in Northeastern Tanzania: Social Repercussions of an Economic Transformation" (typescript, May 1977; 65 pp.); D. Nurse, *Classification of the Chaga Dialects: Language and History on Kilimanjaro, the Taita Hills, and the Pare Mountains* (Hamburg: Helmut Buske Verlag, 1979).

34. K. M. Stahl, *A History of the Chagga People of Kilimanjaro* (London: Mouton, 1964); S. Feierman, *The Shambaa Kingdom: A History* (Madison: University of Wisconsin Press, 1974); K. A. Jackson, "The Dimensions of Kamba Pre-colonial History," in B. A. Ogot (ed.), *Kenya Before 1900* (Nairobi: East African Publishing House), pp. 174–261.

35. Ehret, "Invention of Highland Planting Agriculture."

36. Using data in R. Vossen, *Eastern Nilotic,* and idem, *Towards the Comparative Study of Maa.*

37. Ambrose, "Archaeology and Linguistic Reconstructions," first proposed this correlation, which has since received general acceptance.

38. P. Robertshaw, *Early Pastoralists of South-Western Kenya* (Nairobi: British Institute in Eastern Africa, 1990).

39. C. Ehret, "The Eastern Kenya Interior, 1500–1800," in A. Odhiambo (ed.), *Essays on Kenya History in Honor of B. A. Ogot* (Basel: P. Schlettwein, 2001); Ehret, *Southern Nilotic History.*

40. Ehret, *Southern Nilotic History.*

41. Ambrose, "Archaeology and Linguistic Reconstructions."

42. P. Robertshaw and D. Collett, "A New Framework for the Study of Early Pastoral Communities in East Africa," *Journal of African History* 24 (1983): 289–331.

43. C. Ehret, *Ethiopians and East Africans: The Problem of Contacts* (Nairobi: East African Publishing House, 1974), presents linguistic evidence for these locations; see also Ehret, *African Classical Age,* chap. 2.

44. Ehret, *Historical Reconstruction of Southern Cushitic,* pp. 108, 385–388.

45. M. L. Bender, "The Languages of Ethiopia: A New Lexicostatistical Classification and Some Problems of Diffusion," *Anthropological Linguistics* 13, no. 5 (1971): 165–288.

46. For this history see H. C. Fleming, "Ethiosemitic Language History: Testing Linguistic Hypotheses in an Archaeological and Documentary Context," *Ethnohistory* 15 (1968): 353–388.

47. Bender, "Languages of Ethiopia"; C. Ehret, "Social Transformation in the Early History of the Horn of Africa: Linguistic Clues to Developments of the Period 500 BC to AD 500," in T. Bayene (ed.),

Proceedings of the Eighth International Conference *of Ethiopian Studies,* vol. 1 (Addis Ababa: Institute of Ethiopian Studies, 1986).

48. C. Ehret, "Social Transformation."

49. W. Y. Adams, "The Coming of Nubian Speakers to the Nile Valley," in Ehret and Posnansky, *Archaeological and Linguistic Reconstruction,* pp. 11–38.

50. R. Thelwall, "Linguistic Aspects of Greater Nubian History," in Ehret Posnansky, *Archaeological and Linguistic Reconstruction,* pp. 39–52.

51. Thelwall, "Linguistic Aspects of Greater Nubian History"; M. Bechhaus-Gerst, *Sprachwandel durch Sprachkontakt am Beispiel des Nubischen im Niltal* (Cologne: Rüdiger Köppe Verlag, 1996).

52. T. Shaw, "Holocene Adaptations in West Africa: The Late Stone Age," *Early Man News* 3–4 (1984): 51–82, is an early identification and summary of these developments.

53. R. G. Armstrong, *The Study of West African Languages* (Ibadan, Nigeria: Ibadan University Press, 1964); L. E. Wilson, "The Evolution of Krobo Society: A History from c. 1400 to 1692" (Ph.D. diss., UCLA, 1980); idem, *The Krobo People of Ghana to 1892: A Political and Social History* (Athens, OH: Ohio University, Center for International Studies, 1991); Klieman, "Peoples of the Western Equatorial Rainforest," chap. 2; idem, *"The Pygmies Were Our Compass,"* chap. 2.

54. J. Vansina, *Paths in the Rainforests: Toward a History of Political Tradition in Equatorial Africa* (Madison: University of Wisconsin Press, 1990), chap. 2; Klieman, *"The Pygmies Were Our Compass,"* chap. 2.

55. Klieman, *"The Pygmies Were Our Compass,"* pp. 43–51.

56. K. Klieman, "Hunters and Farmers in the Western Equatorial Rainforest" (Ph.D. diss., UCLA, 1997); idem, *"The Pygmies Were Our Compass,"* chap. 2; Bastin, Coupez, and de Halleux, "Classification lexicostatistique des langues bantoues."

57. Wilson, *Krobo People of Ghana,* chap. 2.

58. The cognates were identified through application of the systems of regular sound correspondences in C. Ehret, *Modeling Historical Linguistic Reconstruction: Proto-Southern African Khoesan* (forthcoming); for identification of cognates in selected languages, see C. Ehret, "Transformations in Southern African History: Proposals for a Sweeping Overview of Change and Development, 6000 BC to the Present," *Ufahamu* 26 (1997): 54–80.

59. The primacy of Africans in the invention of ceramic technology in world history is considered in more detail in chap. 6.

60. We need here to distinguish the process of cultivation from the process of domestication. It can be argued that, in the earliest periods of Sudanic agriculture, crossbreeding of wild with cultivated sorghum continued to be common and that distinct, fully domesticated varieties of sorghum did not appear until centuries after this grain first began to be cultivated.

61. F. Wendorf and R. Schild, "Nabta Playa and Its Role in Northeastern African Prehistory," *Journal of Anthropological Archaeology* 17, no. 2 (1998): 97–123; R. Kuper and S. Kröpelin, "Climate-Controlled Holocene Occupation in the Sahara: Motor of Africa's Evolution," *Science* 313 (11 August 2006): 803–807.

62. See chaps. 2 and 6 for selections of this evidence.

63. The counts are those of the author, combining evidence from several lists in Bender, "Languages of Ethiopia" (reevaluated for actual cognation using the sound-change rules presented in C. Ehret, *The Historical-Comparative Reconstruction of Nilo-Saharan* [Cologne: Rüdiger Köppe Verlag, 2001]), with additional unpublished lists for other languages of the Nilo-Saharan family.

64. See S. Starostin, "Comparative-Historical Linguistics and Lexicostatistics," in C. Renfrew, A. McMahon, and L. Trask (eds.), *Time Depth in Historical Linguistics,* vol. 2 (Cambridge: McDonald Institute for Archaeological Research, 2000), pp. 223–259, for arguments germane to this issue.

PART TWO

Applications

History in the Sahara

Society and Economy in the Early Holocene

This chapter presents the first of four studies exemplifying in different ways the application of linguistic testimony to writing history as historians write it—to the overall courses of social, cultural, economic, demographic, and other developments among the peoples of particular regions and ages of history. These studies proceed chronologically, with this chapter tackling the transformative changes of the early Holocene transition from gathering and hunting to herding and farming in the Saharan belt of Africa. Several elements of the wider history of the Holocene Sahara, relating to the roles of Nilo-Saharan peoples in these developments, served previously as illustrations of method in chapter 2. A primary contribution of the chapter to world history is its revelation of how deep and ancient are the African roots of the Afrasian family. Chapter 7 focuses on developments equally transformative, but of a quite different nature, taking place in the Horn of Africa in the last thousand years BCE. Chapter 8 models how one undertakes the challenging task of uncovering the histories of peoples who have left no modern-day direct descendant communities; its regional and time focus is eastern Kenya in the past 2,000 years. Finally, chapter 9 tracks the spread of American crops in East Africa during the Atlantic Age of the last 500 years, presenting this history as a model for discovering the particular ways in which ideas and things have spread in different ages from centers to peripheries in world history.

An earlier version of this chapter was published as C. Ehret, "Linguistic Stratigraphies and Holocene History in Northeastern Africa," in Marek Chlodnicki and Karla Kroeper (eds.), *Archaeology of Early Northeastern Africa* (Poznan: Poznan Archaeological Museum, 2006), pp. 1019–1055; used by permission.

THE PEOPLING OF THE HOLOCENE SAHARA

For the whole of the Holocene, greater northeastern Africa has formed a zone of ongoing encounter between speakers of Nilo-Saharan languages and speakers of Afrasian (Afroasiatic) languages. The history of cultural change among these groupings of peoples and the history of interfamilial language contacts over this long period left its mark in myriad ways in the vocabularies of the Afrasian and Nilo-Saharan languages. We gain access to the early eras of this history by laying out the linguistic stratigraphies of both families. With this base established, we can then situate the appearance of new vocabulary of subsistence (and of other areas of culture) in the stratigraphy, according to when it first came into use. We can similarly identify the words adopted from languages of one family into languages of the other, situate the times and directions of the particular word borrowings within the stratigraphy, and seek out the cultural and sociolinguistic significance of different individual loanwords as well as sets of loanwords.

From these varied bodies of evidence several important conclusions emerge. The most important of all is that *both* language families, Afrasian as well as Nilo-Saharan, *originated in Africa*. This point can hardly be too strongly emphasized, considering how often scholars in non-African fields of study still presume that, somehow, the Afrasian family had an Asian homeland. This idea has its roots in old, unexamined Western views about Africa. Much recent work in biological anthropology continues to start off from this presumption, and, as a result, scholars too often still allow this view to shape, a priori, the interpretation of the DNA evidence.

A second discovery is that, from the very early periods, cultural and technological influences have flowed in both directions, from Nilo-Saharans to Afrasians as much as from Afrasians to Nilo-Saharans. In addition, the regions extending from the Red Sea westward along the line of climatic transition in the central Sahara, from Mediterranean subtropical to African tropical regimes, have formed a long-term zone of shifting language-family boundaries and interfamilial influences. Last, the areas between the Red Sea and the Nile have been affected by significant episodes of population and language replacement over the course of the Holocene era. These findings have major implications for future work on the archaeology and the biological anthropology of the peoples of northeastern Africa in the Terminal Pleistocene and Holocene eras.

ON THE AFRICAN ORIGIN
OF THE AFRASIAN LANGUAGE FAMILY

The cumulative work of many scholars on the historical reconstruction of the Afrasian language family, from Greenberg's work in the late 1940s down to the most recent publications, makes an overwhelming case for situating the origins of

Afrasian, and nearly all of the history of the peoples who spoke languages of that family, in Africa.[1] Only Semitic, itself a relatively late offshoot of an otherwise African subbranch of the family, has an Asian history at all.

The Africanness of the Afrasian family is evident first and foremost from a simple look at the geographical locations of the six universally recognized deep divisions of the family. Three of the six are, in fact, not just African, but wholly *sub-Saharan* African. These are Cushitic, the languages of which are spoken from just north of the Ethiopian Highlands to as far south as central Tanzania; Omotic, located entirely in the Ethiopian Highlands; and Chadic, found far to the west, in the countries of Nigeria, Niger, Cameroon, and Chad. A fourth division, Berber, consists of languages of North Africa and the Sahara; a fifth, comprising ancient Egyptian and its descendant form, Coptic, was spoken in the midst of the eastern Sahara. Just a single branch of the six, Semitic, ended up in the far southwestern corner of Asia.

Knowing the subgrouping of a language group allows us to make inferences as to the most probable location of the common ancestor language of the group as a whole. To make these inferences we apply the principle of parsimony to the linguistic geography of the languages involved. We say that the best explanation for the locations of the languages in later times is the history that requires the fewest movements of peoples to account for those locations. Let us apply this principle to the six major divisions of Afrasian, one by one, and then to the family as a whole.

Cushitic Divergence and History

Cushitic has four deep divisions: Beja, Agäw, Eastern Cushitic, and Southern Cushitic. The four divisions fall into two primary branches, one consisting of the single language Beja and the other comprising the Agäw and Eastern and Southern Cushitic subbranches.[2] The evidence of shared phonological innovation indicates that Eastern and Southern Cushitic form a combined, tertiary East-South Cushitic branch.[3] The Beja dialects are spoken today in the Red Sea hills regions of Sudan and northern Eritrea; the Agäw languages, in Eritrea and northern and central Ethiopia; and the Eastern Cushitic languages, all through the Horn from Eritrea to northern Kenya. Modern-day Southern Cushitic populations reside in parts of Kenya and Tanzania. The overall scheme of Cushitic relationships can be depicted as a tree (figure 6).

Applying the principle of parsimony, the most straightforward accounting of early Cushitic history depicts a successive southward advance of Cushitic speakers in four major early stages. The original Cushitic speech territory lay in either of two adjacent areas: the southern Red Sea hills, where the Beja and their North Cushitic forebears have long resided; or the northern edges of the Ethiopian Highlands, where the lands of the rest of the Cushites begin. The Proto-Cushitic society diverged into daughter societies either because the distant ancestors of the Beja moved northward into the Red Sea hills or because the ancestors of the Proto-Agäw-East-South

Figure 6. Family Tree of the Cushitic Subbranch of Afrasian

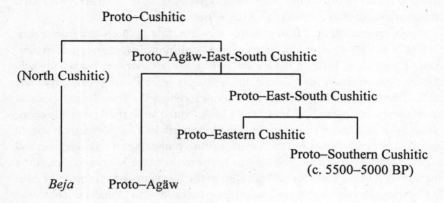

Cushitic community spread southward along the northern edges of the highlands. At the second stage, the Proto-Agäw-East-South society itself diverged into two daughter societies. The Proto-Agäw emerged in the far northern Ethiopian Highlands; the Proto-East-South Cushites settled in more easterly parts of the highlands, probably especially moving south along the Ethiopian Rift Valley.[4] Finally, the Southern Cushitic offshoot of the Proto-East-South Cushites moved still farther south, into Kenya and eventually Tanzania. Archaeological correlations show that the Proto–Proto–Southern Cushitic expansion into Kenya began in the mid- or later fourth millennium BCE;[5] hence the dating of Proto–Southern Cushitic in figure 6. The evidence that Proto-Sahelian borrowed its words for "goat" from an already distinct ancestral Beja language in the later seventh millennium[6] supports the conclusion that the initial divergence of Proto-Cushitic into the Beja (North Cushitic) branch and Agäw-East-South-Cushitic branches began before 6500 BCE, 3,000 to 4,000 years earlier.

Omotic Prehistory

The Omotic division of the Afrasian family has two primary branches, North and South Omotic. The South Omotic branch is today restricted to the farthest southern part of the Ethiopian Highlands. The northern branch, in contrast, extends across a much wider part of southwestern Ethiopia. There is indirect evidence, in the form of loanwords in the Agäw languages, indicating that other Omotic languages, of possibly a third branch, were once spoken considerably farther north in the highlands.[7] The simplest history, taking into account only the extant languages, would place the Proto-Omotic origins in the farther southern part of the Ethiopian plateau, with the North Omotic emerging as a northward and northeastward extension of Omotic peoples across the southern half of the highlands. But the evidence of ancient Omotic loanwords in the Agäw languages of the northern and central highlands indicates a former broader spread of Omotic peoples within the highlands as a whole.

Chadic, Berber, and Egyptian Language History

The Chadic languages today cover a large expanse of territories running across the southern parts of the Chad Basin in the central Sudan belt of Africa. Scholars who have worked closely and extensively with these languages divide them into either three or four primary branches,[8] spread out east to west across this expanse of lands. Either subclassification depicts essentially the same broad history. The Proto-Chadic language was spoken most probably somewhere in the areas west and southwest of modern-day Lake Chad. At the Proto-Chadic period, on the order of about 7,000 years ago, a much vaster Lake Mega-Chad occupied the heart of the basin. The initial period of Chadic divergence into either three or four daughter societies would have spread Chadic communities all across the areas immediately west and south of that lake, from the plains north of the Jos Plateau on the west, to the Mandara Mountains in the middle, to as far east as the Guerra Mountains.

The Berber languages at the earliest stage of their so-far-traceable history were most likely spoken in central North Africa. Two different eras of major Berber expansion can be discerned from the linguistic record.[9] The earliest stage spread the ancestors of the Zenaga to the western Sahara and of the Kabyle to northern Algeria, with the ancestral speech community of the remainder of the Berbers, which we might call the Proto-Libu (i.e., Libyans), taking shape in some other part of central and western North Africa. An eastern outlier of this period of Berber expansion is likely to be reflected in the Middle Kingdom Egyptian records of warfare with peoples who attacked from the west around the close of the third millennium BCE. The second period of Berber expansion, involving peoples of the Libyan grouping of Berbers, lay probably in around the late second millennium and the early first millennium BCE, when renewed attacks on Egypt from the west are recorded. Only after this period, and possibly not until the coming of camels to the region around 2,000 years ago, did the Tuareg spread into the central Sahara.

The Egyptian language, as far back as we can trace, was spoken along the Egyptian Nile. A single language, although characterized at different periods by significant dialect differences, it gives us no internal evidence for a wider history of expansion than what we know from the written record.

Semitic Language History

The sole Asian division of the Afrasian family, Semitic, itself gave rise in later times to two African offshoots: (1) Arabic, which has spread into North Africa, the Sahara, and parts of the eastern Sudan since 638 CE; and (2) Ethiosemitic, a group consisting of about fifteen languages spoken today in Ethiopia and Eritrea, which all derive from a South Arabian language brought into the northern Ethiopian Highlands in about the sixth and fifth centuries BCE.[10] But the original split in Semitic was a dual one, separating Eastern Semitic, consisting of Akkadian in all its versions, from Western Semitic, comprising all the rest of the branch.[11] The subclassification of Semitic into Akkadian (Eastern) and Western subbranches locates its original center of divergence in the ancient period along a line that fell between Syria-Palestine and northern Mesopotamia. The most parsimonious history of Semitic has two alternative forms:

1. Proto-Semitic was spoken in northern Mesopotamia. Its speakers broke into two speech communities when one of those communities, ancestral to the Western Semites, moved away westward into Syria-Palestine.
2. Proto-Semitic was spoken in Syria-Palestine. Its speakers broke into two speech communities when one of those communities, ancestral to Akkadian, moved away eastward into northern Mesopotamia.

Because of the many indications that non-Semitic languages predominated throughout Mesopotamia and all around its northern and eastern flanks in the prestate eras—and that Akkadian therefore was originally intrusive to that region—the second solution seems by far the more probable of the two. The Syria-Palestine regions, as the part of Asia nearest and more directly connected to Africa, also make much better sense as the Proto-Semitic territory, considering the solely African locations of all the rest of the Afrasian family. If indeed the early Byblos language belongs to the eastern branch along with Akkadian, this further consolidates the case for an original Syria-Palestine homeland for Proto-Semitic.[12]

Locating Proto-Afrasian

So the linguistic geography of the Afrasian languages as a whole is resoundingly African. Even if the six major divisions of the family—Omotic, Cushitic, Chadic, ancient Egyptian, Berber, and Semitic—formed coequal primary branches of the family, each equidistantly related to each other branch—an inherently improbable situation—the inference of an African origin for the family would be overwhelmingly supported. An African homeland would more than meet the requirement of parsimony in such an instance: just a single population movement out of Africa would be required to account for the distribution of the branches. If an Asian origin were postulated, on the other hand, an immensely improbable five separate movements of peoples, all through one narrow isthmus or across the Red Sea to Africa, would have to be postulated.

The only basis on which the hypothesis of an Asian origin for Afrasian could be entertained would be a subclassification in which Semitic formed one of two primary branches of the family, and the other branch included the whole rest of the family. The old name *Hamito-Semitic* on the surface might seem to imply such a division. But no one who has worked widely on the African branches of the family any longer considers this idea even remotely likely. The wide acceptance nearly everywhere today, even among the majority of Semitists and Egyptologists, of the name Afrasian or Afroasiatic for the family came about because of the general recognition that Semitic does not constitute a primary branch all by itself and that the family is overwhelmingly and fundamentally an African one.

But the problems with an Asian origin for the family are far greater than even these considerations might suggest. Different lines of investigation—based on grammar, lexical innovation patterns, and a mix of grammatical and lexical evidence—have led several scholars separately to the conclusion that there actually is a particular division of Afrasian that may indeed form a primary branch of the family all by itself. That group is Omotic, the division of Afrasian located today in the southern Ethiopian Highlands, farthest south in Africa—in terms of the overall distribution of its languages—of any of the six divisions.[13] We now have available, in addition, a proposed overall classification of the interrelationships of the six divisions, based on the history of sound change in the family and backed up by further evidence of pronominal, lexical, and grammatical innovation. Again according to this classification, Omotic stands off from the rest of the family.[14]

The outline of the subclassification of the Afrasian family appears in appendix 1. Summaries of the unique phonological and/or grammatical innovations of each branch, subbranch, and sub-subbranch of the family accompany the outline.[15]

The history implied by the Afrasian linguistic stratigraphy begins with the Proto-Afrasian speech community inhabiting a region no farther north than the southern half of the far eastern Sahara. The primary divergence between Omotic and all the rest of the family allows two equally probable histories. One history places the Proto-Afrasian community in the Ethiopian Highlands. Afrasian then diverged into two branches, one ancestral to Omotic and a second, Erythraic, whose speakers spread northward into the areas of Africa immediately west of the Red Sea. Alternatively, the Proto-Afrasians initially lived immediately north of the Ethiopian Highlands, and the ancestral Omotic society then diverged from the Proto-Erythraic community by moving south into the highlands.

A tree of the Afrasian relationships allows for a clearer visualization of the chronological sequence and thus the historical implications of the classification (figure 7).

The overall hierarchy of relationships requires that at later periods the Erythraic peoples commenced a series of successively wider expansions, while the Omotic speakers remain restricted to Ethiopia. The Cushitic relationship tree (see figure 6) indicates that the Cushitic peoples spread by stages farther south through the Horn of Africa. The Proto–North Erythraic speakers, in contrast, moved northward, most probably to the areas surrounding Egypt, and diverged subsequently into Proto-Boreafrasian and Proto-Chado-Berber.

Figure 7. Family Tree of Afrasian Branch Relationships

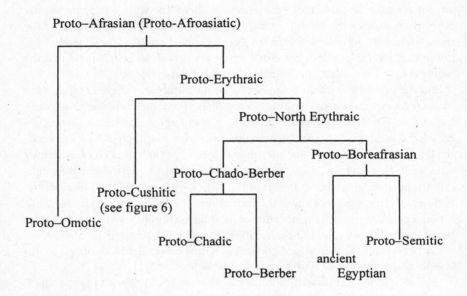

Early Chado-Berber speakers, in view of modern language distributions, would have emerged as a distinct grouping of Afrasians through an expansion of their linguistic forebears westward across the Sahara. The subsequent resettlement of one branch of Chado-Berber southward from the central Sahara accounts for the presence of the Chadic languages in the Chad Basin. The Berber languages derive from a later Chado-Berber language spoken somewhere in North Africa.

Boreafrasian also gave rise to two groups of people. One descendant group would have remained in the Egyptian regions and evolved into the later ancient Egyptians. The other group of early Boreafrasians would have moved at some point across Sinai into the Levant. Their much later descendants in language would have been the Semitic speakers of the past 6,000 years.

Future work may well revise or overturn parts of this picture; other parts are likely to last. The strongest claim here is that Omotic and Cushitic derive from the first and second periods of divergence within the family. The evidence is pervasive that Egyptian, Semitic, Berber, and Chadic are significantly more closely related to each other than they are to either Cushitic or Omotic, and that Omotic above all, and Cushitic to lesser extent, stand off from the rest of the family. What this means is that the most probable lands of the Proto-Afrasians lay not just in Africa, but

Table 11. Representative Sample: Afrasian Cognate Retentions

Ari (South Omotic)													
8	Mocha (North Omotic)												
1	0	Iraqw (Southern Cushitic)											
2	1	8	Cadale Soomaali (Eastern Cushitic)										
0	1	2	10	Yaaku (Eastern Cushitic)									
1	2	6	9	5	Awngi (Agaw)								
1	2	4	7	5	7	Beja (Northern Cushitic)							
0	0	2	0	2	1	0	Ngizim (West Chadic)						
0	1	1	1	1	1	1	9	Matakam (Central Chadic)					
0	1	1	1	1	1	0	7	5	Tuareg (Berber)				
0	1	1	1	1	1	0	6	5	30	Kabyle (Berber)			
1	2	3	2	1	2	2	3	3	6	5	Middle Egyptian		
2	2	2	2	1	2	1	3	4	4	3	6	Sudan Arabic (Semitic)	
2	3	1	2	1	3	2	3	4	3	3	5	26	Tigre (Semitic)

specifically either in the southeasternmost parts of the Sahara, along the west side of the Red Sea, or, alternatively, still farther south, in the Ethiopian Highlands.

Dating Early Afrasian History

There is another kind of evidence—cognate counts in a one-hundred-meaning list of basic vocabulary—that can be brought to bear on the problem of Afrasian sub-classification and history. It is not determinative evidence by itself, and in any case the time depth of differentiation within the Afrasian family is so great that the rates of retention of exactly the same root words with their meanings unchanged in languages of distant branches of the family are exceedingly low. Nonetheless, these data conform roughly in their indications to the other evidence of subclassification. Most important, they bring us to an abrupt awareness of just how long ago the Proto-Afrasian language must have been spoken.

A sample of lexical retention counts is provided here, drawing on the evidence of several languages from each of the major divisions of the Afrasian family. To give some reflection of the degree of diversity within each division, the languages were chosen from distantly related subgroups in each division (table 11).

Because the Afrasian figures are so low, two points need special emphasis. First of all, the determination of what is cognate and what is not is based on the rigorous establishment of regular sound correspondences across the family. Neither impression nor guesswork is involved here.[16] In addition, the knowledge of the regular correspondences allows one to avoid counting word borrowings as if they were true cognates. Failure to separate out borrowings can lead to a false inflation of the scores of Arabic with many of the Berber languages and of those between a number of the Cushitic and Omotic languages.

Second, the reader needs to know just what it is that this kind of lexicostatistics does count. The focus of the exercise is not simply on the counting of cognates, as many works seem to imply, but rather on the counting of a particular category of cognates—namely, lexical retentions. What one counts up is the number of times, in the one-hundred-meaning list, in which a pair of related languages have *retained* the very same root word with the *very same meaning* ever since their divergence out of their most recent common ancestor. In both Ari of the Omotic branch and Iraqw of the Cushitic branch, for instance, nearly half of the items on the one-hundred-meaning list can be traced back to Proto-Afrasian roots,[17] yet only one of the one hundred has retained its original meaning unchanged down to the present in both languages. The rest have changed their meanings over the millennia since the Proto-Afrasian period—so far in the past did that time period lie. The direct cognate, for example, of the Ari word *gooli* 'tail', an item on the one-hundred-meaning list, is Iraqw *gwalay* 'female genitals', different in meaning although reconstructably the same root.

One caveat: the Egyptian figures come from Middle Egyptian, a version of the language spoken almost 4,000 years ago; thus, Egyptian had less time for lexical change than the other cited languages, all of them spoken today. For this reason the Egyptian cognate-retention counts are skewed higher with the other languages than if we had a modern-day descendant of Middle Egyptian to draw our data from. We need to adjust our figures to account for this time difference. When we do so, the Middle Egyptian percentages of cognate retention with Chadic, Berber, and Semitic drop down to around 2 percent and, with Omotic and Iraqw, down to an average of 1 percent.[18] Table 12 gives these Middle Egyptian figures, as adjusted to account for the fact that those figures come from 4,000 years ago rather than from the present. (The adjusted numbers are marked with asterisks.)

The figures between the deep divisions of Afrasian are too low and too little differentiated to allow a detailed hierarchy of relationships to emerge, such as can be argued from other kinds of linguistic evidence (see table 11). But taken at face value, they do reveal one thing: three distinct levels of Afrasian relationships appear in the numbers. Chadic and Berber share distinctly more lexemes in the basic list (tables 11 and 12), confirming the probability of their forming a Chado-Berber sub-branch of North Erythraic. Chado-Berber, Egyptian, and Semitic divisions fall in the next range, with their figures with each other no lower than 2 percent. Cushitic

Table 12. Adjusted Afrasian Intergroup Median Cognation

Omotic					
0-2	Cushitic				
0-1	0-2	Chadic			
0-1	0-1	5-7	Berber		
1	1	2*	2*	Egyptian	
2-3	1-3	3-4	3	2-3*	Semitic

and Omotic appear consistently more distant, both from each other and from the North Erythraic languages (Chadic, Berber, Egyptian, Semitic). The shared root-and-meaning retentions between any particular Omotic or Cushitic language and any particular North Erythraic language in general run no higher than 2 percent, and the great majority fall at either 0 or 1 percent. The Semitic languages chosen for the sample tend to run about a percentage point higher across the board with the other groups, so that figures as high as 3 percent between Tigre and Omotic or Cushitic and between Arabic and Cushitic can be found. But overall, the pattern of three tiers holds.

The lexical-retention counts, in other words, are consistent with the conclusions reached from other, better kinds of evidence—that out of the earliest periods of divergence of Afrasian there arose three deep divisions of the family: Omotic, Cushitic, and North Erythraic. Just one branch, North Erythraic, then gave rise to all the remaining languages of the family: Chadic, Berber, Egyptian, and Semitic. Once again, the evidence strongly places Afrasian origins and the first stages of differentiation within the family no farther north than the southern half of the eastern Sahara.

The most striking insight these data give us, however, is that the Proto-Afrasian language must have been spoken a great many thousands of years ago. Consider the Indo-European family: the percentages of cognate retention in the one-hundred-meaning list between its most distantly related, modern spoken languages center around the middle and high teens, with one language, Armenian, dropping somewhat lower because of the numerous non-Indo-European loanwords in its basic vocabulary. The most commonly accepted archaeological correlations date the early Indo-European society to the fourth millennium BCE.[19] The retention counts between the most distant Afrasian languages—far lower, at 0–3 percent—must therefore surely reflect a time span thousands of years longer than Proto-Indo-European's generally accepted 6,000 years. Just how may thousands of years is an issue one can dispute. But if, just for the sake of argument, we treat the formula used in glottochronology as if it made sense so far back in time, we discover that figures of 0–3 percent, with a median of about 1 or 2 percent, should correspond to a time span of somewhere in the range of 15,000 or more years between the time the Proto-Afrasian language was spoken and the present.

LINGUISTIC STRATIGRAPHY, SUBSISTENCE, AND DATING

But we have a better and more direct way of establishing time spans of linguistic history. We can work out the linguistic stratigraphy of early Afrasian subsistence practices, and we can compare those findings to uncover plausible archaeological correlations. The basic framework of a linguistic stratigraphy is provided by the subclassification of the family (figures 7 and 8).

To be traceable to a particular stratum in the history of Afrasian-speaking peoples, a word must occur (with regular sound correspondence, of course) in at least one language of each of the branches going back to that particular stratum. To be reconstructed for the Proto-Boreafrasian stratum, for example, the root must appear (with regular correspondences) in ancient Egyptian and in one or more Semitic languages. The reason is that Egyptian and Semitic are the two primary branches of Boreafrasian. If we view the Afrasian family tree (see figure 7), we see that their lines of descent diverge out of that node. Proto-Boreafrasian is their most recent common ancestor, and it is along those two lines of descent that the particular root word would separately have been transmitted in use down to later Egyptian and Semitic speakers.

Similarly, a word must be found in Chadic or Berber languages *and* in ancient Egyptian or Semitic if we are to reconstruct its use back to the Proto–North Erythraic node. To trace back to the still earlier Proto-Erythraic stratum, reflexes of the root must appear in languages of both the Cushitic and North Erythraic lines of descent. Finally, to be considered a sure Proto-Afrasian term, reflexes of the root, showing regular sound correspondences, need to be discovered in one or more languages of the Omotic primary branch of the family as well as in languages of the sister Erythraic primary branch.

With these principles in mind, we can move on to the historical interpretation of the extensive lexical data relating to subsistence foods and practices of the earliest Afrasian societies. In appendix 1, where this kind of evidence is presented, the outline notations from figure 8 identify the lines of descent of the languages in which the roots appear. This allows the reader to refer back to the outline classification of Afrasian (see figure 8) to verify the claims about the ages of particular roots.

Were the Early Afrasians Cultivators?

What sequences of subsistence developments do the lexical data reveal for early Afrasian speaking peoples? The Proto-Afrasian people and their descendants

Figure 8. Outline Classification of the Deep-Level Divisions of Afrasian

I. Omotic
II. Erythraic
    A. Cushitic
    B. North Erythraic
        1. Chado-Berber
            a. Chadic
            b. Berber (Amazight)
        2. Boreafrasian
            a. Egyptian
            b. Semitic

clearly utilized grasses and/or grains for food. A significant body of root words shows that the earliest Afrasian communities used parts of grasses for food. Even more roots relating to this kind of subsistence can be traced to the Proto-Erythraic stratum,[20] as is apparent in appendix 1. The evidence from this latter stratum clearly refers to the use of grass seeds in subsistence. The Proto-Afrasian (PAA) lexicon also indicates the eating of such seeds.

The PAA term for a kind of flour, however, actually may initially have applied to the grinding of sedge tubers, a practice known from earliest northeastern African archaeology of wild-grass collection. Keeping this point in mind, it can be argued that the PAA term *ʕeyl- originally referred to the eating of grass seeds (i.e., grains) in the form of whole kernels. The respective ancient Egyptian and Omotic meanings ("kernels" and "flour") indicate that the term probably originally applied to grain prepared for eating; but the preponderant meanings suggest that the original reference of this old root word was to whole grains.

Taken as a group, these data allow us to propose the following two-stage development of early Afrasian subsistence use of the Gramineae.

1. The Proto-Afrasians certainly ate grains. The lexical evidence is consistent with their having eaten them whole rather than ground. The evidence available so far would as well fit the hypothesis that they used another kind of grass food—the tubers of sedges. Determinative word evidence that they did so is as yet lacking, however.
2. The evidence from the Proto-Erythraic stage onward specifically indicates the use of grains, with the grinding of flour and the making of flat bread as well as the eating of whole grains.

Appendix 2 presents the array of the so-far-reconstructed early Afrasian root words relating to the subsistence use of grasses. This appendix divides the data up according to whether we can trace the particular root words in question back to the Proto-Afrasian, the Proto-Erythraic, or, in the case of three root words, the Proto–North Erythraic period.[21]

The words indicative of the subsistence utilization of grasses or wild grains by the earliest Afrasian-speaking peoples are many. But despite the size of this body of evidence, not one word certainly diagnostic of the cultivation of grains can be reconstructed for any of first several periods of Afrasian history. No words for a cultivated field and no words for tools specifically and only used in cultivation, such as the plow, appear in the data. A variety of verb roots of reference to digging can be identified, but none specifically and universally applies to cultivation.

One old Afrasian root, *-mar- 'to dig', has been cited by various scholars as a candidate for such a verb of cultivation.[22] It gave rise to a Proto-Chadic root word that distinctly meant "cultivated field." But in the Semitic languages and Egyptian it occurs as a noun for a digging implement, either a hoe or a digging stick—a tool not diagnostic of farming because gatherer-hunters before the eras of agriculture also commonly used such digging implements. And above and beyond that problem, its Cushitic reflex, seen in the Southern Cushitic noun *maraʔ- 'burrow, den' (verb stem plus a Southern Cushitic noun-forming suffix, *-Vʔ-), directly implies that the root originally applied to the digging of a hole and not to farming.[23]

In a recent article, Alexander Militarev has made the opposing claim—that the Proto-Afrasians were food producers. There are two fundamental problems with his arguments and data. The first is that the actual meanings of the reflexes he cites under each of his roots contradict his claim. The reflexes each include words that do have agricultural meanings in some languages or subgroups of Afrasian, but in each case the same roots apply to preagricultural activities, items, or landscapes in other languages, undermining the claim of reconstructed agricultural meanings for the roots.[24] The second fatal objection is that Militarev's proposed roots mostly can be shown not to be valid, phonologically regular reconstructions. All but perhaps one of the purported roots are visibly composite in origin. That is, they combine into one root the reflexes of from two to as many as four or five distinct and separate early Afrasian roots.[25]

The complete lack of determinative evidence of cultivation in the early Afrasian strata contrasts sharply with the picture for later periods. In each of the protolanguages of the major divisions of the family, root words distinctly indicative of farming occur. In the subgroups of deepest time depth, the words are not numerous, but they consistently apply to aspects of cultivation. The Proto-Agäw-East-South Cushitic language contained a verb meaning "to cultivate, till" and a noun for "cultivated field,"[26] while Proto-Chadic had, as just noted, the word *mar 'cultivated field'. The subsistence vocabularies of the Proto-Berber and Proto-Semitic languages provide copious evidence that their speakers were indeed farmers.[27] (The Proto-Omotic vocabulary has not yet been adequately enough studied to include its data in the picture.)

To sum up, throughout the early stages of Afrasian history, the lexical evidence is exceedingly strong that grains or grasses played a key role in subsistence. At the same time, however, there is no evidence before the Proto-Cushitic, Proto-Chadic, Proto-Berber, and Proto-Semitic languages that these sources of food were anything but wild plants. The answer to the question asked by the title of this section seems to be, No, the early Afrasians were not cultivators.

Were the Early Afrasians Herders of Domestic Animals?

But if the early Afrasians were not tillers of the soil, might they still have been raisers of livestock?

The diagnostic evidence for postulating herding is a little different in nature from that indicative of cultivation. Again the reconstruction of certain verb roots is important, including roots with such meanings as "to drive to pasture" and "to drive to water." And there is a herding noun equivalent to the term for "cultivated field"—namely, a word for "livestock pen." But in addition, the domestication of an animal can be identified from the existence of certain breeding terms. It is not enough to reconstruct separate words for the male and female of a particular animal, distinct from the generic term, because gatherer-hunter peoples often themselves make these distinctions for especially important meat animals. What is diagnostic of herding, however, is the presence of the particular breeding terms for "castrated male" or for "young female that has not yet borne young" (e.g., heifer). Milking is another activity requiring domestication for its success. The diagnostic terms in this semantic field are verbs for "to milk" and nouns for such things as "sour milk," "buttermilk," and "butter." The noun "milk" is, of course, nondiagnostic by itself, as are also verbs with the meaning "to produce milk," since all mammals, including humans, make milk.

None of these several kinds of term diagnostic of livestock raising can be certainly reconstructed back to the early stages of the Afrasian family. Only at the Proto-Cushitic, Proto-Chadic, Proto-Berber, and Proto-Semitic stages, separately in each case, did such vocabularies come into certain existence. Proto-Cushitic, for example, had two verbs for "to herd" and a noun "livestock pen," among others.[28]

But there is one other kind of evidence that can be diagnostic of herding, and that is the presence of terms naming animals that were domesticated elsewhere and were not native in their wild state to the areas where those terms are used. In the case of the Afrasian languages of Africa, such animals would be the goat and the sheep, both domesticated in far southwestern Asia. A number of possible old Afrasian terms for goat and sheep have been proposed.[29] Most of these turn out not to be valid reconstructions or to have more probably referred originally to one or another species of antelope or other wild ungulate.

Table 13. Words for Domestic Stock Spread by Word Borrowing

---

1. *book- 'he-goat'

    II.A. Cushitic: Beja *book* 'he-goat'

    II.B. Chadic: Mafa *ɓɔk* 'goat'; cf. PCh *bkr 'he-goat'?

2. *gayd- 'goat'

    II.B.1. Berber *i-ɣayd 'kid'

    II.B.2. proto-Semitic *gdy 'goat'

3. *b-g- 'sheep'

    I. Omotic: Gonga *bägg- 'sheep': loan from Agaw

    II.A. Cushitic: Agaw *bäg - 'sheep'

    II.B.1. Chadic: Central Chadic: Bachama group *baga ~ *bäga 'sheep'

    II.B.2. Semitic: Ethiopic *bɨgg- is a loan from Agaw

4. *dz-r- 'ram (?)'

    II.B.1. Chadic: some central Central Chadic *(n)zər- 'ram' (Eg. *r* word-final regularly corresponds to Central Chadic *l, not *r)

    II.B.2. Egyptian *zr* 'ram,' *zr.t* 'ewe'

5. *k-rr- 'young sheep (?)'

    II.B.1. proto-Berber *kärr-/*-krär- 'sheep'

    II.B.2. proto-Semitic *krr 'male lamb'

Nevertheless, after weeding out the inapplicable cases, a few terms do remain that consistently refer to either goats or sheep. They appear in table 13. The first four terms fail the test of fully regular sound correspondence in either their vowels or their consonants. Their distribution in the Afrasian languages must thus be attributed to borrowing spread. The fifth item may show regular sound correspondences: the Proto-Semitic vowel remains to be determined. But in this instance, because Proto-Afrasian *k and *r did not undergo sound shifts and remained unchanged in Proto-Semitic or Proto-Berber, the word could be either a loan or a shared retention in the two groups.

Items 1 and 2 in table 13 are both extraordinarily widely spread *Wanderwörter*, which must anciently have diffused with the spread of goats north, west, and south out of the Levant. Root 1 diffused from the Chadic languages of the Chad Basin as far south by 3000 BCE as southern Cameroon, because the form seen in Mafa was adopted into the Proto-Bantu language as *-boko 'he-goat' and later carried south and east by Bantu expansions.[30] This root also appears in Indo-European— for example, German *bock* and English *buck* 'he-goat, male deer, etc'. Root 2, found in just the Semitic and Berber subgroups of the Afrasian family, seems similarly to have been a *Wanderwort* with also a northward expansion, appearing in the Indo-European root *ghaido- 'he-goat' (the source of the English word *goat*). Items 3–5 spread mostly from one Afrasian branch to another, indicating the spread of the animal named from one already established Afrasian-speaking region to another. Item 5 may also have spread anciently to the Proto-Sahelian peoples of the Nilo-Saharan family, if it is the source of Proto-Sahelian *k'er 'ewe lamb' (see appendix 3).

To sum up, the lexical evidence relating to livestock raising does not sustain the proposition that the Afrasian peoples kept livestock in the early eras of their history. The few terms for goats and sheep appearing in more than one branch of the family are best explained as words that diffused from one Afrasian group to another along with the spread of those two animals from Asia into Africa, beginning between 6500 and 6000 BCE. Just as was true for cultivation, secure lexical reconstructions attesting to livestock raising appear *only* at the Proto-Cushitic, Proto-Chadic, Proto-Berber, and Proto-Semitic periods.

EARLY NILO-SAHARAN LANGUAGE HISTORY

Stratifying Nilo-Saharan History

Having presented the evidence for the early Afrasians, we proceed now to consider the Nilo-Saharan speakers and their roles in early northeastern Africa. A recent, detailed Nilo-Saharan family stratigraphy has been published elsewhere. A simplified version of that stratigraphy appears here (figure 9), leaving out the complexities of lower-level internal subgroupings within the Central Sudanic, Koman, Saharan, Maban, and Eastern Sahelian divisions of the family.[31] The dating scale along the right side of the chart rests on the archaeological correlations of the ninth to seventh millennia BCE for the Northern Sudanic, Saharo-Sahelian, and Sahelian stages in the linguistic stratigraphy[32] and separately on correlations of developments of the last two millennia BCE for the Nubian and Rub strata.[33] The correlations of the ninth to seventh millennia seem, if anything, even more securely founded in the light of the most recent reevaluations of the eastern Saharan archaeology.[34] The intervening stages of Nilo-Saharan divergence have been given notional dates in the stratigraphy according to their relative lexicostatistical distances.[35] The question marks following these interpolated dates denote their lack as yet of proposed specific correlates in the archeological record. The dates along the right-hand side of the stratigraphy,

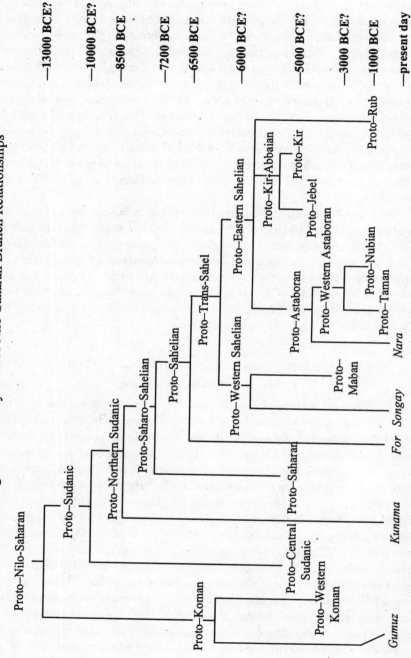

Figure 9. Family Tree of Nilo-Saharan Branch Relationships

the reader will note, are not necessarily proportionally spaced, because salient historical nodes cluster more closely in some eras than in others.

Early Nilo-Saharan Subsistence and Technologies

The evidence for the timing of the emergence of food production is strikingly clear and consistent in the Nilo-Saharan stratigraphy. For the Proto-Nilo-Saharan and Proto-Sudanic stages, no food production can be reconstructed. The Proto–Northern Sudanic language, in contrast, contained vocabulary indicative of the raising specifically of cattle, along with lexicon requiring the use of grains as food, but not diagnostic of their having been cultivated. The succeeding stage, Proto-Saharo-Sahelian, added vocabulary of cultivation along with lexicon indicative of more extensive cattle raising and also, for the first time, terminology descriptive of large, complex sedentary homesteads, including granaries and round houses. The still-later period, Proto-Sahelian, added further words to the agricultural and cattle-herding lexicon, as well as a set of words relating to goats and sheep. Appendix 3 lays out each of these sets of lexical "documents" according to the linguistic stratum to which they can be traced back.[36]

The linguistically attested steps in the shift of Nilo-Saharans to a food-producing economy are exactly those of the archaeology of the earliest cattle raisers of the southern eastern Sahara between 8500 and the sixth millennium BCE (see chapter 2):

first, cattle raising and ephemeral settlements already with pottery;
then, as of the later eighth millennium, larger, more sedentary settlements
    with granaries and round houses and prima facie evidence of possible
    cultivation; and
finally, sometime after 7000 BCE, the appearance of sheep and goats.

The evidence that the earlier two strata—the Proto-Nilo-Saharan and Proto-Sudanic—preceding the Proto–Northern Sudanic era were pre–food producing is not simply negative. Two positive kinds of evidence exist.

First, in Proto–Northern Sudanic and Proto-Saharo-Sahelian, every root word diagnostic of food production for which there is a known etymology—and this means the majority of such terms—derives from an earlier root word of originally non-food-producing connotation.[37] These word histories, in other words, directly reveal the readaption of old vocabulary to describe new knowledge and practice. This pattern continued in the Proto-Sahelian language, except for the adoptions at that period of loanwords for sheep and goats from Afrasian languages. The borrowing of these words demonstrates the spread of these animals to Nilo-Saharans who were already food producers. The chronological placement—that is, the linguistic stratigraphy—of this evidence is in keeping with the archaeology of the southern eastern Sahara, which also places the spread of sheep and goats subsequent to the development of cattle raising (and probably cultivation).

Second, the two deep branches of Nilo-Saharan—Koman and Central Sudanic, which diverged before the Proto–Northern Sudanic period in the stratigraphy—each developed its own vocabularies of food production by two processes:

1. deriving their own new food-producing terms out of earlier Nilo-Saharan non-food-production lexicon; and
2. borrowing key food-producing words from descendant languages of proto–Northern Sudanic.

The latter kind of evidence reveals that the Koman and Central Sudanic development of food production rested on the prior creation of this kind of economy by the Northern Sudanians and their descendants.

For the Proto-Sudanic period, preceding the Northern Sudanic era, a small set of data relating to the economy and technology of the Proto-Sudanic period has been given tentative identification. It consists of three verbs, one meaning "to grind (a tool)" and the others "to grind (grain)" and "to heap up (especially grain)," along with a very, very provisionally proposed noun for a jar or pot of some kind. These terms direct our attention to some of the things we might look for in seeking to identify the archaeology of the immediate pre-cattle-raising ancestors of the proto–Northern Sudanians. They may already have been collectors of wild grains or grasses and would already have been making ground stone tools, and they may possibly have been experimenting with pottery making (see appendix 2).[38]

What have not been properly investigated as yet are the lexicons of fish and fishing in early Nilo-Saharan. The little we can propose as yet about the material culture of the Proto-Sudanic stratum allow the possibility that the Proto-Sudanians were the instigators of the spread of the Aquatic economy of the tenth to eighth millennia across the Sudan belt. In this scenario the Northern Sudanians could be understood as an offshoot of the Proto-Sudanic community that chose an alternative subsistence response to the changing climate of the era—a strategy adapted to the dry eastern Saharan areas away from the more favored river and lake environments where their sister peoples of the Sudanic branch predominated. In this way we could parsimoniously account for the shared pottery traditions and other features common to both the Aquatic peoples and the eastern Saharan cattle raisers.

The ceramic technology of these peoples directs the attention of historians to a very important story for world history—namely, the global primacy of sub-Saharan Africans in the invention of ceramic technology. Pottery making was already a fully established and not at all incipient technology in the archaeology of the southern half of the eastern Sahara by 8500 BCE, as early as the claimed dates for pottery in Japan. But Saharan pottery making was not even the first ceramic technology in Africa. The earliest known pottery in all of human history comes from West Africa, from the modern-day country of Mali, and dates to the centuries 10,000–9500 BCE. The archaeology of the makers of this pottery belongs to the West African Microlithic Complex,[39] a set of archaeological traditions everywhere associated with peoples speaking languages of a third African family, Niger-Congo. For historians the question still to be answered is, Did ceramic technology among Nilo-Saharan speakers in the eastern and other parts of the Sahara diffuse to them a thousand or more years later from far-away West Africa, or were these two separate and independent African developments of this key early technology?

SUMMING UP EARLY AFRASIAN
AND NILO-SAHARAN HISTORY

The Afrasians

The now very extensive evidence we have from the stratification of language history from greater northeastern Africa places two families of languages, Afrasian and Nilo-Saharan, anciently all across these regions. (There may well once have been other language families there, but if so their languages long ago became extinct in the face of the expansion of these two families.) The history of peoples speaking languages of both these families goes back to pre-food-producing eras, well before 10,500 BP.

The Afrasian family originated in all probability in either of two locations: in the northern Ethiopian Highlands or in the areas immediately north of the highlands. There is an interesting bit of supporting zoological-vocabulary evidence for placing them in the Horn: their reconstructed lexicon shows that at the Erythraic stage of their history, they knew of the donkey, PAA *k^{w}er-, and a second equine species, Proto-Erythraic *for-.[40] The second term denotes a zebra in Cushitic languages but an onager in Semitic, so either meaning might seem plausible as the original. But in fact there appears to have been only one zone with a high probability of early Afrasian settlement that was also a region in which two species of wild equine coexisted in the late Pleistocene—namely, the steppe climate areas of the northern and eastern Horn of Africa, where the territories of the wild donkey and the zebra overlapped.

The evidence of reconstructed subsistence lexicon shows that the Proto-Afrasians and their Erythraic descendants must particularly have emphasized the collection of wild grasses and/or wild grains. Just this kind of economy was present at the end of the Pleistocene in or near the regions where the linguistic arguments best place the Proto-Afrasians. Wild-grass collecting goes back before 15,000 years ago in the Nubian Nile regions and has been claimed to be present in the same period around Diredawa on the northern edges of the Ethiopian Highlands.[41] What is lacking currently is knowledge of subsistence in the highlands themselves in the Terminal Pleistocene. But since this period was arid, with probably much more extensive areas of grassland in the highlands than in the early and mid-Holocene, it would not be at all surprising if we were to discover that wild-grass or grain collection was practiced there as well.

The unassailable lexical evidence of food production among Afrasian peoples goes back only to the proto-periods of the major existing subgroups of the family—to the Proto-Cushitic, Proto-Chadic, Proto-Berber, and Proto-Semitic periods. If we consider the interbranch Afrasian cognate-retention percentages (see tables 11 and 12), the branch with the deepest internal time depth is Cushitic. The lowest percentage range in Cushitic, representing the time since the first divergences within Cushitic took place, centers on a median of 5–6 percent. The range of deepest cognation in Northern Sudanic, with a median slightly lower at around 3–4 percent,[42] indicates that the Proto-Cushitic period fell perhaps slightly later than Proto–Northern Sudanic. If, as the proposed archaeological correlations imply, the Proto–Northern Sudanic period lay in the ninth and early eighth millennia BCE, then the Proto-Cushitic period not unreasonably might be placed at around the eighth millennium. This datum implies that we should not expect the earliest archaeological evidence of livestock raising among Afrasians to go back much before 8000 BCE.

Overall, four successive periods can be identified in the linguistic stratigraphy of the earliest periods in Afrasian history with Proto-Boreafrasian and Proto-Chado-Berber both belonging to the fourth period:

1. Proto-Afrasian
2. Proto-Erythraic
3. Proto–North Erythraic
4. a. Proto-Boreafrasian
   b. Proto-Chado-Berber

The reconstructed lexicons of subsistence in each successive stratum reveal the people, all through these successive periods, to have made a strong subsistence use of grasses or grains, but there is no probative evidence at any of the periods indicating the cultivation of those plants.

These four stages of Afrasian history most likely belong to the eras following the close of the last ice age and extending through the first amelioration of African climates, coincident with the Allerød Interstadial, ca. 14,100 to 12,800 years ago; the cool, dry Younger Dryas period, ca. 12,800 to 11,500 years ago; and the first stage of the second era of climatic amelioration, after 11,500 years ago. We can examine this historical period most fruitfully by starting with its more recent events and then moving back in time.

The far-flung Proto-Chado-Berber spread across North Africa and the northern Sahara marks the closing episode in this approximately 5,000-year historical period of early Afrasian expansions. Both the geographical locations and the material culture of the ancestral Chado-Berber stratum, as argued from the linguistic evidence, closely match up with those of the early Capsian archeological culture of the ninth and tenth millennia (map 2). The projected linguistic time depth of the Proto-Chado-Berber period is consistent with this correlation as well.

Chado-Berber's sister sub-subbranch, Boreafrasian, has an apparently somewhat

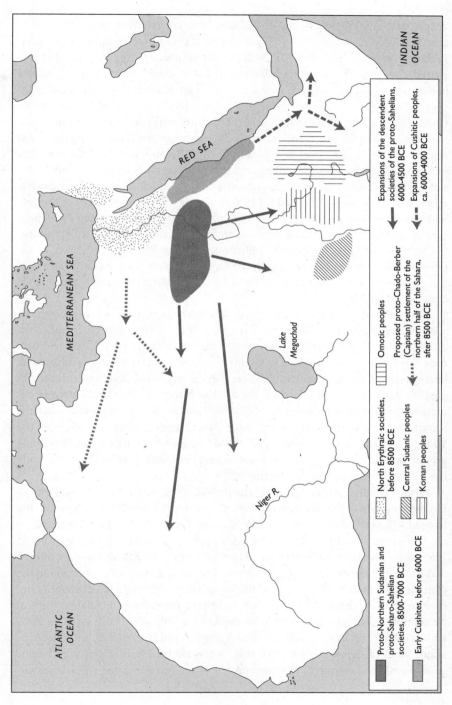

MAP 2. Afrasians and Nilo-Saharans, ca. 8500–4000 BCE

Proto-Northern Sudanian and proto-Saharo-Sahelian societies, 8500–7000 BCE

Early Cushites, before 6000 BCE

North Erythraic societies, before 8500 BCE

Central Sudanic peoples

Koman peoples

Omotic peoples

Proposed proto-Chado-Berber (Capsian) settlement of the northern half of the Sahara, after 8500 BCE

Expansions of the descendent societies of the proto-Sahelians, 6000–4500 BCE

Expansions of Cushitic peoples, ca. 6000–4000 BCE

ATLANTIC OCEAN

MEDITERRANEAN SEA

RED SEA

INDIAN OCEAN

Lake Megachad

Niger R.

deeper stratigraphic time depth. The adjusted cognate retention range of 2–3 percent for Boreafrasian is around 50 per cent of the 5–7 percent figure for Chado-Berber divergence (see table 12). Each further 50 percent drop in percentages of shared cognates in the one-hundred-word list normally reflects an additional period of language divergence with a median span of somewhat more than 2,000 years. (See table 9 in chapter 5 for this pattern.) Thus the correlation of Proto-Chado-Berber with the earliest Capsian of the ninth millennium BCE would place the beginning of the divergence of Proto-Boreafrasian into daughter languages at around the eleventh or twelfth millennium BCE. Because just two later branches of Boreafrasian existed—ancient Egyptian, which remained in Africa, and ancestral Semitic, which emerged in the adjacent Levant—the Borefrasan divergence is most parsimoniously accounted for by postulating a single movement of the earliest pre-Proto-Semitic speakers from Egypt into the Levant (see map 2).[43] There is in fact an apparent archaeological counterpart of just this linguistic hypothesis: the Mushabi culture of the eleventh millennium BCE in the southern Levant, which Ofer Bar-Yosef traces back to origins in Egypt,[44] closely fits the qualifications of this hypothesis (provided that the proposals of Mushabi's Egyptian provenance continue to hold up).

When did the two still-earlier Afrasian divergences, first of the Proto-Erythraic speakers and then of their Proto–North Erythraic descendants, take place, and when did the Proto–North Erythraic ancestors of the Boreafrasians and Chado-Berbers move northward from the Horn to Egypt? Considering that these expansions most likely preceded the thirteenth millennium BP, the triggering developments remain obscure. If as a recent work argues, the Allerød Interstadial period of warmer climate in the Northern Hemisphere, 12,100–10,900 BCE, did not affect the eastern Sahara, and hyperarid conditions in the Sahara ended abruptly only after the Younger Dryas, at around 8500 BCE,[45] then the expansions of the North Erythraic groups as far north as Egypt took place during very unfavorable times, with only the Nile as a possible corridor northward.

Farther south in Africa, however, the period of the Allerød Interstadial probably did coincide with warmer temperatures and higher rainfall.[46] One possibility in need of investigation is that conditions in the Red Sea hills, which stretch along the far eastern periphery of the Sahara, may have ameliorated during the Allerød Interstadial, as they seem to have done farther south. Today these areas get rainfall that the rest of the eastern Sahara does not. They have their own connection to the climatic systems of the Red Sea, and this connection might well have brought rain, even in periods when the interior eastern Sahara, dependent on Atlantic tropical circulation, might have had none. If so, the Red Sea hills might have included areas with seasonal rain during and even before the Allerød Interstadial, and thus contained areas of steppe environment able to provide the kinds of grain- and wild-grass-based food resources that are attested in the reconstructed subsistence vocabulary of the early Afrasian peoples. The areas immediately inland from the Red Sea, in that case, would have been the route of the northward expansion of early Afrasian speakers out of the Horn of Africa, rather than the Nile.

The Nilo-Saharans

The Nilo-Saharan family clearly originated west of the Ethiopian Highlands, in the Middle Nile Basin. The distribution of the extant descendant languages of the three earliest branchings of the family—Koman languages along the eastern side of the basin, Central Sudanic in the far southwest of the basin, and early Northern Sudanic (as argued here) in the southern eastern Sahara (see map 2)—places the Proto-Nilo-Saharans most likely in the heart of the basin, probably (considering the aridity of climate in the Terminal Pleistocene) in areas south of the confluence of the White Nile and the Abbai or Blue Nile.[47]

The gathering-hunting and fishing lexicon of early Nilo-Saharan remains to be adequately studied, so there is much still to learn in this case. It appears from the reconstructed lexicon that, by the period immediately preceding the Proto–Northern Sudanic node of the Nilo-Saharan tree, some Nilo-Saharans may already have begun to collect wild grains (see appendix 2, section A, roots 1 and 3). This development may well have been a result of encounters by the forebears of the Northern Sudanians with Afrasian peoples east of the Nile, as they spread north into the Sahara following the advancing tropical-rainfall belts after the end of the Younger Dryas. That is a matter much in need of future investigation. The lexical data hint that the first making of pottery in the Sahara and Sudan may possibly trace back to the period before 10,500 years ago as well.

If we examine the linguistic stratigraphy of the Northern Sudanic division of Nilo-Saharan, we discover two main stages in the spread of food-producing ways of life. In the first era, extending from perhaps before 8500 down to the seventh millennium BCE, cattle raising took hold, followed by the development of a more sedentary living style, with round houses and granaries, and a probably more varied food production that included the cultivation of sorghum and eventually gourds. But the societies that evolved out of this beginning were very few. As of the seventh millennium, just three—the pre-Kunama, the Proto-Saharans; and the Proto-Sahelians—can be identified (see figure 9; also figures 1 and 2 in chapter 2). For up to 2,500 years, the geographical spread of this new economy must have remained relatively restricted.

The second era, which began with the breakup of the Proto-Sahelian society, would have been marked, in contrast, by a rapid radiation of new societies out over very large regions. Referring to the Nilo-Saharan family tree (see figure 9), one can see that a succession of divergences followed. The Proto-Sahelian language gave rise to the ancestral For and Proto-Trans-Sahel; Proto-Trans-Sahel in turn diverged into Western and Eastern Sahelian divisions; and Western Sahelian then broke up into Songay and Maban branches. At the same time Eastern Sahelian diverged into three branches: Astaboran, Rub, and Kir-Abbaian. And Astaboran and Kir-Abbaian then each further broke up into subgroups. All these divergences have been argued to have taken place between the late seventh and early fifth millennia BCE.[48] The distribution of the descendant languages of this series of rapid divergences ended up as far apart as the Songay (Western Sahelian) in the areas just east of the Niger Bend and the Nara (Eastern Sahelian: Astaboran subgroup) on the slopes of the Ethiopian Highlands.

The history of the divergence and spread of Nilo-Saharan food producers thus has an excellent overall fit with the archaeology of the establishment and spread of the new economy. The first divergences within Northern Sudanic imply a long-term, relatively restricted occurrence of the earliest stages of food production in the eastern Sahara. The era of the wide spread of cattle raising across the southern half of the Sahara, around the sixth millennium BCE, is just the period in which the linguistic evidence would situate the great radiating out of the speakers of the descendant languages of the Sahelian sub-subbranch of Northern Sudanic across those same regions (see map 2).

HISTORIES OF CONTACT

The second fundamental contribution of linguistic stratigraphy studies is what they can tell us about cross-cultural encounter. With this point we return to some issues raised at the very beginning of this chapter. The long presence of Nilo-Saharan and Afrasian language families, in adjacent territories across large expanses of northeastern Africa, certainly should be directly attested in multiple periods of word borrowing from one family to the other. In addition, there should be examples of later language expansions overlaying earlier spreads of languages belonging to the same family, apparent in intrafamilial word borrowing. Both kinds of histories abound. The Nilo-Saharan materials relating to both interfamilial and intrafamilial contacts in the southern and eastern Middle Nile Basin have received considerable attention.[49] Our studies of similar phenomena in the northern Middle Nile Basin and surrounding regions are much less advanced. Nevertheless, we can give preliminary identification to several important periods of interfamilial contact involving Afrasian and Nilo-Saharan speakers, as well as to intrafamilial contacts among Nilo-Saharan speech communities.

Intersocietal Interactions

The earliest contacts clearly identified so far were of the Proto-Sahelians with probably two different Afrasian-speaking peoples. These encounters would date to roughly the seventh millennium BCE on the basis of the proposed archaeological correlations of the Proto-Sahelian period. The first two root words in table 14 are of the kind that normally reflects considerable bilingualism and intimate cross-

Table 14. Afrasian Loanwords in Proto-Sahelian

Loanwords indicative of general cultural impact:

1. PSah *har 'rain; to flow' Proto-Afroasiatic (PAA) *har- 'flow'
2. PSah *hinzah 'three' PAA *xaynz- 'three' (Chadic, Omotic; but *not* retained in Cushitic or Berber)

Loanword reflecting culturally specific adoption of new item of culture:

3. PSah *ay 'goat' Beja *ay* 'goat' (< proto-Cushitic (PC) *ʔaz- 'sheep, goat'; *z > y /V_ is a specifically Northern Cushitic (Beja) sound change)
4. PSah *nay 'goat' Beja *naʔi* (< PC *ʔanaʕ-)
5. PSah *k'er 'ewe lamb/kid' See table 13, item 5

cultural interactions. The adoption of a new word for "three" is particularly arresting, because the borrowing of numerals usually goes along with a significant amount of word borrowing in other areas of culture (most likely fitting loanword category 3B or 3C; see chapters 2 and 4). So the presence of these two loanwords strongly suggests that we will eventually discover more such Afrasian loans in Proto-Sahelian. The borrowing of the old Afrasian root word for "three" in particular—because it was maintained in Chadic but not in Cushitic, Egyptian, Berber, or Semitic[50]—favors the conclusion that these contacts were with the linguistic forebears of the Chadic branch of Afrasian before they moved south out of the Sahara.

The last three borrowed root words in table 14, represent an entirely different contact history—a spread by diffusion from the east, specifically from a very early language of the North Cushitic branch. This branch of Cushitic has a single representative still spoken today, Beja. The spread of these words most probably accompanied the spread of goats and sheep from very early North Cushites to the Proto-Sahelian livestock raisers. They are examples of a category-1 loanword, as defined in chapter 4.

Important early influences flowed in the opposite direction as well. The Red Sea hills may have been a region of recurrently shifting ethnic and linguistic boundaries during the middle Holocene. The very early North Cushites would most likely have inhabited the southern half of that zone in the period immediately preceding the fifth millennium BCE. But intriguingly, the extant North Cushites of the present

Table 15. Sample Sahelian (Kir-Abbaian) Loanwords in Beja

Beja	Nilo-Saharan source	Commentary
1. farr/fafar 'to jump, hop'	proto-Saharo-Sahelian (PSS) *p^haar 'to jump (about)' (proto-Nilo-Saharan (PNS) *p^haar 'to run about, run away')	shows PSS semantic shift; Beja *fir* 'to fly' is a distinct root, derived from proto-Afrasan *-pur-/*-pir- 'to fly'
2. foor 'to flee'	PNS *p^hor 'to flee'	
3. gara, 'fenced-in homestead'	PNS *gaar 'to encircle (as homestead fence)'	
4. as- 'five' (preserved today in Beja only as base of numerals 6-9)	Proto-Kir-Abbaian *as 'five'	from proto-Sahelian *has 'fingers' (loss of *h and meaning innovation, 'five,' are specifically Kir-Abbaian changes)

day, the Beja, appear to derive from a later reexpansion across the region. Beja contains a notable set of Nilo-Saharan loanwords. Only a few words of what was probably once a much large set of loans have yet been identified (see table 15). The types of words borrowed indicate that we are dealing here with a category-3B or -3C borrowing pattern, which commonly reflects the spread of the borrowing language into the lands of the source language. In this situation people gradually, over a period of generations, give up the earlier language in favor of the new language, but as part of the process they take words from their former language into their new one. The loanwords in this instance, like the Afrasian loanwords in Proto-Sahelian, include everyday verbs and numerals. Again as for the Proto-Sahelian borrowing set, we can expect that future study will reveal the presence of more such loanwords.

The particular source of the Nilo-Saharan loans in Beja was a language of the Sahelian group. The borrowed numeral for "five" was even more specifically an innovation of the Kir-Abbaian subbranch of the Eastern branch of Sahelian, allowing us to place the source language in that subbranch. This evidence tells us that at some period in the last 5,000 years BCE, a Kir-Abbaian people inhabited large parts of the southern Red Sea hills region. Then North Cushitic–speaking people, the an-

Table 16. Sahelian Loanwords in Ancient Egyptian

ancient Egyptian	Nilo-Saharan attestation
1. *bdt* 'bed (of gourds, etc.); *bddw-k3* 'watermelon' (Late Eg. *bdt* 'cucumber, gourd')	proto-Sahelian (PSah) *bud̪ 'edible gourd'
2. *s3* 'cattle byre' (earlier *sr)	proto-Saharo-Sahelian *sar 'enclosure'
3. *mrw* 'bulls' (-*w* is Eg. pl. suff.)	proto-Trans-Sahel *maawr 'ox'
4. *pg3* 'trough' (earlier *pgr)	proto-Saharo-Sahelian *pooKur 'wooden vessel'
5. *ds* 'jar'	proto-Sudanic *DɔS 'waterpot (?)'
6. *t3* 'kind of beer' (earlier *tr)	proto-Sah *Ter 'fermented grain'

cestors in language of the Beja, reexpanded and assimilated these particular Kir-Abbaians into their society.

Eastern Sahelian Influences on the Ancient Egyptians

Another notable spread of Nilo-Saharan loanwords to an Afrasian language occurred in ancient Egyptian. The borrowed words so far identified in this instance tend to be terms for items of material culture, principally relating to food production and use (table 16). They constitute an example of category-2A word borrowing—namely, a semantically restricted set of loanwords (see chapter 4, figure 5). They reflect, in other words, the adoption by ancient Egyptians of a particular field of new cultural knowledge from a Nilo-Saharan people. The loanwords include terms relating not just to crops and food processing, but also to cattle and cattle raising, suggesting that Egyptian ideas about cattle may be beholden as much to southern, Sudanic influences as to North African or Levantine influences—or more so. The available diagnostic markers place the source language of the loans specifically in the Eastern Sahelian group of Nilo-Saharan. The phonology of at least two of the loanwords (original *r > ancient Egyptian consonant transliterated as 3) places the time of borrowing very early in Egyptian history, most probably in the predynastic era.

Future studies in this vein will surely find more examples of cultural influences in ancient Egypt coming from the south. When we undertake such studies, we must not neglect the possibility that we will uncover Nilo-Saharan loanwords in other semantic areas of ancient Egyptian vocabulary, reflective of other kinds of south-to-north influences.

SUMMING UP

The long-term histories of the Afrasian and Nilo-Saharan language families raise two very important points about world history at the intersection of Africa with Eurasia. The points are crucial because they force reexaminations of long-accepted Western and Middle Eastern views on history that simply cannot be sustained any longer:

1. Afrasian is an African family every bit as much as is Nilo-Saharan. Its origin region lay well south in Africa, and nearly all of the history of the Afrasian-speaking societies played out in Africa. Only a single offshoot of the family, Semitic, left the continent.
2. Both language families began their earliest periods of expansion within northeastern Africa long *before* the development of food production. Those expansions were driven by other factors—subsistence, environment, and technology—and not by the possession of herding or cultivation.

For both families, their subsistence strategies, as attested in reconstructed lexicon, have strong echoes in the archaeology of subsistence change between 15,000 and 6,000 years ago across greater northeastern Africa. We do not have to look farther afield to find the archaeological correlates of their linguistic stratigraphies.

The early Afrasians, from the evidence of their reconstructed lexicon of subsistence, stand out in particular as having been exploiters of wild grasses (and wild grains). In later periods, from the ninth to the sixth millennium BCE, the different branches of the family separately turned to food production, and to different kinds of animal raising and different crops, depending on the different climatic zones they inhabited, and the different influences they had come under, by that time.

The Nilo-Saharans before the Northern Sudanic period in their history can be less certainly identified with any particular kind of gathering and hunting. But from the Proto–Northern Sudanic stage of 8500–7500 BCE onward, the history of subsistence lexicon shows these particular Nilo-Saharans to have been central participants in an African creation, first, of cattle raising, and then, of the cultivation of Sudanic crops.

Contemporaneously across much of the southern Sahara in the period following 8500 BCE, however, other Nilo-Saharan speakers pursued a highly productive food-collecting system based on aquatic resources. We can identify the aquatic-based people as probable Nilo-Saharans because of their close cultural relationship, notably in ceramic styles, to the earliest cattle raisers, identified with the Proto–Northern Sudanic society. The Proto–Northern Sudanic cattle keepers, as suggested earlier, could be considered a regional offshoot of the aquatic Nilo-Saharans, differing in subsistence practices because they moved into lands with little surface water and poor access to aquatic food sources and so were forced to develop a new way to make effective use of those lands.

From at least the early middle Holocene, we are already able to identify some of the cases of interfamilial and intrafamilial contacts among Nilo-Saharans and Afrasians. An Eastern Sahelian people, notably, influenced predynastic Egyptian material culture, including customs relating to cattle raising. Other Eastern Sahelians became a major component in the demic ancestry of the North Cushitic (Afrasian) Beja peoples of the Red Sea hills region. Diffusion of material culture also sometimes passed the other direction, as we see in the case of the spread of goats and sheep from southwestern Asia, via Afrasian peoples of the eastern Sahara, to Proto-Sahelian people of the southern half of the Sahara region as early as the seventh millennium. The potential of this kind of study for attaching detail and complexity to the course of cultural and economic change and interaction among societies is immense, as a number of studies of African history farther south are already beginning to show.[51]

These proposals raise a strong challenge to archaeologists, historians, and biological anthropologists to resituate the geography of our thinking about the histories of the peoples of northeastern Africa. These peoples were fundamentally African; they were not intruders from outside the continent, contra long-held Western ideas about the histories of these regions. Along the way this chapter offers a provisional overall scheme of human history in greater northeastern Africa over the long term of the Holocene, and a first look at some of the more specific elements in the story from the perspective of the linguistic evidence.

NOTES

1. Greenberg's work was first brought together in one volume, as J. H. Greenberg, *Studies in African Linguistic Classification* (New Haven, CT: Compass Publishing Company, 1955). I. M. Diakonoff's last work on this topic, "The Earliest Semitic Society," *Journal of Semitic Studies* 43 (1998): 209–219, still clearly places Afrasian (Afroasiatic) origins in northeastern Africa, although this fact has been misrepresented by some recent commentators; on this issue see C. Ehret, S. O. Y. Keita, and P. Newman, "The Origins of Afroasiatic," *Science* 306 (3 December 2004): 1680–1681.

2. R. Hetzron, "The Limits of Cushitic," *Sprache und Geschichte in Afrika* 2 (1980): 7–162, builds this case on the basis of the history of morphological innovations in the branches of Cushitic. Some scholars have gone so far as to remove Beja entirely from Cushitic, but the shared innovatory evidence in the lexicon makes the case for its membership in Cushitic a solid one. C. Ehret, "Proto-Cushitic Reconstruction," *Sprache und Geschichte in Afrika* 8 (1987): 7–180, first published the defining sound change of the East-South subgroup of Cushitic, the highly specific shift, proto-Cushitic *nt to *tt /#ʔV_V#. Idem, "The Primary Branches of Cushitic: Seriating the Diagnostic Sound Change Rules," in John Bengtson (ed.), *In Hot Pursuit of Language in Prehistory: Essays in the Four Fields of Anthropology*, pp. 149–160 (Amsterdam and Philadelphia: John Benjamins, 2008), provides a detailed up-to-date layout of the diagnostic sound changes leading from proto-Cushitic to the protolanguage of each branch.

3. A full listing and subclassification of the Agäw languages appears in D. Appleyard, *Comparative Dictionary of the Agaw Languages* (Cologne: Rüdiger Köppe, 2006). Similarly for the Eastern Cushitic languages, see C. Ehret, "Yaakuan and Eastern Cushitic: A Historical Linguistic Overview," in G. Takacs (ed.), *Semito-Hamitic Festschrift for A. B. Dolgopolsky and H. Jungraithmayr*, pp. 128–141 (Berlin: Diet-

rich Reimer, 2008). Chapter 8, figure 13, gives a detailed subclassification of the Southern Cushitic languages, extinct and still spoken.

4. C. Ehret, "Cushitic Prehistory," in M. L. Bender (ed.), *The Non-Semitic Languages of Ethiopia* (East Lansing: Michigan State University, 1976), pp. 85–96.

5. S. Ambrose, "Archaeological and Linguistic Reconstructions of History in East Africa," in C. Ehret and M. Posnansky (eds.), *The Archaeological and Linguistic Reconstruction of African History* (Berkeley and Los Angeles: University of California Press, 1982), pp. 104–157.

6. C. Ehret, *Reconstructing Proto-Afroasiatic (Proto-Afrasian): Vowels, Tone, Consonants, and Vocabulary* (Berkeley and Los Angeles: University of California Press, 1995), root 1508. See also idem, "Proto-Cushitic Reconstruction"; idem, "Nilo-Saharans and the Saharo-Sudanese Neolithic," in T. Shaw and others (eds.), *The Archaeology of Africa: Food, Metals and Towns* (London: Routledge, 1993), pp. 104–125; and elsewhere.

7. Ehret, "Cushitic Prehistory"; idem, *Reconstructing Proto-Afroasiatic.*

8. P. Newman, "Chadic Classification and Reconstructions," *Afroasiatic Linguistics* 5, no. 1 (1977): 1–42; H. Jungraithmayr and K. Shimizu, *Chadic Lexical Roots*, vol. 2 (Berlin: Reimer, 1981); H. Jungraithmayr and D. Ibriszimow, *Chadic Lexical Roots*, 2 vols. (Berlin: Reimer, 1994).

9. C. Ehret, "Wer waren die Felsbildkünstler der Sahara?" trans. W. Pichler and C. Hintermann, *Almogaren* 20 (1999): 77–94; C. Ehret, "Who Were the Rock Artists? Linguistic Evidence for the Holocene Populations of the Sahara," in Alfred Muzzolini and Jean-Loïc Le Quellec (eds.), *Symposium: Rock Art and the Sahara*, in *Proceedings of the International Rock Art and Cognitive Archaeology Congress* (Turin: Centro Studi e Museo d'Arte Preistorica, 1999).

10. Some scholars have offered impressionistic assertions that the Proto-Ethiosemitic language might have been spoken in the Horn well before the sixth century, but H. C. Fleming, in "Ethiopic Language History: Testing Linguistic Hypotheses in an Archaeological and Documentary Context," *Ethnohistory* 15 (1968): 353–388, and I, in chap. 7 in this volume, have both argued that there is no good reason to think that this Semitic offshoot reached there much, if at all, earlier than the epigraphic records indicate.

11. R. Hetzron, "La division des langues sémitiques," in A. Caquot and D. Cohen (eds.), *Actes du premier congrès international de linguistique sémitique et chamito-sémitique* (The Hague and Paris: Mouton, 1974), pp. 182–194; idem, "Genetic Classification and Ethiopian Semitic," in J. Bynon and T. Bynon (eds.), *Hamito-Semitica* (The Hague and Paris: Mouton), pp. 103–127. There remain alternative views to Hetzron's on how Western Semitic diverges, but his arguments and data continue to make a more compelling and—this is crucial—a more comprehensively integrated case than any competing view.

12. For a recent study reaffirming these conclusions and proposing a history of how Semitic languages initially dispersed out of these regions, see A. Kitchen and others, "Bayesian Phylogenetic Analysis of Semitic Languages Identifies an Early Bronze Age Origin of Semitic in the Near East," *Proceedings of the Royal Society B: Biological Sciences* 276, no. 1668 (2009): 2703–2710.

13. H. C. Fleming, "The Classification of West Cushitic within Hamito-Semitic," in D. McCall, N. Bennett, and J. Butler (eds.), *Eastern African History* (New York: Praeger, 1969), pp. 3–27; idem, "Chadic External Relations," in H. E. Wolff and H. Meyer-Bahlburg (eds.), *Studies in Chadic and Afroasiatic Linguistics* (Hamburg: Buske Verlag, 1981), pp. 17–31; M. L. Bender, *Omotic: A New Afroasiatic Family* (Carbondale: University Museum, Southern Illinois University, 1975); C. Ehret, "Omotic and the Subclassification of the Afroasiatic Language Family," in R. Hess (ed.), *Proceedings of the Fifth International Conference on Ethiopian Studies* (Chicago: University of Illinois, 1980), pt. 2, pp. 51–62.

14. Ehret, *Reconstructing Proto-Afroasiatic.*

15. The classification presented in appendix 1 has been updated on the basis of earlier proposals in P. Newman, *The Classification of Chadic within Afroasiatic* (Leiden: Universitaire Pers, 1980), supported by new lexicostatistical evidence (table 12) and by findings on lexical innovation (app. 1), that Chadic

and Berber should be combined in a Chado-Berber group. Newman's essay includes, in its tabling of data evidence of uniquely shared Chadic and Berber pronominal innovations, an especially strong support for this conclusion.

16. Ehret, *Reconstructing Proto-Afroasiatic*, lays out systematically and in detail the regular sound correspondences and sound changes, with extensive supporting data, that characterize this family and provide the system of criteria for judging whether or not individual words are cognate.

17. C. Ehret, *Reconstructing Proto-Afroasiatic*, vol. 2 (in preparation).

18. The cognate lists used in these counts are available electronically from the author. These figures run so low because they count only shared retentions in languages of exactly the same roots with exactly the same meanings. Many other words in each language derive from old Proto-Afrasian (PAA) roots but have changed meaning since PAA.

19. The only alternative claim, originated by Colin Renfrew, ties Indo-European to the first spread of agriculture into Europe 2,000 to 3,000 years earlier than that. This possibility is flatly contradicted by the evidence of the reconstructed Proto-Indo-European vocabulary of technology, which places the earliest Indo-European expansions in the era when wheeled vehicles were coming into use—that is, in the fourth millennium BCE. They also raised horses, animals that in domestic form did not spread west into Europe until after 3500 BCE. It conflicts also with the evidence of non-Indo-European agricultural loanwords in each of the European branches of the family, which reveal that the early Indo-European speakers everywhere, except in the southern boreal forest zone, spread into regions where farming was already established.

20. As reconstructed in Ehret, *Reconstructing Proto-Afroasiatic*; also idem, *Reconstructing Proto-Afroasiatic*, vol. 2, and Orel and Stolbova, *Hamito-Semitic Etymological Dictionary*.

21. Most the roots cited in app. 2 are not yet published and will not appear until vol. 2 of *Reconstructing Proto-Afroasiatic*, currently under preparation, is published. To make this evidence available, a selection of the reflexes of the roots in particular Afrasian languages along with branch reconstructions of the roots, when available, are included in the table.

22. See J. H. Greenberg, "Historical Inferences from Linguistic Research in Sub-Saharan Africa," in J. Butler (ed.), *Boston University Papers in African History*, vol. 1 (Boston: Boston University Press, 1964), pp. 1–15.

23. C. Ehret, *Historical Reconstruction of Southern Cushitic Phonology and Vocabulary* (Berlin: Reimer, 1980), p. 342.

24. A. Militarev, "The Prehistory of a Dispersal: The Proto-Afrasian (Afroasiatic) Farming Lexicon," in P. Bellwood and C. Renfrew (eds.), *Examining the Farming/Language Dispersal Hypothesis* (Cambridge: MacDonald Institute, 2003), pp. 135–150.

25. C. Ehret, "Applying the Comparative Method in Afroasiatic (Afrasian, Afrasisch)," in Rainer Voigt (ed.), *"From Beyond the Mediterranean": Akten des 7. internationalen Semitohamitistenkongresses (VII. ISHaK), Berlin 13. bis 15. September 2004* (Aachen: Shaker Verlag, 2007), pp. 43–70.

26. W. T. Amaruda, "Linguistic Evidence for Cereal Plow Agriculture in Ethiopia and the Horn" (unpublished paper, African History Seminar, UCLA, 1971); C. Ehret, "On the Antiquity of Agriculture in Ethiopia," *Journal of African History* 20 (1979): 161–177; idem, "Wer waren die Felsbildkünstler der Sahara?"; idem, "Who Were the Rock Artists?"

27. I. M. Diakonof, "Earliest Semites in Asia: Agriculture and Animal Husbandry, According to the Linguistic Data," *Altorientalische Forschungen*, 8 (1981): 23–74.

28. Ehret, "Antiquity of Agriculture in Ethiopia"; idem, "Proto-Cushitic Reconstruction"; idem, "Wer waren die Felsbildkünstler der Sahara?"; idem, "Who Were the Rock Artists?"; idem, "A Linguistic History of Cultivation and Herding in Northeastern Africa" (in press).

29. Orel and Stolbova, *Hamito-Semitic Etymological Dictionary*.

30. C. Ehret, *An African Classical Age: Eastern and Southern Africa in World History, 1000 B.C. to A.D. 400* (Charlottesville: University Press of Virginia, 1998), p. 105.

31. C. Ehret. *A Comparative Historical Reconstruction of Proto-Nilo-Saharan* (Cologne: Rüdiger Köppe Verlag, 2001).

32. See chap. 2; also C. Ehret, "Linguistic Stratigraphies and Holocene History in Northeastern Africa," in M. Chlodnicki and K. Kroeper (eds.), *Archaeology of Early Northeastern Africa* (Poznan: Poznan Archaeological Museum, 2006), pp. 1019–1055; and idem, "Nilo-Saharans and the Saharo-Sudanese Neolithic."

33. R. Thelwall, "Linguistic Aspects of Greater Nubian History," in Ehret and Posnansky, *Reconstruction of African History*, pp. 39–52; C. Ehret, "Population Movement and Culture Contact in the Southern Sudan, c. 3000 B.C. to A.D. 1000," in J. Mack and P. Robertshaw (eds.), *Culture History in the Southern Sudan*, Memoir No. 8 (Nairobi: British Institute in Eastern Africa. 1983), pp. 19–48; idem, *African Classical Age*; idem, "Language Family Expansions: Broadening Our Understanding of Cause from an African Perspective," in P. Bellwood and C. Renfrew (eds.), *Language and Agricultural Dispersals* (Cambridge: McDonald Institute for Archaeological Research, 2003), pp. 163–176.

34. F. Wendorf and R. Schild, "Nabta Playa and Its Role in the Northeastern African History," *Anthropological Archaeology* 20 (1998): 97–123; F. Wendorf, R. Schild, and associates, *Holocene Settlement of the Egyptian Sahara*, vol. 1, *The Archaeology of Nabta Playa* (New York: Kluwer Academic/Plenum Publishers, 2001); R. Kuper and S. Kröpelin. "Climate-Controlled Holocene Occupation in the Sahara: Motor of Africa's Evolution," *Science* 313 (11 August 2006): 803–807.

35. For these figures, see M. L. Bender, "The Languages of Ethiopia: A New Lexicostatistical Classification and Some Problems of Diffusion," *Anthropological Linguistics* 13, no. 5 (1971): 165–288; Thelwall, "Linguistic Aspects of Greater Nubian History"; and chap. 5 of this volume.

36. For published substantiations of the reconstructions in appendix 3, see the etymological dictionary in Ehret, *Comparative Historical Reconstruction of Proto-Nilo-Saharan*, along with C. Ehret, "Linguistic Evidence and the Origins of Food Production in Africa: Where Are We Now?" in Dorian Fuller and M. A. Murray (eds), *African Flora: Past Cultures and Archaeobotany* (forthcoming).

37. Chap. 2 lays out several examples of cultivating and pastoral root words that derive from older Nilo-Saharan words of originally non-food-producing meanings; see also Ehret, "Proto-Cushitic Reconstruction"; idem, "Wer waren die Felsbildkünstler der Sahara?"; and idem, "Who Were the Rock Artists?" Idem, *Comparative Historical Reconstruction of Proto-Nilo-Saharan*, provides detailed derivational evidence on all the roots cited in appendix 3.

38. In most cases in appendix 3, in contrast to appendix 2, just the root words and their meanings are presented. The reason for this contrasting treatment of the data is that the particular reflexes of the root words, and the systematic sound correspondences establishing their validity, have already been published in Ehret, *Comparative-Historical Reconstruction of Nilo-Saharan*, to which the reader may refer. Several root words not previously published are also included in appendix 3, however, and in these cases cognate reflexes are cited.

39. E. Huysecom and others, "The Emergence of Pottery in Africa during the Tenth Millennium BC: New Evidence from Ounjougou (Mali)," *Antiquity* 83 (2009): 905–917.

40. Ehret, *Reconstructing Proto-Afroasiatic*, vol. 2.

41. J. D. Clark, "The Origins of Domestication in Ethiopia," in R. E. Leakey and B. A. Ogot (eds.), *Proceedings of the Eighth Panafrican Congress of Prehistory and Quaternary Studies* (Nairobi : International Louis Leakey Memorial Institute for African Prehistory, 1980), pp. 268–270.

42. See chap. 5.

43. Proto-Semitic, of course, was a much later descendant version of the original pre-Proto-Semitic language and was spoken in the Levant at around the sixth or fifth millennium BCE; see I. M.

Diakonoff, "Earliest Semitic Society," and Kitchen and others, "Bayesian Phylogenetic Analysis," for this dating.

44. Ofer Bar-Yosef, "Pleistocene Connexions between Africa and Southwest Asia: An Archaeological Perspective," *African Archaeological Review* 5 (1987): 29–38; S. O. Y. Keita, "Explanation of the Pattern of P49a,f *TaqI* RFLP Y-Chromosome Variation in Egypt," *African Archaeological Review* 22, no. 2 (June 2005): 61–75.

45. Kuper and Kröpelin, "Climate-Controlled Holocene Occupation."

46. L. M. Kiage and K. Liu, "Late Quaternary Paleoenvironmental Changes in East Africa: A Review of Multiproxy Evidence from Palynology, Lake Sediments, and Associated Records," *Progress in Physical Geography* 30 (2006): 633–658.

47. C. Ehret, "Language Family Expansions: Broadening Our Understanding of Cause from an African Perspective," in P. Bellwood and C. Renfrew (eds.), *Examining the Farming/Language Dispersal Hypothesis* (Cambridge: McDonald Institute for Archaeological Research, 2002), pp. 163–176.

48. Ehret, "Nilo-Saharans and the Saharo-Sudanese Neolithic."

49. Ehret, "Population Movement and Culture Contact in the Southern Sudan,"; idem, *Comparative-Historical Reconstruction of Proto-Nilo-Saharan;* idem, "Language Contacts in Nilo-Saharan Prehistory," in H. Andersen (ed.), *Language Contacts in Prehistory: Studies in Stratigraphy* (Amsterdam and Philadelphia: John Benjamins, 2003), pp. 135–157.

50. Ehret, *Reconstructing Proto-Afroasiatic*, p. 228.

51. J. Vansina, *Paths in the Rainforests: Toward a History of Political Tradition in Equatorial Africa* (Madison: University of Wisconsin Press, 1990); idem, *How Societies Are Born: Governance in West Central Africa before 1600* (Charlottesville: University of Virginia Press, 2004); C. Ehret, *An African Classical Age: Eastern and Southern Africa in World History, 1000 B.C. to A.D. 400* (Charlottesville: University Press of Virginia); D. L. Schoenbrun, *A Good Place, a Green Place: Agrarian Change, Gender, and Social Identity in the Great Lakes Region to the Fifteenth Century* (Portsmouth, NH: Heinemann, 1998); K. Klieman, *"The Pygmies Were Our Compass": Bantu and Batwa in the History of West Central Africa, Early Times to c. 1900 C.E.* (Portsmouth, NH: Heinemann, 2003).

Social Transformation in the Horn of Africa, 500 BCE to 500 CE

The establishment of Semitic languages in the Horn of Africa during the last millennium BCE accompanied a major set of social historical transformations. Languages new to an area do not displace other languages from use for trivial reasons of taste or fashion, but normally because the social formations associated with the new languages are spreading at the expense of previous social formations. The patterns of relationship among the Ethiosemitic languages show that two focal points of spread of the new tongues soon arose, the one much neglected by historians being in probably the upper Awash River watershed. The patterns of word borrowing in the languages require that the Semitic speakers were initially a tiny minority and indicate that they added little if any new technological or agricultural knowledge to that already present on the south side of the Red Sea. The establishment and spread of Ethiosemitic languages among the populations of the Horn cannot be attributed thus to technological advantage. Rather, it seems probable that the Semitic speakers held the key ground in the spread of new kinds of relations of production or exchange.

BUILDING THE LINGUISTIC STRATIGRAPHY

The chronological framework for this reconstruction of early history in the northern Ethiopian Highlands is provided by the subclassification of the Ethiosemitic

This chapter revises C. Ehret, "Social Transformation in the Early History of the Horn of Africa: Linguistic Clues to Developments of the Period 500 BC to AD 500," in T. Bayene (ed.), *Proceedings of the Eighth International Conference of Ethiopian Studies,* vol. 1 (Addis Ababa: Institute of Ethiopian Studies, 1988), 639–651; used by permission.

Figure 10. Outline Subclassification of Ethiosemitic

I. North Ethiosemitic
   A. **Tigre**
   B. **Tigrinya**
II. South Ethiosemitic
   A. Cross-Rift
      1. Western Cross-Rift
         a. **Amharic**
         b. **Argobba**
      2. Eastern Cross-Rift
         a. **Harari**
         b. **Zway, Walani**
   B. Outer South Ethiosemitic
      1. Gafat-Soddo
         a. **Gafat**
         b. **Soddo**
      2. Gurage
         a. Chaha-Mäsqan
            i. **Mäsqan**
            ii. Chaha-Ennemor
               (1) **Chaha, Geto**
               (2) **Ennemor**
         b. **Mesmes**

languages. The combined findings of morphological and lexical reconstruction support the scheme of relationships shown in figure 10. (The names of individual languages appear in boldface.)

This classification rests on the work of Robert Hetzron, who built his conclusions on identifying shared innovations in morphology.[1] His results agree broadly, and often in detail as well, with the evidence of lexicostatistics[2] (see appendix 4) and shared lexical innovation (see appendix 5).

From this evidence, plus that of loanwords and linguistic geography,[3] it is possible to chart the early historical periods and locations of Ethiosemitic-speaking societies in the Horn of Africa. This history begins with the Proto-Ethiosemitic-speaking community.[4] The evidence of loanwords in the Proto-Ethiosemitic language allows us to resolve a number of issues in the history of the earliest Ethiosemitic-speaking community. This evidence helps us pinpoint the location of this society. It reveals something of the demographic impact of this new society on the northern Horn, and it gives us an indication of the length of time this society existed as a single societal grouping.

LOCATING AND DATING THE EARLIEST
ETHIOSEMITIC COMMUNITIES

The Proto-Ethiosemitic language can be shown, by the simple application of the standard fewest-moves principle of linguistic-historical inference, to have come from the Arabian side of the Red Sea. All the rest of the Semitic languages, at the earliest periods from which we have direct knowledge, were spoken in other parts of the Arabian Peninsula and farther north, in the Levant and Mesopotamia. The center of diversity of the deep branchings of Semitic can be shown decisively to lie in the Levant, and the origin of Semitic as a whole traced back to about 6,000 years ago in that region.[5] The Ethiosemitic languages, in contrast, form a subgroup of one of the deep branches, South Semitic. The origin region of the settlers who brought the Proto-Ethiosemitic language across the Red Sea can be pinned down even more closely, to Yemen in particular. Proto-Ethiosemitic was a dialect of a language, or a cluster of closely related dialects, spoken in Yemen in the late second and the first millennia BCE. This language is conventionally called Epigraphic South Arabian, from the fact that our documents in this language come from inscriptions.

A major loanword set in the Proto-Ethiosemitic language reveals that the formative period of a distinct Proto-Ethiosemitic community took place on the African side of that sea. Because the particular source language of the loanwords belonged to the Agäw branch of Cushitic (see appendix 5)—the ancient territories of which extended from the northern fringe of the Ethiopian Highlands south to Lake Tana— we can argue that the speakers of Proto-Ethiosemitic established their early settlements in the northern parts of the Ethiopian Highlands.[6] This placement of the Proto-Ethiosemitic speakers is further confirmed by epigraphic evidence dating to the mid- and later first millennium BCE at sites such as Yeha in modern-day far northern Ethiopia and Eritrea.

The Agäw loanword set in Proto-Ethiosemitic fits the "intensive general" category of borrowing. The most notable characteristic of this kind of borrowing is the significant penetration of loanwords into even the one-hundred-word list of core vocabulary meanings. This kind of word borrowing has both demographic and chronological implications. (See chapter 4.)

It implies, first, that the speakers of the borrowing language were a persistently minority community, for a long time fluent in the donor language as well as their own before, finally, the language of the majority population began to drop from use in favor of the originally minority tongue. More than that, intensive general word borrowing in instances where a majority community switches to a former minority language usually indicates that the originally minority speech community formed at first only a tiny minority of the overall population.

Second, it appears from a number of examples in other regions of Africa that

borrowings in basic vocabulary, under circumstances of intensive general influence, tend to be added at a rate of about one to three per century.[7] As many as
six Agäw loans were adopted into the Proto-Ethiosemitic core vocabulary, indicating that the Proto-Ethiosemitic period lasted from two to six centuries.

Harold Fleming's suggestion four decades ago that South and North Ethiosemitic derived from separate South Arabian settlements has direct relevance to
whether we settle for a longer or shorter chronology here.[8] Contrary to Fleming's
suggestion, the Proto-Ethiosemitic people must initially have formed a single settlement in the northern Horn. The presence of the intensive general Agäw word
borrowing in Proto-Ethiosemitic, which must have taken place in Africa, puts this
conclusion beyond doubt. Fleming's proposal rested on the fact that he did not find
a clear lexicostatistical indication of a separate Proto-Ethiosemitic period when he
compared the Ethiosemitic basic vocabularies with the partial evidence available
in the Epigraphic South Arabian inscriptions. This finding suggests that the period
of word borrowing from Agäw must have been relatively short and thus that the
Proto-Ethiosemitic period is likely to have lasted nearer to two or three centuries
than to four to six centuries.

DEVELOPMENTS AFTER THE END
OF THE PROTO-ETHIOSEMITIC ERA

The end of the Proto-Ethiosemitic period was marked by the beginning of the divergence of the language into Proto–North and Proto–South Ethiosemitic dialects.
As we can now decisively argue, this divergence into two successor communities
emerged in situ in the Horn of Africa.

The Proto–North Ethiosemitic–speaking society developed among those whose
settlements continued to be located in the northern highland fringes. Over the next
some centuries the North Ethiosemitic communities may have remained for a while
a minority before finally beginning to grow by extensive linguistic assimilation of
Agäw populations. At least two more loanwords in basic vocabulary appear to have
come into Proto–North Ethiosemitic (see appendix 5), indicative of possibly a continuing intensive general influence from Agäw lasting one or two centuries. Thereafter, however, only much less heavy types of word borrowing appear in the evolution of the North Ethiosemitic tongues, showing that North Ethiosemitic speech
communities had begun to take on the characteristics of a majority population in
their particular regions of habitation.

Early South Ethiosemitic Communities Resettle to the South

The Proto–South Ethiosemitic society coalesced around a group of Ethiosemitic
speakers who settled far away to the south, in the upper Awash River country. Two

mutually confirmatory lines of evidence place them there. One is the linguistic geography of the South Ethiosemitic languages. They divide, as we have seen (see figure 10), into a northern branch—Cross-Rift, the languages of which can be traced back to the areas straddling the Awash watershed—and an Outer South Ethiosemitic branch, whose members, except for Gafat, concentrate in the areas immediately south of the upper Awash.

The second line of evidence is provided by a major set of loanwords datable to the Proto–South Ethiosemitic language. These loans come from an Eastern Cushitic language and apparently specifically from a language of the Highland Eastern Cushitic subgroup. The Highland Eastern Cushitic subgroup includes Sidamo, Hadiya, Kembatta, and several other languages. These languages are spoken today in the areas extending along the Ethiopian Rift Valley, south of the upper Awash watershed, adjacent to the areas implied by the linguistic geography to have been the Proto–South Ethiosemitic homeland.[9]

A smaller but still significant set of Agäw loanwords is also limited to South Ethiosemitic. The presence of these loanwords could be explained by a history in which the Proto–South Ethiosemitic community began to emerge initially as a separate group of people in the northern highland fringe, with their adoption of the Agäw loans taking place before they moved south to a new settlement region. An alternative solution is that the first speakers of the evolving Proto–South Ethiosemitic dialect, when they resettled in the upper Awash areas, moved in along a seam between Eastern Cushitic– and Agäw-speaking territories, with the Highland Eastern Cushites living in the upper Awash River area itself and the Agäw living in the highlands just west of that area. If so, the Agäw would have been a somewhat less important component than Eastern Cushites in the amalgam of peoples incorporated into the Proto–South Ethiosemitic society. Agäw country in later times lay not so far to the west of the probable South Ethiosemitic settlement areas in the upper Awash region, and could quite reasonably be presumed to have extended at one time as far east almost as the Rift, there touching on the Eastern Cushitic lands in and to the east of the Rift Valley. What adds to the reasonability of this solution is the observation that the Agäw loanwords in South Ethiosemitic at times show better comparability with forms of the roots found in southern, rather than northern, Agäw tongues. (Note, in particular, the loanword for "water" in appendix 5.)

The Cushitic loanwords in Proto–South Ethiosemitic again have the semantic distributions characteristic of the intensive general category of borrowing. The Proto–South Ethiosemitic people must at first have formed a tiny, intrusive minority element, which only after a period of time began to amalgamate parts of the much larger indigenous population into their expanding new speech area. Five loanwords in the Proto–South Ethiosemitic core vocabulary come from the Eastern Cushitic people involved in this social history, and three from the Agäw (see appendix 5). If these loanwords derive from partially contemporaneous influences from both

Highland Eastern Cushites and Agäw, the period of the establishment and subsequent growth of the Proto–South Ethiosemitic society is likely to have lasted around three or four centuries.

The Proto–South Ethiosemitic society thereafter began to diverge into two clusters of communities through a new expansion into areas on the immediate southern end of the Proto–South Ethiosemitic homeland. This southward movement set off a succession of further divergences, as one can see by referring back to the outline subclassification. The Proto–Outer South Ethiosemites moved farther into Highland East Cushitic–speaking lands before diverging into separate Proto-Soddo-Gafat and Proto-Gurage communities, with the Proto-Soddo-Gafat only a short time later diverging into pre-Soddo and pre-Gafat. Judging from how few the grammatical and lexical innovations are that distinguish these divergences, this succession of historical developments is likely to have run its course over a period of no more than two or three centuries. The pre-Gafat, from the known locations of their Gafat descendants in medieval times,[10] probably stem from a community that moved away westward, to areas south of the upper Abbai. The pre-Soddo and the Proto-Gurage evolved in or near the areas immediately south and southwest of the upper course of the Awash, where their modern linguistic descendants reside today. The Proto-Gurage in particular expanded farther into former Highland East Cushitic country. The fact that the Soddo, in Ethiopian popular thinking, are included today among the Gurage testifies to the long, close relations that ensued over the past 1,500 years between the ancestors of the Soddo and of the Gurage proper.

The Proto-Cross-Rift people comprised those South Ethiosemitic people who continued to reside in the original areas of Proto–South Ethiosemitic settlement in the upper Awash regions. That they did not expand into the territories of other peoples is supported by the fact that no new loanwords in core vocabulary can be dated to this period in the linguistic stratigraphy.

After no more than perhaps a couple of centuries, however, the Proto-Cross-Rift society itself underwent a further split into two daughter communities. This development probably arose somewhat after the earliest divergences of the Proto–Outer South Ethiosemitic communities were taking place, but still during the first half or middle of the first millennium CE. The Western Cross-Rift people, from whose dialect the Amharic and Argobba languages derive, expanded more widely within the upper Awash region, as their adoption of further core vocabulary, particularly from Highland East Cushitic communities, indicates (see appendix 5). The Proto–Eastern Cross-Rift society can be argued, from the locations of its modern-day descendant communities, to have coalesced around Cross-Rift groups who moved just to the east or southeast, into portions of the far upper Shebeelle River watershed. Their new settlement areas also appear, from the loanword evidence (see appendix 5), to have been lands previously occupied by Highland Eastern Cushites.

The secondary expansions of the early South Semitic peoples initiated a variety of contact situations with surrounding Cushites. Only a very uneven and tiny sampling of the evidence for such contacts has so far been identified, and except for core vocabulary items it is often not possible yet to know whether or not a particular root word has a wider distribution than has been noted for it. Later Gurage expansions continued the process of interaction with and the absorbing of Highland Eastern Cushites initiated in Proto–South Ethiosemitic times, and the close relations between Gurage and Highland peoples extended right into recent times, as loanwords limited to narrow subgroups of Gurage attest (appendix 5). Gafat has possibly some Highland Eastern Cushitic loanwords of its own; if so, this evidence supports its very early location in areas close to the Proto-Gurage.

The Proto-Cross-Rift people and their descendants, the Proto–Western Cross-Rift society, appear for a while to have continued to interact with both Agäw and Eastern Cushites.[11] Such contacts would be in keeping with the indications of linguistic geography that the Proto-Cross-Rift and later Western Cross-Rift peoples remained in much the same areas as the Proto–South Ethiosemitic community. The early Eastern Cross-Rift peoples, on the other hand, entered generally into close interactions, as their easterly trend of expansion portended, with Eastern Cushites whose language or languages did not belong to the Highland branch (see appendix 5). On the whole, loanwords in core vocabulary became less common in the later eras, indicating that the South Ethiosemitic societies had become more numerous, established populations—and no longer exceedingly small and intrusive minorities.

Dating the Early Stages of South Ethiosemitic Settlement

To put these developments into some kind of chronological framework, glottochronology can be brought into play. Chapter 5 offers numerous examples of the applicability of this technique in African history. In the case of Ethiosemitic language history, glottochronological dating of the key developments tends to fall closely in line with the dating indicated by other kinds of evidence and with the time spans suggested by the loanword evidence. We begin our chronological considerations with the Proto-Ethiosemitic era.

The initial divergence of Proto-Ethiosemitic into separate South and North Ethiosemitic branches is marked by a cognation range in core vocabulary centering on 43–49 percent. In glottochronological reckoning (see chapter 5) this range would be equivalent to an estimated rough median divergence period of about 2,500 years ago. One additional problem must addressed, however, in proposing approximate dates in this and other Ethiosemitic cases. It has been found in several African examples that word borrowings into core vocabulary *after* two languages have begun to diverge out of their common mother language distort cognate retention figures in a particular fashion. They tend to depress the shared cognation in direct proportion to the combined number of the loanwords in the two vocabularies.[12] Considering the numbers of loanwords that have entered both North and South Ethiosemitic core vocabularies since the end of Proto-Ethiosemitic times, the figure of 2,500 years must be seen as the upper limit for the breakup of Proto-Ethiosemitic rather than a median date. The end of the Proto-Ethiosemitic period would therefore best be placed more recently than 500 BCE, most probably in about the fourth or third century in linguistic dating.

How long before that period should we place the initial settlement of the ancestral Proto-Ethiosemitic community in the northern Horn? The evidence, examined just above, of intensive general word borrowing from an Agäw language, including as many as six Agäw loanwords in core vocabulary, indicates that the settlement of the first Ethiosemitic speakers took place at least two to three centuries before the divergence of the Proto-Ethiosemitic society into Proto–North and Proto–South Ethiosemitic branches began, at least to midmillennium and perhaps to the sixth or seventh century.

There is no need to press the Proto-Ethiosemitic settlement any further back in time to account for the differences between early Ethiosemitic and Epigraphic South Arabian. Fleming's examination of lexical change suggests that the differences between the language of the earliest Ethiosemites and the language of populations in Yemen in those times would have been small.[13] Some scholars have impressionistically argued from the differences in grammar between Epigraphic South Arabian of the first millennium BCE and the early Ethiosemitic of the fifth or fourth century BCE in the northern Ethiopian Highlands that the Proto-Ethiosemitic speakers had already lived in the northern Horn for quite a few centuries by that time. But the disparity between the spoken and written forms of a language is too much a historical commonplace to require much comment. Written versions commonly retain archaic forms long discarded in spoken use. In any case, Proto-Ethiosemitic need not have derived from the same dialect as that which formed the basis for most Epigraphic South Arabian writing. Indeed, we would expect it not to have been, for the South Arabian settlers in the Horn are more likely to have come from the nearby Arabian coastlands just across the Red Sea—from seaports if they were traders—than from those interior areas of Yemen, where the principal South Arabian populations and the centers of government and literacy tended to lie.

The Proto–South Ethiosemitic society arose around an apparently small group of Ethiosemitic speakers who moved to the upper Awash area at the end of Proto-Ethiosemitic times. This development can be expected to date to perhaps midway through the second half of the first millennium BCE. The subsequent breakup of the developing Proto–South Ethiosemitic society into a succession of several descendant communities is marked by a cognation range centering around 48–59 percent,

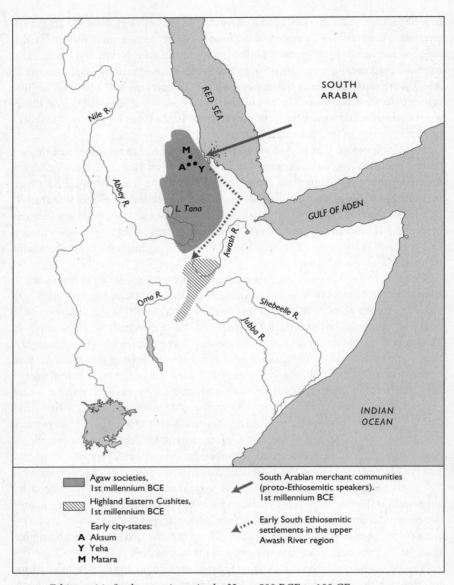

MAP 3. Ethiosemitic Settlement Areas in the Horn, 500 BCE to 100 CE.

its median figure of 54 percent (see appendix 4) indicating a time of about 2,000 years ago for the beginning of this divergence. In the South Ethiosemitic case, later word borrowing by South-branch languages from each other has probably some-times raised the percentages of apparent cognation, partially compensating for the expected depression of cognation from the penetration of Eastern Cushitic loans into basic vocabulary. Soddo seems especially to have been affected by word borrowing from its close relatives, as is evident from its consistently higher-than-expected cognate percentages with nearly all the rest of South Ethiosemitic (see appendix 4). It would be not improbable, then, for the beginning of South Ethiosemitic differentiation to have fallen fairly close to the 2,000 years suggested by the cognation counts, perhaps somewhere around the first or second century CE.

This dating places the incipient South Ethiosemitic breakup about three or four centuries after the Proto-Ethiosemitic period ended. Such a date fits very well indeed with the independent evidence of intensive general borrowing in basic vocabulary. This evidence includes seven word borrowings from Cushitic languages in the core vocabulary of Proto–South Ethiosemitic, implying a time span of three to four centuries for the Proto–South Ethiosemitic era. The slightly higher ranges of cognation, centering in the very high 50 percents, between the two primary subgroups of Cross-Rift and the two primary subgroups of Gurage South Ethiosemitic indicate that the second and third stages of divergence of South Ethiosemitic into at least six emergent societies, spread out around the eastern, southern, and southwestern sides of the upper Awash country—the Proto–Western Cross-Rift, Proto–Eastern Cross-Rift, pre-Gafat, pre-Soddo, pre-Mäsqan, and Proto-Chaha-Ennemor—should have been complete by the fifth or sixth century CE (map 3).

EARLY ETHIOSEMITIC COMMUNITIES AND THEIR CUSHITIC NEIGHBORS

The questions of how and why the Ethiosemitic tongues were able to become established as indigenous languages in northeastern Africa can be answered as yet only by inference and speculative proposals.

Some solutions can be decisively discounted. The first Ethiosemitic speakers did not come as technologically advantaged conquerors. It may perhaps be possible that the South Arabian settlers introduced iron to the Horn. But what little as has yet been investigated of northeastern African iron-working terminology suggests that metallurgy in some form was already known and that the root *bir-t- used for "iron" throughout the Horn today was borrowed into early Ethiosemitic from a Cushitic source.[14] Nor did the early Ethiosemitic settlers apparently introduce any significantly different agricultural knowledge or practice to the regions of their settlement.

From the kinds of agricultural words borrowed we can say something, however, about the relations of the early Ethiosemitic speakers with the peoples among whom they settled. They were, in the first place, not farmers. Understandably, the names of crops new to South Arabian immigrants, such as t'ef, finger millet, and nug, an indigenous Ethiopian oil plant, came into Ethiosemitic from the Cushitic languages. But to a surprising extent the names even for crops and agricultural implements of ancient acquaintance to Semitic peoples in Asia were also borrowed from the indigenes.[15] This surpassing lack of agricultural orientation is strongly attested for the Proto-Ethiosemitic community, which borrowed such terms as those for wheat, mashed chickpeas, flax, and plowshare—all items known much more anciently to Semitic speakers. This orientation continued in evidence among the Proto–South Ethiosemitic settlers of the upper Awash, who adopted additional basic cultivating lexicon such as words for barley, wheat bread, and chickpeas. The early Ethiosemitic people surely all consumed the products of the local cultivators, but just as surely they seem not to have been themselves the cultivators.

Two possibilities present themselves. The Ethiosemitic speakers may have formed a ruling class with a distinctive language of their own, supporting themselves by extracting a surplus from the still-Cushitic-speaking cultivators. But this is, linguistically speaking, an inherently unstable situation, in which either the ruling class will soon take up the language of the ruled, or the ruled will begin increasingly to shift to the rulers' language. Alternatively, the Ethiosemitic speakers may have followed a particular occupational specialization that allowed them to operate outside narrow linkages to particular localities but obliged them to obtain their food by purchase from the cultivators.

Both possibilities could in fact have been operative in successive eras. A fundamental theme in Red Sea history in the last millennium BCE is the expansion of long-distance trade. The trade came at first overland through the western side of Arabia, with South Arabians as the distant suppliers of desired goods. But several principal products, among them tortoiseshell and frankincense, were also produced in the drier northern fringe of the Horn, and so the attention of traders would soon have been drawn to the areas across the Red Sea from South Arabia. It can be proposed that the early Ethiosemitic language was brought into the Horn by traders from South Arabia, who as transmitters of goods between societies would have stood outside the normal social networks of the cultivating Cushitic population and who would by occupation have been noncultivators. Their language, because of its connections to outside trade links, would have become the lingua franca and therefore have been used as a second language by many of the Agäw of the northern Horn.

In time, it can be suggested, some traders would have begun to contract marriage with daughters of local chiefs or notables, for the obvious reason that such alliances would have benefited both traders and chiefs in channeling and securing the flow of goods. If so, then eventually the opportunities could have arisen for the offspring of marriages of that kind to parlay their combination of chiefly descent and familial access to the trade into a wider political power. Thus might a ruling class, whose home language was Proto-Ethiosemitic, have begun to evolve and its language thereafter begun to spread among the general populace.

The Proto–South Ethiosemitic settlers, from the patterns of their word borrowings from surrounding peoples, seem likely to have replicated the kinds of relations of the Proto-Ethiosemitic period, but in a new and distant locale. From that evidence it seems not at all improbable that the earliest Proto–South Ethiosemitic speakers were also traders, coming from the established Ethiosemitic-speaking areas on the north edge of the highlands and seeking to open up new sources of supply of goods, such as ivory and rhinoceros horn. The proposed dating of the Proto–South Ethiosemitic era to roughly the last three centuries BCE raises the possibility that the Proto–South Ethiosemitic intrusion into the upper Awash regions began as a commercial response to the added Ptolemaic presence in the Red Sea trade beginning in the late 300s BCE and the growth of the Indian Ocean trade connection over last three centuries BCE.

The social basis for the long-term maintenance and expansion of the South Ethiosemitic peoples between the first and tenth centuries CE is unclear, however. In the north the rise of small kingdoms and eventually of a state, Aksum, in which the language of the dominant stratum and of the core areas of the state was Ethiosemitic, and the continuing major importance of trade as a source of revenue supporting the state, are well attested. All these developments would have favored the gradually widening establishment of the North Ethiosemitic languages in the countryside as well as the towns. But the evidence is lacking as yet for continuities between the early period of South Ethiosemitic expansion and the much later state-building period from the ninth century CE onward in the upper Awash and northern Ethiopian Rift Valley areas. If the South Ethiosemitic settlers came for trade, the political consequences of their settlement remain unknown. In Gurage and perhaps elsewhere, South Ethiosemitic languages spread to peoples who, except for shift of language, seem to have either carried on or soon reverted back to earlier Cushitic patterns of culture and governance, without major lasting change. Other social mechanisms of language shift than those associated with exchange relations will probably have to be sought if we are to explain the secondary expansions of the early South Ethiosemitic speech areas.

WHERE DO HISTORIANS GO FROM HERE?

The primary goal in this exercise has been to examine what the linguistic evidence can add to our understanding of the history of the period of early establishment of Ethiosemitic languages in the Horn of Africa. It is strongly evident that the people who brought the Proto-Ethiosemitic language into the northern Ethiopian Highlands in the middle centuries of the first millennium BCE were initially a tiny minority intrusion among the long-established Cushitic Agäw populations of the region. They did not become prominent because of any technological or agricultural innovations they had to offer. Rather, as the epigraphic, documentary, and archaeological records imply, they must originally have been the instigators and mediators of a new set of commercial relations, whose influence subsequently radiated out through trade from a few small urban centers during the second half of the first millennium BCE. In this way their language would have gained wide currency as a lingua franca. In time, their descendants of mixed Agäw and South Arabian ancestry would have been able to parlay economic importance into political power, further solidifying the importance of their language as the medium through which governance was carried out. This factor, we can propose, was particularly potent in the establishment of Proto–North Ethiosemitic and its dialect Ge'ez as the language of the Aksumite state in the first half of the first millennium CE.

This is only the beginning of the history we will eventually be able to write for these regions from the linguistic evidence. The centuries-long spread of the South Ethiosemitic languages into the Eastern Cushitic–speaking Ethiopian Rift Valley regions and into the formerly Agäw-speaking central portions of the Ethiopian Highlands reflects a complex social history as yet entirely unstudied for the periods before the thirteenth century. The lexicons of the Agäw languages still spoken today in Eritrea and in northern and central Ethiopia are archives registering a myriad of as-yet-uninvestigated encounters of Cushites and Ethiosemitic speakers all across those regions, lasting into and through the age of the medieval Solomonic kingdom. Investigating these topics with the resources of linguistic historical reconstruction is an engaging prospect for the future.

For those readers who wish to further explore different issues of interpretation from those already raised here, appendices 4 and 5 offer additional perspectives, confronting important issues in the interpretation of linguistic evidence for history. Appendix 4 presents the matrix of cognate retention counts among the various Ethiosemitic languages. Following the matrix is a discussion of a variety of issues involved in formulating and interpreting data of this kind. Some of the points raised have wide applicability to the problems associated with processing this kind of evidence. Appendix 5 presents the core vocabulary loanwords so far identified for different strata in the evolution of Ethiosemitic. Except for David Appleyard's work, the numerous Cushitic loanwords found in other parts of the lexicons of these languages remain to be studied.

NOTES

1. R. Hetzron, *Ethiopian Semitic: Studies in Classification*, Journal of Semitic Studies Monograph no. 2 (Manchester, UK: Manchester University Press, 1972); idem, "Genetic Classification and Ethio-

pian Semitic," in J. Bynon and T. Bynon (eds.), *Hamito-Semitica* (The Hague: Mouton, 1975), pp. 103–127; idem, *The Gunnän-Gurage Languages* (Naples: Istituto Orientale di Napoli, 1977).

2. M. L. Bender, "The Languages of Ethiopia," *Anthropological Linguistics* 13, no. 5 (1971): 165–288.

3. The overall lexical counts do not make a clear case that Soddo and Gafat are any closer to each other than either is to Gurage. But a few lexical innovations, in the form of shared loanwords from Cushitic languages, do appear to confirm both Hetzron's Gafat-Soddo and Outer South Ethiosemitic levels. See apps. 4 and 5 for particular data on shared innovations. One difference from Hetzron's classification in the scheme followed here has to do with the placement of Mesmes. For reasons discussed in app. 4, Mesmes is best placed as the lexical figures indicate, while the relationships among Chaha, Geto, and Ennemor remain as Hetzron proposed them.

4. In some theoretical statements, a proto-period is treated as if it were the instant in time at which the protolanguage first begins to diverge into dialects. But in the real world no such single moment of divergence normally exists. In historical practice, it is useful to allow the proto-period to cover the two, or three, or four centuries immediately preceding the unmistakable manifestations of the first divergence of that protolanguage into dialects.

5. Hetzron, works cited in n. 1 above. The solitary view of the scholar Grover Hudson that the Ethiosemitic languages are highly diverse and the source from which the rest of Semitic spread cannot be sustained. Ethiosemitic in all respects forms a very closely related group, roughly of the same order of diversity as the Germanic subgroup of Indo-European, whereas the Semitic family as a whole has the same kind of internal time depth and diversity as Indo-European. For a recent substantiation of both Hetzron's and the standard subclassifications of Semitic, and for the dating, locations, and proposed archaeological correlations of the Proto-Semites and their earliest daughter societies with the early Bronze Age in the Levant 6,000 to 5,000 years ago, see A. Kitchen and others, "Bayesian Phylogenetic Analysis of Semitic Languages Identifies an Early Bronze Age Origin of Semitic in the Near East," *Proceedings of the Royal Society B: Biological Sciences* 276, no. 1668 (2009): 2703–2710.

6. C. Ehret, "Cushitic Prehistory," in M. L. Bender (ed.), *The Non-Semitic Languages of Ethiopia* (East Lansing, Michigan State University, 1976).

7. Arguments for this kind of time relation are presented in chap. 4. In addition, C. . Ownby, "Early Nguni History: The Linguistic Evidence and Its Correlation with Archaeology and Oral Tradition" (Ph.D. diss., UCLA, 1985), identifies a number of loanword sets of intensive general characteristics in different Nguni dialects and subdialect groupings. The time spans allowed by oral tradition and archaeological dating for the borrowing sets involved fit with the rate of one to three per century. The same kind of basic vocabulary borrowing rate is indicated in the borrowings of Maasai words by Okiek groups over the past four to five centuries in Kenya. For these latter cases, see the appendices in C. Ehret, *Southern Nilotic History: Linguistic Approaches to the Study of the Past* (Evanston, IL: Northwestern University Press, 1971).

8. H. C. Fleming, "Ethiosemitic Language History: Testing Linguistic Hypotheses in an Archaeological and Documentary Context," *Ethnohistory* 15 (1968): 353–388.

9. Considerable numbers of, especially, borrowed culture lexicon reflective of this history have been presented in D. L. Appleyard, "The Semitic Basis of the Amharic Lexicon" (Ph.D. diss., School of Oriental and African Studies, University of London, 1975), and in idem, "Linguistic Evidence of Non-Semitic Influence in the History of Ethiopian Semitic: Lexical Borrowing in Ge'ez and Other Ethiopian Semitic Languages," *Abbay* 9 (1978): 49–56. Items of basic vocabulary borrowed from early Highland Eastern Cushitic into proto–South Ethiosemitic appear in app. 5 of this book.

10. W. A. Shack, *The Central Ethiopians* (London: International African Institute, 1974), p. 148.

11. A number of loanwords have this implication, provided that they are actually innovations dating to those periods; examples of such loanwords include the words for "goat," "bamboo," and "castrated animal" (Appleyard, "Linguistic Evidence of Non-Semitic Influence"). Further possible cases appear in app. 5 of this book.

12. Chapter 4; also Ehret, *Southern Nilotic History,* p. 94; idem, *Historical Reconstruction of Southern Cushitic* (Berlin: Reimer, 1980), pp. 385–388; idem. "Testing the Expectations of Glottochronology against the Correlations of Language and Archaeology in Africa," in C. Renfrew, A. McMahon, and L. Trask (eds.), *Time Depth in Historical Linguistics,* vol. 2 (Cambridge: McDonald Institute for Archaeological Research, 2000), pp. 373–400.

13. Fleming, "Ethiosemitic Language History."

14. C. Blakney, *On "Banana" and "Iron": Linguistic Footprints in African History,* Hartford Studies in Linguistics, no. 13 (Hartford, CT, 1963).

15. W. T. Amatruda, "Linguistic Evidence for Cereal Plow Agriculture in Ethiopia and the Horn," (unpublished paper, advanced seminar in African history, Department of History, UCLA, 1971); Appleyard, "Linguistic Evidence of Non-Semitic Influence"; C. Ehret, "On the Antiquity of Agriculture in Ethiopia," *Journal of African History* 20 (1979): 161–177.

8

Recovering the History of Extinct Societies

A Case Study from East Africa

One of the more fascinating capacities of linguistic methodology is its ability to allow historians to identify extinct societies and even to reconstruct many elements of the histories of those extinct communities. The lexical documents supporting this kind of historical reconstruction are loanwords from the extinct languages, preserved in the lexicons of the later languages of a region. The particular kinds of loanwords preserved in this fashion, of course, reveal the kinds of cultural influences the extinct society had on its successors. At the same time, those same loanwords—because they relate to the knowledge, beliefs, cultural practices, and material life of the extinct society—give direct testimony about the life and cultural activities of the extinct community. In addition, from how the loanwords are pronounced today in the borrowing languages we can often deduce how the words must originally have been pronounced in the extinct language. In turn, this kind of evidence, along with semantic and morphological innovations in the borrowed words, frequently allow us to take the further step of situating the extinct language in the stratigraphy of its language family and, from this evidence, to infer the broad history of how the extinct society diverged and spread into new areas.

Just as a warning, this particular chapter inserts more technical linguistic analysis within the text than the rest of the chapters in this section of the book. The reason is that, in this case, differences in how loanwords are pronounced are key to identifying the extinct languages, and thus the extinct societies that spoke them.

This chapter develops its story from the materials contained in C. Ehret and D. Nurse, "The Taita Cushites," *Sprache und Geschichte in Afrika* 3 (1981): 125–168, although with revisions and corrections of the data and with a different focus for the narrative; used by permission of Rüdiger Köppe Verlag.

But, having read this far in the book, the reader may be ready for a few additional challenges. The technical aspects include formulaic statements of the regular sound-change rules along with tables of borrowed words that illustrate those rules. The rules are stated in a kind of linguistic shorthand, but a quick primer on how to "read" the shorthand is provided.

HISTORY IN THE TAITA HILLS OF KENYA

The Taita Hills, located at a historical crossroads of population movement through eastern Kenya and far northeastern Tanzania, provide an especially illustrative set of examples of the power of these approaches. The region has had a long and complex history of encounter and merger of people of diverse ethnic backgrounds. The oral traditions of the communities of this region recognize the diversity of their historical roots,[1] and linguistic evidence amply confirms the testimony of tradition.

The Taita Hills remain an area of relative linguistic diversity down to the present. Two distinct Bantu languages dominate the region today—Dawida on the main range of peaks, and Saghala of the Teri Valley on a neighboring lesser range. Four Dawida dialects are distributed through the main range, one to each of the four major drainage systems of the range.[2] A fifth dialect of Dawida, which has been confusingly called "Hill Saghala," is spoken on the same mountain as the Saghala language proper. Kasighau, spoken on a third, still smaller range nearby, is a sixth dialect of Dawida.

The region was one of much greater ethnic diversity in the past, home not only of a variety of Bantu-speaking populations, but of several distinct Southern Cushitic societies as well. Loanwords in the present-day Bantu languages, Dawida and Saghala, reveal the former presence of at least two separate and historically important Southern Cushitic societies in and around the region of the Taita Hills. The sorts of word borrowing that took place reflect long-term situations of extensive bilingualism, or more probably multilingualism, and indicate that these Southern Cushitic societies once formed a significant, and probably majority, proportion of the Taita population. In all likelihood these peoples constituted the original pre-Bantu agricultural settlement of the hills and the surrounding regions. The traditions of the modern-day peoples of the region remember two earlier peoples: a pastoralist society, the Mbisha, and a gathering-hunting society, the Asi. *Mbisha* seems likely to have been the pastoralists' name for themselves, but *Asi* is a general northeastern Bantu term applied to any foraging people. In order not to prejudge the economic orientation of the two Southern Cushitic peoples who have left loanwords in Dawida and Saghala, we follow a convention of Indo-European studies and distinguish the two Southern Cushitic languages as "Taita Cushitic A" and "Taita Cushitic B."[3]

Southern Cushites in Early East African History

The presence of Southern Cushitic–speaking populations in East Africa extends back over 5,000 years. The Proto–Southern Cushitic society established itself in northern Kenya in the latter half of the fourth millennium BCE. Its early settlements can be identified with the archaeological sites of the Savanna Pastoral Neolithic of those regions.[4] The reconstructed Proto–Southern Cushitic (PSC) vocabulary confirms that the speakers of this language were herders of cattle, goats, and sheep—and both bled and milked their cattle for sustenance—and that they were acquainted with the cultivation of several crops, especially the grains sorghum and finger millet.[5]

Over the next 2,000 years, various descendant communities of the Proto–Southern Cushites carried Southern Cushitic languages into northeastern Uganda, northern and central Tanzania, the Lake Nyanza (Lake Victoria) region, and the eastern Kenya Coast and interior.[6] The arrival of Southern Nilotic–speaking peoples in western Kenya in the early first millennium BCE led to a long-term assimilation of considerable numbers of Southern Cushites into their societies.[7] In similar fashion, the scattering out of Mashariki Bantu-speaking communities across southern Kenya and northern Tanzania set in motion regional histories of the merger of erstwhile Southern Cushites into those communities.[8] In each case, the borrowing ; Southern Cushitic words took place, yielding us in some instances quite large bodies of loanwords, allowing us to identify a variety of no-longer-existing Southern Cushitic societies.

Figure 11 presents an overall classification of the group. The names of languages spoken today appear in boldface; the names proposed for the so-far-identified extinct Southern Cushitic tongues are italicized;[9] and the names of languages that were still spoken in the twentieth century, but are now apparently extinct, appear in italic boldface. Roland Kiessling argues for a different breakdown of the West Rift subgroup, putting Alagwa with Iraqw and Gorowa rather than with Burunge.[10]

From this outline we can construct the tree of descent of the Southern Cushitic languages, extinct and extant, in figure 12. The approximate dates of this history, entered along the right side of tree, rest on multiple archaeological correlations, some of which were presented in chapter 5.[11] The solid lines of language descent mark histories for which we have archaeological correlations allowing us to assign approximate dates. Dashed lines indicate histories for which the time spans involved are undetermined. And the dotted lines, with which some of the dashed lines end, represent the extinction of those lines of descent.

SOUTHERN CUSHITES IN THE TAITA HILLS REGION

One of the specific regions of the early secondary expansion of Southern Cushitic peoples, it can now be argued, lay in and around the Taita Hills of southeastern

Figure 11. Outline Classification of Southern Cushitic

I. Dahaloan
   A. **Dahalo**
   B. *Highland Dahaloan*
II. Rift-Mbugu
   A. Mbuguan
      1. *North Mbuguan*
      2. **Ma'a**
   B. Rift
      1. *North Rift*
      2. *Tale Southern Cushitic*
      3. East Rift
         a. *Asa*
         b. South Rift
            i. *Kw'adza*
            ii. *Iringa Southern Cushitic*
      4. West Rift
         a. Burungean
            i. **Burunge**
            ii. **Alagwa**
         b. Iraqwan
            i. **Iraqw**
            ii. **Gorowa**

Kenya. The classification as given in figures 11 and 12 does not yet include the Taita Cushitic communities, but we will remedy that later, in figure 13. The evidence for the former presence of two distinct societies in the region is strong and varied. The primary testimony consists of large numbers of Southern Cushitic loanwords limited to either or both of the Dawida and Saghala languages.

Identifying Loanwords

In order to identify loanword evidence in the first place, it is necessary to know the grammatical rules of word formation in both the donor and borrowing languages of the loans. In particular, we need to be able to separate out the *stems* of words from any *suffixes* or *prefixes* added to those stems. Suffixes and prefixes are part of what we call the *morphology* of a language.

In Bantu languages, such as Saghala and Dawida, each noun consists of a stem to which prefixes marking singular and plural are attached. For example, the

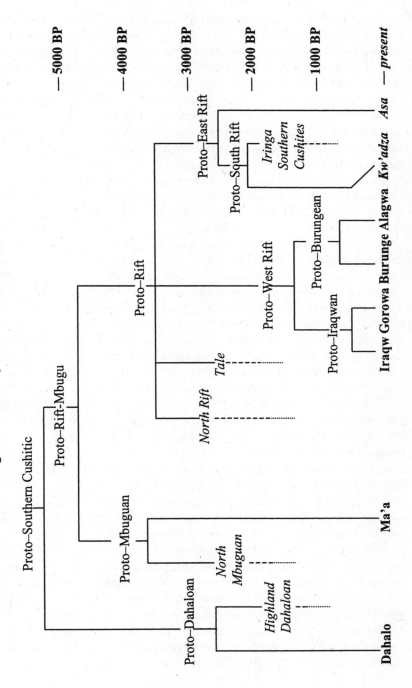

Figure 12. Family Tree of Southern Cushitic

Saghala noun *mrigo* 'log' consists of a singular prefix m- plus the stem -rigo. The plural prefix of this word is mi-, so the plural of "log" is *mirigo* in Saghala.[12] The stems of verbs also cannot stand alone in Bantu languages. But in contrast to nouns, they can take both suffixes and prefixes. For this reason we write a verb stem with hyphens before and after—for example, Saghala -*kogan*- 'to meet'.

Both of these Saghala word stems, the noun for "log" and the verb for "to meet," happen to be loans from a Taita Cushitic language. In the case of -*kogan*-, there is an additional wrinkle: the final part of the stem, -an-, is actually a Saghala suffix implying reciprocity. If we remove that suffix also, we get the true stem, *-kog-. This stem came into early Saghala as a borrowing of the Southern Cushitic root *kok- 'to listen, notice'. When Saghala added the reciprocal extension, -an-, it gave the word the literal meaning "to notice or listen *to each other*"; hence the current meaning of the verb: "to meet." (The term *extension* denotes a suffix that adds to or modifies the meaning of the verb to which it is attached.)

Southern Cushitic languages normally are suffixing languages, although prefixes exist, too. Verbs in Southern Cushitic may add any of several Cushitic verb extensions to a verb root. A very common Southern Cushitic verb suffix is the extension *-t-, which gives the verb a sense of ongoing or extended action. When we find in a Taita Bantu language the verb -*barit*- 'to go visiting', this knowledge allows us to break that verb down into two parts: a root, *-bari-, from the Southern Cushitic verb *bariy- 'to travel'; plus *-t-, the Southern Cushitic verb extension connoting action that lasts for a period—that is, "to travel for an extended time"; hence "to go visiting." The morphological evidence—the fossil Southern Cushitic verb extension—in this instance reveals -*barit*- to be a borrowing from a Southern Cushitic language.

This word also contains two further markers of the direction of borrowing, both phonological in nature. The original sound *b of Proto-Bantu became *w* (or sometimes *v*) everywhere in Dawida and Saghala words. Except immediately following the consonant *m*, the consonant *b* simply should not exist in these two Bantu languages of the Taita Hills. So, in nearly every case, the presence of *b* is a dead giveaway of borrowing. Similarly, Proto-Bantu *t became *r* in the Dawida language, so the presence of a *t* in a Dawida word is also normally a marker of the borrowing of that word. In the case of -*barit*-, both *b* and *t* are present, confirming the morphological evidence that this verb is indeed a Southern Cushitic loanword.[13]

Once in a while one can even discover the presence of an otherwise unrecognized loanword because it contains the fossil remnant of an earlier suffix or other morphological marker or a noninherited sound. Saghala has *bigati* 'blood' where Dawida has *paga* for the same meaning. These two words appear clearly to be separate borrowings of the same underlying root word. We know they are borrowings because they start with the consonants *b* and *p*, both of which occur as first consonants *only* in word borrowings in the two languages. The Saghala word differs most notably in having an additional suffixed element, *-at-. Now *-at- is not a Bantu noun suffix, but it *is* an old Southern Cushitic noun suffix. We cannot be entirely certain that these words are from a Southern Cushitic language because the underlying root has not yet been found in any of the extant Southern Cushitic languages, but the fossil suffixation does seem to require this conclusion.

To sum up, we know that the words *paga* and *bigati* are borrowings because their first consonants, *p* and *b*, appear only in borrowed words. We believe they were probably adopted from Southern Cushitic languages because one of the two shapes contains an evident Southern Cushitic noun suffix. On the other hand, the difference in suffixation (in the *morphology*) tells us that two separate borrowings of the word took place. The difference in the first vowel in the two words requires, moreover, that the sources of the borrowings be two different languages, although conceivably fairly closely related ones.

Characterizing the Southern Cushitic Source Languages

How do we identify the past existence of particular languages? Our ability to attribute loanwords to a particular extinct language depends in the end on how much evidence the loanwords preserve of the histories of regular sound change that took place in that extinct tongue. An extinct language, like any other, underwent a history of phonological evolution out of its a protolanguage. But because that language is extinct, its words come down to us filtered through the medium of another, still-spoken language. The words that we have from the extinct Southern Cushitic languages of the Taita Hills region are preserved only indirectly, in the word borrowings in the Taita Bantu languages, Dawida and Saghala. But the word borrowings are so numerous, and our knowledge of PSC reconstruction so well advanced, that this evidence is enough to build a strong case.

To be able to interpret the evidence of sound-change history contained in the loanwords from an extinct language, we need first to know what the consonants and vowels of its protolanguage were. With that information at hand, we can then look for these sounds in the borrowed words and identify what sound changes affected them.

Proto–Southern Cushitic (PSC), the distant ancestor of the Taita Cushitic languages, and, of course, of all the rest of the Southern Cushitic languages, had at least thirty-nine consonants:[14]

*b	*d, *ɗ	*dz	*dl		*g	*gʷ	*ʕ
*p	*t	*ts	*tl		*k	*kʷ	*ʔ
*p'	*t'	*ts'	*tl'	*c'	*k'	*kʷ'	
*f	*s		*ɬ	*š	*x	*xʷ	*ħ, *h
*m	*n			*ɲ	*ŋ	*ŋʷ	
	*l, *r						
*w	*y						

Proto-Southern Cushitic also had six vowels,

*i	*ɨ	*u
*e		*o
	*a	

and a diphthong, *ay.[15] All the vowels as well as the diphthong could also occur long. We write the long vowels of Proto–Southern Cushitic as doubled vowels:

*ii	*ɨɨ	*uu
*ee		*oo
	*aa	
	*aay	

The two Taita Cushitic languages had different histories of regular sound change, with their different sound changes each modifying these inherited sets of Proto–Southern Cushitic consonants and vowels in different fashions. By discovering their varying sound-change rules, we can work out their relationships to each other and to the other, still-spoken Southern Cushitic languages. From that evidence we can in turn find out a good deal about the histories of peoples who spoke the Taita Cushitic languages.

In stating sound-change rules, linguists and linguist-historians often use a sort of shorthand. In this shorthand a slash(/) means "in the environment of," and a low horizontal line (_) denotes the location of the consonant or vowel affected by the rule. As we have already learned in this book, an asterisk identifies a reconstructed sound or root word. The acronym "PSC" of course refers to Proto–Southern Cushitic.

Consider the example of rule 3 in list 2 below, relating to Taita Cushitic B:

PSC *dl > r /V_.

This expression is to be read: "The Proto–Southern Cushitic consonant *dl became r (*dl > r) in Taita Cushitic B in the environment of a preceding vowel (/V_)." That is to say, original *dl became r in this extinct language when it followed a vowel. In this shorthand, the capital letter V is used when the sound change happens with any vowel; if a specific vowel environment causes a sound change, then of course these rules will give the specific vowel. Similarly, a capital C represents an unspecified consonant.

Another important sign, the pound sign (#), marks either the beginning or end of a word. Thus rule 6 of list 1,

PSC *g > k /#_

should be read, "The Proto–Southern Cushitic consonant *g became k (*g > k) in Taita Cushitic B at the beginning of words (/#_)."

Identifying Loanwords from Taita Cushitic A

At least nine sound-change rules are known to have characterized the extinct Taita Cushitic A language:

List 1. Taita Cushitic A Sound-Change Rules

1. PSC *d > r /#_ (i.e., at the beginning of a word);
2. PSC *CaCaC > CuCuC, when the three consonants are /r/ and PSC *t and *k (or *k^w) in any order;
3. PSC *tl' > t;
4. PSC *f > *p, *x > *k, *x^w > k^w;
5. PSC *p > *b, *t > *d, *k and *k' > g /V_;
6. PSC *g > k, *g^w > k^w /#_;
7. PSC *e and *o > a /_h and /_$\hbar$;
8. PSC *l > r /i_ and /u_;
9. PSC *d > r /V_

Interestingly, it is often possible to discover the historical order in which particular sound-change rules took place, even from such indirect evidence as loanwords. In this list, for example, rule 2, changing PSC *a to *u*, followed the shift of PSC *d to *r* by rule 1. The reason we know this is that rule 2 changed *a to *u* not just in words that originally had *r in the Proto–Southern Cushitic language, but also in words in which rule 1 had previously changed the original PSC *d to *r*. Similarly, rule 5 operated later than rule 4 because it affected not just the original PSC *p, *k and *k^w, but also the new *p, *k, and *k^w created by rule 4. The ordering of the rest of the rules is uncertain.

The Taita Cushitic A language also differed from Taita Cushitic B in preserving unchanged certain old Southern Cushitic consonants that did undergo sound changes in the Taita Cushitic B. We might call these "nonrules."

a. Notably, Saghala borrowings from Taita Cushitic A retained the Proto–Southern Cushitic consonant PSC *ł, which is pronounced like the consonant written *ll* of the Welsh language. Over the course of the twentieth century the Saghala speakers made a further sound change of their own, converting the borrowed *ł to *š. This is the sound represented by the letters *sh* in English words. This same consonant also turns up as š in Dawida borrowings from Taita Cushitic A. In contrast, in Taita Cushitic B loanwords in both Saghala and Dawida, *ł became *l, showing that this particular sound change took place in the Taita Cushitic B languages before the words were adopted into Saghala and Dawida.

b. A second such feature was the Taita Cushitic A preservation of Proto–PSC *a before the consonant *m. In Taita Cushitic B loanwords, PSC *a became *o when followed by *m.

c. Taita Cushitic B also changed some PSC *a to *i in first syllables of words when the following consonant was *b, *d, or *g, whereas the Taita Cushitic A language maintained original *a.

d. Taita Cushitic A loanwords also retained PSC *r when followed by the vowel *e. But in the loanwords from Taita Cushitic B, original Southern Cushitic *r became *l in this environment.

e. Taita Cushitic A appears to have retained the PSC consonant cluster *nk, while in Taita Cushitic B this cluster simplified to the nasal consonant *ŋ (this sign is pronounced like *ng* in the English word *singer*).

f. Finally, Taita Cushitic A also kept the PSC palatal consonants *š (English *sh*) and *c', which apparently became, respectively, *s and *ts in Taita Cushitic B.

Table 17 provides a sample of loanwords in Saghala that exhibit the Taita Cushitic A sound changes 1–9 or maintain the additional Taita Cushitic A characteristics a–f. A selection of loanwords from Dawida illustrating some of the same rules and characteristics appears in table 18. A further sample of Taita Cushitic A loanwords, consisting of items that occur today in both Dawida and Saghala, makes up table 19.

To help the reader sift this evidence, the first column in each table gives the stem of the borrowed word as it appears today in Saghala or Dawida, while the second column gives the old Southern Cushitic root word which was the source of the loan. The third and fourth columns then provide the phonological and morphological information that reveals the source languages of the loans. Column three identifies, in particular, the sound changes in the word that took place in the source language *before* the word was borrowed by Saghala or Dawida. Column four identifies the sound changes and morphological modifications that took place in Saghala or Dawida *after* the borrowing of the root. The sound-change rules appear as they do in list 1, written in the shorthand fashion already described preceding list 1. The same format is followed in tables 20–28 in this chapter.

Several abbreviations occur in the tables for the names of the protolanguages of the various earlier stages in Southern Cushitic history: PSC for Proto–Southern Cushitic; PR, Proto-Rift; and PWR, Proto–West Rift. To see where these periods fit in the overall scheme of Southern Cushitic history, the reader should refer back to the Southern Cushitic family tree in figure 12.

Table 17. Taita Cushitic A Sound Changes: Examples from Loanwords in Saghala

Loanword in Saghala	Southern Cushitic borrowed root	Taita Cushitic A sound change(s) *before* borrowing	Sound changes or morphology added in Saghala *after* borrowing
m-rigo 'log'	PR *dik'ayo 'thick stalk' (from PSC *ɗik'-)	rule 1: PSC *ɗ > r; also rule 5: PSC *k' > g /V_	noun class prefix *m-*
turuga 'wild dog'	PWR *takʷar- 'wild dog'	rule 2: PSC *a > u in /t_r_kʷ/; also rule 5: PSC *k > g /V_; metathesis of *kʷ and r	
-tag- 'to sell'	PR *tlaxʷ- 'to buy' (PSC 'to obtain')	rule 3: PSC *tl' > t; also rules 5, 6: PSC *x > *k, then *k > g /V_	
ki-tangara 'platform' (root + SCush *-r- noun suff.)	PR *tl'ak- 'platform' (pre-PR *tl'ank-)	rule 3: PSC *tl' > t; 'nonrule' (e): preserves pre-PR *nk	*nk > *ng* is Saghala rule
-tsub- 'to lick'	pre-PR *ts'if- 'to lick,' in PR *ts'if- 'tongue'	rules 4 and 5: PSC *f > *p, then *p > b /V_	
-kog-an- 'to meet'	PSC *kok- 'to listen, notice'	rule 5: PSC *k > g /V_	*-an-* reciprocal extension, i.e., 'notice each other,' hence 'meet'
-seget- 'to bleed' (root + PSC *-t verb extension)	PSC *sak'- 'blood'	rule 5: PSC *k' > *g /V_ (for *a > e change, see list 3 and table 23)	
-fwah- 'to have diarrhoea'	PSC *gʷah- 'to flow out (of bodily fluids)'	rule 6: PSC *gʷ > *kʷ /#_ (beginning of word)	*kʷ > *fw* is a regular Saghala sound change

(continued)

Table 17 *(continued)*

Loanword in Saghala	Southern Cushitic borrowed root	Taita Cushitic A sound change(s) *before* borrowing	Sound changes or morphology added in Saghala *after* borrowing
-kakah- 'to gnaw' (SCush reduplication)	PSC *k'eħ- 'to bite'	rule 7: PSC *e and *o > a /_ħ	
-ah- 'to pick fruit'	PWR *oh- 'to grasp' (PSC *ʔoh- 'to put')	rule 7: PSC *e and *o > a/_h	
-kurum-u- 'to be stunned'	Rift: Kw'adza *kul- 'to dream,' + -m-, the SCush stative verb extension	rule 8: PSC *l > r /u_	-u- is Saghala passive extension
-ɬah- 'to hurt'	PSC *ɬahaħ- 'to hurt'	'nonrule' (a): preserves PSC ɬ (> š in recent Saghala	
-kušu- 'to pluck (fowl)'	PSC *xiɬ- 'to peel, scrape off'	rule 3: PSC *i > *u /x_C; also *x > *k: Taita Cushitic A rule 4); Taita Cushitic A 'nonrule' (f): *ɬ > ɬ (> š)	
sambe 'kudu'	Rift: Kw'adza semaʔayo (from root *samaʔ- or *samaʕ-)	'nonrule' (b): preserves *a before *m	

Identifying Loanwords from Taita Cushitic B

Taita Cushitic B stands out as a quite distinct language from Taita Cushitic A. A different set of sound changes, often running counter to those of Taita Cushitic A, characterized its loanwords in Saghala and Dawida. PSC *x became *h*, for example, and *f remained *f* in Taita Cushitic B, instead of becoming *k* and *p*, as they did in Taita Cushitic A; and the nasal cluster *nk simplified to *ŋ in Taita Cushitic B, while becoming *ng* in Taita Cushitic A. To carry this theme further, both the Taita Cushitic languages change certain PSC *r to *l*, but in sharply contrasting environments. In

Taita Cushitic A *r became *l* when directly *followed* by a PSC high vowel *i or *u, while in Taita Cushitic B *r became *l* when it directly *preceded* a PSC front vowel *i or *e. At least thirteen sound-change rules overall appear to have been specific to Taita Cushitic B.

List 2. Taita Cushitic B Sound-Change Rules

1. PSC *tl' > dl, *ɫ > l; rules (2) and (3) followed this sound change:
2. *dl > d /#_;
3. *dl > r /V_;
4. PSC *u > o /#C_C, when 1st C is k, k', or g and 2nd C is l, r, or t.
5. *ɗ > d;
6. PSC *x > h, *x^w > hw;
7. PSC *o > u and *a > o /_m;
8. PSC *e > i /_m, /_n, or /_ŋ;
9. PSC *a > i /#C_C, where 2nd C is *b, *d, or *g
10. PSC *r > l /_e or /_i;
11. PSC *mp > m, *nk, *nk^w, *nk', and *nk$^{w'}$ > ŋ;
12. PSC palatal consonants (š, č') > alveolar sounds (s, ts);
13. PSC *ħ > Ø /#Ce_-# (Ø = zero, i.e., *ħ was deleted when it was the last consonant of a stem).

The first three sound changes in list 2 form a sequence. In addition, rule 4 followed rule 3, because this rule changed the vowel *u to o not just before PSC *r, but also before an r that had been created from *dl by rule 3. The ordering of the remainder of the shifts is not yet known.

Taita Cushitic B also maintained several older Southern Cushitic consonants that had undergone sound changes in Taita Cushitic A. These "nonrules" included the following:

a. PSC *d stayed *d /V_ (in Taita Cushitic A *d > r /V_ by Taita Cushitic A rule 9);
b. PSC *g and *g^w stayed *g and *g^w (in Taita Cushitic A loans, they became *k and *k^w by Taita Cushitic A rule 6);
c. PSC *f stayed f (in contrast to Taita Cushitic A sound change rule 4);
d. PSC *p, *t, *k, *k^w, *k', and *k$^{w'}$ stayed *p, *t, *k, *k^w, and *k', *k$^{w'}$ /V_ (in contrast to Taita Cushitic A sound change rule 5);
e. PSC *l stayed l /i_ (in contrast to Taita Cushitic A sound change rule 8);
f. PSC *e stayed e /_ħ (in contrast to Taita Cushitic A sound change rule 7).

A selection of the Taita Cushitic B loanwords in Saghala appears in table 20. Table 21 presents a further selection of such loanwords in Dawida, and table 22 presents a sample of those occurring today in both Dawida and Saghala.

Table 18. Taita Cushitic A Sound Changes:
Examples from Loanwords in Dawida

Loanword in Dawida	Southern Cushitic borrowed root	Taita Cushitic A sound change(s) *before* borrowing	Sound changes or morphology added in Dawida *after* borrowing
ki-gutu 'hip'	PSC *kutl'- 'buttocks' (Iraqw *kutl-ʔama*, stem + SCush *-ama noun suff.)	rule 3: PSC *tl' > *t	*ki-* noun class prefix; *k > g is a Dawida sound change (Dahl's Law)
kwaru 'hare'	PR *kʷaʕ- 'hare' (pre-PR *xʷaʕ-, + SCush *-r- noun suff.)	rule 4: PSC *xʷ > *kʷ	
-pugurus- 'to turn over'	PSC *birik'- 'to turn round,' + SCush *-s- tr. suff.	rule 5: PSC *k' > g /V_	*b > p
i-kara 'desert'	PSC *gara 'wilderness'	rule 6: PSC *g > k /#_	*i-* noun class prefix
m-bama 'boil'	Dahalo *baʔama* 'scab'	'nonrule' (b): preserves PSC *a before *m	*m-* Dawida noun class prefix
paga 'blood'	(not known in extant Southern Cushitic languages)	'nonrule' (c): preserves *a as *a* (by Taita Cushitic B rule 9, *a > *i, in this root in table 4)	
-cw- 'to circumcise'	Dahalo *t'uʕ-* 'to pluck, remove' (*c'uʕ-)	'nonrule' (f): preserves PSC *c' as Dawida *c*	

The Relationships of Taita Cushitic A and Taita Cushitic B

Having identified the characteristic sound changes of the two extinct languages, we now address two key issues for turning the linguistic evidence into history—namely,

Table 19. Taita Cushitic A Sound Changes:
Examples from Loanwords in Both Saghala and Dawida

Loanword in Saghala and Dawida	Southern Cushitic borrowed root	Taita Cushitic A sound change(s) *before* borrowing	Sound changes or morphology added in Saghala or Dawida *after* borrowing
*n-dana 'bow'	PR *tl'an- 'arrows'	rule 3: PSC *tl' > *t	*n-* noun class prefix; *n- + -t > nd* in Dawida, Saghala
*-tag-an-y- 'to cut'	PSC *tl'ak'- 'to cut'	rule 3: PSC *tl' > *t; rule 5: PSC *k' > g /V_	*-an-y-* are Saghala and Dawida verb extensions
*-šabwa 'wide, broad'	PSC *ɬaf- 'to grow'	rules 4 and 5: PSC *f > *p, then *p > b /V_; 'nonrule' (f): *ɬ > ɬ (> š)	
*lagaya 'chest'	PSC *lax- or *laxʷ- 'lung' + SCush *-aya noun suff.	rules 4 and 5: PSC *x or *xʷ > k, then *k > g	
*fwandi 'ram'	PR *gʷand- 'ram'	rule 6: PSC *gʷ > kʷ /#_	*kw > fw:* early Saghala sound change
*-kur- 'to meet'	PSC *kul- 'to meet'	rule 8: PSC *l > r /u_	
*are 'python'	proto-East Rift *ʔarar- (PR *ʔar-)	'nonrule' (d): preserves *r before *e	

determining the relationships of the extinct Taita Cushitic A and B languages to the rest of Southern Cushitic *and* the relationship of the two with each other.

In historical linguistics the crucial evidence for placing a language in a particular subgroup of languages is its sharing of unique innovations with other languages of that group. To understand why this kind of evidence is determinative, we need to think back about how linguistic evolution proceeds. Over the course of time, every living, spoken language develops numerous innovations in lexicon (words and their meanings), sounds (phonology), morphology, and syntax (sentence and

Table 20. Taita Cushitic B Sound Changes: Examples from Loanwords in Saghala

Loanword in Saghala	Southern Cushitic borrowed root	Taita Cushitic B sound change(s) *before* borrowing	Sound changes or morphology added in Saghala *after* borrowing
-ruf-uk- 'to thicken (porridge)'	PSC *ɬuf- 'to swell'	rule 1: PSC *ɬ > l; also 'nonrule' a: PSC *f > f	*l > r; -uk- is Dawida intr. verb extension
dumu 'heights'	Rift: Iraqw *tloma* 'mountain' (PSC *tl'oma 'swelling, raised area')	rule 2: PSC *tl' > d /#_; also rule 7: PSC *o > u /_m	
-gor- 'to talk, discuss, advise'	PSC *gur- 'to advise'	rule 4: PSC *u > o /g_r	
dah- 'to knock'	PSC *ɗaħ- 'to knock'	rule 5: PSC *ɗ > d	
-kup-ul- 'to pour out'	Rift: Iraqw *qip-* 'to pour' (< *k'ip-)	*p > *p by Taita Cushitic B 'non-rule' (d)	-ul- is Saghala verb extension
hwaru 'hare'	*xʷaʕar- 'hare' (see table 17 for more on this word)	rule 6: PSC *xʷ > hw	
sahala 'gall'	PSC *sax- 'gall,' + SCush *-l- n. suff.	rule 6: PSC *x > h	
sombe 'fly-whisk' (fly-whisk is made from animal's tail)	PSC *šam- 'tail'	rule 7: PSC *a > o /_m (for *m > *mb, see List 3, rule 5)	
doma 'eland'	PR *dama 'eland' (PSC *ɗooɗaama)	rule 7: PSC *a > o /_m	
biɣati 'blood'	SCush *-at- noun suff.	rule 9: PSC *a >i /#C_g	*g > ɣ

(continued)

Table 20 *(continued)*

Loanword in Saghala	Southern Cushitic borrowed root	Taita Cushitic B sound change(s) *before* borrowing	Sound changes or morphology added in Saghala *after* borrowing
n-gwale 'hartebeest'	W. Rift *gʷaraʕ- 'hartebeest'	rule 10: PSC *r > l /_e or /_i	
tele 'ring'	PSC *teer- 'ring'	rule 10: PSC *r > l /_e or /_i	
tamahi 'oryx'	Dahalo *tampakkano* 'antelope sp.' (*tampax- + PSC *-an- noun suff.)	rule 11: PSC *mp > m; also rule 4: PSC *x > h	
li-fusa 'feather'	PSC *punc'- 'to pluck (feather)'	rule 12: PSC *c' > ts	*li*- noun class prefix; *pu > *fu* and *nts > *s* are Saghala sound changes after borrowing
-de- 'to do'	PR *tl'eħ- 'to do'	rule 13: PSC *ħ > Ø /#Ce_-#; also rules 1 and 2: PSC *tl' > *dl > *d /#_	
gudi 'penis'	PSC *gɨd- 'penis'	'nonrule' (a): PSC *d stayed d /V_; 'nonrule' (b): PSC *g > g /#_	
-baf-uk- 'to explode'	PSC *baaf- 'to splatter'	'nonrule' (c): PSC *f stayed f	*-uk-* is Saghala intr. extension
ki-patsi 'breakfast'	PR *pats- 'daylight'	'nonrule' (d): PSC *p stayed p	*ki*- noun class prefix
-uk- 'to rise'	PSC *ʔuk'- 'to rise'	'nonrule' (d): PSC *k' stayed *k'	*k' > *k*
n-doli 'gazelle sp.'	PSC *ʔaadool- 'sp. of antelope'	'nonrule' (e): PSC *l stayed *l /_i	*n*- noun class prefix
gweha 'jackal'	Rift root *gʷeħ- 'jackal' seen in Burunge *gweħera* (root + SCush *-r- noun suff.)	'nonrule' (f): PSC *e stayed e /_ħ; also 'nonrule' (b): PSC *gʷ stayed gʷ	

Table 21. Taita Cushitic B Sound Changes: Examples from Loanwords in Dawida

Loanword in Dawida	Southern Cushitic borrowed root	Taita Cushitic B sound change(s) *before* borrowing	Sound changes or morphology added in Dawida *after* borrowing
dime 'day'	PR *tlehem- 'day'	rules 1 and 2: PSC *tl' > *dl > d; also rule 8: PSC *e > i /_m	
i-ridia 'hair' (root + PSC *-iya noun suff.	PSC *rad- 'feathers'	rule 9: PSC *a > i /#C_d; 'nonrule' (a): PSC *d stays d /V_	Dawida noun class prefix *i-*
-se- 'to sit, stay'	PSC *seħ- 'to sleep, rest'	rule 13: PSC *ħ > Ø /#Ce_-#	
-ger- 'to talk'	Rift: Iraqw *gehar-* 'to announce'	'nonrule' (b): PSC *g stayed g /#_	

Table 22. Taita Cushitic B Sound Changes: Examples from Loanwords in Both Saghala and Dawida

Loanword in Saghala and Dawida	Southern Cushitic borrowed root	Taita Cushitic B sound change(s) *before* borrowing	Sound changes or morphology added in Saghala or Dawida *after* borrowing
-kot- 'to dig'	PSC *k'ut- 'to dig'	rule 4: PSC *u > o /k'_t; 'nonrule' (d): PSC *t stayed t /V_	
-tim- 'to try'	PSC *tem- 'to try'	rule 8: PSC *e > i /_m	
gafa 'beard'	PSC *gamfa 'chin'	'nonrule' (b): PSC *g stayed g; also 'nonrule' (c): PSC *f stayed f	*mf > f

phrase structure). When a language begins to diverge into separate daughter languages, many of the innovations that arose before the divergence will persist in use in those daughters. The persistence of these shared common developments reveals a period of common ancestry of the daughter languages, a period when they were still one language spoken by one society. That shared period of common ancestry is what defines them as members of a particular genetically related group of languages.

The loanwords from the Taita Cushitic A and Taita Cushitic B languages in Saghala and Dawida reveal a number of diagnostic innovations allowing us to fit these two languages into the Southern Cushitic family tree. The most important of these innovations are in phonology (see lists 3 and 4 and tables 23–25), but innovations in the meanings and morphology of particular words provide additional evidence on the relationship of these two extinct languages.[16]

Taita Cushitic A and Taita Cushitic B had many differences in their sound-change histories, as lists 1 and 2 reveal. Nevertheless, there are several pieces of evidence indicating that they most probably formed a subgroup of their own. Uniquely in Southern Cushitic, Taita Cushitic A and Taita Cushitic B shared a sound-change innovation deleting the labial element in any of the Southern Cushitic labiovelar consonants, $*g^w$, $*k^w$, $*x^w$, or $*k^{w'}$, when it was not the first consonant in a word. In those cases Proto–Southern Cushitic $*g^w$ became simple $*g$, $*k^w$ became $*k$, $*x^w$ became $*x$, and $*k^{w'}$ became $*k'$ (or $*k$) in both Taita Cushitic A and Taita Cushitic B. Also, both Taita Cushitic A and Taita Cushitic B apparently changed PSC $*a$ to $*e$ when it preceded the PSC consonant $*k'$; and they changed the PSC vowel $*i$ to $*u$ when it followed a $*k$, $*k'$, or $*x$. The two extinct languages both also changed all PSC $*i$ to $*u$; but this sound change took place independently elsewhere in Southern Cushitic, so it does not carry the same diagnostic weight. Also, PSC $*m$ became Taita Cushitic $*mb$ in one restricted environment.

List 3 presents "shorthand" versions of these shared sound-change rules:

List 3. Taita Cushitic Shared Sound-Change Innovations

1. PSC $*C^w$ > Taita Cushitic $*C$ /V_;
2. PSC $*a$ > Taita Cushitic $*e$ /#C__(n)k'-;
3. PSC $*i$ > Taita Cushitic $*u$ /k_C, /k'_C, and /x_C;
4. PSC $*i$ > Taita Cushitic $*u$;
5. PSC $*m$ > Taita Cushitic $*mb$ /#sV_V# and /#šV_V#

Table 23 offers a selection of loanwords exemplifying these shared sound-change rules and showing that the rules appear in loanwords from both Taita Cushitic A and Taita Cushitic B in Saghala and in Dawida.

In addition, other shared sound-change innovations common to Taita Cushitic A and Taita Cushitic B show that their closest relationships were to the Rift branch

Table 23. Shared Sound-Change Innovations of Taita Cushitic: Examples in Loanwords in Saghala and Dawida

Loanword in Saghala or Dawida	Southern Cushitic borrowed root	Shared Taita Cushitic A and B sound change(s)	Sound changes or morphology added in Saghala or Dawida *after* borrowing
turuga 'wild dog' (table 17)	PWR *takʷar- 'wild dog'	rule 1: PSC *kʷ > *k /V_ (> *g by Taita Cushitic A rule 5)	
-tag- 'to sell' (table 17)	PR *tlaxʷ- 'to buy' (PSC 'to obtain')	rule 1: PSC *kʷ > *k /V_ (> *g by Taita Cushitic A rule 5)	
-neŋ-eš- 'to penetrate' (table 21)	PSC *ɲankʷ'-	rule 2: *a > *e /#C__(n)k'; also rule 1: PSC *kʷ' > *k /V_ (*nk > *ŋ: Taita Cushitic B rule 11)	
-seget- 'to bleed' (table 17)	PSC *sak'- 'blood'	rule 2: PSC *a > *e /#C__(n)k' (*k' > *g: Taita Cushitic A rule 5)	
-kup-ul- 'to pour out' (table 17)	Rift: Iraqw *qip- (from earlier *k'ip-)	rule 3: PSC *i > *u /K_C; *p > *p by Taita Cushitic B 'nonrule' (d)	*-ul-* is Saghala verb extension
-kušu- 'to pluck (fowl)' (table 17)	PSC *xiɬ- 'to peel, scrape off'	rule 3: PSC *i > *u /K_C (x > *k: Taita Cushitic A rule 4; Taita Cushitic A 'nonrule' (f): *ɬ > ɬ > š)	

(continued)

Table 23 *(continued)*

Loanword in Saghala or Dawida	Southern Cushitic borrowed root	Shared Taita Cushitic A and B sound change(s)	Sound changes or morphology added in Saghala or Dawida *after* borrowing
-pugurus- 'to turn over' (table 18)	PSC *bɨrɨk'- 'to turn round,' plus SCush *-s- tr. suff.	rule 4: PSC *ɨ > *u; metathesis of *g* and *r* (*k' > *g: Taita Cushitic A rule 5)	
gudi 'penis' (table 20)	PSC *gɨd- 'penis'	rule 4: PSC *ɨ > *u; *d > *d by Taita Cushitic B 'non-rule' (a)	
sambe 'kudu' (table 17)	Rift: Kw'adza sema?ayo 'kudu' (root *sama?- or *samaʕ-)	rule 5: PSC *m > mb /#sV_V#; *a > *a: Taita Cushitic A 'nonrule' (b)	
sombe 'fly-whisk' (table 20)	PSC *šam- 'tail'	rule 5: PSC *m > mb /#sV_V# (PSC *a > *o /_m: Taita Cushitic B rule 7)	

of Southern Cushitic. The Taita Cushitic A and Taita Cushitic B loanword sets both reveal a number of sound-change innovations that are specifically characteristic of the languages of the Rift branch of Southern Cushitic. List 4 lays out the sound changes of this kind so far identified. Table 24 provides examples of the changes in particular loanwords.

List 4. Sound Changes in Taita Cushitic Diagnostic of Rift Southern Cushitic Affiliations

1. PSC *ŋ (the sound of *ng* in English *singer*) > Proto-Rift (PR) *ng /V_ (this consonant stayed *ŋ* in the Mbuguan branch but became *n* in the Dahaloan branch);
2. PSC *e > PR *o /#ʕ_n or /#ʕ_ŋ ([ʕ] is a pharyngeal consonant, articulated far back in the throat);
3. PSC *ʔV > Ø /#__CVC- in PR ([ʔ] is called a glottal stop; initial syllables in PSC words beginning with the glottal stop consonant *ʔ were lost in Proto-Rift)

4. PSC $*C_1V > \emptyset /\#\_\_C_1VCV$ in PR (the first syllable of PSC words was lost in 3-syllable or longer words *if* the first two consonants were identical);
5. PSC $*h > \emptyset$ /CV_VC in PR ($*h$ was deleted when it was the middle consonant in a three-consonant word);
6. PSC $*t' > PR$ ts' (this is actually an earlier sound change of the Proto-Rift-Mbugu period, which preceded the Proto-Rift era: see figures 11 and 12).

The common ancestor of Taita Cushitic A and Taita Cushitic B appears, however, to have diverged from the line of descent leading to Proto-Rift *before* the full evolution of the Proto-Rift language had run its course (fig. 13). This history is shown by the lack of certain diagnostic Rift sound-change rules in the Taita Cushitic A and Taita Cushitic B loanwords. Both languages, for example, retained the Proto-Cushitic consonant $*c'$ apparently unchanged in all positions in a word; in contrast, in Proto-Rift this consonant underwent a sound change to $*s$ in the middle of words, although it stayed $*c'$ at the beginning of words. In addition, Taita Cushitic A and Taita Cushitic B did not share Proto-Rift's simplification of $*mp$ and $*nk$ to $*p$ and $*k$, respectively. Taita Cushitic A retained these nasal clusters unchanged; Taita Cushitic B changed them in a quite distinct direction: $*mp > m$ and $*nk > ŋ$.

Examples of loanwords lacking these Proto-Rift sound changes appear in Table 25.

To sum up, the Taita Cushitic A and Taita Cushitic B languages, because of their divergent sound-change histories, must have long been separate languages before they came into contact with the Bantu languages, Saghala and Dawida. Nonetheless, the evidence of shared sound changes in the two (list 3 and table 23) best fits the conclusion that they formed one subgroup of Southern Cushitic: they were descendants of an intermediate protolanguage, Proto–Taita Cushitic. Their closest relationship was to the Rift branch; this conclusion is required by their sharing in a number of the diagnostic sound-change innovations of the Rift branch (list 4 and table 24). But they diverged from the Rift line of descent sometime before the Proto-Rift, as their lack of some of the diagnostic Rift sound changes indicates.

An expanded family tree of the Southern Cushitic languages (see fig. 13) shows how we can integrate these findings into our previous family tree (see fig. 12) to produce a new, more encompassing dendogram. In keeping with the linguistic evidence for the relationships of Taita Cushitic A and Taita Cushitic B to each other and to other Southern Cushitic languages, this tree groups Taita Cushitic A and Taita Cushitic B as daughter languages of Proto-Taita Cushitic, and it combines the Taita Cushitic and Rift groups as two sister subbranches in an expanded "Taita Cushitic-Rift" branch.

Again in figure 13, as in figures 11 and 12, the names of extant Southern Cushitic languages appear in boldface; the names of extinct branches and languages, in italics; and the names of recently extinct languages, in italicized boldface.

Figure 13. Expanded Family Tree of Southern Cushitic

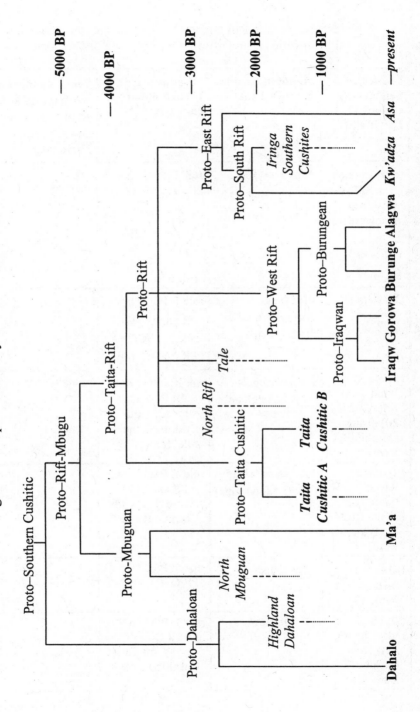

Table 24. Diagnostic Rift Branch Sound-Change Innovations: Taita Cushitic Loanwords in either Saghala or Dawida

Loanword in Saghala (S) and/or Dawida (D)	Southern Cushitic borrowed root	Diagnostic Rift branch sound change(s)	Sound changes or morphology added in Saghala or Dawida *after* borrowing
(S) m-riginga 'root' (Taita Cushitic A loanword)	*ɗik'iŋa < PSC *ɗik'- 'stalk,' plus PSC *-ŋ noun suff.	rule 1: PSC *ŋ > PR *ng /V_V; PSC *ɗ > r: Taita Cushitic A rule 1, PSC *k' > g /V_: Taita Cushitic A rule 5	
(S), (D) *-onge- 'to get drunk'	PR *ʕong- 'to get drunk' (PSC *ʕeŋ-)	rule 1: PSC *ŋ > PR *ng /V_V; rule 2: PSC *e > PR *o /#ʕ_n/ŋ	
(S) n-doli 'kind of gazelle' (table 20) (Taita Cushitic B loanword)	PSC *ʔaadool- 'sp. of antelope'	rule 3: PSC *ʔVV > PR Ø /#_CVC-; *d > *d: Taita Cushitic B 'non-rule' (a)	*n-* noun class prefix
(S) doma 'eland' (table 20) (Taita Cushitic B loanword)	PR *dama 'eland' (PSC *ɗooɗaama)	rule 4: PSC *C_1V > PR Ø /#_C_1VC-; *a > o /_m: Taita Cushitic B rule 7	
(S) -šah- 'to hurt' (table 17)	PSC *ɬahaħ- 'to hurt'	rule 5: PSC *h > PR Ø /CV_VC	
(D) dime 'day' (table 21) (Taita Cushitic B loanword)	PR *tlehem- 'day'	rule 5: PSC *h > PR Ø /CV_VC; *e > i /_m: Taita Cushitic B rule 8	

(continued)

Table 24 *(continued)*

Loanword in Saghala (S) and/or Dawida (D)	Southern Cushitic borrowed root	Diagnostic Rift branch sound change(s)	Sound changes or morphology added in Saghala or Dawida *after* borrowing
(D) -ger- 'to talk' (table 21)	Rift: Iraqw *gehar-* 'to announce'	rule 5: PSC *h > PR Ø /CV_VC	
(S) -hots- 'to rub, scrub, polish'	Dahalo *ɦoot'-* 'to scratch' (PSC *ɦoot'-)	rule 6: PSC *t' > *ts'	*ts' > *ts*

Table 25. Rift-Branch Sound Changes Lacking in Taita Cushitic: Examples from Loanwords in Saghala and Dawida

Loanword in Saghala (S) and/or Dawida (D)	Southern Cushitic borrowed root	Missing diagnostic Rift branch sound change(s)	Sound changes or morphology added in Saghala or Dawida *after* borrowing
(S) i-ɣace 'deserted site' (Taita Cushitic A loanword)	PSC *xanc'- 'deserted site'	PSC *c' > PR *s /Vn_; PSC *c' as *c: Taita Cushitic A 'nonrule' (f)	*nc > c is Saghala rule
(D) li-fusa 'feather' (table 20) (Taita Cushitic B loanword)	PSC *punc'- 'to pluck (feather)'	PSC *c' > PR *s /Vn_; preservation of PSC *nc' as *nc; *nc > *nts by Taita Cushitic B rule 12)	*pu- > *fu-*; *nts > *s* is Dabida rule
(S) ki-tangara 'platform' (table 17) (Taita Cushitic A loanword)	PR *tl'ak- 'platform' < pre-PR *tl'ank-)	rule 3: PSC *tl' > t; Taita Cushitic A 'non-rule' (e): pre-PR *nk > *nk	*nk > *ng* in Saghala

(continued)

Table 25 *(continued)*

Loanword in Saghala (S) and/or Dawida (D)	Southern Cushitic borrowed root	Missing diagnostic Rift branch sound change(s)	Sound changes or morphology added in Saghala or Dawida *after* borrowing
(D) tamahi 'oryx' (table 20) (Taita Cushitic B loanword)	Dahalo *tampakk-ano* 'sp. of antelope'	rule 3: pre-PR *mp > m; Taita Cushitic B rule 11; also Taita Cushitic B rule 4: PSC *x > h	
(D) -neŋ-eš- 'to penetrate' (table 21) (Taita Cushitic B loanword)	PSC *ɲankʷ'-	rule 1: PSC *kʷ' > *k /V_; rule 2: *a > *e /#C__(n)k'; *nk > *ŋ: Taita Cushitic B rule 11)	

CONSTRUCTING A HISTORICAL NARRATIVE

Locating the Early Taita Cushitic

Fitting the Taita Cushitic languages into the Southern Cushitic tree of language descent allows us to begin uncovering the broad processes of history in the Taita Cushitic societies. In previous studies it was clear that the spreading out of Rift Southern Cushitic communities coincided in most areas with the expansion of the Oldishi varieties of the "Savanna Pastoral Neolithic" across southern Kenya and northern Tanzania, beginning in the second millennium BCE and continuing into the first millennium BCE. The areas across which Oldishi sites are found are exactly the areas where the language evidence identifies the presence of earlier Rift peoples of the last 1,500 years BCE, and the linguistic reconstruction early Rift Southern Cushitic culture and economy closely fits the observed features of Oldishi culture and economy.[17]

The Taita Cushitic placement on the family tree widens our perspective on this history. It shows that the beginning of the spreading out of Southern Cushites across southern Kenya and northern Tanzania took place in the Proto-Taita Cushitic-Rift period, one stage earlier in time than the Proto-Rift era, conceivably in the very early second millennium BCE. The eventual location of the Taita Cushites in and around the Taita Hills, an area to the immediate east of the known Rift Southern Cushitic regions, suggests that their ancestors arose out of an early eastward expansion away from the Rift Valley region of central southern Kenya. Their original lands may have lain in the Kaputie plains north of Kilimanjaro and west of the Taita Hills.

Society and Economy among the Early Taita Cushites

The usual sources for revealing the cultures and economies of earlier societies, of course, are reconstructed word histories (see chapter 2). In the case of the Taita Cushitic peoples, however, these resources are available to us only indirectly, in the form of loanwords that happened to have been borrowed into the Saghala and Dawida languages. Though unevenly distributed across the cultural vocabulary, these loanwords nevertheless shed light on a variety of elements of life and livelihood anciently present in the Taita Cushitic societies. Tables 26–28 provide a partial list of the salient loanwords.

The indications of the borrowed words in Saghala and Dawida favor the conclusion that the Taita Cushitic A speakers were in fact the pastoral farming Mbisha society remembered in the historical traditions of the Taita Hills, while the Taita Cushitic B speakers were the gatherer-hunter "Asi" people. Taita Cushitic A words for "butter" and for the platform for keeping watch over the fields, among others, occur in Saghala. A term, "ram," in both Dawida and Saghala is also of Taita Cushitic A origin (table 26). In contrast, the shared Saghala and Dawida verb for "to hunt" is a Taita Cushitic B loanword (table 27). Even more notably, Saghala acquired at least three of its terms for large antelope species from the Taita Cushitic B language (see table 31), in contrast to a single large-animal term adopted from Taita Cushitic A (see table 30). The key indicator among the four is the loanword from the Taita Cushitic B language specifically distinguishing the female kudu from the male. The employing of separate terms for the female and the male of large game animals is common among the East African gatherer-hunter peoples, but not among cultivators and herders. Five further Southern Cushitic loanwords indicative of cultivation or herding—for "weeding," "porridge," "ram," and "he-goat" in Saghala, and for "ox" in Dawida—lack diagnostic markers of which Taita Cushitic language they came from, so their evidence is not determinative one way or the other.

The borrowed culture vocabulary also reveals that the pastoral farming Mbisha society apparently followed the ancient Cushitic practice of circumcising young men (tables 26 and 28), a custom that does leave direct material evidence in the archaeology.[18] Whether the Asi people, the proposed speakers of Taita Cushitic B, had this practice is unclear.

Encounters with New Populations

About a thousand years ago both Taita Cushitic societies began to face the challenge of new groups of settlers moving into their lands.[19] The ancestral Saghala com-

Table 26. Culture and Economy: Taita Cushitic A

Loanword in Saghala (S) and/or Dawida (D)	Southern Cushitic source	Taita Cushitic A sound change(s) *before* borrowing	Sound changes or morphology added in Saghala or Dawida *after* borrowing
(S) tarašu 'butter'	Kw'adza *tala?eto* 'fat': root *tara?-	root + SCush *-š pl. suff; PSC *š as *š*: Taita Cushitic A 'nonrule' (a)	
(S,D) *fwandi 'ram'	PR *gʷand- 'ram'	Taita Cushitic A rule 7: PSC *gʷ > kʷ /#_	*kw > *fw*
(S) ki-tangara 'platform [for watching and protecting fields]"	See table 17	See table 17	
(S) tib- 'to plant'	Rift: Iraw *ti?ip-* 'to bury"	Taita Cushitic A rules 4, 5	
(S,D) *n-dana 'bow' (*-tana)	PR *tl'an- 'arrows'	Taita Cushitic A rule 3: PSC *tl' > *t	n- noun class prefix; *n- + -t > *nd* in Dawida, Saghala
(D) -cw- 'to circumcise'	Dahalo *t'uʕ-* 'to pluck, remove' (*c'uʕ-)	Taita Cushitic A 'nonrule' (f): PSC *c' > c	

munities may have been the earliest to arrive, possibly coming from the coastal belt. The ancestral speakers of Dawida moved into the region, it can be proposed, from the Pare Mountains region to the west (see map 4). These encounters led to a period of multilingualism, probably lasting several centuries, in which large numbers of loanwords passed from the Taita Cushitic languages into Saghala and Dawida. The oral traditions suggest that the lands of the pastoralist Mbisha people included the plains all about the Taita region. The burial cairns found in these areas, which are an archaic feature of Cushitic cultures, are thus likely to have been the work of the Mbisha. The Asi people may have lived in the plains also and coexisted with Mbisha herders and cultivators by focusing their activities on the wild resources of those

Table 27. Culture and Economy: Taita Cushitic B

Loanword in Saghala (S) and/or Dawida (D)	Southern Cushitic source	Taita Cushitic B sound change(s) before borrowing	Sound changes or morphology added in Saghala or Dawida after borrowing
(S) ma-hado 'calabash seeds'	*had-, seen in Ma'a *i-haleto* 'round calabash' (stem + SCush *-t- noun suff.)	Taita Cushitic B 'nonrule' (a): PSC *d > *d /V_	*ma-* noun class prefix (pl.)
(S,D) *-diβ- 'to hunt'	PSC *dab- 'to hunt'	Taita Cushitic B rule 9: PSC *a > *i /#C_b	

areas, as gatherer-hunters did in the past in other parts of East Africa. Alternatively, the Asi communities may have been highland foragers in the Taita Hills. If they were the predecessors of the early Dawida and Saghala speakers in the higher-elevation areas, it would go far in explaining the depth of penetration of Taita Cushitic B loanwords into the Dawida and Saghala lexicons.

Applying the categorizations of word borrowing, as presented in chapters 2 and 4, allows one to build a broad understanding of how this history of cross-cultural encounter unfolded. The Taita Cushitic loanwords in Saghala and Dawida divide up into at least four separate sets, according to which language borrowed the words and which Taita Cushitic language the words came from. Tables 29–33 present the analytically salient portions of this evidence. The fourth column in each table defines the kind of borrowing, whether in "core" vocabulary (items on the Swadesh one-hundred-word list), "peripheral basic" vocabulary, or large-animal terminology. To keep the tables to manageable size, only a small selection of peripheral basic items are cited, and borrowed terms in the culture lexicon are left out.

When we examine the evidence in these tables, in every case—whether Taita Cushitic A loanwords in Saghala or Dawida, or Taita Cushitic B loanwords in Saghala or Dawida—we find a particular borrowing pattern. The borrowings include either two or three loanwords in the Swadesh one-hundred-meaning list of core vocabulary, the part of the lexicon most highly resistant to word borrowing.[20] In addition, the loanword sets contain numerous borrowings in the peripheral basic vocabulary and usually borrowed terms for large animals. This pattern of borrowing all across the lexicon, but with only a very few items in core vocabulary, might remain

Table 28. Culture and Economy: Taita Cushitic A *or* Taita Cushitic B

Loanword in Saghala (S) and/or Dawida (D)	Southern Cushitic source	Diagnostic sound change(s)	Sound changes or morphology added in Saghala or Dawida *after* borrowing
(S) -al- 'to weed'	PSC *ʔaal- 'to sift, clean'		
(S) m-swara 'porridge'	PR *sor- 'prepared grain'		*m-* noun class prefix
(S) bauru 'ram'	Rift: Burunge *baʔuru* 'oryx' (PSC *babaʔ- 'sp. of antelope')	PR rule 4: PSC *C_1V > PR Ø /#__C_1VC-; addition of *-uru noun suff.	
(S) jigau 'he-goat'	PSC *-awu noun suff. (-*au*); root not identified as yet in SCush		
(D) m-biria 'ox'	PSC *-iya noun suff. (-*ia*); root not identified as yet in SCush		
(S) -ciɣ- 'to circum-cise'	Verb root underly-ing PR *tsʼig- 'band of circum-cised youths' (also PSC *tsʼig-?)	Proposed source of /c/: PSC *tsʼ; Taita Cushitic outcomes of *tsʼ are not otherwise known	*g > ɣ

from a short period of category-3A borrowing ("intensive"), lasting a century or two. Alternatively, it may be the outcome of category-3B borrowing ("heavy general") carried on over a period of a number of centuries.

In this particular instance, it appears that the Saghala and Dawida settlements in the Taita Hills began as long ago as the late first millennium CE and early second millennium, but that they did not become the dominant populations of the region until the last few centuries.[21] This dating allows as much as 500 to 600 years of interactions with the then-majority Taita Cushitic communities and so favors the solution that the Taita Cushitic loanword sets in Dawida and Saghala are cases of "heavy general borrowing," category 3B, each lasting a number of centuries.

Interpreting the History behind the Word Borrowing

A heavy general set of loanwords, as argued in chapter 4, commonly accompanies a particular kind of history of interaction between societies. The loanwords in such a set come from an originally majority society of a region. An incoming, initially minority population, after a period of coexistence and extensive bilingualism, begins to absorb the preexisting people of the region into their society, with the consequence that the assimilated group brings many of the words of their former language into their new language.

This is the kind of history we must envision for the Taita Hills region over the period from the late first millennium through the first half of the second millennium CE. Very small intrusive communities speaking ancestral forms of the Saghala and Dawida languages moved separately into different sections of the Taita Hills (see map 4). The beginnings of these settlements date to perhaps 1,200 to 1,000 years ago. For up to five centuries these communities occupied limited niches in the mountainous area, surrounded by the majority, preexisting Taita Cushitic A and Taita Cushitic B peoples.

Then, according to the oral traditions, numerous other Bantu-speaking communities began to move into the hills from around the mid–second millennium CE onward.[22] These groups were rapidly adopted into the existing Dawida and Saghala communities of those times. As this kind of immigration continued, it would have greatly added to the size of the Saghala and Dawida populations. If the Taita Cushites had not already become by this time a declining minority in numbers, the new period of immigration would have finally shifted the demographic balance decisively away from the Taita Cushites and hastened their disappearance as linguistically and culturally distinct populations.

Identifying and giving a broad time frame to the earlier populations of the Taita Hills region is only the beginning of the historian's project. Among the more important historical issues still to be explored is the ancientness of its peoples' reliance on irrigation agriculture and the terracing and manuring of hillside fields. Did these features of economy go back to the Mbisha herders and farmers? Or did the early Dawida, whose closest linguistic relations are with the intensive agriculturist Chaga of Mount Kilimanjaro just to the south, bring these techniques with them when they moved into the region? Extensive and detailed study of the histories of the cultivating and herding vocabularies of the Dawida and Saghala is thus likely to be a rewarding endeavor for the historian who pursues this issue. Ironworking and interregional trade in the varied products of the different environmental zones that meet in the Taita Hills are topics that strongly beckon for historical and archaeological attention as well.

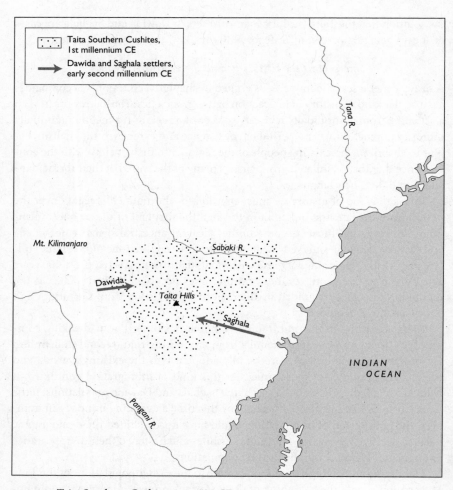

MAP 4. Taita Southern Cushites, ca. 1000 CE

Table 29. Taita Cushitic A Loanwords in Saghala Basic Lexicon

Loanword in Saghala	Southern Cushitic source	Taita Cushitic A sound change(s) *before* borrowing	Semantic category
sisiri 'hair' (partially redup. root)	PR *tsil- 'fur, hide'	Taita Cushitic A rule 8: PSC *l > r /i_	core vocabulary (100-meaning list)
m-riginga 'root'	See table 24	See table 24	core vocabulary (100-meaning list)
-kušu 'feather'	from root seen in verb -*kušu*- 'pluck (feathers),' table 17	rule 3: PSC *i > *u /x_C; also *x > *k: Taita Cushitic A rule 4; Taita Cushitic A 'non-rule' (f): *ɬ > ɬ (> š)	core vocabulary (100-meaning list)
sambe 'kudu'	See table 17	See table 17	large-animal name
-tsub- 'to lick'	See table 17	See table 17	peripheral basic vocabulary item

Table 30. Taita Cushitic A Loanwords in Dawida Basic Lexicon

Loanword in Dawida	Southern Cushitic source	Taita Cushitic A sound change(s) *before* borrowing	Semantic category
paga 'blood'	See table 18	See table 18	core vocabulary (100-meaning list)
li-cuya 'feather' (root + SCush *-iya noun suff.)	*c'uʕ- 'to pluck (feather, etc.)' (Dahalo *t'uʕ*- 'pluck'): semantics: as in -*kušu* 'feather,' table 17	Taita Cushitic A 'nonrule' (f): retention of PCS *c' as c	core vocabulary (100-meaning list)
ki-gutu 'hip'	See table 18	See table 18	peripheral basic vocabulary item

Table 31. Taita Cushitic B Loanwords in Saghala Basic Lexicon

Loanword in Saghala	Southern Cushitic source	Taita Cushitic B sound change(s) *before* borrowing	Semantic category
biɣati 'blood'	See table 20	See table 20	core vocabulary (100-meaning list)
li-fusa 'feather'	See table 20	See table 20	core vocabulary (100-meaning list)
-gwah- 'to lie down'	PSC *gʷaɦ- 'to sit'	'nonrule' (b): PSC *gʷ stayed *gʷ	core vocabulary (100-meaning list)
gudi 'penis'	See table 20	See table 20	peripheral basic vocabulary item
sahala 'gall'	See table 20	See table 20	peripheral basic vocabulary item
-uk- 'to rise'	PSC *ʔuk'-	'nonrule' (d): PSC *k' stayed *k' (> k in Saghala)	peripheral basic vocabulary item
doma 'eland'	See table 20	See table 20	large-animal name
tamahi 'oryx'	See table 20	See table 20	large-animal name
i-galu 'female kudu'	Rift: Asa giałoku 'male oryx,' giałatu 'female oryx' (root *giał-)	Taita Cushitic B rule 1: PSC *ł > l; Taita Cushitic B 'nonrule' (b): PSC *g stayed *g	large-animal name

Table 32. Taita Cushitic A *or* B Loanword in Saghala Basic Lexicon

Loanword in Saghala	Southern Cushitic source	Taita Cushitic sound change(s) *before* borrowing	Semantic category
-sag- 'to die'	PSC *sag- 'to lie down, rest'; semantics: euphemism, 'lie down' > 'die'	(none)	core vocabulary (100-meaning list)

Table 33. Taita Cushitic B Loanwords in Dawida Basic Lexicon

Loanword in Saghala and Dawida	Southern Cushitic source	Taita Cushitic B sound change(s) *before* borrowing	Semantic category
i-ridia 'hair' (root + PSC *-iya noun suff.	See table 21	See table 21	core vocabulary (100-meaning list)
-se- 'to sit, stay'	See table 21	See table 21	core vocabulary (100-meaning list)
-ger- 'to talk'	See table 21	See table 21	peripheral basic vocabulary item
dime 'day'	See table 21	See table 21	peripheral basic vocabulary item

NOTES

1. P. G. Bostock, *The Peoples of Kenya: The Taita* (London: MacMillan, 1950); E. H. Merritt, "A History of the Taita of Kenya to 1900" (Ph.D. diss., Indiana University, 1975); S. Liszka, "A Preliminary Report of Research on the Origins and Internal Migrations of the Taita People," University of Nairobi Discussion Paper no. 57 (Nairobi, 1974).

2. G. G. Harris, *Casting Out Anger: Religion among the Taita of Kenya* (Cambridge: Cambridge University Press, 1978), p. 4.

3. The Indo-European case in point is that of the two extinct Tocharian languages of Central Asia, usually distinguished as Tocharian A and Tocharian B.

4. S. H. Ambrose, "Archaeology and Linguistic Reconstruction of History in East Africa," in C. Ehret and M. Posnansky (eds.), *The Archaeological and Linguistic Reconstruction of African History* (Berkeley and Los Angeles: University of California Press, 1982), pp. 104–157; C. Ehret, *An African Classical Age: Eastern and Southern Africa in World History, 1000 BC to AD 400* (Charlottesville: University of Virginia Press), esp. chap. 3.

5. Ehret, *African Classical Age*, pp. 87, 174.

6. C. Ehret, *Southern Nilotic History: Linguistic Approaches to the Study of the Past* (Evanston, IL: Northwestern University Press, 1971); idem, *Ethiopians and East Africans: The Problem of Contacts* (Nairobi: East African Publishing House, 1974); idem, "Population Movement and Culture Contact in the Southern Sudan, c. 3000 BC to AD 1000," in J. Mack and P. Robertshaw (eds.), *Culture History in the Southern Sudan*, British Institute in Eastern Africa Memoire no. 8 (Nairobi, 1983), pp. 19–48; idem, "Aspects of Social and Economic Change in Western Kenya, 500–1800," in B. A. Ogot (ed.), *Kenya Before 1900* (Nairobi: East African Publishing House, 1977), pp. 1–20; D. Schoenbrun, *A Green Place, a Good Place: Agrarian Change, Gender, and Social Identity in the Great Lakes Region to the 15th Century* (Portsmouth, NH: Heinemann, 1998); Ehret, *African Classical Age*, pp. 85–86 and elsewhere; D. Nurse, *Classification of the Chaga Dialects: Language and History on Kilimanjaro, the Taita Hills, and the Pare Mountains* (Hamburg: Buske Verlag, 1979).

7. Ehret, *Southern Nilotic History*.

8. Ehret, *African Classical Age*, chap. 6 and elsewhere.

9. Evidence for the extinct Highland Dahaloan language appears in D. Nurse, "Reconstruction of Dahalo History through Evidence of Loanwords," *Sprache und Geschichte in Afrika* 7, no. 2 (1986): 267–305; and idem, "History from Linguistics: The Case of the Tana River," *History in Africa* 10 (1983): 207–238. For the extinct Mbuguan languages, see Ehret, *Ethiopians and East Africans*, pp. 78, 84–85; also idem, "Yaakuan and Eastern Cushitic: A Historical Linguistic Overview," in G. Takacs (ed.), *Semito-Hamitic Festschrift for A. B. Dolgopolsky and H. Jungraithmayr* (Berlin: Dietrich Reimer, 2008), pp. 128–141. For North Rift Southern Cushitic, see idem, *Southern Nilotic History*, app. B.2; and idem, "Social and Economic Change in Western Kenya." For Iringa Southern Cushitic, see idem, *African Classical Age*, pp. 192–193, 331–332. For Tale Southern Cushitic, see D. Schoenbrun, *A Green Place, a Good Place*. Ehret, *African Classical Age*, pp. 63–68, 325–330, identifies three distinct dialects of the extinct Tale Southern Cushitic language.

10. The evidence for the revised primary division of Southern Cushitic into Dahaloan and Rift-Mbugu branches appears in C. Ehret, "Extinct Khoesan Languages of East Africa," in R. Vossen (ed.), *The Khoesan Languages* (Abingdon: Routledge, forthcoming); for Alagwa, see R. Kiessling, *Die Rekonstruktion der südkuschitischen Sprachen (West-Rift)* (Cologne: Rüdiger Köppe Verlag, 2002).

11. See also Ambrose, "Archaeology and Linguistic Reconstruction," and Ehret, *African Classical Age*, esp. chaps. 3 and 6, for further dating proposals.

12. A hyphen is the conventional way of marking the beginning or the end of a stem or an affix.

13. See chap. 2 for more on the importance of sound change in determining word histories.

14. C. Ehret, *The Historical Reconstruction of Southern Cushitic Phonology and Vocabulary* (Berlin: Reimer, 1980), proposes several other provisional consonants that are not valid and should never have been included in the book.

15. Ehret, *Historical Reconstruction of Southern Cushitic*, interprets the diphthong as a mid-central vowel with two allophones. But the reconstruction, as here, of a diphthong *ay (occurring also long, as *aay) is required by the wider Cushitic and Afrasian language family evidence; see C. Ehret, *Reconstructing Proto-Afroasiatic (Proto-Afrasian): Vowels, Tone, Consonants, and Vocabulary* (Berkeley and Los Angeles: University of California Press, 1995); and idem, "Proto-Cushitic Reconstruction," *Sprache und Geschichte in Afrika* 8 (1987), pp. 7–180.

16. C. Ehret and D. Nurse, "The Taita Cushites," *Sprache und Geschichte in Afrika* 3 (1981): 125–168, identifies some of these other kinds of innovations.

17. Ambrose, "Archaeology and Linguistic Reconstruction," is the early articulator of this connection; see also Ehret, *African Classical Age*, pp. 97, 98, 173.

18. There are, of course, additional Southern Cushitic loanwords in Dawida and Saghala that turn up more widely in Kenya and Tanzania Bantu languages, but these borrowings reflect earlier contacts between Bantu and Cushites, which took place elsewhere than in the Taita Hills. They identify earlier eras of encounter between the newly arriving Mashariki Bantu communities of 2,000 to 1,500 years ago and their Southern Cushitic predecessors, but not the particular, later histories of contact that the loanword sets limited to the Taita Bantu languages reveal. See, for example, table 4B in Ehret, *African Classical Age*, p. 329.

19. Ehret, "East African Interior," p. 617; idem, "Between the Coast and the Great Lakes," in D. T. Niane (ed.), *Africa from the Twelfth to the Sixteenth Centuries*, vol. 4 of *General History of Africa* (UNESCO, University of California Press, and Heinemann, 1984), pp. 489–492.

20. Several other words in Dawida and Saghala basic vocabulary can be identified as loans, but since their sources cannot yet be specified, they have not been included here. Among them are Dawida -tini 'small' (which could be either a Nilo-Saharan or Eastern Cushitic loanword) and koi 'dog' and Saghala -mojori 'one' and cucu 'dog'.

21. C. Ehret and D. Nurse, "History in the Taita Hills: A Provisional Synthesis," accepted for publication in *Kenya Historical Review* 8 (1980), but the journal ceased publication just before the issue in question was to appear.

22. Liszka, "Internal Migrations of the Taita People"; also Merritt, "History of the Taita of Kenya."

Cultural Diffusion
in the Atlantic Age

American Crops in Eastern Africa

A closing theme of importance for the use of language evidence in history revolves around what the diffusion of individual words for new items of culture can reveal about the diffusion of things and ideas. A historical context highly illustrative of the revelatory powers of this documentation is the Atlantic Age. Unprecedented changes pervaded the world over the course of that age, from the middle fifteenth century into the twentieth century. New items of material culture, new crops, and new ideas passed back and forth across and around the world, following the expanding new networks of exchange and movement of people and goods. With those movements of things and ideas spread the words that named them.

By no means is the Atlantic Age alone in this respect. A similarly powerful flow of things and ideas out of and through the ancient Levant is evident in the diffusion of innumerable words for new products, new crops, new technology, and new gods and beliefs westward through the Mediterranean world over the course of the second and first millennia BCE and the very early first millennium CE. Other similarly complex influences, documented in the lexical evidence, spread in the preceding millennia within, and northward and eastward from, Mesopotamia and Anatolia. Still other major spheres of interaction before the Atlantic Age, where lexical documentation has the same historical explanatory power, encompassed the Indian Ocean, Mesoamerica, and East Asia. Many separate periods of diffusion outward of cultural influences, beliefs, and technology from China stand out,

This chapter revises C. Ehret, "East African Words and Things: Agricultural Aspects of Economic Transformation in the Nineteenth Century," in B. A. Ogot (ed.), *Kenya in the Nineteenth Century* (Nairobi: Anyange Press, 1986).

for example, in the word borrowing evidence in Japanese, Korean, and Southeast Asian languages.

This chapter deals with one arena of such change, eastern Africa, belonging to the Atlantic Age, and it focuses on just one of the numerous facets in this unprecedented history—the introduction and long-distance spread of new crops. In doing so it illustrates the power of the study of lexical diffusions to reveal both expected and unexpected facets of the movement of things, people, and ideas; to provide information where written documentation fails; and to raise questions and issues of global relevance for understanding the formative age of the world we live in.

For eastern Africa in the overall span from the 1400s to the 1900s, the nineteenth century stands out as a period of especially rapid transformation. The characteristic and unifying theme of the period was the penetration deep into the East African interior of motivations and interests generated outside the continent—spread during most of the century through the expanding web of WaSwahili trading contacts and culminating at the end of the nineteenth and beginning of the twentieth century in the rather abrupt European imposition of direct political and economic control.

But although this common thread running through nineteenth-century events helps give sense and order to that history, it cannot be considered the summation of all significant change. The interest of East African nineteenth-century history lies primarily in the variety of ways peoples responded locally to new knowledge and in the cumulative transformations brought about by the availability and acquisition of new tools and possessions. These transformations took place both ahead of and after direct contact with WaSwahili or Europeans. Studies in local political history have been and remain popular approaches among historians of East Africa to uncovering nineteenth-century developments. The equally essential historical task of locating, in time and space, the specific changes in knowledge and material culture that took place among East Africans in that era have only too often been left aside.

One aspect of such cumulative change, often of considerable eventual economic importance, was the introduction of crops native to the Americas. A number of such crops became known at the East African coast prior to the nineteenth century. Some spread inland only with the establishment of WaSwahili caravan routes or colonial communications, while others spread significantly earlier in time.

The linguistic investigation of agricultural change reminds us also that the boundaries and spheres of interaction do not extend immutably back in time. In the nineteenth century and before, human contact and the spread of ideas and things were not constrained by present-day political borders. In addition, the distinctiveness of nineteenth-century transformations stands out clearly only when those transformations are seen in comparison to what came before, and so the depiction of the earlier patterns of crop spread form an essential backdrop to the discussion of nineteenth-century developments.

Along with the principal American crops, at least one crop of Asian origin—

rice—has played a notable part in the agricultural changes of recent times. The reasons are twofold. Most significantly, rice appears to have spread inland during the same eras in which a number of the American crops took hold among peoples of the interior, so its wider diffusion is part of the same history. On the other hand, it was also a crop that arrived much more anciently at the East African coasts than the American crops. Considering the history of Asian rice in conjunction with the history of American crops in eastern Africa throws into sharper relief the factors that explain how and when the new crops spread.

NEW CROPS IN NINETEENTH-CENTURY INTERIOR EASTERN AFRICA

Broad beans (*Phaseolus* sp.), cassava, and peanuts (*Arachis hypogaea*), all of Amerindian origin, and curiously rice, a crop of Southeast Asian origin long known at the East African coast, all appear to have begun spreading inland no earlier than the first half of nineteenth century, at first by WaSwahili and sometime later by colonial agency.

American Beans (Phaseolus *sp.*)

The American broad bean seems to have had a particularly checkered history. Its original adoption in East Africa was by the WaSwahili at the coast, evidenced by the KiSwahili word *haragwe*, which appears to be a borrowing, perhaps indirectly, of some European form of the word seen in English *haricot*.[1] Immediately inland a variety of innovated terms turn up, indicative of a gradual adoption of and longer acquaintance with the plant. For example, the North Mijikenda peoples applied the earlier Bantu root *-kunde, originally "black-eyed pea," to the crop, and the Lugulu and Kagulu of the central Tanzania coastal hinterland used a different term, *mpanda*, of uncertain earlier meaning. But farther inland, wide block distributions of particular terms for "broad bean" occur, reflecting more rapid and more recent spreads. Moreover, it is often the KiSwahili root that overleaps the near-coastal roots.

In central and western Tanzania the same word as in Swahili, but with the phonetic shape -halage (or -halagi), is nearly universal, and its distribution extends northward from the Gogo-speaking area via the Burunge and Langi languages as far as the West Chaga dialects. This form of the KiSwahili term clearly derives from contacts reaching back to the Swahili coast via central Tanzania. But since most of these languages have the sequence gw, the loss of w shows that they cannot have adopted the word and the crop directly from the WaSwahili of the caravan era. The probable alternative solution is that the crop was introduced during the eighteenth- and very early nineteenth-century era of Nyamwezi caravan trade with the coast, and spread originally by Nyamwezi agency, somewhat ahead of the spread of the rise of KiSwahili as the new lingua franca.

In the eastern Kenya interior, on the other hand, the KiSwahili term for the American bean was directly adopted, with such phonetic modifications as the phonologies of the particular languages required. In a shape maintaining the gw and adding the Bantu plural prefix *ma-, the *haragwe* root for "broad bean" extends from Taita- and Kamba-speaking areas north to Marakwet. It turns up also in the Oromo dialects along and south of the Tana River, although the Oromo term north and east of the river is different and reflects a different direction of spread of the new kind of bean: from Somalia and/or Ethiopia. In much of interior Kenya as far inland as the Rift Valley, then, broad beans appear to be an introduction no earlier than the establishment of the WaSwahili caravan trade in the second half of the nineteenth century and, conceivably, dating in fact to the early colonial era. What makes the latter solution possible is that in one major area along the WaSwahili routes into central Kenya—namely, in the central and eastern Kilimanjaro areas inhabited by the Chaga—the words (-boni, -bonu) are borrowings of German *Bohne,* dating the Chaga adoption of this crop to the German colonial era of the 1880s to 1910s. That is to say, WaSwahili traders apparently did not spread the crop into this region, but instead it is likely to have reached places still farther inland, such as the Marakwet areas of Kenya, also only during the colonial era. The KiSwahili term would have spread in this era because the colonial rulers were wont to use KiSwahili in dealing with Africans.

In western Kenya, in contrast, American beans may be a somewhat earlier introduction. The crop, in any case, spread there from the west, as the distribution of a root, *-ganda, shows.[2] This root is found through the Luhyia dialects, including Gisu. It spread to Luo in the shape *oganda* and from Luhyia to Kalenjin in the shape *makant-, with the fossilized Bantu *ma-* class-5 plural prefix embedded in it. The Terik, Nandi, Pok, Kony, and Keyo dialects of Kalenjin all have this version of the root. The term spread thus as far east as the Rift Valley (where it met up with the farthest westward spread of -*haragwe*), in a shape diffused purely from Kalenjin dialect to Kalenjin dialect, with no hint of intermediate KiSwahili or English transmission. Hence the crop must have been known in Kalenjin areas no later than the close of the nineteenth century and thus in the Bantu-speaking areas west of the Kalenjin still earlier than that. It is possible that broad beans reached the region from the south via central Tanzania, but it is also possible that the crop spread from the west coast of Africa or up the Nile Valley from a northern or northeastern African area of introduction.

The Introduction of Cassava

The pattern of names for cassava, with one significant difference, closely resembles that for the broad bean. In particular, again KiSwahili has a term differing from those used immediately in from the coast, whereas the KiSwahili term then widely recurs through the farther interior. KiSwahili *muhogo* comes presumably via Portuguese, ultimately from Tupi-Guarani *mandioca*, and so reflects the first introduction of the crop from the Americas.

Along the coastal belt of northern Tanzania and Kenya a second root, *manga* (singular commonly *lianga*), prevails. The probable source of this form is an older local Bantu term for a root tuber crop, *-langa. This root is present in two KiSwahili words: *danga* for a yam species (*Dioscorea alata*) and *mwanga* 'arrowroot'. The first form changed earlier eastern Bantu *l to *d*, a nonregular sound shift indicative of KiSwahili's having borrowed that term, although from an as-yet-unidentified source. The second form, *mwanga*, from an original singular form, *mu-langa, attests the regular KiSwahili loss of earlier eastern Bantu *l between vowels. This sound shift is also found in Bondei, a language spoken in the immediate hinterland of the WaSwahili coastal towns of northern Tanzania.[3] The shape *manga* thus derived from an original plural shape, *ma-langa. The loss of *l shows that the application of this root word to the new crop, cassava, most likely took place in Bondei, since this meaning shift did not take place in KiSwahili itself, the other language with regular *l loss. The focal region of the adoption and first spread of the plant up and down the coast is therefore likely to have been in coastal areas of far northeast Tanzania around the lower Pangani River, where the Bondei live. The general spread of *manga* north and south in the coastal hinterland shows that cassava became known to peoples of the coastal hinterland before the heavier WaSwahili penetrations of the nineteenth century.

The spread of the *manga* term for "cassava" inland to Kilimanjaro and to the Kamba of the Kenya interior suggests further that knowledge and use of the crop preceded the WaSwahili caravan trade into those areas also. In the case of the Kamba, the late-eighteenth- and early-nineteenth-century Kamba trade with the Mijikenda of the coastal hinterland probably accounts for knowledge of cassava.

As these contacts spread still farther inland, to the Rift Valley area of Kenya, other new terms derived from words for earlier root crops were applied to cassava. The Gikuyu substituted the noun class prefix *mo- for the original *n- of *ngwace* 'sweet potato' to derive a new term, *mogwace*, for "cassava." The Tem (Sonjo) of the Rift Valley of far northern Tanzania took an older term, *ndooma*, for probably "arrowroot" and reapplied it to the new crop.

Farther inland still, south and west of the Tem and westward from the Gikuyu, forms of KiSwahili *muhogo* again are found everywhere. A key difference from the evidence for words for broad beans is that all the forms appear to be direct borrowings from KiSwahili, implying that in most cases cassava became known in the deeper East African interior only during the colonial era. Luo *muogo* and other similar shapes in Western Kenya languages support this conclusion.

Peanuts in Eastern Africa

The terms used to name the American peanut raise additional issues of how we infer history from word distributions. One has to do with the contrastive distributions associated with old items of culture versus items of recent spread. Several different roots are applied in different areas of East Africa to the native African (Bambara) groundnut, *Vigna subterranea*. This result is in keeping with the expectation that things that been around through many hundreds or thousands of years of language change will develop a variety of names in different languages. In contrast, just two terms for the peanut (*Arachis hypogaea*), both probably of KiSwahili provenance, cover wide blocks of languages across much of East Africa—just the kind of distribution indicative of recent borrowing spread.

Both of the widespread words for the peanut are root terms of African origin—each, however, originally naming a different indigenous African plant. The old Bantu root *njugu originally named the African groundnut in the Proto-Bantu language.[4] In early Northeast Coastal Bantu, from which the KiSwahili, Mijikenda, Seuta (Shambaa, Zigula, Bondei), and Ruvu languages (e.g., Gogo, Zalamo, etc.) descend, the word probably still had that meaning. The Upland Bantu group—consisting of the Thagiicu, Chaga, and Dawida languages—shifted the application of the term to a different older African crop, the pigeon pea (*Cajanus indicus*). The other widespread term for the American peanut, *-kalanga, probably originally named the wild plant *Desmodium abscendans,* which the WaSwahili today call karanga mwitu—that is, "kalanga of the woods," or wild kalanga—to distinguish it from the peanut.

These two terms readapted to apply to the introduced crop, the peanut, have mostly complementary distributions across East Africa. In general, derivatives of *njugu occur in languages along the Kenya and northern Tanzania coastal belt and extend from there northwestward into central Kenya and west to Lake Nyanza (Lake Victoria). Through central, northern, and western Tanzania, where *njugu normally continues to apply in Bantu languages to the African groundnut, the alternative term, *kalanga,* means "peanut." In central Tanzania, the Southern Cushitic language Iraqw has adopted its form of the word, *karanga,* directly from KiSwahili since it maintains the *r* of the KiSwahili version. In contrast, nearby Burunge, a closely related Southern Cushitic language, adopted its word *kalanga* probably from its southern neighbor language, Gogo, which attests *l* instead of *r*. For the same reason, the Langi and Sandawe languages spoken west of Burunge and north of Gogo can be argued to have obtained their words for "peanut" from either Burunge or Gogo.

The peanut may, like broad beans and cassava, have gone through an initial prenineteenth-century period of establishment along the coast. But on the other hand, there is no different set of coastal hinterland names for the crop requiring such an intermediate historical stage. Both widespread terms for the peanut come directly from KiSwahili; and at least as far as central and western Tanzania is concerned, the spread of the peanut followed to some extent the pattern of nineteenth-century trade links. In north-central Tanzania, knowledge of the plant apparently preceded direct WaSwahili penetration, which was mostly a colonial-era phenomenon there, and so can be dated back to the precolonial times. But even there, the direct Iraqw adoption of the KiSwahili word, and hence probably adoption of the crop only during colonial times, reinforces the impression of the recentness of the spread of the peanut. A number of instances of *njugu in Kenyan, especially Western Kenyan, languages also are surely direct adoptions from KiSwahili root—for example, Luo *njugu* and Gusii *encugu*—and therefore reflect the probable introduction of the crop to these areas only during the colonial era.

The Great Lakes region marks the edge, however, of the spread of peanuts from the Indian Ocean coasts. Another root, occurring as *emaaito* in Bukusu just south of Mount Elgon, must be traced back toward the north and then the west. Like Päkot *ama:ide:* and Lotuko *amayilo,* it derives from the Ateker root seen in Teso: *emaide.* This term itself many come from a root that occurs west of the Nile in the Central Sudanic language Bongo in the shape *manda.* The reason we can make this connection is that Ateker languages lack *nd* and the speakers of these languages therefore hear the sound of *nd* in *manda* as simple *d.* In these southern Nile watershed regions the probable ultimate source of the peanut was a spread of the crop from the west, from the distant Atlantic coast of Central Africa. David Lloyd has shown that at least one variety of peanut was grown in Zande lands by no later than the early nineteenth century.[5] As that evidence indicates, the crop had indeed spread early enough eastward from the Atlantic coast through north-central Africa to account for its arrival by the nineteenth century in northern Uganda and a subsequent spread to Mount Elgon as early as or earlier than the countervailing colonial-era introduction of the crop into the region from the east.

The Establishment of Rice in the East African Interior

Rice, though of Asian rather than American origin and of far more ancient standing on the coast than crops of the American complex, appears from the naming evidence to have spread into most of the East African interior no earlier than the nineteenth century.

The establishment of the crop along the immediate coast probably dates back into the first millennium CE. Of the three key KiSwahili terms—*mpunga* for the plant, *mchele* for the cleaned whole grain, and *wali* for cooked rice—one, and possibly two, have apparent Indonesian origins, directly connecting the adoption of the crop to people speaking a very early form of Malagasy. The word *wali* can be attributed to an Austronesian root, appearing as *vary* 'rice' in modern-day Malagasy dialects of Madagascar. The phonological changes in the ancestry of Proto-Swahili would have regularly changed *v to *w* and substituted *l for *r*.[6] The -*punga* root is possibly cognate with the otherwise isolated term *mhunga* in Shona of Zimbabwe for "bulrush millet."[7] But an alternative Indonesian source also exists for it, a root seen in the Malay term *bunga* for "rice," so KiSwahili *mpunga* is also a possible borrowing from very early Malagasy speakers.[8]

In the immediate neighboring languages behind the coast, the -punga root has long been applied to the rice plant. The testimony of that fact are the old regular sound shifts of those languages that have affected the pronunciation of *-punga. In particular, a series of sound changes, Proto-Bantu *p > *f > h, took place in certain Mijikenda dialects of the southern Kenya coastal hinterlands and also in the Seuta languages (Bondei, Shambaa, and Zigula) of the northern Tanzania coastal hinterland, changing *-punga to *hunga*. Since this pair of sound changes had already taken place in Proto-Seuta, spoken around 1,000 years ago, the use of the word *-punga for "rice" and therefore the raising of, or at least familiarity with, the crop itself must date to the first millennium in the coastal hinterland belt of northern Tanzania.

If we turn our attention farther inland, however, universally throughout Tanzania and also farther south in the Zambezi River regions, wherever the *-punga root is used, it is pronounced with the same first consonant, /p/, as in KiSwahili. In languages where *p* continues to be the modern-day reflex of Proto-Bantu *p, the sound correspondences appear to be regular. In languages where Proto-Bantu *p has regularly changed to another sound, normally *f* or *h*, nevertheless these languages also retain *p* in their word for "rice." For example, Shona spoken in the Zambezi regions has *h* as its proper, regular correspondent of *p in *rnhunga* 'bulrush millet', but it has *p* in its word for "rice," *mpunga*. The phonological evidence thus shows a rapid and relatively recent borrowing spread of the crop and, moreover, that the adoption of rice came usually directly from KiSwahili speakers or through diffusion from other peoples who had been in direct contact with the WaSwahili. The generally unbroken block distribution of the shape -punga with initial *p* through Tanzania and much of east-central Africa also favors a very recent spread of the crop. Finally, the borrowing of some subsidiary terminology here and there from KiSwahili adds further confirmation as to how knowledge of rice was acquired. For example, Shona *mufake* 'cooked plain rice', reshaping KiSwahili *nafaka* 'grain' by substituting the familiar and grammatically proper mu- prefix for the unfamiliar initial syllable na-, shows that it was precisely WaSwahili people, presumably the merchants who traveled to Zimbabwe in the first half of the second millennium CE, who were the source of the crop for the Shona.

Through most of Kenya, on the other hand, versions of the KiSwahili word for cleaned whole rice, *mchele*, rather than -punga have widely become the general name for the crop. The difference in naming would appear to reflect a difference in the manner in which rice became known. In western Tanzania, WaSwahili settlement at places like Tabora apparently led to the establishment of rice as regular crop. In interior Kenya rice would have been introduced as a transported food, grown and already processed elsewhere, as indeed it has widely remained to the present

in highland areas. The first knowledge of rice in those regions as provisions probably dates not earlier than WaSwahili caravans of the second half of the nineteenth
century, and in some cases highland Kenyans would have become acquainted with
rice only in the twentieth century.

Like the root words for cassava and the broad bean, then, the terms for rice show
an older coastal distribution, in this case dating back to the first millennium, and
a recent overleaping of the near coastal languages by words coming from KiSwahili.
In East Africa, this secondary spread of rice appears to date no earlier than the middle and later nineteenth-century expansions of caravan trade. At its farthest extension, the KiSwahili term -punga reached the Manyema and northeastern Congo
regions invaded by the Swahili-Arab slave trade toward the end of the century.

In the Zambezi regions to the south, the KiSwahili word spread well up the river
and to the south of it into Zimbabwe. Though the Portuguese of those regions ate
rice, they were not the introducers of the crop to the interior, and so it is quite probable that the use of rice began to take hold along the lower Zambezi much earlier
than in the East African interior, starting to spread inland before the Portuguese
arrival in the sixteenth century. The -punga term also appears as far north and west
as the Katanga area of the southeastern Democratic Republic of Congo, where the
introduction of rice may well be attributable to the Nvamwezi trader and adven-
turer Msiri, who set up a predatory state in that region in the second half of the
nineteenth century and had come from the already Swahili-influenced areas of western Tanzania.

Rice had also been diffusing as a crop eastward from the Atlantic coast for some
centuries. In this region rice had been introduced by the Portuguese, as is clearly
attested by the predominance through the Congo Basin of words, with shapes such
as -roso and the like, derived from Portuguese *arroz*. Rice had apparently spread as
far as eastern Congo by the close of the nineteenth century because it is there that
the distribution of -roso meets up with the distribution of the -punga root. In at
least one case, both roots co-occur in a single language: Mangbetu has both *na-ma-
punga* and *ne-roso* for "rice" (na- and ne- are Mangbetu prefixes).

An entirely separate root for "rice," seen in Acholi and Shilluk *alabo* and Naath
lap, implies a third route of introduction of the crop in the Middle Nile Basin. The
root probably originally named wild African rice; such at least is the meaning of
the Dinka reflex *lop*. Thus the Nilotes may have reapplied an older native, Proto–
Western Nilotic term to the Asian rice introduced from the Arabs to the north.

Through all of Africa south of the Nilotes in the Sudan, rice is clearly Asian rice.
The crop entered into the agricultural practices of the southern half of the continent through KiSwahili and still earlier Indonesian agency along the east coast, and
through Portuguese agency along the Atlantic coasts of Central Africa, spreading
beyond the coastal hinterlands only during the past 500 years and in fact, in many
regions, only in the past 150 years.

AMERICAN CROPS IN EAST AFRICA
BEFORE THE NINETEENTH CENTURY

Three crops of origin in the Americas—maize, the sweet potato, and tobacco—appear to have spread into the African interior significantly earlier than the crops previously discussed. Both maize and sweet potatoes had ready analogues in existing African crops, and so direct transference of names from the older to the new crop often took place, or, alternatively, descriptive modifications of the older names were made. The frequency with which new names are thus applied to these crops as they spread inland makes for problems in tracing their particular paths of diffusion.

The Multiple Spreads of Maize into the Interior

Maize spread by at least two, and possibly three, directions into the East African interior. One direction, as one might expect, was from the WaSwahili of the eastern coasts of the continent.

The initial WaSwahili knowledge of the plant came via the Indian Ocean sealanes, as evidenced in the WaSwahili perception of maize as *mahindi,* "the Indian (grain)." The East Ruvu dialects (Zalamo, Lugulu, Doe, Kami, etc.) of the lower Ruvu River regions of eastern Tanzania took up the crop directly from the WaSwahili, as their use of the *mahindi* root shows. As maize then spread farther inland from Ulugulu to Ugogo, the farmers of this region applied another term to maize, *mutama,* originally a old Northeast Coastal Bantu root word for sorghum.

Through northeastern Tanzania and parts of central and eastern Kenya the spread of forms of a different old eastern Bantu root word, *-pemba,* probably originally meaning grain in general, depicts a second line of transmission of maize inland from the coast.[9] This route of the spread of maize inland from the northern Tanzania Coast followed the Pangani Valley to the Pare Mountains and from there north to Kilimanjaro, the Taita Hills region, and the eastern highlands of Kenya.

The distribution of the *mapemba* term clearly identifies a borrowing spread because the root word, when it means "maize," repeatedly fails to show regular sound correspondences. Moreover, in several cases the borrowed shape of the word with the meaning "maize" coexists in one and the same language with a form of the root that shows the proper regular sound correspondence and maintains the original Bantu application to indigenous African grains. An example is the Shambaa language, which has *mapemba* for "maize" and *uhemba* for "sorghum." The word for sorghum shows regular Shambaa *h* for Proto-Bantu *p, but the word for maize fails to show the shift. We can tell that the original source of the widespread borrowed version of the *mapemba* word for maize must have been KiSwahili because only KiSwahili has maintained *p for original Bantu *p, whereas the rest of the languages involved had a regular sound change of *p to *h* or have deleted *p entirely.

The evidence of the borrowing spread inland of *-pemba with a p and the meaning "maize" is thus clear. But there is an interesting twist to this history. KiSwahili
itself no longer uses the word *mapemba, instead calling maize *mahindi*. What apparently happened was that when knowledge of maize first reached WaSwahili via
the Indian Ocean trade of the sixteenth century, some of the KiSwahili, apparently
those of the northern Tanzania and far southern Kenya coasts, thinking the Portuguese had brought it from India, took to calling it *mapemba mahindi*, "Indian
grain." Speakers of inland languages, whose word for "sorghum" was pronounced
*mahemba, would have understood *mapemba with its *p as a distinct word. To
them the adjective *mahindi* would have been unnecessary, allowing them to sim-
plify the name of the new crop to just *mapemba. The WaSwahili made an alternative simplification, calling it just *mahindi*—that is, "the Indian one"—and in the
process dropped the term *mapemba* from their language.

A distinct, more limited area of the introduction of maize from the east coast
was in the hinterland of the Kenya Coast. The Mijikenda of this region applied
reflexes of still another older eastern Bantu root to maize. This term, *-sele, originally meant "cleaned whole grain" in early Mashariki Bantu. Its Mijikenda reflex
was *ma-tsere. The alert reader may notice that this is the same root word separately drafted into use in early KiSwahili as the term for uncooked whole-grain rice.

The second direction of the introduction of maize into East Africa was from the
south, from Malawi and Zambia and probably ultimately from Portuguese visitors,
traders, and settlers in the lower Zambezi region. The words for maize in the Njombe
subgroup of Bantu languages spoken in the southern highlands of Tanzania—such
as Kinga *amatsebere*, Bena *ilidzebele*, and Hehe *matsabeli*—are borrowings of an
old root for "bulrush millet," *kebele, found in Tumbuka and Nyanja-Cewa, two of
the Nyasa Bantu languages, which have long been spoken in Malawi and adjacent
parts of Mozambique. The lack of regular sound correspondence in the Njombe
languages attests to this direction of introduction. The regular outcome of the root
in the Njombe group should have been *-kebele. In the Nyasa languages, in contrast, the original *k regularly became a *c (pronounced like *ch* in English *church*)
before the vowel *e. The pronunciation *ts or *dz was the nearest approximation
of *c that existed in the phonologies of the Njombe languages, and so the Njombe
languages converted the Nyasa languages' sound *c into *ts or *dz, depending on
the particular language involved. The spread of maize from the Malawi region also
reached as far northwestward as the edges of Katanga in Congo, where Lamba shows
the same root in the shape *kancevele*.

Recent work by Catherine Cymone Fourshey adds new detail to our understanding of the northward spread of maize from the Zambezi basin into southern
Tanzania. She shows that at least two other terms of older Bantu application to
grains—*-konde, originally "thick stalk," and *-saka, an old eastern Bantu word for
sorghum—reveal the spread of maize, respectively, from Malawi into the areas at

the north end of Lake Malawi and via eastern Zambia into the areas east of the southern end of Lake Tanganyika.[10]

A third direction of the spread of maize is visible in western Kenya. The establishment of the crop along the east side of Lake Nyanza (Lake Victoria) can be seen in the distribution of a root of the shape *-duuma (alternative shape *-dumua) in Bukusu and other Luhyia dialects, in Luo, and in Gusii and Kuria. In Gusii and Kuria the root turns up with a *t as *-tuuma, showing the word to have been borrowed into those languages from Luhyia dialects spoken north of the Wami Gulf of Lake Nyanza in which *d regularly became t. This sound substitution indicates that the word, and thus the crop, were introduced into the region from around the north side of the lake.

The further diffusion of maize from the east side of the lake eastward into the Kenya highlands is apparent in the distribution of a second root word for maize. Its initial shape is reflected in the Luo word banda, to which Gusii added a Bantu noun-class prefix, creating a new shape, ecibanda. In a still unidentified Luhyia dialect, a different prefix, *i-, was added, giving rise to the root shape *ipanda in Terik, Nandi, and as far east as the Kalenjin communities of the Kenya Rift Valley. The eastern limit of this spread was the areas north of Nakuru. Keyo dialects normally have only the *ipanta root, but Tuken has both it and an alternative form, alpai(ek), from Maasai ol-paeki used to the east and south. Marakwet communities, on the other hand, all have the *alpai root, indicative of the spread of knowledge of maize from the east and south. It seems that maize or at least knowledge of it was reaching the Rift Valley area of Kenya from the west at about the same time as from the east.

But how was this eastward spread of maize from the lake region connected to the introductions of maize to eastern Africa? The answer to this question is unclear on the evidence so far available. It could be that the plant spread from Malawi through western Tanzania into the Great Lakes region and thence to western Kenya, or from the Tanzania Coast to western Tanzania and from there to the Great Lakes. Other possibilities are that maize could have reached this region from the Sudan to the north or via the Congo Basin from the Atlantic coast of Central Africa. The latter route is a distinct possibility deserving of further investigation. We know already, from the distribution of terms for maize in the southern savanna belt of Africa, that this crop diffused from western Angola eastward to the western parts of Zambia between the sixteenth and nineteenth centuries,[11] so it may conceivably have spread similarly far eastward from the Atlantic in those eras through the rainforest zone as well.

How Early Did Maize Spread into the Deeper Interior?

We have two indications of the possible age of the knowledge of maize in the East African interior. Barabaig (Datooga) hagu 'maize' is a loanword from an earlier form

of the lraqw language. Modern Iraqw and its dialect Gorowa both use the root shape
*ʕay- as the stem of their names for maize. This word is their regular reflex of the
Proto-Cushitic and Proto–Southern Cushitic root word *ʕaag-, originally denoting a sorghum species. The Barabaig shape of the root, *hagu*, and so therefore the
crop it named, thus necessarily must have been present in the region before the *g
became *y in Proto-Iraqw-Gorowa. (The addition of *h* is a Barabaig language substitution for the pharyngeal consonant ʕ, which it lacks.) That is to say, the word
for maize came to Barabaig from Iraqw-Gorowa sometime before the emergence
of separate Gorowa and Iraqw dialects—a development of uncertain date, but surely
before the nineteenth century. On the other side of the coin, the Datoga adoption
of this root word would not have predated their expansion into the lraqw-Gorowa-
speaking areas of Mbulu and Hanang, a historical development belonging according to oral tradition to around the seventeenth century. Hence a seventeenth- or
eighteenth-century introduction of maize into north-central Tanzania west of the
Rift can be postulated.

   A second indication of the age of maize comes from the Rift Valley areas of central
Kenya. There the spread of the *ipanta root right across Kalenjin territories indicates
that maize diffused to those areas either before the Il-Wuas-in-Kishu Maasai con-
quests of the eighteenth century broke up the continuity of Kalenjin settlement
across the Uasingishu plateau or after the collapse of Il-Wuas-in-Kishu power in
the mid–eighteenth century. That is, maize reached the Rift Valley region either in
or before the early eighteenth century or else during the second half of the nineteenth century. What supports the earlier dating is that Maasai dialects almost uni-
formly show the *ol-paeki* root despite their vast spread at the end of the nineteenth
century, from central Kenya to central Tanzania. To account for this situation, we
must presume that the knowledge of maize reached the Maasai while they were yet
a relatively compact territorial grouping of communities—a condition beginning
to fail as early as the later seventeenth century and certainly no longer obtaining in
the middle eighteenth century.[12] If, as proposed, the *ipanta word for maize was
spreading to the western edge of the Kenya Rift Valley just as early, then the spread
of the knowledge of maize from the west also occurred before the mid–eighteenth
century.

   Maize appears, then, from the cumulative indications of the evidence, to have
spread relatively rapidly through eastern Africa from a variety of directions during
the sixteenth to eighteenth century. It may possibly have spread just as early to the
Great Lakes region from the Congo Basin to the west, although more likely the
acquaintance of Great Lakes peoples with maize came indirectly via Tanzania from
areas to the south. In many cases, the word evidence may imply only the bare knowledge or the sporadic cultivation of the crop. Still, the plant itself appears to have
been widely known in the deep interior of East Africa well before its twentieth-
century emergence as the major grain crop in many areas.

The Problem of the Sweet Potato: Multiple Introductions?

As for sweet potatoes, a variety of root words for this crop occur in usually contiguous patches of languages whether the languages belong to the same language family or not and, where the languages are related, frequently without regular sound correspondences. This kind of distribution and this kind of phonological pattern, of course, indicate the relatively recent spread of the item in question. There are, however, two notable exceptions to the usual patterns of contiguous occurrence of root words for sweet potato. Some of the data, in other words, is consistent with a much more ancient introduction.

One set of words for sweet potato in the Tanzania coastal hinterland, represented by Shambaa *kiogwe*, Zalamo *vibogwa*, and similar forms in neighboring languages and dialects, derive apparently from the same root as KiSwahili *myugwa* 'taro'. From the northern and central coastal hinterlands of Tanzania, sweet potatoes spread inland in the north to the Pare Mountains, where Asu has *kiogwe*, a visibly direct adoption of the Sambaa form, and inland farther south to the Uluguru Mountains, where Lugulu maintains the Zalamo form as *bogwa*.

An alternative Lugulu word for sweet potato, *hoka*, exists also. Since *h* in Lugulu comes from earlier Bantu *p, the original root shape of this word was *-poka. This root turns up still father inland in the Sandawe word *mpokhaa*. This form, because it maintains the embedded Bantu noun class prefix element m-, must he derived from a Bantu language, possibly closely related to Lugulu, but not yet identifiable from the available evidence. The most likely source of the Sandawe word would be the neighboring Gogo language of central Tanzania, but the evidence to settle the matter has not yet been gathered. In either case, however, the presence of this term in Sandawe shows that the spread of the sweet potato reached the Sandawe by borrowing from a Bantu language.

A second set of terms—seen in Dawida and Saghala *ikaji*, the Thagiicu (Gikuyu, Kamba, Meru, etc.) term *-kwaaje, Temi (Sonjo) *ngwaazi*, and Maasai *en-kwase*—marks a spread of sweet potatoes through the intermediate regions between the coast and the Rift. The Maasai word is clearly borrowed from a Thagiicu language. But the Thagiicu, Temi, and Taita shapes cannot be explained as borrowings from each other, nor do they show regular sound correspondence. Rather, they must be reckoned separate borrowings from a Southern Cushitic root, *kac'-. The Iraqw reflex of this root, *kasito?o*, plural *kasiis*, means "yam" (*Dioscorea* sp.).[13] But the presence of the consonant *j in the Dawida and Saghala languages and in Proto-Thagiicu shows that the word was borrowed from one or more now-extinct Southern Cushitic languages in which the original *c' sound was retained (or became *j), and not from Iraqw or any of its close relatives, in which *c' became *s.

Moreover, in the Thagiicu languages the uniformity of application of the root to sweet potatoes, together with the regularity of the sound correspondences, favors one of two solutions. Either the term reconstructs back to the Proto-Thagiicu language, spoken in the very early second millennium CE, or the term spread among Thagiicu groups during the later first half of the second millennium while the Thagiicu still formed a compact set of communities along the southern slopes of Mount Kenya and very little sound change had yet occurred.[14] Either way we are dealing with strong indications that the knowledge of sweet potatoes goes back before the earliest European contact with East Africa in 1497. What pushes back the possible arrival of sweet potatoes in the region even earlier than that is the derivation of these terms for sweet potato from probably two different Southern Cushitic languages, one in which original *k became *kw, as in the Thagiicu version of the word, and one in which original *k was maintained, as in the Saghala and Dawida borrowings.

A third set of words for sweet potato occurs at the Kenya Coast and in the coastal hinterland, represented by Giryama *kirazi,* Lower Pokomo *kiazi,* KiSwahili *kiazi,* and the like, and in north-central Tanzania in Langi *keraji* (plural *viraji*). This form derives from an early Mashariki noun root *-lagi for some species of yam; it is, for example, a word for yam in the Nyanja-Cewa language of Malawi. The same root is used for sweet potato in the Southern Cushitic languages neighboring Langi— Gorowa *wirasi,* Burunge *birasi,* and Alagwa *kirasimo.* The Southern Cushitic forms of the root lack regular sound correspondences with each other, and they all are, in any case, recent separate loanwords apparently from Langi, as their retention of fossilized Langi noun class prefixes shows. But the shape of the root in Langi does not derive from such a source. It maintains perfectly regular sound correspondence with the KiSwahili forms. Either the Langi usage was a case of a separate meaning shift of the original root from "yam" to "sweet potato," dating as recently as the nineteenth-century introduction of the crop implied by the Southern Cushitic versions of the root, or else it reflects a very early meaning shift dating to the first millennium CE.

In western Kenya, the spread of terms for sweet potato followed a pattern of spread very closely resembling that for maize. One root, occurring as *rabuon* in Luo, as *lipuoni* in Luhyia dialects, and as *ropuon in the southern half of the Kalenjin area, has a spread extending from Lake Nyanza to the Rift Valley, occurring as far east as the Keyo and Marakwet dialects. The Kalenjin shapes are direct borrowings from Luo because they retain the Luo ra- prefix element (in the assimilated shape ro-). Hence the Kalenjin knowledge of sweet potatoes dates no earlier than the establishment of Luo populations in Western Kenya in the sixteenth and seventeenth centuries. The Luhyia similarly borrowed their form of the *rabuon root from Luo, substituting their own *li- noun class prefix for Luo ra-.

A third version of this particular root word appears in the Sabiny and Päkot dialects of Kalenjin as, respectively, *tapono* and *toponik.* The tV- element substituted for initial ra- appears to be an Ateker (Eastern Nilotic) reinterpretation of the morphology of the root. The Ateker peoples, such as the Teso, inhabit areas just north of the Kalenjin and had strong earlier historical contacts with Luo-speaking peoples.[15] The words seen in Sabiny and Päkot are thus ultimately of Luo origin, although reaching them indirectly via an Ateker people.

If sweet potatoes were brought into eastern Uganda and western Kenya by the Luo, as the lexical evidence requires, then the crop is likely to have been known in northern Uganda in the seventeenth or sixteenth century, because this was the region and time from which the early Luo settlements emanated. How sweet potatoes might have reached this region, however, remains in need of further investigation.[16]

Only one root of really vast territorial spread turns up—namely, *-loolo, possibly originally denoting a red variety of sweet potato, or so reflexes as far scattered as Lugulu *ndolo* in eastern Tanzania and Lamba *cilolwe* in Zambia attest. In the simple shape of noun class prefix plus stem, this root shows the sort of scattered distribution and the differences in morphology (prefixation, in this case) typical of a really old word.

All along the eastern side of East Africa, down even into northern Mozambique, however, an additional prefix has been added to this root, preceding the original Bantu noun class prefix *n-, seen in the Lugulu reflex—for example, KiSwahili *kindoro* (*ki-n-lolo) and Gikuyu *mondooro* (*mo-n-loolo). The KiSwahili doubly prefixed shape has apparently undergone a further secondary spread inland, with progressively greater phonetic skewing as it spread westward from the Tanzania Coast.[17] In central Tanzania, Gogo *ikondolo* skews the vowel of former prefix *ki-, assimilating it to the *o of the final two syllables, and in addition attaches a new noun class prefix, *i-, to the skewed stem shape. The same form recurs as far inland as Lamba in Zambia, where it provides a second Lamba word for sweet potato, *kandolo*, lacking the usual Lamba sound change *o > *we, evident in the other, and older, Lamba version of the same root, *cilolwe*.

These versions of the root do not name "red" varieties of sweet potato in Lamba, nor apparently in Gogo, although the latter evidence needs to be checked in the field to see whether the available references are correct. In Lamba the occurrence of a phonologically noncorresponding form of the root can be proposed to be due to late-nineteenth-century contacts with East Africa established through the military adventures in the region of the Msiri, who had direct trading links with East Africa and the WaSwahili trade networks. The overall distribution of the varieties of the *-lolo root for "sweet potato" thus implies two spreads of the crop in Tanzania and southern Central Africa. The first, it can be proposed, was a very old spread of a red variety of sweet potato reflected in the remnant occurrences of the *-lolo root with a single prefix. The older Lamba shape, *cilolwe*, would be a retention of this root in the deep interior. The second diffusion of sweet potato varieties would belong to last few centuries and be reflected in the spread of the phonologically skewed shapes of the *-lolo root, ultimately deriving from the eastern Tanzanian root shape seen in KiSwahili *kindoro.*

In three cases—those of the *-kwaje, *-kaji, and *-lolo roots—it is difficult to find any way to fit the spread of sweet potatoes into a time span allowing for the introduction of the plant from the Americas by European sea trade. We can hardly resolve the issue for East Africa, let alone the wider continental frame: there are simply too many gaps in the necessary knowledge of the whole naming vocabulary of root and tuber crops. But there is clearly a reasonable basis for proposing the hypothesis that, at least in parts of the eastern portion of the continent of Africa, the introduction of one sort of sweet potato long predates the European arrival, that it came into East Africa through the Indian Ocean, and that ultimately it can be traced back to the pre-Columbian spread of the sweet potato from the Americas to Oceania. The introduction of additional varieties and the further diffusion of the crop in Africa then took place in the centuries since the rise of the Atlantic connection established by the Portuguese.

The Special Case of Tobacco

Tobacco, in contrast to maize and sweet potatoes, apparently had no readily analogous category of plants in the earlier East African agricultural repertoire, for its spread was accompanied almost wholly by borrowed names for it. The patterns of diffusion revealed by the names do not seem to reflect the restrictions of climate and prior agricultural proclivity as much as do those of some of the other introduced crops of American origin. In particular, it appears that knowledge of tobacco was most commonly transmitted through trade and that therefore the naming distributions might reflect patterns in the movement of goods from society to society in pre-nineteenth-century times.

In languages of the lower Zambezi region and south of there into northern South Africa, borrowed words for tobacco of the shape *fola* (in Venda), *fodia* (in Shona and Nyanja), and the like, derived from Portuguese *folha* 'leaf', are now widespread, showing the Portuguese to have been the direct source of the plant. The particular meaning of the Portuguese source of this borrowed word implies, further, that tobacco must have spread first in that region as a trade item in the form of tobacco leaves, before beginning to be grown locally.

Three other root words account for the diffusion of tobacco from the Zambezi northward to southern East Africa. A root word of uncertain origin, *-sayo, occurs in the Njombe languages Kinga, Bena, and Hehe of the southern highlands of Tanzania, while the Gogo and Kagulu languages, spoken immediately north of the Njombe languages, in central Tanzania, applied to tobacco the same old Bantu root word, *-konde 'thick stalk', which the Bantu societies around the north end of Lake Malawi drafted into use to name a different introduced crop, maize.[18] All across far southeastern Tanzania and northern Mozambique, the distribution of a third distinct root word, *-sona, marks the spread of tobacco inland through all the Rufiji-Ruvuma Bantu languages and as far west as the Tumbuka language of northern Malawi.

This third term raises an interesting historical issue. In many languages of the Rufiji-Ruvuma group, it shows a regular sound change of the original *s to *h*, and in some languages a further regular sound change took place, entirely deleting *h*. The change of *s to *h* was a quite early sound change of that group, implying that the word is old among those languages,[19] seemingly of too early an origin in time for its spread to have taken place as late as the arrival of the Portuguese at the East African coast. Intriguingly, however, the *-sona root bears a striking resemblance to the old Indo-Aryan root word for hemp; Hindi *san* and Punjabi *sanu* are examples of the modern-day reflexes of this ancient term. This suggests a possible historical explanation: that the distribution of *-sona may actually go back to an early introduction and spread of the use of cannabis inland via the Indian Ocean trade well before 1500 and that, with the introduction of tobacco by the Portuguese, the old term was shifted everywhere to the new, more addictive commodity.[20]

Across nearly all the rest of East Africa, different versions of the Taino (Native American of the Caribbean region) word *tabako* predominate.[21] This is, of course, the same word from which English *tobacco* also comes. The varied forms of this root reveal a variety of routes of diffusion of the plant into the interior regions of eastern Africa, dating clearly to after 1497. In most of Kenya and Tanzania a pattern of progressively greater phonetic skewing of this root word took place as the term and the item it names, tobacco, spread farther from the area of initial introduction.

The step-by-step diffusion of tobacco into the interior can be followed by tracing inland the successive stages in the skewing of the pronunciation of the words for tobacco. The original East African form of this word, naturally enough most closely resembling in shape the Native American source word, appears in KiSwahili *tumbako*. This word reached KiSwahili indirectly, via India,[22] indicating the establishment of the plant first in India before its introduction to the East African coastal towns.[23]

One chain of progressively more skewed word shapes traces the spread inland of the knowledge of tobacco from the Kenya Coast as far as the Rift Valley.

1. At the first stage of this spread, evidenced by Pokomo *ntumbaku* and some North Mijikenda *dumbaku*, the original final -o of the KiSwahili version of the word was assimilated to the preceding *u of the word; that is to say, those languages changed the pronunciation of the second back rounded vowel from *o* to *u*, making it identical (assimilating it) to the first back rounded vowel in the word, *u*.
2. The word *kumbaku* for tobacco in Giryama, and in Dawida of the Taita Hills

region, reveals the second stage of skewing. Their form of the word retains the first assimilation, of final *o* becoming *u*, and adds to that a second assimilation of the two voiceless stop consonants of the word: the first voiceless stop, *t*, shifted to *k*, becoming identical with the second voiceless stop of the word.

3. Saghala, also spoken in the Taita Hills region, with its form *kimbaku* took the skewing to still a further stage by interpreting initial ku- of the *kumbaku* stage as the Bantu locative prefix ku-, inappropriate in this grammatical context, and so replaced it with a suitable Bantu noun class prefix, ki-.

4. Kamba, spoken farther inland between the Taita Hills and the eastern highlands of Kenya, carried the process one stage further by treating the initial element ki- as an unnecessary, redundant prefix; deleting it; and reinterpreting the new initial consonant *m-* as a manifestation of one of the regular noun class prefixes of Bantu. (The change of the final vowel in the Kamba term *mbake* 'tobacco' remains to be accounted for, however.)

5. Gikuyu and the other Thagiicu languages, spoken still farther inland, around and south of Mount Kenya, then adopted the Kamba form but substituted the semantically more fitting mo- noun class prefix of plant names in place of Kamba m-, which normally attaches to animal names.

A separate route in the spread of tobacco diverged at the Taita Hills region:

6. The *kumbaku* shape seen in Dawida spread east and northeastward to the Maasai, producing the general Maasai term for tobacco, *ol-kumpau*. The loss of the second *k* in the word is a relatively recent Maasai sound change, and *mb* regularly becomes *mp* in Maasai borrowings from other languages. Tobacco would thus have first reached the Maasai in southern central Kenya from the Taita Hills, and the presence of a Maasai sound change along with the wide general use of the term by Maasai groups today suggests that the knowledge reached them before their wide expansions southward, and thus possibly by as early as the late seventeenth century.

To the south, in Tanzania, the crucial first stage of phonetic skewing in those regions was a consonant assimilation opposite to that seen in the Kenyan instances:

1. The second voiceless stop assimilated instead to the first, *k* becoming *t*, as exemplified by *tumbatu* for tobacco in the Shambaa language spoken just inland from the northern Tanzania Coast.

This assimilation was followed by additional skewings of the pronunciation as the term spread inland with the spread of tobacco.

One line of diffusion of the *tumbatu* term followed the Pangani River inland to Kilimanjaro:

2. The Chaga dialects apparently mark the end point of this route of transmis-

sion: they deleted the initial syllable, tu-, apparently interpreting it as the old Bantu diminutive plural class prefix *tu-, inappropriate in the context, and began to treat the residual shape *mbatu as composed of their regular reflex *m- of the old Bantu noun class singular prefix *mu- of plant names, plus a stem, *-batu.

The full *tumbatu* shape spread also from northeastern Tanzania westward across the present Maasai plains to the highland areas of north-central Tanzania. This region appears to have formed a major interior dispersal point of tobacco. Different sequences of skewed pronunciation marked these further dispersals:

3. In Langi the original *tumbatu* changed to *tumbetu,* brought about by a vowel height assimilation of the vowel *a*. (What this means is that the *a* became *e*, which is pronounced with the tongue higher in the mouth than *a*. The *a* was influenced to move to a higher position of pronunciation because the vowels on each side of *a* in *tumbatu*, both of them *u*, are pronounced with a high tongue position).

4. The *tumbetu* form in Langi was then in turn borrowed by the near western neighbor language Barabaig (Datoga) as *dumbedida*. (The change of original *t* to *d* is normal in Barabaig, which does not have the consonant *t* in these positions in a word; and the ending -ida is a Barabaig suffix.)

5. In early Iraqw, the shape *tumbatu* can be reconstructed to have developed two alternate pronunciations, *tumbato* and *tumato*. (These two forms, along with the present-day Iraqw term *tumati,* arose through the replacement of original -*u* by the Iraqw noun suffixes -*o* and -*i,* a common process of suffix substitution in the language.)

6. In the shape *tumato,* with the simplification of *mb* to *m,* the term subsequently spread to the nearby Sandawe language.

7. In the same shape it spread north to the western highlands of Kenya, accounting for the widespread presence of *tumato* (secondary form *tumatet*) for tobacco in the modern-day Kalenjin dialects. The direct spread of this word shape to the Kalenjin across the intervening Mara and Loita regions implies that the diffusion of tobacco northward to the western highlands must date to before the expansion of Maasai into the Mara and Loita plains in around the late seventeenth century.

8. From the Kalenjin the *tumato* shape of the word then spread to the neighboring Bantu-speaking Gusii people.

9. Still another line of dispersal of tobacco out of north-central Tanzania passed westward via early Iraqw to the Takama Bantu languages—Nyamwezi and Sukuma—which occupy much of western Tanzania. The form -tumbati found in the Takama groups must have been borrowed after the Iraqw substitution of -*i* for original final -*o,* but before the Iraqw simplification of original *mb* to *m*.

10. As knowledge of tobacco subsequently spread north from the Sukuma along the west side of Lake Nyanza (Lake Victoria), a further skewing of pronunciation took place: a dissimilation of the two identical consonants *t* of *tumbati,* such that the first *t* became *k.* This change created a new word shape, -kumbati. This new shape developed apparently in the Suguti group of Bantu languages spoken along the southeastern shores of Lake Nyanza. It then spread northward along the east side of the lake, with the farthest north spread of this form reaching the slopes of Mount Elgon, where it appears in the Bukusu dialect of Luhyia as *si-xumbari* 'lump of tobacco' (si- is an added Bukusu noun class prefix; *t regularly becomes *r* in Bukusu, and *k becomes *x*).

The northward spread of tobacco along the eastern side of the lake must therefore have been contemporaneous with the parallel northward diffusion of tobacco from north-central Tanzania into the immediately adjacent areas to the east inhabited by the Gusii and Kalenjin peoples. That is to say, the knowledge of tobacco, on this evidence, would have reached both the lakeshore areas and the western highlands of Kenya by probably no later than the late seventeenth century. This dating is further confirmed by the fact that the -*kumbati* term is not used in the Luo language today spoken in the intervening Winam Gulf area, south of the Luhyia and north of the Kuria. The spread of the term thus must predate the growing establishment of Luo communities in more and more of that area by the later seventeenth and eighteenth centuries.[24]

11. The *tumbato* word for tobacco was apparently transmitted southward, as well, from the Nyamwezi, to the Corridor region of southwestern Tanzania, but with a more severe phonetic skewing, in the form -tumba, with the loss of the whole final syllable of the word.

But tobacco did not enter East Africa only from the east side of the continent. The second principal direction of the spread of tobacco into eastern Africa was from the northwest. In these areas the basic term for tobacco has the root shape -taba, also derivable ultimately from the Taino term, and has a vast continuous distribution reaching into Uganda and western Kenya from the Middle Nile Basin and extending back westward across the Sudan belt of Africa all the way to Senegal. Apparently introduced into Senegambia by the Spanish or Portuguese, tobacco spread so rapidly across the Sudan belt as to reach all the way to western Kenya as early as it reached those areas from the much nearer Indian Ocean coasts.

For East African history what is most revealing is the interface of the -taba root with skewed varieties of the -tumbako root. In Bukusu, *eraba,* from -taba (the sound change of *t to *r* is regular), is the generic term for tobacco. The coexisting presence of the -kumbati term in Bukusu as *sixumbari* 'lump of tobacco' can be explained

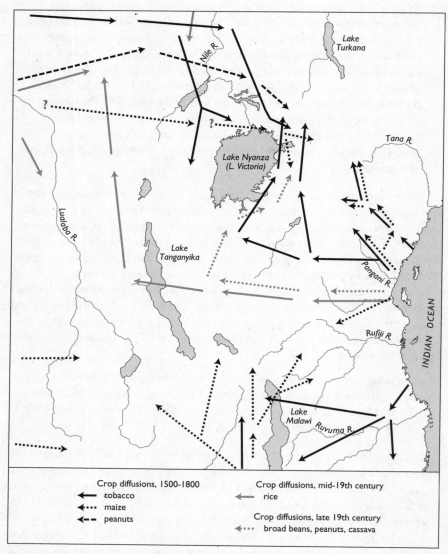

Lake Turkana

Nile R.

Tana R.

Lualaba R.

Lake Nyanza
(L. Victoria)

Lake Tanganyika

Pangani R.

INDIAN OCEAN

Rufiji R.

Lake Malawi

Ruvuma R.

Crop diffusions, 1500-1800
◄— tobacco
◄···· maize
◄– – peanuts

Crop diffusions, mid-19th century
◄— rice

Crop diffusions, late 19th century
◄···· broad beans, peanuts, cassava

MAP 5. The Diffusion of American Crops in East Africa, 1500–1900

by a dual introduction of tobacco. The initial acquaintance of Bukusu speakers would have been with tobacco in a processed form, as a "lump of tobacco," coming to them in trade from their southern neighbors, but with the crop itself arriving somewhat later from the north, bringing with it the name -taba.

When did these events take place? The spread of tobacco into the Mount Elgon area as a trade item from the south, we have already proposed, is likely to have to have preceded the full establishment of the Luo in western Kenya. On the other hand, the spread of tobacco as a crop appears likely to date after Luo populations had become well established north of the Winam Gulf. The reason is that Luo *ndawa* 'tobacco' does not correspond regularly with the Acholi *taba* and other northern Luo forms of this root. It is, instead, a shape that, because it contains the Luhyia noun class prefix *in- (in the shape *n-*), must have been a loanword in Luo from one of the Luhyia dialects. This evidence means that the -taba word for tobacco must have reached northern Uganda only after the founders of many of the Kenya Luo communities had already left those regions—thus no earlier than probably the later seventeenth century. The various lines of evidence conjoin in implying that knowledge of tobacco as a trade item was reaching western Kenya from the south by sometime in the seventeenth century and that the knowledge of the tobacco plant itself, coming from northern Uganda and southern Sudan, dates to no later than the eighteenth century.

The still-earlier spread inland of tobacco from the Kenya and northern Tanzania coasts, as well as from the coasts of the lower Zambezi regions to the south, would have begun in the sixteenth century. In Zimbabwe tobacco was a direct Portuguese introduction. In East Africa, the transmission of a Native American term for tobacco via Portuguese to India and then back from India to the WaSwahili coastal peoples shows that tobacco reached the northern and central WaSwahili towns by a more circuitous route. The southern arm of the spread of tobacco inland was the most rapid, extending to western Tanzania and then reaching northward into western Kenya by two parallel lines of spread before the eighteenth century. Tobacco, it also appears, often spread as a commodity ahead of its spread as a locally grown crop. An almost equally early and territorially much more rapid spread of the plant took place from the northwest into western Kenya via the Middle Nile Basin, coming ultimately from the far Senegambian coasts (map 5).

DIFFERING CROP HISTORIES
AND THEIR WIDER IMPLICATIONS

In the cumulative picture, the nineteenth century stands out as a significant period in the spread in eastern Africa of new crops from the Americas and the spread inland of at least one crop of southern Asian origin already raised for centuries on the coast. The introduction of American crops along the coast in the sixteenth and seventeenth centuries did not necessarily lead to their immediate spread into the interior. On the other hand, some of these crops did begin to penetrate early into the interior. Tobacco, which became a widely exchanged commodity, apparently diffused rapidly and widely early on, reaching the Great Lakes region probably before the end of seventeenth century. Maize spread also appears often to predate the nineteenth century, but it is not at all evident that it was as rapid or as early as the spread of tobacco. Presumably the adoption of maize was governed more by climatic constraints and agricultural predilections of peoples along the ecologically possible routes of spread.[25] One variety of sweet potato is even conceivably very ancient in East Africa and may have reached the continent from the Americas via the Indian Ocean and South Pacific. But other American crops spread beyond the coast only in the later nineteenth or even twentieth century.

In the spread of certain crops the long-distance trade contacts established in the nineteenth century seem to have been crucial. This importance is clearly evident for rice, for which WaSwahili agency in its establishment in the East African interior and as far as the eastern Democratic Republic of Congo is everywhere attested in the naming data. Rice is simply the most striking illustration of this pattern, since it is not even an American crop, but rather an Indonesian and Southeast Asian plant probably established at the coast since the first millennium and yet still not more widely spread until 150 years ago. As well, American beans of the *Phaseolus* genus were known at the coast for some time before the nineteenth century, and WaSwahili trade links apparently spread them to peoples in several parts of the Tanzania and Kenya interior in the nineteenth century. Also the diffusion of new varieties of sweet potatoes probably took place by this means, as at least Lamba *kandolo* for "sweet potato" suggests for Zambia and adjoining areas of Katanga in Congo.

Other crops became established widely probably only in the colonial era. In the case of cassava, the use of the KiSwahili word is so widespread that, even without documentary confirmation, one would have to suppose establishment of the crop in many parts of East Africa only in that period, the point in time when KiSwahili finally became used almost universally in interethnic communication. Broad beans as well did not attained their full spread until the colonial era—Marakwet, where the KiSwahili term for the crop was directly adopted, and Kilimanjaro, where the German word was used among the Chaga, being examples. Peanuts also in several areas must have been a twentieth-century adoption.

Only the surface has been touched here of all that could be learned about recent agricultural history from a detailed investigation of the myriad of plant variety names in each East African language's agricultural vocabulary and through intensive oral historical research into the agricultural past. The task is worthy of our interest and attention. It is a task to which local historians interested in the areas in which they live can make significant contributions. How much can be accomplished in this sort of historical study is well illustrated in the doctoral thesis of David Lloyd on nineteenth-century agricultural change in northeastern Congo. This work is essential reading for those who wish to study precolonial agricultural history.[26]

There are, in addition, implications here for more than just the history of crops. To the extent that a new crop spread at first as a commodity, the routes of spread will reveal the lines of exchange relations between peoples and often uncover trade routes otherwise unknown to us. For example, the spread of tobacco names in particular implies south-to-north trade orientations of peoples of north-central and western Tanzania and the adjacent areas of Kenya around the seventeenth century. Similarly, the distribution of tobacco names through northeastern Tanzania and southeastern Kenya, as also names of maize, shows that the nineteenth-century caravan trade tended to move along the older main lines of contact and movement of goods of the eighteenth and seventeenth centuries from coast to interior. In central Tanzania, on the other hand, the late-eighteenth- and nineteenth-century trade route opened up between the coast and Unyamwezi appears to have been a truly new connection not presaged in the earlier patterns of crop spread from the coast.

Obviously we would be mistaken to suppose that any absolute barriers stood between the East African interior and the Indian Ocean world before the late eighteenth century. But we would be equally mistaken to suppose that the interior areas faced more, usually, than culturally peripheral historical influences coming from outside those areas. The dominant historical factors were locally generated conditions, simply because the seventeenth- and eighteenth-century communities of the central East African interior interacted through interlocking local networks exchanging small amounts of surplus production, rather than through overarching and all-encompassing networks that imposed high commodity demand on the suppliers. That kind of demand began to be the case only toward the very end of the eighteenth century. The immensely rapid spread of tobacco across the Sudan belt— over 6,000 kilometers from Senegal to the African Great Lakes in 250 years, as compared with 600 to 1,000 kilometers in 250 years from the East African coast to the Great Lakes—brings out very clearly how undeveloped and localized the East African trade links were, how different not only in degree but in kind East African interior trade was, from that of the Sudan belt in the sixteenth to eighteenth century. The diffusion of peanuts all the way from the Atlantic coast of Central Africa to western Kenya in 300 years or less, but not inland from the Indian Ocean coast until the colonial era, similarly reveals the importance of the long-existing long-distance trade networks in the Congo Basin.

The nineteenth century brought a leap upward in the rate and scale of impact of new things and ideas, and of forces generated outside the continent, on the minds and lives of East Africans. Some of the agricultural elements of that history have been brought to attention here, but they form only a segment of the whole range of material and other cultural changes that began well before the nineteenth century and continue to take place now. More important, eastern Africa itself was just one small arena in an age of transformative change around the globe. The testimonies of the myriad spreads of new words for all the varieties of cultural change set in motion since 1500 deserve the attention of historians, and not just in eastern Africa, but across the rest of the world as well.

NOTES

1. The attribution of this root in the *Standard Swahili-English Dictionary* to a Persian word for an unidentified kind of grain seems unwarranted. *Haricot* is of disputed origin, but a common attribution of the term is to the Nahuatl name (*ayecotli*).

2. The asterisk indicates a reconstructed original or underlying shape for a root word and not necessarily the root as pronounced in any particular language today.

3. This sound shift also took place, but at a very recent point in time, in the major dialect of Shambaa, spoken just inland from Bondei.

4. C. Ehret, *An African Classical Age: Eastern and Southern Africa in World History, 1000 BC to AD 400* (Charlottesville: University of Virginia Press, 1998), p. 105.

5. D. T. Lloyd, "The Precolonial Economic History of the Avongara-Azande c. 1750–1916" (Ph.D. diss., UCLA, 1978).

6. It is possible to argue that *wali* is a form of the early Mashariki Bantu noun root *-gali, present in KiSwahili *ugali* 'porridge', but was borrowed from another, unidentified Bantu language (with irregular loss of former *g); but a straightforward borrowing of the Proto-Malagasy term is the more parsimonious solution here.

7. The Shona term can be proposed to derive from the earlier Bantu verb root *-pung- 'to fan', which took on the meaning "to clean grain by winnowing" in early Mashariki Bantu; see C. Ehret, "Agricultural History in Central and Southern Africa, ca. 1000 BC to AD 500," *Transafrican Journal of History* 4 (1974): 1–24; and idem, *African Classical Age*, pp. 129.

8. KiSwahili *mchele* is a straightforward, regular reflex of Mashariki Bantu *-sele 'individual grain', itself a noun derivative of earlier Bantu *-sel- 'to clean.' which in early Mashariki Bantu took on the specifically grain-processing meaning "to sift grains"; Ehret, "Agricultural History in Central and Southern Africa."

9. Some colonial observers suggested the derivation of this term from the name of Pemba Island. This idea is insupportable on the face of it and shows that those who proposed it were simply unacquainted with the evidence, long known to linguists, of the old eastern Bantu root *-pemba for grain species.

10. C. C. Fourshey, "Agriculture, Ecology, Kinship and Gender: A Social and Economic History of Tanzania's Corridor, 500 B.C. to 1900 A.D." (Ph.D. diss., UCLA, 2002).

11. C. Ehret, "Agricultural History in Central and Southern Africa, ca. 1000 BC to AD 500," *Transafrican Journal of History* 4 (1974): 1–25; Ehret, *African Classical Age*, p. 272.

12. C. Ehret, "The Eastern Kenya Interior, 1500–1800," in E. S. Atieno Odhiambo (ed.), *African Historians and African Voices* (Basel: P. Schlettwein, 2001).

13. C. Ehret, *The Historical Reconstruction of Southern Cushitic Phonology and Vocabulary* (Berlin: Reimer, 1980).

14. Ehret, "Eastern Kenya Interior."

15. C. Ehret and others, "Some Thoughts on the Early History of the Nile-Congo Watershed," *Ufahamu* 5, no. 2 (1974): 85–112; C. Ehret, "Population Movement and Culture Contact in the Southern Sudan, c. 3000 BC to AD 1000," in J. Mack and P. Robertshaw (eds.), *Culture History in the Southern Sudan: Archaeology, Linguistics and Ethnohistory* (Nairobi: British Institute in Eastern Africa, 1983), pp. 19–48.

16. To the west of Uganda, the word among the Mangbetu (Central Sudanic) people of Congo, -bondo, is a possible further related form.

17. The Swahili version of this root itself was borrowed from an as yet unidentified Bantu language of the coastal region, possibly no longer spoken, in which *l between vowels was retained as an /r/ sound. In Swahili, the regularly corresponding shape should be *kindoo, with loss of the *l.

18. Fourshey, "Agriculture, Ecology, Kinship and Gender." Bantu peoples applied the same root word, although much more anciently, to the banana across much of western central Africa.

19. D. Nurse, "The Diachronic Background to the Language Communities of Southwestern Tanzania," *Sprache und Geschichte in Afrika* 9 (1988): 15–115.

20. Allen Thurm, a graduate student in African Studies at the University of California, first presented this material and this argument in a research seminar paper in 1969.

21. Interestingly, in the Taino language of the Caribbean this word referred not specifically to the tobacco plant but to a roll of tobacco leaves and a Y-shaped pipe for smoking tobacco through the nostrils. Spanish speakers converted it into the general term for tobacco, and from Spanish the word spread in that meaning to many other languages.

22. The Indian languages converted the medial *b* of the word into a prenasal consonant, *mb*, as we see in the Hindi terms *tambaku, tumbak*.

23. The same shape of the root turns up in modern Shambaa and Dawida. But its presence there may be due to twentieth-century feedback from the use of KiSwahili in the colonial era, because both of these languages, like the other near-coastal Bantu languages, possess alternative shapes of the word with first-stage skewings of the KiSwahili pronunciation.

24. The history of the expanding settlements of Luo communities in these centuries is detailed in B. A. Ogot, *History of the Southern Luo* (Nairobi: East African Publishing House, 1977).

25. The evidence does not suggest any particular association of maize with provisioning the slave trade as it did on the western side of Africa. Rice seems instead to have taken on that role in East Africa, notably in the nineteenth century.

26. Lloyd, "Precolonial Economic History."

Outline Classification of Afrasian (Afroasiatic): Diagnostic Branch Innovations

I. Omotic

Defining innovations

a. Merging of Proto-Afrasian (PAA) labiovelars with velars except before the vowel *i

b. Asymmetrical devoicing of two PAA voiced affricates (*j > *c, *dz > z)

II. Erythraic

Defining innovations found in both Cushitic and North Erythraic but not in Omotic

a. Merging of PAA voiced and voiceless affricates into one voiced and one voiceless consonant (PAA *j and *dz > *dz; *c and *ts > *ts)

b. Co-occurrence constraint disallowing two different labial consonants in same root

c. Shift to assigning grammatical gender to nouns in place of PAA marking only of natural gender

d. New masc./fem. 3rd person singular pronouns, *su/*si

e. New masc./fem. 3rd person plural pronoun, *sun/*sin

f. New 2nd person subordinate masc./fem. pronouns, *ku, *ki

A. Cushitic

Defining innovations

a. PAA *b > *m preceding *n as the 2nd consonant in a root

b. Devoicing of PAA *g to *k following *d or *w in the same root

B. North Erythraic

Defining innovation

a. Reduction of the vowels from a PAA system of ten long and short vowels (*i, *ii, *e, *ee, *a, *aa, *o, *oo, *u, and *uu) to a system of one back, one front, and two central vowels (*u, *i, *a, and *ə)

1. Chado-Berber
   Defining innovations
   a. Innovated pronoun shapes[1]
   b. Lexical innovations[2]
2. Boreafrasian
   Defining innovations
   a. Development of an array of co-occurrence constraints against sequences of sibilants in the same root
   b. Merging of velar and palatal nasals with *n

NOTES

1. P. Newman, *The Classification of Chadic within Afroasiatic* (Leiden: Universitaire Pers, 1980).

2. James Bynon, "Berber and Chadic: The Lexical Evidence," in J. Bynon (ed.), *Current Progress in Afro-Asiatic Linguistics: Papers of the Third International Hamito-Semitic Congress* (Amsterdam and Philadelphia: John Benjamins, 1984), pp. 241–290, lists a large number of old root words shared by Proto-Chadic and Proto-Berber, at least four of which, for "know," "drink," "wind," and "breast," stand out as innovations unique to the core vocabularies of these two branches.

APPENDIX TWO

Proto-Afrasian and Proto-Erythraic Subsistence

A. PROTO-AFRASIAN SUBSISTENCE LEXICON

1. *maaw-/*maay- 'grain seed'
   I. Omotic: Mocha maawo 'cereals'
   II. Proto-Cushitic (PC) *maay 'grain; grain seed ' (So. Cush. 'granary');
   Chadic: East Chadic *may 'sorghum'; Egyptian mymy 'seed corn of emmer (?)';
   Semitic *my 'grain, seed grain, whole grains'

2. *tl'eff- 'grain sp.'
   I. Omotic: Proto-Gonga (PG) *t'eepp- 'wheat'
   II. Cushitic: Proto-Agäw *tab-/ taf- 'teff'; E. Cush.: Soomaali dheef 'food, sustenance')

3. *ʕeyl- 'grain processed for eating (in the form of kernels?)'
   I. Proto-Omotic *il- 'flour'
   II. Proto-Cushitic *ʕeyl- 'grain, cereal'; Egyptian inyt 'kernels'

4. *dzayj- '(coarse?) flour'
   I. Omotic: Bench žaču 'millet flour';
   II. Egyptian zzw 'dust'; Semitic: Arabic jaðiið 'coarse flour'

5. *-xuum- 'to separate ears of grain'
   I. Omotic: Zayse huum- 'to winnow'
   II. Egyptian ḥms 'ear of wheat' (stem plus *-s noun suffix; Coptic hms, hēms)

6. *zar- 'grain seed, grass seed'
   I. Omotic: Proto–North Omotic (PNO) *zar- 'seed'
   II. Chadic: Ngizim ɗari 'grain with bran removed'; Semitic: PS *zrʕ 'to sow; seed')

B. ADDITIONAL PROTO-ERYTHRAIC SUBSISTENCE LEXICON

7. *buz- 'flour'
   - II.A. Cushitic: Soomaali budo 'flour'
   - II.B. Chadic: Bole buɗu 'flour'
8. *kw'aʔ- or *-kw'aaʔ- 'grain (coll.)'
   - II.A. Cushitic: So. Cush.: Kw'adza kw'aʔateto 'granary' (stem *kwaʔ- plus So. Cush. n. suffixes)
   - II.B. Egyptian ḳ33 'grains (?)'
9. *boor- 'grain sp.'
   - II.A. Cushitic: Dullay *boor-t- 'barley'
   - II.B. Proto-Semitic *br(r) 'corn, wheat' (A. burr)
10. *musay-/*misay- 'grain sp. (sorghum[?])'
    - II.A. Cushitic: Proto-East-South Cush. *mušʌŋ-/*mišʌŋ- 'sorghum' (stem plus Cush. *-ŋ noun suff.)
    - II.B. Egyptian msy 'kind of grain'
11. *daadl- 'grain sp.' (uncertain sp. in each case)
    - II.A. Cushitic: Oromo daad'a
    - II.B. Egyptian dḍ
12. *ʕaag- 'grain'
    - II.A. Proto-Cushitic *ʕaag- 'sorghum sp.'
    - II.B. Egyptian cgwt 'a preparation of grain'; Chadic: Ngizim aagaw 'pounded, cooked grain'
13. *baz- 'grain'
    - II.A. Cushitic: Proto–Eastern Cushitic (PEC) *baz(z)- 'flour'
    - II.B. Egyptian bd.t 'emmer, spelt'; Semitic: Arabic bazr, bizr 'seed, grain'
14. *puzn- 'flat bread'
    - II.A. Cushitic: PHEC, Oromo *budden- 'flat bread'
    - II.B. Egyptian pzn 'a loaf'
15. *faʕ- or *faaʕ- 'cooked grain'
    - II.A. Cushitic: Proto–West Rift *faʕ- 'porridge'
    - II.B. Egyptian pct 'a cake or loaf' (PAA *f > Eg. p in this environment)

C. ADDITIONAL LEXICON IN PROTO-NORTH ERYTHRAIC

16. *ɣunz- or *ɣʷinz- 'sp. of grain'
    - II.B.1. Chadic: Hausa gunɗu 'Pennisetum' (Chadic *ɣ > Hausa /g/)
    - II.B.2. Egyptian ḫnd 'kind of cereal'
17. *ław 'grain (coll.)'
    - II.B.1. Chadic: some C. Chadic *ław 'sorghum'
    - II.B.2. Egyptian š 'garden'; Semitic: Arabic šauna-t, pl. šawānī 'granary, barn' (< *ław-n, stem plus *n noun suff.)
18. *bayn- 'grindstone'
    - II.B.1. Chadic: Proto-Chadic *bəna
    - II.B.2. Egyptian bnwt

Development of Nilo-Saharan Lexicons of Herding and Cultivation

A. PROTO-NORTHERN SUDANIC

Lexicon That Is Diagnostic of Livestock Raising

1. *ndʸɔw 'to milk': Kunama; E'rn Sahelian (Taman; Jebel; Rub)
2. *sʸuuk 'to drive (domestic animals)': Kunama; Saharan; E'rn Sahelian (Nubian)
3. *yaaṭ 'to water (livestock)': Kunama; Saharan
4. *ɔrɔh 'thornbush livestock pen': Kunama ora, ola 'thornbush pen'; Saharan (Zaghawa oru 'livestock, herd'); E'rn Sahelian (Kir: Didinga ɔlɔ' 'village (enclosed in thornbush fence)')

Lexicon That Is Not Diagnostic of Herding or Cultivation

5. *yaayr 'cow (generic)': Kunama; Songay; E'rn Sahelian (Nara; Kir)
6. *way or *'way 'grain': Kunama; For; E'rn Sahelian (Astaboran, Kir)
7. *ke:n 'ear of grain': Kunama; Songay
8. *p'ɛl 'grindstone': Kunama; E'rn Sahelian (Kir)

Other Material-Culture Lexicon

9. *saap or *saab or *saaɓ 'temporary shelter': Kunama; Songay; E'rn Sahelian (Kir)
10. *ted 'to make pot': Kunama: Maban; E'rn Sahelian (Kir)

B. PROTO-SAHARO-SAHELIAN STAGE

Lexicon That Is Diagnostic of Cultivation

11. *dʸipʰ 'to cultivate': Saharan; Songay; E'rn Sahelian (Jebel)
12. *tɔɔk(ɔp) 'to cultivate': Saharan; Songay; E'rn Sahelian (Rub)
13. *tʰaypʰ 'to clear plot for cultivation': Saharan; Songay; E'rn Sahelian (Jebel; Rub)

14. *kʰay 'to clear (weeds, stubble)': Saharan; Songay; E'rn Sahelian (Kir)
15. *od̶ ʸomp 'cultivated field': Saharan; E'rn Sahelian (Kir)

Lexicon That Is Not Diagnostic of Cultivation

16. *ŋak or *ŋag or *ŋaʃ 'to grind (grain) coarsely': Saharan; E'rn Sahelian (Kir)
17. *pʰeθ 'to winnow': Saharan; Songay; E'rn Sahelian (Kir)

Other Material Culture: Residential Lexicon

18. *ɓoreh 'thornbush cattle pen': Saharan; E'rn Sahelian (Rub)
19. *kʰal 'fence': Saharan; Songay; E'rn Sahelian (Kir)
20. *dɔŋ or *d̶ɔŋ or *d̶ʸɔŋ 'yard, enclosure of homestead': Saharan; For; E'rn Sahelian (Kir)
21. *d̶ ʸor 'open area of settlement': Saharan; E'rn Sahelian (Nubian; Jebel; Kir)
22. *piḍah 'granary': Saharan; For
23. *d̶onk'ol 'circular roll of reeds/grass which supports roof of round house': Saharan; E'rn Sahelian (Kir)

Additional Lexicon That Is Diagnostic of Livestock Raising

(18. *ɓoreh 'thornbush cattle pen')
24. *yokw 'to herd': Saharan; Songay; E'rn Sahelian (Kir; Rub)
25. *Wer 'young female domestic animal, heifer': Saharan (Zaghawa orı 'young camel'; E'rn Sahelian (Kir: Didinga oli 'heifer'; Nilotic; Rub: pre-Soo *weras, pl. *weret 'ewe-lamb, young female kid')
26. *opu 'adult male domestic animal, bull': Saharan (Zaghawa obu 'he-goat'); E'rn Sahelian (Kir: Temein opʋn 'bull')
27. *ŋgeṭ 'to milk': Saharan; E'rn Sahelian (Kir)
28. *ṭʰa 'milk (n.)': Saharan; E'rn Sahelian (Nara; Kir) (derivation of this term from the PNS root for "white" implies milk in quantity, hence diagnostic of milking)

C. PROTO-SAHELIAN STAGE

Lexicon That Is Diagnostic of Sheep and Goat Raising

29. *ay 'goat': For; E'rn Sahelian (Kir)
30. *ǰent 'he-goat': Songay; E'rn Sahelian (Rub)
31. *Wɛd 'sheep': For; E'rn Sahelian (Nubian; Kir-Abbaian)
32. *meŋkʰ 'ram' or 'sheep': Maba 'sheep'; E'rn Sahelian (Kir 'ram')
33. *Weḷ 'ram': For; E'rn Sahelian (Kir; Rub)
34. *k'er 'female sheep, goat (?)': Songay 'female kid'; E'rn Sahelian (Kir 'sheep')
35. *θagw 'young male goat or sheep (?)': Songay 'male kid'; E'rn Sahelian (Kir 'sheep', 'cow that has not yet borne young')

Additional Cattle Terminology That Is Diagnostic of Herding

36. *owiŋ or *o'wiŋ 'bull': For; E'rn Sahelian (Kir)
37. *maawr 'ox': Maban; E'rn Sahelian (KA: Kir)

38. *yagw or *yaɗw 'young cow': Songay 'young bull'; E'rn Sahelian (Nubian 'small stock'; Kir 'heifer')
39. *kaa or *kaah 'large livestock enclosure': Songay 'nomad encampment; livestock pen'; E'rn Sahelian (Kir 'homestead [enclosed in thornbush fence]')

Additional Cattle Terminology

40. *Ṭ'ɛ or *Ṭ'ɛh 'cow (generic)': Maban; E'rn Sahelian (Astaboran, Kir)
41. *hɛw 'cow (generic)': For úú; Songay háw

Additional Lexicon That Is Diagnostic of Cultivation

42. *pʰad 'to cultivate': Songay; For; E'rn Sahelian (Kir)
43. *t'um 'to sow, plant': Songay; E'rn Sahelian (Kir)
44. *pʰaal̩ 'bush, uncultivated land': For; E'rn Sahelian (Nubian, Kir)

Additional Crop and Food-Preparation Lexicon

45. *ɗuT 'a kind of gourd': Songay; E'rn Sahelian (Rub)
46. *kʰul 'a kind of gourd': Songay; E'rn Sahelian (Kir)
47. *Kɛdɛh 'bottle gourd': For; E'rn Sahelian (Kir)
48. *buḍ 'edible gourd': For; E'rn Sahelian (Kir)
49. *p'ent'uh 'winnowing tray': Songay; E'rn Sahelian (Kir)

Interpreting the Ethiosemitic Cognation Matrix

METHODOLOGICAL PRELIMINARIES
TO INTERPRETING A COGNATION MATRIX

The shared cognation retention counts for languages or subgroupings of languages of equally distant relationship from each other tend to a normal distribution. Commonly, the number of languages deriving from any particular ancestral language in any particular case are too few, and thus the figures are too few, to form a smooth bell curve. Nevertheless, that is the phenomenon involved in this kind of reckoning.

Before we examine the diagnostic distributions in the following matrix, we need to take account of a factor, intrusive and extraneous to the usual processes of lexical replacement in a language's history, that has the effect of skewing the cognation counts upward. This factor— word borrowing among closely related languages—can often add further bumpiness to the distribution curve. When a language borrows a word from a closely related language, this event may happen before any sound changes have taken place that would clearly identify the word as a loan. Also, when pronunciation differences are still small between two diverging languages, the speakers of the borrowing language often readjust the pronunciation of the borrowed word to fit their way of pronouncing, thus removing the effects of the sound changes in the closely related language from which the word came. As a consequence, borrowings between still mutually intelligible dialects of a language or between closely related languages often cannot be distinguished phonologically from commonly inherited roots. Thus they appear to be normal shared retentions; they get counted as retentions; and their presence inflates the apparent cognation retention rate (table 34).

Several instances of this effect stand out in the matrix. They appear in italicized boldface to allow easy identification. For these counts, even the possibility of explaining them as far extremes on the bell-shaped normal distribution curve is of vanishingly small probability. The alternative solution is thus that such counts reflect undetected word borrowing

Table 34. Ethiosemitic Cognation Matrix

Tigre	Tigrinya	Amharic	Argobba	Harari	Zway	Walani	Gafat	Soddo	Mäsqan	Chaha	Geto	Ennemor	Mesmes
	Tigrinya												
64													
52	56	Amharic											
45	53	79	Argobba	(Cross-Rift South Ethiopic)									
49	47	59	56	Harari									
52	51	60	57	70	Zway								
43	45	56	57	70	79	Walani							
46	49	65	57	52	53	59	Gafat						
47	49	66	64	61	61	63	62	Soddo	(Outer South Ethiopic)				
43	45	56	57	59	55	59	54	69	Mäsqan				
44	43	55	55	54	58	62	52	70	80	Chaha			
44	43	53	52	52	55	58	51	69	76	89	Geto		
43	43	50	53	54	55	55	49	66	70	81	83	Ennemor	
40	40	45	50	49	55	49	48	58	58	56	59	68	Mesmes
(box 1)		(box 2)											

between the languages involved. The four notably anomalous cases are those of Amharic with Tigrinya, Amharic with Gafat, Mesmes with Ennemor, and Soddo with the rest of South Ethiosemitic.[1]

The direct consequence of the presence of undetected word borrowings between related languages is that the undetected loans will be counted as if they were actual common retentions. If such loans are relatively numerous, they will significantly raise the apparent cognation percentage of the borrowing language with the language from which the loanwords come.

This kind of borrowing has a corollary effect, however, that helps us to determine the direction of borrowing and thus confirm the conclusion that borrowing is in fact involved. What is this effect? The cognate retention counts of the borrowing language with languages closely related to the particular source language of the loans will also be skewed higher. The reason for this secondary effect is that the closely related tongues, because of their close relationship, will retain many (but not all) of the same words as those borrowed from their near relative. Thus their scores with the borrowing language will tend to be inflated, but to a lesser extent. For example, Amharic's overly high apparent cognation with Tigrinya (56 percent) can in part be attributed to word borrowing by Amharic from Tigrinya because

Amharic also has an overly high score, though offset somewhat lower (52 percent), with Tigre, the closest relative of Tigrinya. By the same token, Tigrinya can also be argued to have borrowed words from Amharic, since Tigrinya's count with Amharic's closest related language, Argobba, is similarly overly high (53 percent), although once again not as high as with Amharic, the inferred donor language.

The direction of influence is not so clear in the case of the anomalously high Amharic and Gafat figure of 65 percent. It is probable that some of the early expansions of Amharic, between 1300 and 1500, were into areas speaking early Gafat. Such a history might well have brought Gafat loanwords into Amharic and thus in part account for the inflated Gafat–Amharic percentage. In addition, recent loan activity from Amharic to Gafat during the centuries of Gafat's decline can be expected to have further raised the apparent cognation of the two languages. Both possibilities deserve careful investigation.

Ennemor should be considered the more probable borrowing language in the Mesmes–Ennemor interaction, because no upward skewing of Mesmes's scores with Ennemor's nearest congeners is apparent. Hetzron groups Ennemor with Mesmes, but his genetic grouping of Ennemor and Mesmes depends on the presumption that the morphological developments he identified were not borrowed.[2] Such borrowing is relatively infrequent, but it does take place. Here the lexical evidence indicates intensive language interference between Mesmes and Ennemor and, except for the one figure of Mesmes–Ennemor itself, a very sharp break between Mesmes and the rest of the group to which Ennemor belongs. Even the high skewed cognation between the two languages is distinctly below the general range of cognation among Ennemor and its other near relatives. More likely than not, then, morphological interference accompanied lexical borrowing in this instance, making Mesmes seem more closely related to Ennemor than is actually the case.

Soddo provides the most striking examples of anomalously high percentages. Its highest range is 66–70 percent with the Chaha-Mäsqan languages, with which it is geographically joined. Its 47 and 49 percentages with North Ethiosemitic languages clearly places it outside that group. Soddo thus can be accounted a South Ethiosemitic tongue with an extraordinarily high rate of word borrowing in basic vocabulary, probably on the order of about 15 percent, from Chaha-Mäsqan—a situation that reflects probably centuries of close social interactions between Soddo speakers and their immediate neighbors. A second major influence of Soddo in recent centuries would appear to have been Amharic, with which Soddo has an apparent 66 percent retention rate. As expected, the corollary effect confirming this history for the Soddo language is present: the Soddo scores with the rest of South Ethiosemitic are also overly high, but offset lower at 58–64 percent.

INTERPRETING THE PERCENTAGES AND THEIR IMPLICATIONS FOR HISTORY

Once these skewed ranges and individual figures are removed, the rest of the figures fall into coherent distributions and distinguish a sequence of subgroupings and language divergences. The deepest level of divergence within Ethiosemitic is represented by a range of cognate retentions figures running 40–52 percent (leaving aside the presumed skewed

Amharic and Argobba figures), with a median at 45 percent. This range, outlined on three sides in the matrix and called "box 1," distinguishes the North Ethiosemitic branch, consisting of Tigre and Tigrinya (and of course Ge'ez, the written early ancestral form of Tigrinya)[3] from the South Ethiosemitic branch. The unity of the South Ethiosemitic branch is attested by a second range of figures, found in "box 2." Leaving aside the higher-skewed figures for Soddo, these run at 49–59 percent (plus two outside figures of 45 and 62), with a median of 55 percent.

Gafat counts run anomalously low with the Gurage languages, at 48–54 percent, considering the morphological and lexical innovatory evidence for its closer relationship to that group than to the Cross-Rift (Amharic, Harari, etc.) group. One possible reason is that the available one-hundred-meaning list for Gafat is missing nine words, and at least five of these nine are highly retained in Outer South Ethiosemitic, showing cognate forms right through the rest of the group. Having the Gafat equivalents for these items would likely raise the Gafat percentages several points with its nearest related languages, into the higher 50 percents, better in line with expectations.

The more recent divergences within South Ethiosemitic are of course reflected in the various groupings of higher cognate retention counts in the matrix. These ranges are set off by different kinds of dotted lines in the matrix to facilitate identification. A tight range of 57–60 percent differentiates the two Western Cross-Rift languages, Amharic and Argobba, from Eastern Cross-Rift, suggesting that Proto-Cross-Rift may have begun to diverge sometime in the first two to three centuries CE. The incipient split between Argobba and Amharic, at 79 percent, can be estimated to have begun by or somewhat before the establishment of the Solomonic dynasty in 1270. The divergence of Proto–Eastern Cross-Rift into Harari and Zway-Walani branches is marked by Harari-Zway and Harari-Walani figures of 70 percent, suggesting an expansion of this group along the eastern side of the northern part of the Ethiopian Rift region sometime in the later first millennium CE, with Zway and Walani at 79 percent with each other diverging into two communities in the first half of the second millennium.

The deepest divergence of Proto-Gurage into separate Mesmes and Chaha-Mäsqan subgroups, marked by figures of 56–59 percent shared cognate retention (leaving aside the presumed high-skewed Mesmes–Ennemor figure of 68 percent), would have begun earlier than suspected, at a time before 500. This means that the first immigration of South Ethiosemitic groups into the Gurage region most likely would have to date back to relatively early in the first millennium CE. The subsequent divergence of Proto-Chaha-Mäsqan into Mäsqan and the ancestor language of Chaha and Ennemor, marked by cognate retention percentages of 70, 76, and 80, respectively, would belong in that case to around the late first millennium.

NOTES

1. Core vocabulary counts used here are modified from M. L. Bender, "The Languages of Ethiopia: A New Lexicostatistical Classification and Some Problems of Diffusion," *Anthropological Linguistics* 13, no. 5 (1971): 165–288.

2. R. Hetzron, *Ethiopian Semitic: Studies in Classification,* Journal of Semitic Studies Monograph no. 2 (Manchester, UK: Manchester University Press, 1972); idem, "Genetic Classification and Ethio-

pian Semitic," in J. Bynon and T. Bynon (eds.), *Hamito-Semitica* (The Hague: Mouton, 1975), pp. 103–127; idem, *The Gunnän-Gurage Languages* (Naples: Istituto Orientale di Napoli, 1977).

3. This is the conclusion in H. C. Fleming, "Ethiopic Language History: Testing Linguistic Hypotheses in an Archaeological and Documentary Context," *Ethnohistory* 15 (1968): 353–388, and is supported by the modified cognate figures in Bender, "Languages of Ethiopia."

Cushitic Loanwords in Ethiosemitic Core Vocabulary

The lists of borrowings presented in this appendix are from core vocabulary. As the discussions of loanword categories in chapter 4 reveal, this kind of indicator goes with intensive borrowing. In the situation of a language spreading into new speech areas, as would have repeatedly been true of Ethiosemitic language history, this category of borrowing would imply that the Ethiosemitic speakers began in each case as an intrusive small minority. As the data reveal, this kind of history again and again accompanied the successive establishment of Ethiosemitic speakers more widely across the Ethiopian highlands.

The particular attestations of roots are given in the following lists below in modified versions of the forms that appear in M. L. Bender, "The Languages of Ethiopia: A New Lexicostatistical Classification and Some Problems of Diffusion," *Anthropological Linguistics* 13, no. 5 (1971): 165–288. Highland Eastern Cushitic reconstructions are based usually on materials in Grover Hudson, *Highland East Cushitic Dictionary* (Hamburg: Buske Verlag, 1989). Southern Cushitic reconstructions come from C. Ehret, *The Historical Reconstruction of Southern Cushitic Phonology and Vocabulary* (Berlin: Reimer, 1980). Eastern Cushitic reconstructions are based on H.-J. Sasse, "The Consonant Phonemes of Proto-East-Cushitic: A First Approximation," *Afroasiatic Linguistics* 7, no. 1 (1979): 1–67; and C. Ehret, "Revising the Consonant Inventory of Proto-Eastern Cushitic," *Studies in African Linguistics* 22, no. 3 (1991): 211–275.

PROTO-ETHIOSEMITIC

1. "cloud": *dämmäna   Agäw: Proto–North Agäw (PNA) *dämmäna ~ *dimmina
2. "egg": *ink'ak'iḥ   uncertain Cushitic source
3. "fish": *ʕasa   Agäw: PNA *(ʕ)asa
4. "hair": *s'igär   Agäw: Bilin šigʷir (from earlier *s'igʷir)

5. "smoke": *t'is   Agäw: Proto-Agäw *t'iz
6. "tail": *c'ira   uncertain Cushitic source

PROTO-NORTH ETHIOSEMITIC

1. "meat": *siga   Agäw: PNA *siɣa
2. "skin": *k'arbät   Agäw: PNA *k'ärb-
3. "swim": *ħambäs   Agäw: Bilin xambäs-

PROTO-SOUTH ETHIOSEMITIC

1. "dog": *wissa   Highland Eastern Cushitic (HEC) *wuš-
2. "fat": *c'omma   HEC *c'omm-; also some Agäw
3. "knee": *gulbät   Proto-Cushitic *gulb-/*gilb-; occurs in Southern Cushitic
                          and Agäw as well, but shape is specifically HEC
4. "skin": *goga   HEC *goga; also Oromo
5. "tongue": *ʔanrabät   Proto–Eastern Cushitic *ʕaanrab-
6. "sand": *(h)asäwa   Agäw: PNS *ašewa
7. "tree": *zaf   Agäw: PNA *zaf
8. "water": *ʔikʷ-   Agäw: Proto-Agäw *äkʷ-

PROTO-WESTERN CROSS-RIFT

1. "egg": *ʔink'ulaliħ   uncertain Cushitic source
2. "skin": *k'oda   Cushitic: HEC *k'oda; also Proto–Southern Cushitic
                          *kʷaad- 'goatskin'
3. "tail": *jer-   EC: Afar *gera
4. "water": *wiha   Cushitic: HEC

PROTO-EASTERN CROSS-RIFT

1. "road": *ʔunga   HEC *ʔunk-
2. "sun": *ʔir-   Eastern Cushitic *ʔar-/*ʔir-

PROTO-ZWAY-WALANI

1. "fire": *jira   HEC, Afar *giir-
2. "heart": *wäzän-   Eastern Cushitic *wazn-; specific source uncertain
3. "white": *gumärä   Eastern Cushitic: Bayso (Soomaali group) gumara

PROTO-OUTER SOUTH ETHIOSEMITIC

1. "egg": *ʔankʷa   separate borrowing of Cushitic root seen in Proto-Ethiosemitic
                          *ʔink'ak'iħ- 'egg'; but source uncertain
2. "red": *bissa   HEC *bišš-

PROTO-GURAGE

1. "egg": *ʔɨnkʼura   separate borrowing of Cushitic root seen in Western Cross-Rift *ʔɨnkʼulaliħ; source uncertain

2. "hair": *dugura   Eastern Cushitic *tʼogor-; source was an uncertain Lowland Eastern Cushitic language in which *t' became *ɖ or *ɗ; heard as *d in Proto-Gurage, which lacks these two sounds

INDEX

Abbai River (White Nile), 159, 175
Acholi, 229, 243
Afar, 262
Afrasian (Afroasiatic) (language family), 11, 16,
    20, 26, 30, 37, 41, 67, 129, 135–151, 153,
    155–167, 219
African Great Lakes, 7, 30, 47, 57, 65, 114, 117,
    122, 227, 232, 233, 244, 245
African groundnut (Vigna subterranea), 226
Agäw, 93, 103, 137–139, 148, 165, 172–177, 180,
    182, 261, 262
Agäw-East-South Cushitic, 137, 138, 148
agriculture (see also cultivation), 16, 55, 132,
    148, 167, 215
Akie, 92
Akkadian, 140
Aksum, 181, 182
Alagwa, 187, 235
Albany (archaeological culture), 123–124
Algonkian (language family), 85, 86, 88, 89, 102,
    107
Allerød Interstadial, 156, 158
Ambrose, Stanley, 6, 42, 118
American, Native, 4, 39, 49, 103, 238
American South, 87
American Southwest, 85
Americas: 5, 41, 222, 225, 233, 237, 243, 244;
    pre-Columbian, 4, 237
Amharic, 175, 183, 257–259
Anatolia, 221

Anglo-Saxon, 102
Aquatic (Aqualithic) (archaeological complex),
    154, 164
Arabia, Arabian peninsula, 172, 177, 180
Arabic, 15, 97, 98, 102, 139, 144, 145, 172, 252
Argobba, 175, 258, 259
Armenian, 145
arrowroot, 225
Asa, 92, 93, 95
Asi, 186, 211, 212, 213
Asia, 4, 37, 41, 46, 136, 137, 139, 140, 149, 151,
    165, 180, 221–223, 227, 243, 244
Astaboran (Nilo-Saharan subgroup), 160, 253,
    255
Asu (Pare), 74, 80, 92, 93, 98, 101, 114, 116, 234
Ateker (Eastern Nilotic subgroup), 227, 235, 236
Atlantic Age, 135, 221, 222
Atlantic Ocean, 88, 122, 124, 227, 229, 232, 237,
    245
Atlantic tropical circulation, 158
Aushi, 112
Austronesian (language family), 39, 49, 227
Awash River, watershed, 170, 173–175, 177, 179–
    181

bananas, plantains, 10, 65, 247
Bantu languages (Niger-Congo language family),
    8, 10, 11, 18, 28–30, 39, 41, 47, 48, 55, 59, 60,
    62–64, 70, 71, 74, 75, 77, 78, 80, 87, 93, 97,
    103, 108, 109, 111, 113–117, 119, 122–124,

Bantu languages *(continued)*
129, 151, 186, 187, 190, 191, 206, 215, 219,
223–226, 228, 230–232, 234, 236–241, 246,
247
Barabaig, 232, 233, 240
barley, 180, 252
basic vocabulary (*see* core vocabulary)
Batwa ("Pygmies"), 8, 47
Bayso, 262
Bechhaus-Gerst, Marianne, 9, 11
Beja, 37, 137, 138, 161–163, 165
Bemba, 111, 112
Bena, 80, 231, 237
Bender, Lionel, 48
Benue-Kwa (branch of Niger-Congo), 121, 122
Berber (Amazigh), 11, 20, 137, 139–142, 144–
146, 148–151, 156, 161, 167
Berti, 36, 40
Bilin, 261, 262
Bisa, 111, 112
black-eye pea (cowpea), 223
Blench, Roger, 10, 11, 20
Blust, Robert A., 18
Bole, 252
Bondei, 225, 226, 228, 246
Bongo, 227
Boreafrasian (branch of Afrasian language
family), 141, 142, 146, 156, 158, 250
boreal forest zone, 167
Bostoen, Koen, 10, 11, 20
Botatwe, 108, 111, 112, 130
Botswana, 124
Boyeldieu, Pascal, 11
bread, 147, 180, 252
broad beans (*Phaseolus* sp.), 223–226, 229, 244
Bukusu, 227, 232, 241, 243
bulrush millet (pearl millet, *Pennisetum*), 227,
231
Burunge, 69, 75, 223, 226, 235
bushpig, 90
butter, 211
Byblos, 140

Cameroon, 121, 122, 137, 151
Camus (language, people), 117, 118
Cape of Good Hope, 86, 124
Capsian (archaeological tradition), 156, 158
caravan (trade, routes), 222–225, 229, 245
Carib, 41
Caribbean, 238, 247
cassava, 223–226, 229, 244

Central Africa, 7, 9, 10, 43, 59, 227, 229, 232,
236, 245
Central Asia, 218
Central Sudanic, 11, 24–28, 31, 34–40, 42, 227,
247
ceramic technology, 10, 38, 43, 78, 108, 109, 111,
113–117, 121, 122, 125, 130, 132, 153–155,
159, 164, 253
Chad (country), 7, 137
Chad Basin, 40, 139, 142, 151
Chadic (language group), 11, 20, 37, 137, 139,
140, 142, 144–146, 148, 149, 151, 160, 161,
167, 251, 252
Chado-Berber (branch of Afrasian language
family), 141, 142, 144, 156, 158, 167, 250
Chaga, 9, 63, 80, 117, 118, 215, 223, 224, 226,
239, 244
Chaha, 179, 183, 258, 259
Chami, Felix, 115, 130
chickpea, 180
Chifumbaze (archaeological complex), 108, 117
China, 221
Chinese, 50
circumcision, 78, 211
Ciskei, 108
Coastlands Bantu, 122, 123
cognate, 11, 28, 29, 47, 67, 125, 127, 132, 144,
158, 167, 168, 227, 259
cognate counts/retentions, 124, 143, 145, 156,
158, 177, 179, 182, 257–260
Comoro Islands, 113
Congo, Democratic Republic of, 111, 112, 229,
231, 244, 245
Congo Basin, 7, 229, 232, 233, 245
core vocabulary (basic vocabulary), 41, 50, 63,
90–98, 106, 107, 109, 112, 114, 116, 117, 122,
123, 125–127, 143–145, 172, 173, 175–177,
179, 182, 183, 213, 216, 220, 250, 258, 259,
261
cow, cattle, 35, 36, 53, 60–62, 125, 253–255
crops: 10, 20, 30, 55, 65, 77, 86, 163, 164, 180,
187, 221–237, 243–245; African, 163, 164,
180, 187, 226, 230, 231, 233, 235; Asian, 222,
223, 225, 227, 243, 244; Sudanic, 164
Cross-Rift (Ethiosemitic subgroup): 174, 175,
176, 179, 259; Eastern Cross-Rift, 175, 176,
179, 259, 262; Western Cross-Rift, 175, 176,
179, 259, 262, 263
Crowley, Terry, 13
cultivation (*see also* agriculture), 7, 10, 27, 29,
30, 33–35, 38, 43, 77, 78, 87, 92, 109, 125,

132, 135, 146, 148, 149, 151, 153, 156, 159, 164, 167, 168, 180, 187, 211, 212, 215, 230, 233, 253–255
Cushitic languages: 11, 37, 41, 137, 140–142, 144–146, 148, 149, 151, 155, 156, 161, 165, 172, 174, 176, 179, 180–183, 219, 249–251; Agäw-East-South Cushitic, 137, 138, 148; East-South Cushitic, 137, 138, 165, 252; Eastern Cushitic, 11, 21, 78, 137, 165, 174–176, 179, 182, 219, 252, 261–263; Highland Eastern Cushitic, 174–176, 183, 261, 262; North Cushitic, 137, 138, 161, 162–163, 165; Southern Cushitic, 11, 21, 26, 27, 32, 48, 61–63, 68–71, 74, 75, 78, 81, 92, 117–119, 137, 138, 148, 166, 186, 187, 188, 190–193, 194, 197, 198, 203, 205, 206, 210, 211, 219, 226, 233–235, 261, 262

Dahalo, 26, 27, 69–70, 74, 92, 119, 203, 205, 219
Daju (Nilo-Saharan subgroup), 11, 37
Dangme, 107, 123
Datoga (see also Barabaig), 118, 233, 240
daughter language, 13, 23–30, 40, 43, 47, 50, 55, 66, 109, 111, 137–139, 158, 175, 183, 199, 203
Dawida, 186, 188, 190, 191, 193, 194, 197, 203–203, 206, 211–215, 219, 226, 234, 235, 238, 239, 247
Diakonoff, I. M., 20
Didinga, 253, 254
Didinga-Murle (Nilo-Saharan subgroup), 37
digging stick, 148
Dinka (see Jyang)
Divinity, 32
Doe, 230
dog, 53, 219, 262
domestic animals, 10, 33, 35–37, 54, 62, 125, 149
Dongolawi, 35, 121
donkey, 53, 63, 155
Drakensburg, 110
Dullay (Eastern Cushitic subgroup), 252

East Africa, xiii, 5, 6, 9, 32, 42, 55, 57, 59–61, 71, 74, 76, 77, 80, 92, 103, 115, 118, 119, 135, 187, 213, 222, 223, 225–227, 229–233, 235–238, 241, 243–245
East African coast, 114, 115, 222, 223, 227, 229, 230, 231, 238, 241, 243, 244, 245, 247
East Asia, 221
eastern Africa, 8–10, 16, 47, 59, 63, 75, 76, 93, 117, 124, 223–225, 232, 233, 238, 241, 243, 245, 246

Egypt: 16, 43, 107, 121, 124, 125, 139, 141, 142, 158, 163, 165; Middle Kingdom, 139
Egyptian: ancient, 16, 137, 139, 140, 142, 144–148, 158, 161, 163, 251, 252; Middle, 144
Elmenteitan (archaeological culture), 118
Embleton, Sheila, 114
English, 32, 37, 53, 54, 71, 74, 85–89, 94, 95, 97, 101, 102, 103, 151, 193, 194, 205, 223, 224, 231, 238
Ennemor, 183, 257–259
Epigraphic South Arabian, 172, 173, 177
Eritrea, 120, 137, 140, 172, 182
Erythraic (branch of Afrasian language family): 141, 146–148, 155, 156, 158, 249, 252; North Erythraic, 141, 144–146, 148, 156, 158, 249, 252
Ethiopia, xiv, 78, 93, 119, 120, 137, 138, 140, 141, 172, 182, 224
Ethiopian Highlands, 40, 78, 120, 137, 138, 140, 141, 143, 155, 159, 160, 170, 172, 177, 181, 182, 261
Ethiopian Rift Valley, 138, 174, 181, 182
Ethiosemitic (Ethiopian Semitic): 93, 103, 107, 120, 139; North Ethiosemitic, 173, 176, 181, 182, 258, 259, 262; Outer South Ethiosemitic, 174, 175, 183, 259, 262; South Ethiosemitic, 173–177, 179–183, 257–259, 262
ethnoscience, 31, 52

farming, farmers (see cultivation)
Feierman, Steven, 48, 104
Fibobe (see also Namakala), 111
field, cultivated, 34, 65, 148, 149, 211, 215, 254
finger millet (Eleusine), 180, 187
fishing, 109, 154, 159
flax, 180
Fleming, Harold C., 166, 173, 177, 260
fly, 91
French, 87, 95, 96, 97, 102, 103
For (Fur) language, people, 34, 37, 40, 159

Gaam (Ingessana), 35, 36
Gafat, 174–176, 179, 183, 258, 259
Garree, 27
gatherer-hunters, 14, 26, 33, 38, 92, 148, 149, 186, 211, 213
gathering (subsistence), 14, 124, 135, 159, 164
Geʼez, 120, 182, 259
German, 97, 151, 183, 224, 244
Geto, 183

Gikuyu (Kikuyu), 28, 29, 80, 98, 225, 234, 236, 239
Giryama, 235, 238
Gisu, 224
glottochronology, 15, 39, 41, 42, 49, 50, 105–107, 125, 126, 129, 145, 176
goat, 29, 33, 37, 38, 42, 43, 53, 59–64, 125, 138, 149–151, 153, 161, 165, 183, 187, 211, 254
Gogo, 80, 87, 223, 226, 230, 234, 236, 237
Gonzales, Rhonda, 65, 115
Gorowa, 233, 235
gourd, calabash, 159, 255
grains (in subsistence), 65, 75–78, 109, 125, 132, 147–149, 153–156, 158, 159, 164, 187, 227, 228, 230, 231, 233, 246, 251–254
granary, 251, 252, 254
grassland, 42, 119, 155
Great Fish River, 124
Greek, 102
Greenberg, Joseph H., 136, 165
grindstone, 125, 147, 252, 253
Guinea coast, 88
Gumuz, 24, 26
Gundu (see also Namakala), 111
Gurage, 175, 176, 179, 181, 183, 259
Gusii, 80, 98, 227, 232, 240, 241

Hadiya, 174
Hanang, 233
Harari, 259
Hausa, 252
Hehe, 80, 231, 237
Heine, Bernd, 11, 17, 19
herding, herders, 14, 26, 27, 33, 35, 37, 38, 64, 65, 68, 78, 92, 135, 149, 153, 164, 167, 168, 186, 187, 211–212, 215, 253, 254
Hetzron, Robert, 166, 171, 183, 258
High Veld, 110
Hindi, 238, 247
hoe, 148
Holocene, 14, 16, 135, 136, 155, 161, 165
Horn of Africa, 16, 30, 33, 135, 137, 141, 155, 158, 159, 166, 171–173, 177, 179–181
house, round, 33, 38, 43, 125, 153, 159, 254
Hudson, Grover, 161, 261
hunting, 109, 125, 135, 159, 164

Ila, 111, 112
Il-Tatua wars, 118
Indian Ocean, 113, 181, 221, 227, 230, 231, 237, 238, 241, 244, 245

Indo-Aryan, 238
Indo-European (language family), 4, 10, 12, 41, 107, 145, 151, 167, 183, 186, 218
Inland Delta (of Niger River), 40
Iraqw, 69, 70, 71, 74, 75, 144, 226, 227, 233, 234, 240
iron, ironworking, 78, 122, 179, 215
Iron Age, 18, 109, 124
irrigation, 34, 215
Ivory Coast, 121

Japan, Japanese, 41, 50, 154, 222
Jebel (Nilo-Saharan subgroup), 253, 254
Jos Plateau, 139
Jyang (Dinka), 31, 34, 229

Kabyle, 139
Kagulu, 223, 237
Kalambo (archaeological culture), 112, 113
Kalenjin: 39, 92, 118, 224, 232, 233, 235, 236, 240, 241; South Kalenjin, 39
Kalundu (archaeological complex), 109, 110
Kamba, 80, 224, 225, 234, 239
Kami, 80, 230
Kanem, 40
Kanuri, 34, 35, 37, 40
Kaonde, 112
Kasai River, 6
Kasighau, 186
Kaskazi (branch of Mashariki Bantu), 55–57, 59, 61, 63, 64, 80
Katanga, 43, 46, 229, 231, 244
Kati, 57, 61–65, 78
Kaufman, Terence, 48, 104
Kembatta, 174
Kenya, xiv, 26, 28, 31, 39, 55, 71, 78, 80, 92, 96, 113, 115, 117–120, 135, 137, 138, 183, 186–188, 210, 219, 224–233, 235, 236, 238–241, 243–245
Kenya coast, 113, 117, 120, 187, 212, 225, 228, 231, 234, 235, 238, 243
Kenya Highlands, 230, 232
Kenya Rift Valley, 119, 210, 224, 225, 232, 233, 235, 238
Keyo, 224, 232, 235
Khoe (branch of Khoesan language family, 124
Khoekhoe, 86
Khoesan (language family), 26, 27, 123, 124
Kiessling, Roland, 187
Kinga, 80, 231, 237
kinship, kin terminology: 66–68; Crow kinship, 66

Kir-Abbaian (Nilo-Saharan subgroup), 160, 162, 163, 254
Klieman, Kairn, 8, 46, 47, 66, 128
Koman languages, 24–27, 34, 38, 151, 154, 159
Kony, 224
Korean, 50, 222
Kuba kingdom, 6
Kunama, 24–28, 34–36, 40, 41, 125, 159, 253
Kuria, 232, 241
Kw'adza, 69, 252
Kwale (archaeological tradition), 114, 115
Kwazulu-Natal, 7, 108–110, 117

Lake Chad, 139
Lake Malawi (Lake Nyasa), 232, 237
Lake Mega-Chad, 139
Lake Nyanza, 56, 57, 80, 187, 226, 232, 235, 241
Lake Tana, 172
Lake Tanganyika, 55, 56, 232
Lake Turkana, 119
Lake Victoria (see Lake Nyanza)
Lala, 112
Lamba, 112, 231, 236, 244
Lamu Archipelago, 113, 115, 116
Lanet (pottery tradition), 117
Langi, 55, 57, 75, 223, 226, 235, 240
Latin, 96, 102
Lenje, 111, 112
Leopard's Kopje (Kutama) (archaeological culture), 110
Levant, 142, 151, 158, 163, 168, 172, 183, 221
lexicon, 199
lexicostatistics, 113, 114, 129, 130, 144, 151, 166, 171, 173
Libyans, 139
Limbo (archaeological culture), 114
Limpopo River, 109, 124
linguistic geography, 14, 42, 137, 140, 171, 174, 176
Lloyd, David, 55, 227, 244
loanwords (see also word borrowing), 9, 15, 29–31, 36, 37, 39, 42, 50, 61, 63, 74, 76–78, 83, 85, 87–89, 91, 92, 94–98, 102, 103, 109, 119, 124, 129, 136, 138, 139, 145, 153, 161–163, 167, 171–177, 182, 183, 185, 186, 187, 188, 190, 191, 193, 194, 197, 203, 205, 206, 211–213, 215, 219, 232, 235, 243, 257, 258, 261
loanwords, individual (see word borrowing: single-word borrowing)
Loita plains, 118, 240

Lotuko (Eastern Nilotic language), 227
Louisiana, 109
louse, 91
Luangwa (archaeological tradition), 111–113
Luba, 43, 46, 112
Luban (Bantu subgroup), 112
Lugulu, 223, 230, 234, 236
Lungu, 112
Luo, Kenya, 96–98, 224, 225, 232, 235, 236, 241, 243, 247
Lunda (Rund) Empire, 6
Lydenburg (archaeological culture), 109, 110

Ma'a (Southern Cushitic language), 48, 69, 70, 74, 92, 93, 95, 98, 101, 104, 119
Maa (Eastern Nilotic language), 108, 118
Maa-Ongamo (Eastern Nilotic subgroup), 108, 117, 118, 119
Maasai, 31, 40, 78, 87, 92, 95, 98, 108, 118, 183, 232, 233, 234, 239, 240
Maasai plains (Maasai steppe), 240
Maba, 254
Maban (Nilo-Saharan language group), 151, 160, 253–255
Madagascar, 227
maize, 86, 230–233, 235, 237, 244, 245, 247
Malagasy, 227, 246
Malawi, 9, 43, 80, 113, 231, 232, 235, 237, 238
Malay, 88, 228
Mali, 40, 154
Mambwe, 112
Mandara Mountains, 139
manuring, 215
Marakwet, 224, 232, 235, 244
Mara Plains, 118, 240
Marra Mountains, 40
Mashariki (Bantu languages), 30, 55, 60–64, 77, 78, 108, 114, 116, 117, 187, 219, 231, 235, 246
Mäsqan, 179, 258, 259
matriliny, matrilineal descent, 18, 66, 68
Maxay, 30
Mbisha, 186, 211, 212, 215
Mbulu, 233
McMahon, April, 129
McMahon, Robert, 129
Mediterranean, 4, 136, 221
Meillet, Antoine, 48
Mesmes, 183, 258, 259
Mesoamerica, 221
Mesopotamia, 140, 172, 221

Mexico, 86, 88
Middle East, 10, 16, 68, 164
Middle Egyptian, 144
Middle English, 89, 97, 102
Middle Nile Basin, 119, 159, 160, 229, 241, 243
Mijikenda, 80, 114, 116, 223, 225, 226, 228, 231, 238
Militarev, Alexander, 148
milk, milking, 30, 36, 37, 53, 65, 149, 187, 253, 254
mitotic metaphor, 23, 24
Mocha, 251
morphology, 107, 126, 165, 171, 185, 189–191, 199, 203, 236, 258, 259
Mount Elgon, 227, 241, 243
Mount Kenya, 235, 239
Mount Kilimanjaro, 215
Mous, Maarten, 48
Mozambique, 110, 111, 113, 124, 231, 236, 238
Msiri, 229, 236
Mushabi (archaeological culture), 158

Naath (Nuer), 129
Nahuatl, 86, 246
Nakuru, 232
Namakala (archaeological traditions), 111, 112
Namibia, 124
Nandi, 224, 232
Nara, 36, 160, 253, 254
Native American, 4, 39, 49, 103, 238
Ndebele: Northern Ndebele, 110; Southern Ndebele, 110
Newman, Paul, 166, 167
Ngizim, 251, 252
Nguni, 95, 108–110, 116, 183
Niger, 137
Niger Bend, 160
Niger-Congo (language family), 10, 11, 28, 29, 121, 122, 155
Nigeria, 137
Niger River, 40
Nilo-Saharan (language family), 11, 14, 24–28, 30, 32–39, 41, 43, 46, 48, 49, 68, 78, 123–125, 132, 136, 151, 153–155, 157, 159, 160, 162, 164, 165, 168, 219
Nilotic (languages): 34–36, 41, 229, 235; Eastern Nilotic, 35, 117; Southern Nilotic, 11, 31, 32, 35, 36, 61–63, 78, 117–119, 129, 187; Western Nilotic, 34, 229
Njombe (Bantu subgroup), 55–57, 80, 231, 237
Nkangala-Nguni, 108, 110

Nobiin, 121
Norman, 95, 97, 102
Northeast-Coastal Bantu, 55–57, 80, 108, 113–116
northeastern Africa, 16, 107, 119, 136, 147, 151, 155, 160, 164, 165, 179, 224
Northern Hemisphere, 158
Northern Sudanic, 24–28, 33–38, 40–43, 68, 125, 151, 153, 154, 156, 159, 160, 164, 253
Nubia, 10, 11, 15, 17
Nubian, 10, 11, 15, 17, 35, 40, 107, 119, 121, 151, 155, 253–255
nug, 180
Numic, 41, 49
Nurse, Derek, 7, 9, 19, 103
Nyamwezi, 80, 223, 240, 241, 245
Nyanja-Cewa, 43, 46, 112, 113, 231, 235
Nyasa Bantu, 231
Nyimang, 34
Nyong-Lomami Bantu, 122, 123

Occam's razor, 39
Oceania, 4, 237
Oceanic (branch of Austronesian language family), 49
Ogowe River, 122
Okiek, 92, 183
Oldishi (archaeological culture), 118, 119, 210
Old Norse, 102
Olmalenge (archaeological culture), 118, 119
Omotic (branch of Afrasian family): 11, 20, 137–142, 144–147, 149, 249, 251; North Omotic, 138; South Omotic, 138
onager, 155
Ongamo, 117, 118
Opo, 34
Oromo, 92, 107, 119, 120, 224, 252, 262
Owmby, Carolan, 18, 109, 110
ox, 211

Päkot, 227, 235, 236
Pangani River, 114, 116, 225, 230, 239
Pare Mountains, 92, 212, 230, 234
pastoralism (see herding, herders)
patriliny, patrilineal descent, 66, 68
peanuts (Arachis), 223, 225, 227, 244, 245
pen, livestock, 33, 38, 43, 149, 253, 254
peripheral basic vocabulary, 90–93, 95–98, 103, 213, 216
phonological reconstruction (systematic), 11, 48
Phuti, 110

pidgin, pidginization, 83, 84, 98, 101
pig, 53
pigeon pea, 226
Pleistocene, Terminal, 136, 155, 159
plow, plowshare, 34, 148, 180
Pok, 214
Pokomo, 80, 114, 116, 235, 238
Portuguese, 229, 231, 237, 238, 241, 243
Posnansky, Merrick, 6
pots, pottery (see ceramic technology)
pre-Proto-Semitic, 158
Proto-Afrasian, 67, 140–148, 150, 155, 156, 166, 167, 249, 251
Proto-Agäw, 138, 251, 262
Proto-Agäw-East-South Cushitic, 137, 138, 148
Proto-Berber, 148, 149–151, 156, 250
Proto-Boreafrasian, 146, 156, 158
Proto-Chadic, 139, 148, 149, 151, 156, 252
Proto-Chado-Berber, 141, 156, 158, 250
Proto-Chaga, 117, 118
Proto-Chaha-Ennemor, 179, 259
Proto-Cross-Rift, 175, 176, 259
Proto-Cushitic, 137, 138, 149, 151, 156, 165, 233, 251, 252, 262
Proto-Daju, 37
Proto-Eastern Cross-Rift, 175, 179, 259, 262
Proto–Eastern Cushitic, 252, 261, 262
Proto–Eastern Nilotic, 35
Proto–Eastern Savanna Bantu, 59, 60
Proto-East Nyanza, 55, 57
Proto-East-South Cushitic, 138, 252
Proto-Erythraic, 141, 146–148, 155, 156, 158, 251
Proto-Ethiosemitic, 166, 171–173, 176, 177, 179–181, 261, 262
Proto-Gonga, 251
Proto–Great Lakes Bantu, 55, 57
Proto-Gurage, 175, 176, 259, 263
Proto-Koman, 24, 25
Proto-Langii-Mbugwe, 57
protolanguage, 23, 26–30, 39, 127, 148, 165, 183, 191, 194, 206
Proto-Libu, 139
Proto-Luhyia, 55, 57
Proto-Maa-Ongamo, 117, 118
Proto-Mashariki, 30, 55, 60, 63, 64, 77, 78, 116
Proto-Mijikenda, 116
Proto-Njombe, 55–57
Proto-Nkangala, 110
Proto-Northeast-Coastal Bantu, 55–57, 113, 116
Proto-Northern Sudanic, 25–28, 33, 35, 38, 40, 41, 43, 68, 125, 153, 154, 156, 159, 164, 253

Proto-North Erythraic, 141, 146, 148, 158, 252
Proto-North Ethiosemitic, 173, 182, 262
Proto–North Nyanza, 55
Proto–North Omotic, 251
Proto-Omotic, 138, 251
Proto-Pokomo, 116
Proto-Rift (Southern Cushitic), 75, 119, 194, 205, 206, 210
Proto-Rift-Mbugu, 206
Proto-Rub, 34, 36
Proto-Rufiji-Ruvuma, 55, 56
Proto-Rukwa, 55
Proto-Sabaki, 116
Proto-Saharan, 25, 26, 33, 38, 40, 42, 43, 159
Proto-Saharo-Sahelian, 25, 26, 28, 33, 34, 37, 38, 40, 43, 125, 153, 253
Proto-Sahelian, 25, 26, 33, 37, 38–40, 42, 43, 125, 138, 151, 153, 159, 160–162, 165, 254
Proto-Savanna Bantu, 59, 60
Proto-Semitic, 68, 140, 148–151, 156, 158, 168, 183, 252
Proto-Soddo-Gafat, 175
Proto-Soomaali, 30
Proto-Southern Cushitic, 68, 70, 71, 138, 187, 191–193, 194, 203, 233, 262
Proto–Southern Nilotic, 32, 35, 36
Proto–South Ethiosemitic, 173–177, 179–181, 183, 262
Proto-Sudanic, 24, 26, 28, 33, 153, 154
Proto-Swahili, 116
Proto–Taita Cushitic, 206, 210
Proto-Takama, 55–57
Proto-Trans-Sahel, 159
Proto–Upland Bantu, 55, 57
Proto–Western Cross-Rift, 176, 179, 262
Proto–Western Lakes, 55
Proto–Western Nilotic, 34, 229
Proto–West Rift Southern Cushitic, 194
Ptolemaic Red Sea trade, 181
Punjabi, 238

rainforests: equatorial (of Africa), 7, 30, 47, 66, 77, 122, 123, 232; West African, 121, 122
ram, 211
Red Sea, 37, 136, 140, 141, 143, 158, 159, 170, 172, 177, 180, 181
Red Sea hills, 16, 137, 158, 161, 165
regular sound change, regular sound correspondence, 11, 12, 28, 29, 37, 132, 144, 146, 150, 167, 186, 191, 192, 196, 197, 205, 206, 225, 228, 230, 231, 234, 235, 238

religion: 8, 9, 29, 31, 32, 65, 66, 97, 98, 102;
   Sudanic, 31, 32
Rendille, 31
rice, 223, 227–229, 231, 244, 247
Rift-Mbugu, 219
Rift Southern Cushitic, 203–204, 205
Rift Valley, Kenya, 232, 233
root word, 27–30, 33–37, 49, 52, 62, 63, 67, 75,
   81, 125, 127, 143–149, 151, 153, 159–161,
   166–168, 174, 176, 179, 186, 190–192, 194,
   223–238, 241, 243, 246, 247, 249, 250, 254,
   256, 261–263
Rossel, Gerda, 10, 11
Rottland, Franz, 11
Rub (Kuliak) (Nilo-Saharan language group), 11,
   34, 36, 151, 160, 253–255
Rufiji Delta, 114
Ruvu (Northeast-Coastal Bantu subgroup), 114,
   116, 226, 230

Sabaki (Northeast-Coastal Bantu subgroup),
   108, 113–116
Sabi (Bantu subgroup): 43, 46, 108, 111–113;
   Central Sabi, 108, 112, 113
Sabiny, 235, 236
Saghala, 80, 186, 188, 190, 191, 193, 194, 197,
   203, 206, 211–214, 215, 219, 234, 235, 239
Sahara: 16, 40, 135–137, 139, 141–143, 145,
   151, 153–156, 158–161, 164, 165; central,
   40, 136, 137, 139, 142; eastern, 14, 33, 40,
   42, 124, 141, 145, 151, 153, 154, 158–160,
   165; northern, 156; southern, 164; western,
   139
Saharan (Nilo-Saharan language group), 24, 26,
   34–37, 125, 151, 253, 254
Saharo-Sahelian (Nilo-Saharan language group),
   24, 27, 28, 34, 41, 125, 151
Sahel (geographical belt), 40
Sahelian (Nilo-Saharan language group): 24,
   34, 38, 40, 125, 151, 160, 162, 254, 255;
   Eastern Sahelian (Eastern Sudanic), 40,
   151, 159, 160, 163, 165; Western Sahelian,
   159, 160
Saidi, Christine, 42
Sala, 109, 110
Salamano (archaeological culture), 112
salt, 30
Sampuru, 117, 118
Sandawe, 226, 234, 240
Sankuru River, 6
Sapir, Edward, 4, 10

savanna, 42, 77
Savanna Pastoral Neolithic (archaeological
   complex), 118, 119, 187, 210
Schoenbrun, David, 7–9, 46, 47, 65
sedges, 147
Semitic: 11, 16, 41, 67, 68, 93, 129, 137, 139–142,
   144–146, 148, 151, 155, 158, 161, 164, 166,
   170, 172, 180, 183, 251, 252; Eastern Semitic,
   140; South Semitic, 176; Western Semitic,
   140, 166
Senegal, 241, 245
Senegambia, 241, 243
Seuta (Northeast-Coastal Bantu subgroup), 114,
   116, 226, 228
Shaiqi, 15, 17
Shambaa, 74, 80, 93, 95, 101, 226, 230, 234, 239,
   246, 247
Shebeelle River, 175
sheep, 33, 37, 38, 42, 43, 53, 59–63, 125, 149–
   151, 153, 165, 187, 254
Shilluk (Ocolo), 229
Shona, 108–111, 116, 227, 228, 237, 246
Sidamo, 174
Sino-Tibetan (language family), 107
Soddo, 175, 179, 183, 258, 259
Soli, 111–113
Solomonic kingdom, 182, 259
Somalia, 7, 224
Songay, 34–36, 40, 159, 160, 253–255
Soo, 254
Soomaali (language), 74
sorghum, 125, 132, 159, 187, 230, 231, 233, 251,
   252
South Arabia, 180
South Arabians, 140, 173, 177, 179, 180, 182
Southeast Asia, 46, 222, 223, 244
Southeast Nyanza communities, 57, 61–65
Southern highlands (of Tanzania), 80, 231, 237
Southern Kaskazi, 56, 60, 63, 64
Southern Nilotic (languages, peoples), 11, 31, 32,
   35, 36, 61–63, 78, 117–119, 129, 187
Southern Nyanza communities, 57, 60, 61
Southern savanna belt (of Africa), 6, 7, 232
South Pacific, 242
Spanish, 85, 86, 87, 89, 97, 102, 103, 241, 247
Spaulding, Jay, 15, 17
Spear, Thomas, 7
Starostin, Sergei, 132
steppe, 42, 155, 158
stone tools, 121, 122, 124, 154
stratigraphy, archaeological, 33, 42

stratigraphy, linguistic, 12, 14, 21, 23–27, 32, 33, 35–38, 42, 43, 55, 69, 105, 107, 108, 124, 136, 141, 146, 151, 153, 154, 156, 158–160, 164, 170, 175, 185
Sudan (country), 117
Sudan (geographical belt), 139, 154, 229, 232, 241, 245
Sudanic (primary branch of Nilo-Saharan language family), 24, 27, 154
Suguti (Bantu subgroup), 241
Sukuma, 80, 240, 241
"Swadesh": 100-meaning list (100-word list), 41, 90, 213; 200-meaning list (200-word list), 41, 90
Swahili (KiSwahili, WaSwahili), 28, 29, 71, 74, 80, 92, 97, 98, 102, 108, 113–116, 222–231, 234–238, 243, 244, 246, 247
sweet potato, 34, 225, 230, 234–237, 244
syntax, 48, 107, 199
Syria-Palestine, 140

Tabora, 228
Tabwa, 111
Taino, 238, 241, 247
Taita Cushites, Taita Cushitic: 188, 190, 191, 192, 203, 205, 206, 208, 210–214; Taita Cushitic A, 186, 193, 194, 196, 197, 198, 203–204, 206, 211, 213, 215; Taita Cushitic B, 186, 192, 193, 194, 196, 197, 198, 203–204, 206, 211, 213, 215
Taita Hills, 186, 187, 190, 191, 210, 212, 213, 214, 215, 219
Takama (Bantu subgroup), 55–57, 80, 240
Tale Southern Cushites, 219
Tama, 36
Taman (Nilo-Saharan subgroup), 253
Tana River, 224
Tana ware tradition (archaeological culture), 114–116
Tanzania, 39, 40, 57, 62, 66, 71, 75, 80, 87, 92, 94, 113–115, 119, 130, 137, 138, 186, 187, 210, 219, 223–226, 228–241, 243
Tanzania coast, 114, 225, 226, 227, 230, 232, 234, 236, 238, 243–245
t'ef, 180
Tem (Sonjo), 225, 234
Temba, 112
Temein, 34, 37, 254
Terik, 224, 232
Teri Valley, 186
terracing, terraced fields, 215

Teso, 227, 236
Thagiicu (Bantu subgroup), 226, 234, 235, 239
Thelwall, Robin, 11, 121
Thomason, Sarah Grey, 48, 104
Tibesti, 40
Tibu, 40
Tigre, 120, 145, 258, 259
Tigrinya, 120, 257–259
tobacco, 230, 237–241, 243–245, 247
Tocharian, 218
Tonga, 111, 112
Transkei, 108, 109
triangular-incised ware (see Tana ware tradition)
Tuken, 232
Tumbuka, 231, 238
Tupi-Guarani, 225
Turkana, 31
Turkic (languages), 41
Tuu (branch of Khoesan language family), 124

Uasingishu plateau, 233
Ubangian (branch of Niger-Congo language family), 39
Uganda, 55, 187, 227, 236, 241, 243, 247
Ugogo, 230
Ulugulu, 230
Uluguru Mountains, 234
Unyamwezi, 245

Vaal River, 109
Vansina, Jan, 5–9, 41, 46, 47
Venda, 237
Vossen, Rainer, 11

Waite, Gloria, 79
Walani, 259, 262
Wami Gulf, 232
Wenje ware (see Tana ware tradition)
Werner, Douglas, 9
West African Microlithic (archaeological complex), 154, 155
Western Rift, 30
wheat, 180, 251, 252
wild grasses (in subsistence), 125, 147–149, 154–156, 158, 164
Wilton (archaeological complex), 123, 124
word borrowing: 5, 6, 15, 18, 30, 31, 37, 61–65, 74, 82, 84, 85, 87–93, 95–98, 101, 103, 107, 114–116, 120, 121, 136, 144, 160, 161, 163, 170, 172, 173, 176, 177, 179, 181, 186, 190, 191, 213, 214, 215, 222, 256–258; extensive

word borrowing *(continued)*
  general word borrowing, 90, 93, 95–98,
    101; grammatically restricted borrowing,
    87, 88; heavy general word borrowing, 36,
    90, 95–98, 101, 214, 215; intensive word
    borrowing, 90–95, 97, 98, 172–174, 177,
    179, 183, 214, 258, 261; light general word
    borrowing, 90, 96, 98, 101; semantically
    restricted borrowing, 85–88, 98, 163; single-
    word borrowing, 31, 37, 84, 136, 221; status-
    restricted borrowing, 88, 89

Xhosa, 108

yam, 30, 225, 234, 235
Yeha, 172

Yemen, 172, 177
Younger Dryas, 156, 158, 159

Zaghawa, 40, 253, 254
Zalamo, 226, 230, 234
Zambezi River, 17, 228, 229, 231, 237, 243
Zambia, 9, 43, 80, 111–113, 130, 231, 232, 236,
  244
Zande, 55, 227
Zayse, 251
zebra, 155
Zhu (branch of Khoesan language family), 124
Zigula, 80, 226, 228
Zimbabwe, 55, 109–111, 227–229, 243
Zulu, 108
Zway, 259, 262

TEXT
10/12.5 Minion Pro

DISPLAY
Minion Pro

COMPOSITOR
Integrated Composition Systems

CARTOGRAPHER
Bill Nelson

PRINTER AND BINDER
Maple-Vail Book Manufacturing Group